THE WAR
THAT MADE
AMERICA

CIVIL WAR AMERICA

*Peter S. Carmichael, Caroline E. Janney,
and Aaron Sheehan-Dean, editors*

This landmark series interprets broadly the history and culture of the Civil War era through the long nineteenth century and beyond. Drawing on diverse approaches and methods, the series publishes historical works that explore all aspects of the war, biographies of leading commanders, and tactical and campaign studies, along with select editions of primary sources. Together, these books shed new light on an era that remains central to our understanding of American and world history.

A complete list of books published in Civil War America is available at https://uncpress.org/series/civil-war-america.

THE WAR THAT MADE AMERICA

Essays Inspired by the Scholarship of

Gary W. Gallagher

Edited by
CAROLINE E. JANNEY
PETER S. CARMICHAEL
AARON SHEEHAN-DEAN

THE UNIVERSITY OF NORTH CAROLINA PRESS
Chapel Hill

This book was published with the assistance of the Thornton H.
Brooks Fund of the University of North Carolina Press.

© 2024 The University of North Carolina Press

All rights reserved

Designed by Jamison Cockerham
Set in Arno and Cutright
by codeMantra

Cover art: (top) from a Civil War envelope for the Manchester Light Battery
and (bottom) from a Civil War envelope featuring a verse from the song
"A Soldier's Tear" (both courtesy of the Liljenquist Family Collection
of Civil War Photographs, Library of Congress, Washington, DC)

Manufactured in the United States of America

LIBRARY OF CONGRESS CATALOGING-IN-PUBLICATION DATA
Names: Gallagher, Gary W., honoree. | Janney, Caroline E., editor. |
Carmichael, Peter S., editor. | Sheehan-Dean, Aaron Charles, editor.
Title: The war that made America : essays inspired by the
scholarship of Gary W. Gallagher / edited by Caroline E.
Janney, Peter S. Carmichael, and Aaron Sheehan-Dean.
Other titles: Essays inspired by the scholarship of Gary
W. Gallagher | Civil War America (Series)
Description: Chapel Hill : The University of North Carolina Press, 2024. |
Series: Civil War America | Includes bibliographical references and index.
Identifiers: LCCN 2023044357 | ISBN 9781469678887 (cloth ; alk. paper) |
ISBN 9781469678894 (paperback ; alk. paper) | ISBN 9781469678900 (ebook)
Subjects: LCSH: Reconstruction (U.S. history, 1865–1877) | United States—
History—Civil War, 1861–1865. | United States—History—Civil War, 1861–1865—
Historiography. | BISAC: HISTORY / United States / Civil War Period (1850–1877) |
HISTORY / Military / United States | LCGFT: Essays. | Festschriften.
Classification: LCC E468 .W368 | DDC 973.7—dc23/eng/20231004
LC record available at https://lccn.loc.gov/2023044357

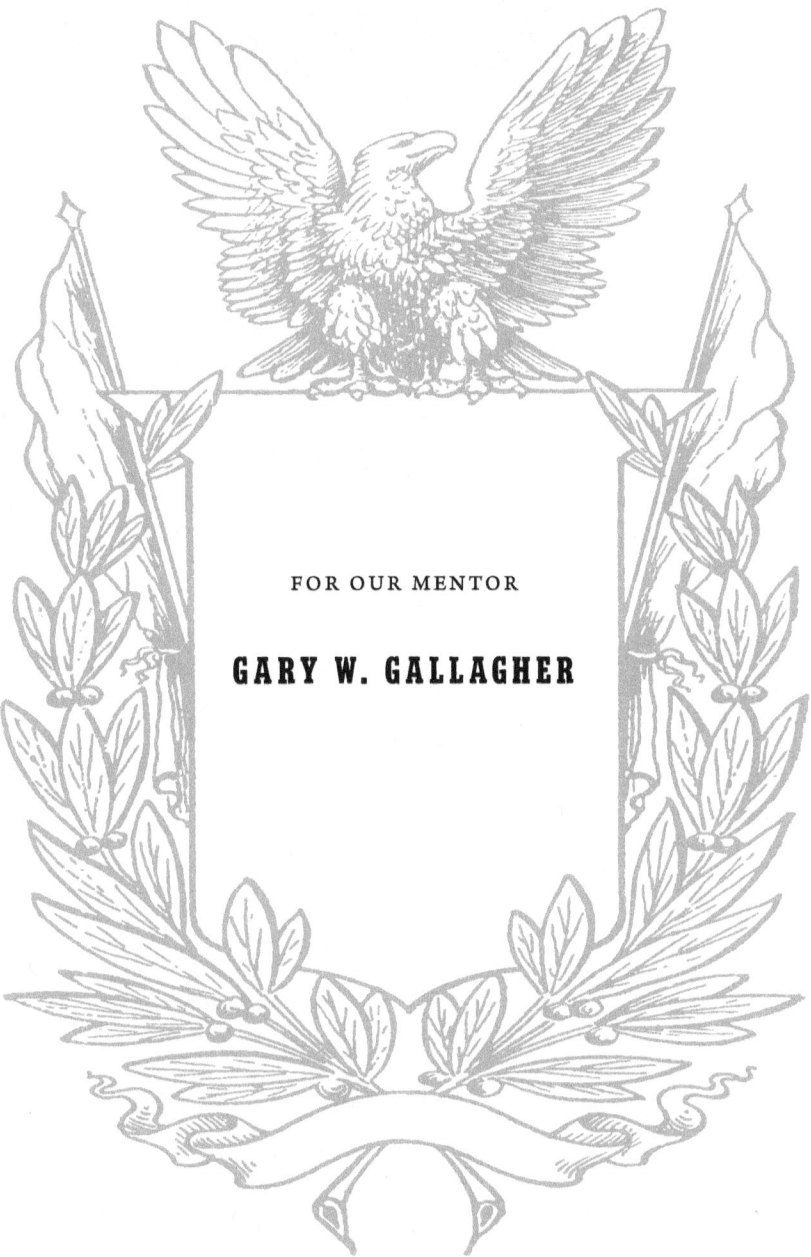

FOR OUR MENTOR

GARY W. GALLAGHER

CONTENTS

INTRODUCTION
Peter S. Carmichael, Caroline E. Janney,
and Aaron Sheehan-Dean · 1

NATIONS AT WAR

Protecting Their Self-Interest:
Native American Governance in the Confederacy
William A. Blair · 17

Apples and Oranges and Hardtack:
On the Uses of Comparison in Civil War History
Aaron Sheehan-Dean · 39

The Confederacy's Use of Nationalism and Vice Versa
Andre M. Fleche · 69

INTERSECTIONS OF WAR

Science and Daring: Robert E. Lee as
Engineer, Soldier, and Modernizer
Wayne Wei-siang Hsieh · 93

Guerrillas, Vengeance, and Mercy after
Appomattox: The Trial of John W. McCue
Caroline E. Janney · 118

Robert Smalls's Tax Title and the Endurance of
Land Redistribution in Port Royal, South Carolina
Cynthia Nicoletti · 141

CONSTRUCTING THE PAST

We Cannot Believe Americans Can Do These Things:
Erasing Violence from the Civil War Record
Peter S. Carmichael · 165

Jubal A. Early, Lee Commemoration, and the
Consolidation of Confederate History, 1870–1890
Kathryn J. Shively · 186

From the Field of Battle to the Field of
History: White Northern Veteran-Writers
and Their Narratives of the Civil War
Peter C. Luebke · 207

EPILOGUE: TAKING THE SHAPE
OF THE CIVIL WAR
*Aaron Sheehan-Dean, Caroline E. Janney,
and Peter S. Carmichael · 227*

Contributors · 251

Index · 253

THE WAR
THAT MADE
AMERICA

Introduction

PETER S. CARMICHAEL
CAROLINE E. JANNEY
AARON SHEEHAN-DEAN

Perhaps no field of United States history has become more diverse, expansive, and generative in the past forty years than that of Civil War history. This was not always the case. The middle decades of the twentieth century were banner years for Civil War historiography. A generation of influential scholars—David Potter, Kenneth Stampp, Benjamin Quarles, David Donald, and more—produced some of their best work.[1] This trend began to tail off by the late 1960s as some nineteenth-century scholars turned their attention to slavery, which was usually treated separately from the war and emancipation. Others focused on the war's causes through the lens of the new political history, which often emphasized ethno-cultural and partisan conflict.[2] What Civil War history was being produced tended to focus on the military and political aspects of the conflict.[3] Even the new military history of the 1970s, which sought to integrate military and civilian experiences by positioning the war within its broader social context, failed to push most Civil War historians beyond the bounds of more traditional top-down works.[4] This narrow focus famously prompted Maris Vinovskis to ask in the title of his 1989 essay "Have Social Historians Lost the Civil War?"[5]

The picture looks very different from the third decade of the twenty-first century. The field of Civil War history is vibrant, with scholars adopting capacious chronological framings that explore the deep roots of sectional animosity and the lasting effects of the conflict on American life. Historians integrate the methodologies of visual and material culture, gender history, race theory, the history of science, and environmental history into their studies of the war. They adopt both national and transnational perspectives on the processes of the era. Significantly, historians situate slavery and emancipation at the center of the war. It is hard to imagine any serious Civil War history today that does not reckon with the process of emancipation and how the war unleashed revolutionary forces that consumed people of all classes and races. Scholars of memory studies have found a wealth of new avenues of inquiry within the field. Military histories still exist, but those penned by scholars place military events within their social, political, legal, and cultural contexts. Perhaps most importantly, the period has been redefined as the Civil War *era*, a shift that signals a more expansive interrogation into the coming, fighting, and aftermath of the war.

The revolution in Civil War scholarship can be traced to the cohort of historians who came of age in the 1970s and early 1980s. They were inspired by the emergence of the social history of the 1960s, and they built upon the approach that history should be written from the "ground up." They also pursued new inquiries—especially around the role of race, slavery, and gender—saw new possibilities in sources ignored or misunderstood, and built the networks and institutions that supported innovative work. Gary W. Gallagher played a central role among this generation of scholars and the changes they brought to the field of Civil War history. Gallagher entered graduate school at the University of Texas when the new political history dominated the scholarly field. Although Gallagher appreciated the importance of this approach and recognized the innovation of historians like Michael Holt and Joel Silbey, he was drawn to topics in war and society. Still more problematic, the bicentennial of the American Revolution created a public audience for that era but not for the mid-nineteenth century. His advisors were worried that he would not find an academic position if his dissertation was a military topic. They pushed him to write about the demise of the Whig Party and the presidential election of 1852, a project he loathed. Three years passed, and Gallagher had hundreds of note cards but had not written a single page. In 1975, he withdrew from the doctoral program, having accepted an archivist position at the LBJ Presidential Library. He would have been finished with the academy had it not been for a fellow graduate student who suggested he check out the papers of Stephen Dodson Ramseur in the Southern Historical Collection at the University of North Carolina.

Although Ramseur was a West Point graduate and rose to prominence in Robert E. Lee's Army of Northern Virginia, no scholar had looked closely at his life or delved into his voluminous letters. Gallagher's major advisor, Barnes Lathrop, blessed the project, but he could give his student only fifteen months to research and write the dissertation. It was a brutal deadline, but Gallagher had a head start. Growing up on his family's southern Colorado farm, Gallagher had read widely, even voraciously, in history, and his passion was the American Civil War. This passion had left him familiar with the key works and manuscript collections relating to Lee's Army of Northern Virginia. When he enrolled as an undergraduate at Adams State College, a small liberal arts school near his home, Gallagher landed in a history department full of active scholars who were also committed teachers. His undergraduate mentors provided Gallagher a knowledge of the era's rapidly evolving historiography that proved more extensive than that of the average graduate student.

Gallagher's dissertation, completed in 1982 and published in 1985 by the University of North Carolina Press as *Stephen Dodson Ramseur: Lee's Gallant General*, did not resemble a classic drums-and-bugles narrative of the general's battlefield exploits. Rather, Gallagher pursued topics that few military biographers had considered. He stressed the importance of Ramseur's relationship with his wife and how their romantic exchanges fueled Dodson's ambitions for military promotion and Confederate fame. Gallagher also noted how ideas of manliness and honor shaped Ramseur's relationship with his comrades. At Chancellorsville, his unit suffered horrible losses, and a devastated Ramseur did not hide his feelings, breaking down and crying in front of his men. Gallagher pointed to the importance of emotional intimacy among survivors in building solidarity in the ranks. Uncovering the layers of Confederate loyalty captivated Gallagher, and Ramseur was the perfect case for such an inquiry. Why did the general give himself to the cause of Southern independence with a blinding devotion? Gallagher's portrait of Ramseur as a diehard rebel conflicted with the dominant scholarly idea that insufficient nationalism and a loss of will triggered a Confederate implosion. Working on Ramseur convinced Gallagher that a reevaluation of the Confederate people at war was needed.

Gallagher disagreed with historians who argued that white Southerners lacked a unifying spirit, were torn apart by class divisions, and were too selfish to stave off a defeat that was, in the end, largely self-inflicted.

He acknowledged the importance of economic and political factors behind the Confederacy's collapse, but he also recognized the persistent efforts of Confederate soldiers and the sacrifices of the civilians who supported them. In subsequent work, Gallagher continued to press for the study of internal factors to be put into conversation with events on the battlefield. He did not see any tension in exploring conventional military aspects of the conflict and acknowledging the importance of the social, cultural, and political dimensions of the war.

This analytical perspective—one that connected battlefront and home front and that integrated military, political, and social history—signaled the start of a new era in Civil War historiography. Over a career that stretched from 1986 to 2018, Gallagher propelled a transformation of the field through his own books and essays, through his teaching and mentorship of a new generation of scholars, through his consistent engagement with National Park Service historians and organizations like the Association for the Preservation of Civil War Sites (now the American Battlefield Trust), and through his long-standing role as an editor of the leading book series in the field.

Gallagher's essays and book-length works expanded on the themes and interests he established in his biography of Ramseur, demonstrating what could be achieved by reappraising the war's military and political dimensions alongside its myriad human impacts, both on the battlefield and on the home front. In *The Confederate War* (1997), Gallagher synthesized his extensive writings on Confederate society into a book of four sharply argued chapters, explaining how losses on the battlefield and destruction of property united white Southerners against a common enemy, even as they criticized their own government for its intrusive and inept measures. He emphasized the importance of Robert E. Lee, not only as a military leader but also as a symbol of the Confederacy as a whole, whose battlefield successes nourished a sense of nationalism among white Southerners. Countering other scholars who concluded that the Confederacy was destined to fail because of structural flaws present from the beginning, Gallagher insisted that Confederates did not give up until the United States had vanquished their armies.

The Confederate War also exemplified Gallagher's aim to recover the totality of historical experience. He stressed slavery's centrality to Confederate identity but showed that human bondage did not weigh down Confederates with guilt or cause them to wonder whether God had abandoned them. Looking behind the lines, Gallagher explored the costs of the war for Southern households, especially poor women, whose letters to Confederate officials demanded relief from the government to help them feed starving children, discipline enslaved people, and protect them from demanding impressment agents. By placing such archival material alongside soldiers' letters and official documents, Gallagher recovered the ways that race, class, and gender interacted on the Southern home front. Anticipating that critics would view serious consideration of Confederate history as old Lost Cause wine in a new bottle, Gallagher's introduction condemned Southern apologists for their abuse of history, for pretending that slavery was benign, and for inventing the popular narrative that Union armies persecuted outnumbered Confederates in a war won by "Butcher Grant's" strategy of attrition.

Building on his attention to the memory of the Civil War, Gallagher's extensive research into Gen. Jubal A. Early revealed how ex-Confederates pursued reactionary politics after Appomattox, a position that rested upon a complex and strident defense of the Confederacy. Most historians had dismissed Early as a failure whose postwar writings were little more than an old man's desperate plea for attention. Gallagher showed that Early was an influential propagandist who orchestrated assaults against anyone, Northern or Southern, who questioned that the Confederate cause was anything but virtuous. In the end, Gallagher decided against a full biography of Early, but he published several influential essays on Early's deft maneuverings in a Southern political world ruled by the Lost Cause.[6]

The Lost Cause created a cultural consensus among white Southerners after the Civil War, but Gallagher found that the memories of the war were too contentious for ex-Confederates, who could not maintain strict intellectual discipline about it. The remarkable memoir of Edward Porter Alexander, which Gallagher edited as *Fighting for the Confederacy: The Personal Recollections of General Edward Porter Alexander* (1989), revealed significant interpretive differences among Confederate veterans. Alexander defended the postwar Southern pariah James Longstreet; he praised Ulysses S. Grant's generalship, particularly his undetected flank march across the James River; and he did not hesitate to point out Lee's shortcomings. Alexander's original manuscript volumes were scattered within the University of North Carolina's Southern Historical Collection. Gallagher not only pieced together Alexander's postwar writings into its original narrative form, but he also transcribed the general's handwriting and meticulously edited the manuscript. Upon its release, *Fighting for the Confederacy* was recognized as an indispensable source on Lee's army—and it remains so today. The work also highlighted Gallagher's career-long support for the work of collecting, editing, and interpreting the voluminous primary source material the war generated.

Gallagher also turned his interest to the disjuncture between history and memory in the North. Popular opinion among modern-day Americans holds that the emancipation of enslaved people must have been the North's chief war aim because it gave white Northerners a moral impetus to fight and die in battles waged far from their homes. Such an interpretation, Gallagher pointed out in *The Union War* (2011), suits American needs in the twenty-first century, but it does not accurately reveal how white Northerners at the time thought about their decision to kill on behalf of their nation. When members of the wartime generation referred to liberty, Gallagher argued that they were not necessarily condemning slavery or embracing emancipation. Millions of white Northerners looked to the legacy of the founders, believing that they had an obligation to the country's unique history as a republic, that they had a duty to fight for its preservation, and that defeating the Rebels would protect their right to self-government.

The idea of Union inspired white Northerners at the most fundamental level, but the concept, as Gallagher notes, was sufficiently capacious and pliable to accommodate antislavery beliefs as the North endorsed emancipation. This framing of the Union war effort stimulated a robust debate among scholars in the field, which has clarified that people occupied different points along a spectrum of antislavery sentiment in the North as well as probed investigations of popular politics.

The Union War also represented a change in the source base upon which Gallagher relied. Song lyrics, patriotic images on envelopes, newspaper illustrations, and regimental histories bolstered a bibliography chock-full of letter collections and published diaries. Gallagher used this cultural material to recreate the context within which the war's participants made political and military decisions. Even as he incorporated these sources, Gallagher eschewed the use of theory, preferring to take historical actors on their terms, not ours.

The study of cultural representations surfaced even more fully in his *Causes Won, Lost, and Forgotten: How Hollywood and Popular Art Shape What We Know about the Civil War* (2008). Based on the Steven and Janice Brose Distinguished Lectures Gallagher delivered at Pennsylvania State University, he examined popular films including *Glory, Gettysburg, Gods and Generals*, and *Dances with Wolves*. To study art, he looked at 2,750 advertisements for contemporary prints and sculptures in Civil War magazines. He framed his study around four interpretive traditions: the Lost Cause, the Union Cause, the Emancipation Cause, and the Reconciliationist Cause. Among movies, Gallagher charted the demise of the Lost Cause in Tinseltown, largely because *Glory* (1989) awakened Americans to long-neglected issues of race in the Civil War and the decisive roles that Black troops played in the war. Still, the Lost Cause was more than holding its own in Civil War art. Prints of Lee and Thomas "Stonewall" Jackson fighting, praying, holding children on their laps, singing songs, and on occasion fighting Yankees proved irresistible to consumers. The Union Cause was virtually invisible in late twentieth-century popular culture, a finding that corresponded with Gallagher's argument that Americans have transformed the Civil War into a triumphant struggle for emancipation to assuage guilt felt over racial injustices today.

Alongside his own research, Gallagher played a pivotal role in training the next generation of Civil War historians. Gallagher began his teaching career at Penn State University in 1986. Over the next decade, he mentored graduate students in the field, encouraging them to pursue their chosen topics through deep and careful reading in the primary sources of the era. In 1998, Gallagher accepted an appointment as the inaugural John L. Nau III Professor at the University of Virginia, where he taught until his retirement in 2018. During his years at UVA and Penn State, Gallagher mentored thirty doctoral students in Civil War history. Although he did not assign dissertation topics, many of his students worked at the same intersection of military, political, and social history that defined much of his own scholarship.

Related to his role as a mentor to both undergraduate and graduate students, Gallagher worked to build connections between the academy and the public audience eager to learn about the Civil War. Alongside his books and essays, Gallagher pursued multiple venues to reach a broad audience. He wrote more than 250 articles and notes for popular magazines such as *Blue and Gray*, the *Civil War Monitor*, and *Civil War Times*. He appeared in more than sixty documentaries on PBS, the History Channel, and other networks. He served as an advisor for the Arts & Entertainment Network's fifty-two-part series *Civil War Journal* (and appeared in many of the episodes). His work in television overlapped with the popularity of Ken Burns's 1990 PBS documentary series on the Civil War. Gallagher also recorded a hugely popular Civil War history course for the Great Courses series. In all this work, he maintained his scholarly rigor while communicating with a popular audience.

Perhaps one of his most lasting contributions to the scholarly community was his role in helping to establish and shape the Society of Civil War Historians. Gallagher served as a charter member of the society in 1985, on the board, and as president from 2000 to 2004. The group had the dual goal of invigorating Civil War history within the Southern Historical Association and attempting to connect academic with public historians and preservation efforts. The organization's current mission is to "promote the study of the Civil War Era and to bring greater coherence to the field by encouraging the integration of social, military, political, and other forms of history."[7] Alongside younger members of the Society of Civil War Historians in the 1990s, Gallagher helped encourage the organization to reach out to historians of all specialties interested in the middle decades of the nineteenth century.

If a hallmark of Gallagher's influence on the field of Civil War history is the integration of military history with social, political, and cultural history, this work of intellectual bridge building found its fullest expression in his role as an editor, particularly of two long-standing book series published by the University of North Carolina Press: Civil War America and Military Campaigns of the Civil War. From 1987 to 2009, Gallagher presided over a series of summer conferences featuring a mix of academic and public historians and including general Civil War enthusiasts in the audience. The papers generally tackled questions of military leadership, strategy, and tactics but were framed within the social and cultural context of the war. Volumes derived from these conferences and substantial post-conference editorial shaping were published in the Military Campaigns series. Gallagher's own essays in the volumes on the 1862 Richmond Campaign, Antietam, Fredericksburg, Chancellorsville, Gettysburg, and the Wilderness reveal how soldier and civilian morale was intertwined with and inseparable from military operations. His conclusions drew from hundreds of letters, diaries, and newspaper accounts. From a deep reading in the primary literature a common argument emerged: Civil War era Americans pinned their hopes to the fate of their armies, but civilian morale and loyalty was often contradictory, fluid, and situational.

Gallagher's greatest impact on the field is arguably his editorship of the Civil War America book series at UNC Press. First conceived with press director Matthew Hodgson in the late 1980s, the series developed a reputation over time as the premier home for scholarly and crossover books in the field. It also demonstrated to other publishers the dynamism and intellectual excitement in Civil War history. Louisiana State University Press created its own Civil War book series in 2002, and other university presses, including Georgia, Kent State, Tennessee, and Fordham, among others, followed suit. The result was a vigorous outpouring of scholarship beginning in the 1990s and continuing today. From 1987 to 2012 Gallagher wrote some 200 single-spaced reader reports and shepherded 115 manuscripts to book publication, offering guidance on scores more that could not be published at UNC Press but found a home elsewhere. The first volumes were almost entirely campaign studies, traditional in their orientation but integrating social and political history. In the late 1990s and into the next decade, however, several new monographs signaled a broader transformation in a field that was growing more expansive and innovative.[8]

Building on the success of these volumes, Gallagher and his UNC Press partners recruited historians whose manuscripts possessed intellectual breadth and methodological dynamism, embracing a vision to tell the stories of Civil War Americans of all backgrounds. One of the important, and novel, signals of the orientation of the series was the inclusion of "era" in the title. Rather than seeking out manuscripts that addressed questions bounded by 1861–65, the series broke down chronological and geographical barriers, placing the conflict in the context of the long nineteenth century and adopting both national and global perspectives. By encouraging scholars to write accessibly and by encouraging manuscripts from historians outside the traditional academy, Gallagher helped ensure that books in the series could speak to both academic and popular audiences.

The culmination of Gallagher's role as an editor came in his collaboration with Michael Parrish on the Littlefield History of the Civil War Era series. Published by UNC Press but underwritten by the Littlefield Fund for Southern History, the series returned Gallagher to his intellectual roots at the University of Texas. Now totaling sixteen volumes, Gallagher conceived of the series as a synthetic treatment of the issues that had long animated his career and the field over the previous thirty years. The range of topics—volumes on religion, gender, memory, and diplomacy accompanied by more classic titles on theaters of war—reveals just how broad and dynamic the field has become. Several titles, including Joseph Reidy's volume on emancipation and Thavolia Glymph's on women, have won top awards in the field.[9]

Gallagher's editorship of the Littlefield series, like his editorship of the Civil War America series with UNC Press, underscores his expansive approach to the study of the Civil War. One result of his editorial vision in the Civil War America series was to encourage research that took women and enslaved people seriously as historical actors, perspectives rarely entertained by Civil War historians before 1990. Similarly, although Gallagher's own scholarship has usually focused on the eastern theater of the Civil War, he has supported (through his editing and encouraging his students' work) a shift in the historiography that takes account of the western and trans-Mississippi theater as well as events in the Mountain West. Gallagher has written extensively about Robert E. Lee and command-level decision-making in both armies, but he has also ensured that scholars paid attention to rank-and-file soldiers, North and South, and mid-level commanders.

The essays in this volume take up three broad themes that are central to Gallagher's body of work: national sentiment, the centrality of military events, and the intersection of history and memory. Contributors have also followed Gallagher's career-long emphasis on close engagement with primary sources and a continued effort to understand historical actors on their own terms. Even as new lines of inquiry develop from the influence of a new generation of historians, we believe the essays gathered here reinforce the ongoing value and vitality of questions that Gallagher helped ensure would be central to the field.

One of Gallagher's most important contributions to the historiography has been his emphasis on nationalism—both that of the Confederacy and that of the Union. But as the first three essays in this collection argue, the story of nations and nationalism *beyond* the United States and the Confederacy proved integral to the American Civil War as well. William A. Blair's essay highlights the fluidity of Confederate diplomacy by analyzing treaty relations with Native American communities. He shows that the Confederacy's willingness to negotiate with Indigenous people did not signal a newfound respect for Indian rights; rather, Confederate actions appear akin to global debates about the relationship between imperialism and racialized rule. Like other recent work on Native Americans, Blair's story reveals both the strategies of rule by dominant powers and the strategies of resistance by subjugated people. Aaron Sheehan-Dean's chapter advocates for the use of comparative history as a method that can help us better understand the war's meaning in American life. It builds on the recent work in global and transnational history to show the new analytical frameworks that are replacing the dominant ones of the last few decades. Andre M. Fleche's essay revisits the concept of Confederate nationalism within a transnational framework. Rather than debating its verity and strength, he asks why white Southerners' response to a political problem took a nationalist form. He argues that white Southerners looked to the examples and ideas about state building among both North and South American nations in an attempt to use the power of the nation-state to protect their interests as slaveholders. Fleche thus provides a keen insight into how the Confederacy attempted to establish itself among the family of nations and, equally as important, into the ways in which its failure to do so played into the South's defeat.

A second dominant theme within Gallagher's scholarship is the centrality of military affairs. What happened on the battlefield imbued American understandings of the war while shaping enslaved people's quest for freedom and framing civilian protests at home. The reverse was true as well.

Campaigns and battles did not occur in a vacuum; they were informed and influenced by social, legal, and political relations. The three essays that compose the second portion of the book build on this premise by examining how social, political, and legal circumstances helped to define the limits of warfare or the change wrought by the war. Wayne Hsieh's chapter challenges conventional notions about the relationship between the nature of warfare and the nature of modernity, especially in the context of a slave society. Rejecting older notions that the North embodied the sole spirit of modernity, Hsieh investigates the tensions between the Southern culture of honor and the bureaucratic institutions and rules of the army, revealing the military as a key part of state development within the slaveholding South. Caroline E. Janney's essay turns to the problem of defining partisan or guerrilla warfare. Exploring the military commission trial of nineteen-year-old John McCue of John S. Mosby's partisan rangers in 1865, she argues that by maintaining deliberately vague definitions of irregulars, the US military could utilize the laws of war to wage battle by judicial means. Of equal importance, she demonstrates the ways in which the military, politics, and the law continually shaped one another even after Appomattox. Cynthia Nicoletti's essay extends this discussion deep into the era of Reconstruction. Following Robert Smalls's efforts to retain land that he had purchased at a tax sale, Nicoletti highlights the intersection of the military, politics, and the law in land redistribution along the coast of South Carolina. An 1862 act aimed at collecting taxes in the insurrectionary states had imposed a strict penalty for nonpayment: the property would be sold after ninety days' delinquency. But the statute had been intentionally designed to ensure noncompliance—made possible by the presence of the US Army. These tax sales, Nicoletti argues, proved to be the sole legal mechanism undergirding wartime land redistribution that survived Presidential Reconstruction. As she notes, "The durability of Black landownership secured through tax titles represented a small victory in a sea of disappointed hopes."

The tension between history and memory has formed a third leitmotif in Gallagher's teaching, public presentations, and writing. While emphasizing the importance of what happened, he reminds us that both the Civil War generation and subsequent generations have remembered and written about historical events and personalities in starkly different ways. "Popular memory often trumps reality," he observes in his most recent volume, "because people almost always act on what they perceive to be the truth, however far that perception might stray from historical reality."[10] The essays in the third section pick up this strand, asking us to consider how we construct history. Peter

S. Carmichael's essay highlights the interplay between historical silences, political discourse, and historical memory. Notwithstanding a robust set of rules for the Union military, the Hicksford Raid in 1864 revealed all the worst elements of the Civil War, from sexual violence to grisly acts of reprisal. But a century later the horrifying violence had been forgotten by a small Virginia community, leading Carmichael to question how and what we remember. Kathryn J. Shively explores Gen. Jubal A. Early's postwar narratives as the starting point for much of the American historical writing about the war. As Shively explains, Early employed the techniques of a historian—impartial tone, an emphasis on evidence, and peer review—to construct a defense and valorization of the Confederacy that held sway for well more than a century. Peter C. Luebke demonstrates the crucial role veterans played in the creation of the American historical profession. He shows the process of archive building as deeply embedded in the contest over the war's meaning and memory. But equally as important, he convincingly demonstrates how veterans employed modern historical methods to write a draft of the war's history that would shape the narrative for decades to come.

Taken together, these essays bear the influence of Gallagher's mentorship and scholarship. They also look forward, extending questions he posed and those he encouraged others to explore, beseeching us to look anew at the evidence and the demands on historians to write relevant and meaningful history. They ask us to reconsider the differences between history and memory, examine our perceptions about the nature of warfare, and evaluate the transnational aspects of the war as well as nationalism. The trajectory from Gallagher's writings to this volume reinforces the vitality and creativity that characterize the field of Civil War history more generally. The volume's title—*The War That Made America*—takes inspiration from Gallagher's belief that this era was the pivotal one in creating the modern world we now inhabit. As the essays make clear, the violence of the conflict reshaped rather than definitively settled the problems that generated the conflict in the first place. As a result, we hope that readers see that despite being one of the most extensively covered topics in the American past, the Civil War continues to provide scholars with an opportunity to connect contemporary events with their historical roots and to help modern readers see the full range of possibilities that inhered in the past.

ll of the contributors to this volume are both friends and colleagues, and we enjoyed the opportunity to work with them again. We thank them for the willingness to participate, for their patience,

and for their fine scholarship. One of the great benefits of studying under Gary Gallagher was his ability to attract and sustain generous and fun people. Our work on this book renewed that sentiment.

We are grateful to everyone at UNC Press who helped make this book possible. Mark Simpson-Vos, a longtime champion of Civil War history, helped us envision the project and challenged us to create a work emblematic of Gary's own contributions to the field. We appreciate his faith in this volume. The outside readers for the Press offered valuable feedback on all parts of the manuscript and the finished book is much stronger as a result—they have our deep gratitude. We also thank Dominique Moore and Thomas Bedenbaugh for their help in managing the process and Julie Bush for her typically excellent copyediting. Alongside the UNC Press staff, we thank our spouses—Spencer, Beth, and Megan—who, though unpaid, have tolerated and even supported this project (and its accompanying text message, emails, and Zoom meetings) with grace and good cheer.

We close by thanking Gary Gallagher for everything he has done as a mentor, friend, and scholar. His example of diligent and serious scholarship combined with wry humor has inspired and sustained us all for many years. As an advisor, he was unfailingly generous in reading drafts, offering ideas, and tolerating the dead ends and delays we conjured. His only injunction, which we have each tried to mirror in our work with graduate students, was to respect the ideas of other scholars and to ground our work in careful reading of the primary source evidence. The work we have done as scholars and the work collected in this volume offers a testament to the wisdom of that approach. We gratefully dedicate this volume to him.

NOTES

1. See, for example, David M. Potter, *Lincoln and His Party in the Secession Crisis* (New Haven, CT: Yale University Press, 1942); Roy F. Nichols, *The Disruption of American Democracy* (New York: Macmillan, 1948); Kenneth M. Stampp, *And the War Came: The North and the Secession Crisis, 1860–1861* (Baton Rouge: Louisiana State University Press, 1950); Benjamin Quarles, *The Negro in the Civil War* (Boston: Little, Brown, 1953); David Donald, *Charles Sumner and the Coming of the Civil War* (New York: Knopf, 1960); Benjamin Quarles, *Lincoln and the Negro* (New York: Oxford University Press, 1962); and David M. Potter, *The South and the Sectional Conflict* (Baton Rouge: Louisiana State University Press, 1968).

2. Ronald Formisano, "The Invention of the Ethnocultural Interpretation," *American Historical Review* 99, no. 2 (April 1994): 453–77.

3. Among the many still valuable studies were Thomas L. Connelly, *Autumn of Glory: The Army of Tennessee, 1862–1865* (Baton Rouge: Louisiana State University Press, 1971); Thomas

B. Alexander and Richard E. Beringer, *The Anatomy of the Confederate Congress: A Study of the Influences of Member Characteristics on Legislative Voting Behavior, 1861–1865* (Nashville: Vanderbilt University Press, 1972); D. P. Crook, *Diplomacy during the American Civil War* (New York: John Wiley, 1975); Joel H. Silbey, *A Respectable Minority: The Democratic Party in the Civil War Era, 1860–1868* (New York: Norton, 1977); and Herman Hattaway and Archer Jones, *How the North Won: A Military History of the Civil War* (Urbana: University of Illinois Press, 1983). Works produced for lay audiences likewise stressed soldiers and campaigns, most notably the Time-Life series, released between 1983 and 1987.

4. Robert M. Citino, "Military Histories Old and New: A Reintroduction," *American Historical Review* 112, no. 4 (October 2007): 1070–90.

5. Maris Vinovskis, "Have Social Historians Lost the Civil War? Some Preliminary Demographic Speculations," *Journal of American History* 76 (1989): 34–58.

6. Gallagher's "Consistent Conservative: Jubal A. Early's Patriotic Submission," in *Becoming Confederates: Paths to a New National Loyalty* (Athens: University of Georgia Press, 2013), 57–82, and "Shaping Public Memory of the Civil War: Robert E. Lee, Jubal A. Early, and Douglas Southall Freeman," in *Lee and His Army in Confederate History* (Chapel Hill: University of North Carolina Press, 2001), 255–82, are the most important.

7. The Society of Civil War Historians, https://scwh.memberclicks.net/about.

8. Noel Fisher's *War at Every Door: Partisan Politics and Guerrilla Violence in East Tennessee, 1860–1869* (Chapel Hill: University of North Carolina Press, 1997); Carol Reardon's *Pickett's Charge in History and Memory* (Chapel Hill: University of North Carolina Press, 1997); James Marten's *The Children's Civil War* (Chapel Hill: University of North Carolina Press, 1998); Stephen V. Ash's *When the Yankees Came: Conflict and Chaos in the Occupied South, 1861–1865* (Chapel Hill: University of North Carolina Press, 1999); and Alice Fahs's *The Imagined Civil War: Popular Literature of the North and South, 1861–1865* (Chapel Hill: University of North Carolina Press, 2001).

9. Joseph P. Reidy, *Illusions of Emancipation: The Pursuit of Freedom and Equality in the Twilight of Slavery* (Chapel Hill: University of North Carolina Press, 2019); Thavolia Glymph, *The Women's Fight: The Civil War's Battles for Home, Freedom, and Nation* (Chapel Hill: University of North Carolina Press, 2020).

10. Gary W. Gallagher, *The Enduring Civil War: Reflections on the Great American Crisis* (Baton Rouge: Louisiana State University Press, 2020), 7.

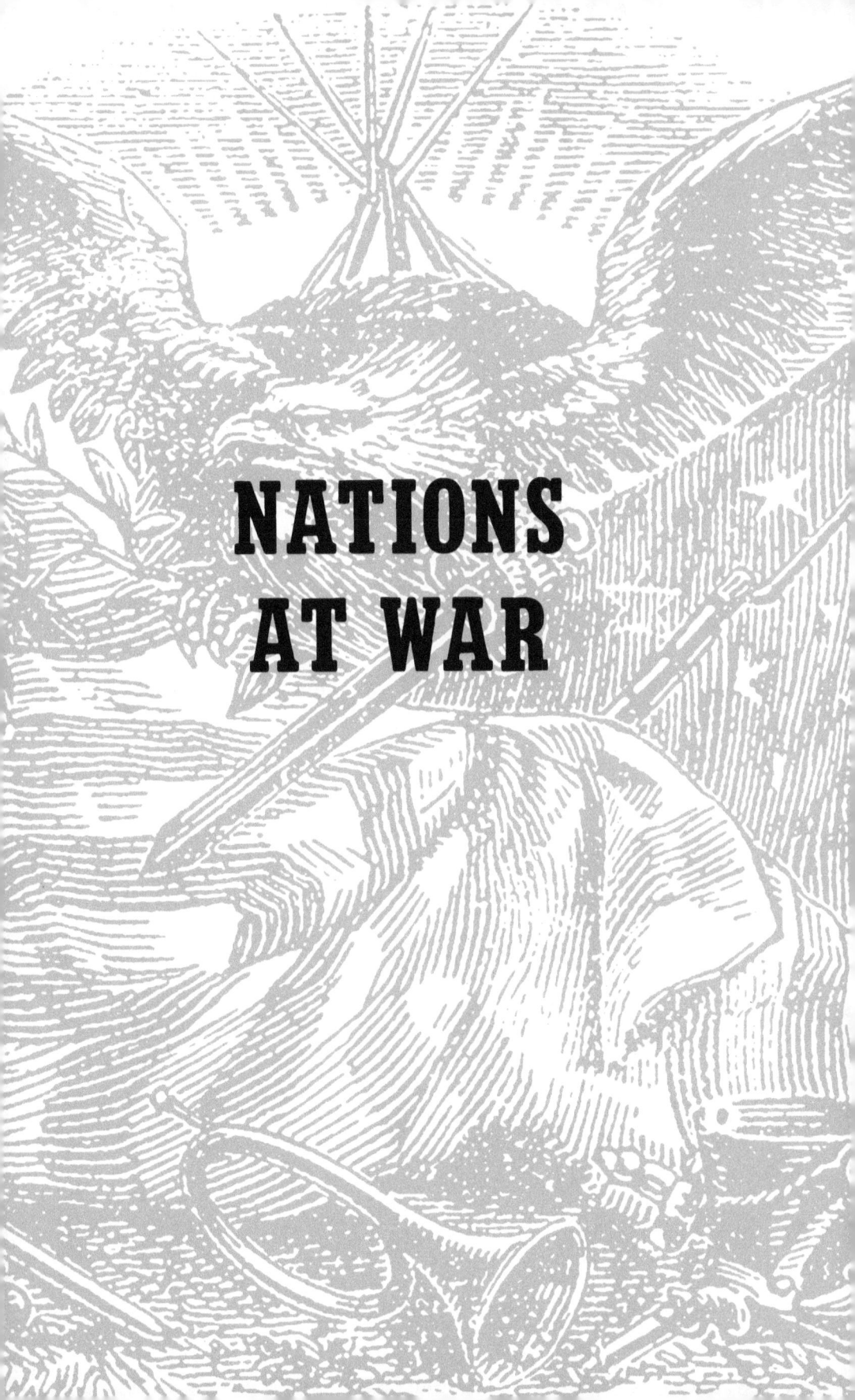

NATIONS AT WAR

Protecting Their Self-Interest

Native American Governance in the Confederacy

WILLIAM A. BLAIR

On May 1, 1863, the Confederacy enacted legislation to regulate elections in Indian Territory. The balloting was to be part of voting throughout the Confederate States for representatives to the Confederate Congress. Native Americans already had sent delegates to that legislative body, elected through Indigenous practices. The new law solidified procedures for electing and seating Indian representatives in Richmond. The Confederacy set the time for voting in Indian Territory for the first Monday of September 1863. The law stipulated who qualified for participation and allowed for absentee balloting by Indians in the army. Warfare apparently disrupted the 1863 election from occurring in Indian Territory, yet the voting for a national delegate represented an example of the remarkable relationship between the Confederacy and Indigenous people, one in which the Anglo war gave Native Americans more bargaining power than they ever had held with the US government.[1]

As unprecedented was that the person who introduced this legislation for Indigenous voting for representation in a white man's legislature was a Native American from the Cherokee Nation. Elias Cornelius Boudinot had received special dispensation from his colleagues to offer the bill in the Confederate House of Representatives. It was not the only time that he drafted legislation. Although not allowed to vote, he often pushed the limits of his involvement. Later he made a passionate appeal for an appropriation of $100,000 to offset destitution among his people—an effort in which he succeeded, while leaving a record of a Native American's speech on the floor of the House. He was not the sole Native American in the Confederate Congress. Richard M. Jones served as a delegate from the Chickasaw and Choctaw Nations, and Samuel B. Callahan represented the Creek and Seminole. Of the three, Boudinot amassed the most visible legislative record, yet they all left their footprints on the political history of the Confederacy.[2]

The Confederate States of America created alliances with the Five Nations not as territories or states but as protectorates. In exchange for Indian help with the war against the Union, the South assumed the responsibility for defending the territory from invasion while respecting home rule for Native Americans. The treaties guaranteed that no outside authority could choose Native leaders or dictate their laws. The pacts created the possibility for district courts in the territory that placed before juries of their peers those Native Americans who were in conflicts with whites from other states. The terms also enabled them to testify in white civil and criminal trials in Confederate state courts, as well as to bring suit. Importantly, the Confederacy assumed the obligations for annuity and other payments owed to the Five Nations by the US government. And selected tribes could have nonvoting representation in the Confederate Congress. Small wonder that historians of the Choctaw and Cherokee Nations have considered the treaties the most favorable made to that point.[3]

It would be wrong, however, to conclude that white Southern leaders had suddenly become racial progressives when it came to Native Americans or to think that such relations would have continued smoothly between the two had the Confederacy won its independence. The Anglo-American government included men who had supported the tragic and destructive dispossession of the Five Nations from their lands in the 1830s. No, what transpired between the two parties came about because it met the self-interest of both sides. Paternalism by whites permeated the relationship as Confederate leaders drew the line against making Native Americans equal partners. The treaties also caused hesitation among Cherokees who saw the relationship as echoing the Supreme Court cases of the 1830s that declared the tribe a dependent nation rather than a separate power. Yet an alliance based on protectorates provided Native Americans with the best course forward through uncertain times. And it allowed the rebel government to keep Native Americans close while also maintaining their distance.[4]

Southern leaders reached out to Native Americans to serve their present military needs and their future nation-building goals.[5] For the more immediate emergency, Indian troops helped stabilize, in the words of one historian, the South's "western flank, preventing Union troops from taking control south of Kansas and Missouri, and engaging in guerrilla-style fighting to keep the enemy off balance." Any friends under arms aided the Confederate cause.[6] The alliance also served Southern white interests in fending off abolition, since the Indian supporters of the Confederacy tended to practice slaveholding and neighboring Kansas was leaning toward becoming a free state. Additionally, an Indian Territory friendly to the rebel government could impede Union invaders from access to the cattle and valuable cotton lands in Texas and Arkansas.[7]

In the longer term, the unprecedented participation in governance earned by Native Americans underscored the geopolitical importance of the region for potential expansion of the Confederate state. Some considered it possible to push white settlement into Indian Territory, while others saw the region as a stepping stone, along with Texas, for extending the Southern government through New Mexico Territory to California. Even before a commissioner negotiated treaties with Native Americans in Indian Territory, Confederate forces in March 1861 occupied what became Arizona. By December it was organized as a territory with a governor. And by January 1862, a nonvoting delegate from Arizona Territory came to the Confederate Congress—serving in a capacity just like the Native Americans who later joined him. The Southwest appealed to Southern leaders, who saw its gold and silver as a way to help pay for the war. The region's acquisition could also lead to the revival of an overland postal route and construction of a railroad along the thirty-second parallel to the Pacific. Indian achievements in their treaties revealed how Confederate leaders imagined the current physical margins of their new nation, as well as its possible future.[8]

But the alliance with Native Americans never fully functioned. In fact, the treaties escalated conflict among Creeks and Cherokees. Union forces hampered the Confederate government's sending of supplies to Native allies, which caused great suffering. The summer of 1863 also witnessed Federal victories in the region that changed the strategic situation permanently in favor of the Union. In such an environment, the election for Confederate representatives does not appear to have been held.[9] That these treaties failed to meet their promise resulted from the strife that rained upon the region. For the Indian delegates who left for Richmond, though, the suffering became a top priority for them to relieve. Through these efforts, they left a mark on the legislative history of the Confederacy.

The Confederate goal for establishing relations with Native Americans emerged immediately after seven Deep South states had created a new government. In March 1861, even before Indigenous people had come within the new government's purview, the Confederacy created a Bureau of Indian Affairs. Southern leaders, however, had to wait for the secession of Arkansas in early May until they could send the emissary from that same state, who was seasoned in handling Indian affairs. Albert Pike, New England–born lawyer and poet who had become an adopted Southerner, crafted the treaties with Indians residing west of Arkansas and south of Kansas. Beginning in late May, Pike traveled throughout Indian Territory for more than five months. As a commissioner chosen by President Jefferson Davis, he met with both single and multiple tribes while drafting nine treaties that became the basis of Native relations with the Confederate States.

The treaties underscored that Native Americans had leverage in negotiating with white people divided by civil war. Pike understood that to win allegiance of the tribes, he had to exceed the terms he had been authorized to grant. At first, he was prevented from proposing that the Confederacy assume the financial obligations of the United States to the Nations. He quickly saw that the lack of such a provision would not wash: it was too important to all the Native leaders. He explained to Davis in his final report, "We proposed to ask them to put their lands, their slaves, their very national existence on the hazard of the die, and take up arms for us, while we should decline to assume to pay them what we and the North together justly owe them." The Confederate Congress ultimately conceded this provision.[10]

Pike could not, however, grant another concession. In the preamble of the treaties, he referred to the Confederate government as forming "the protectorate of the several nations and tribes of Indians" living west of Arkansas and Missouri. Most historians have overlooked the significance of the term "protectorate," but it was not lost on Native Americans. Pike found some opposition, especially among Cherokees, to a relationship that they saw as relegating them to wards needing outside assistance for their defense. The tribes wished to negotiate as independent nations. Cherokees bristled at an alliance that seemingly affirmed "the correctness of the decision of the Supreme Court of the United States in the Cherokee case." This referred to the ruling by Chief Justice John Marshall in *Cherokee Nation v. Georgia* that determined the Natives to be "a Domestic dependent nation," adding, "Their relation to the United States resembles that of a ward to his guardian." The language announced the second-class status of Natives. On this point, however, Pike could not yield, knowing that it could scuttle support of the pacts in Richmond. He gained acceptance from the Nations by underscoring the extent that the treaties allowed for sovereignty over home rule, as well as by providing the annuity payments that were vital to personal security. The promise of military support in the form of munitions and supplies also factored into decisions. Ultimately, the terms proved acceptable enough and were certainly more than what the United States was offering.[11]

"Protectorate" echoed treaties with Native Americans enacted since the formation of the United States. In the agreement at Fort Harmar (1789), for instance, the government employed phrasing that had become common by establishing "friendship and protection" with Indigenous nations. The earliest treaties promised this in exchange for Native Americans returning prisoners or ceding lands. The pacts did little to recognize governance within the Nations except to consider them as foreign powers, caring mostly about land distribution and about policing conflicts that erupted between Native and Anglo societies. In other words, the terms were duplicitous, with the so-called guardian merely looking for ever-expanding concessions of territory on the part of Native Americans.[12]

Having the potential for a delegate to a white legislature also was not new. Both the Treaty of Hopewell (1785) with various groups and the more famous Treaty of New Echota (1835) with the Cherokee allowed for such a possibility with the US Congress. In the case of New Echota, article 7 recognized the Nation as containing people who had made such progress toward "civilization" that "they shall be entitled to a delegate in the House of Representatives of the United States whenever Congress shall make provision for the same." That promise, however, was not realized.[13] Pike again took the initiative to add this provision when not everyone in Richmond considered it necessary.[14]

In his effort to overcome Native objections to functioning as a protectorate, Pike went too far by creating terms that caused a backlash from Confederate leaders. The original draft of the joint treaty with the Chickasaw and Choctaw contained language that suggested that Indigenous people had a path toward statehood and citizenship. Article 28 stated that when the people of the Nation held an election that expressed the desire to become a state, both the Choctaw and Chickasaw Nations would be "admitted into the

Confederacy as one of the Confederate States, on equal terms, in all respects with the original States." All tribal members then would become citizens.[15] Even the Cherokee treaty, although lacking the phrasing for statehood, implied that the Nation enjoyed a status similar to that of territories. It stipulated that Cherokees could send a delegate to advocate for their interests in the Confederate House of Representatives, adding that the person would "be entitled to same rights and privileges as may be enjoyed by Delegates from any Territories of the Confederate States."[16]

President Davis spoke out against these parts of the treaties. When he submitted the pacts to Congress for ratification, he pointed out the danger of what he considered to be an "unconstitutional" arrangement that deprived Congress of its power to determine rules for its body by permitting nonvoting delegates to the House; however, he was as concerned about what he called "the unqualified right of admission as a State into the compact of the Confederacy." He recommended that the provision that gave Indian delegates territorial equivalency be rejected, as well as the language providing for statehood.[17]

Legislators agreed, underscoring the racial bias that lay beneath the seemingly democratic impulse. It was undesirable to give Native Americans an avenue for becoming citizens. Representatives dropped the reference to territorial rights, allowing Native American delegates the ability to represent their people "with such other rights and privileges as may be determined by the House of Representatives." Congress thus retained control over whom it authorized for a seat in the lower house and under what conditions the individual served.[18] Native Americans accepted the amendments, because they cared more about autonomy over their own affairs than about becoming full-fledged members of a Confederate nation. An additional reason for leaning toward the Confederacy came from the concern that the United States would use disorder from war as an excuse for further rapacious land grabs on the part of Unionist whites. Rumors abounded of threats that could come via abolitionists in Kansas, and newspapers twisted comments of then senator William Henry Seward to make it appear as if the Republican Party intended to push Native Americans out of the territory. This raised concerns that the US government would further exploit Native resources.[19]

Ironically, the status of protectorate could be used by Native Americans to defend their interests, something they adroitly displayed during the secession crisis as they rebutted charges of disloyalty. When Northerners accused Native Americans pondering whether to ally with the Confederacy as engaging in "secession," representatives of the Chickasaw and Choctaw conducting business in Washington, DC, rejected the criticism, clarifying that no decisions had yet been made about severing relations with the Union.

Yet the six Indigenous signers of this public letter revealed what they believed to be the limits of allegiance under a protectorate. "The position and relation of the Indian tribes towards the Government of the United States do not seem to be very clearly understood; otherwise the charge of 'secession purposes' would not be made against them." The writers indicated that because their nations had not become an integral part of the Federal Union, they hardly could secede from something they had never belonged to. They added, "They have been regarded by the United States as foreign Governments, with whom treaties have been made, establishing a protectorate over them, and defining clearly their relations to the Federal Government." Although under the protection of the United States, the Nations had "the right of self-government."[20]

Nearly a year and half into the war, the principal chief of the Cherokee Nation, who was in exile in the Northeast, took a similar approach. John Ross in September 1862 wrote a follow-up memorandum after an interview with President Abraham Lincoln in which he explained that his Nation had not been disloyal in aligning with the Confederacy. He reminded the president that the Federal army had withdrawn from Indian Territory in 1861, leaving the region at the mercy of Confederates, which violated the central responsibility of a protectorate. (This line of thought made a deep impression on many within the Indian Nations, in essence laying blame for the Indian alliance with the Confederacy on a breach of obligations by the United States.) He said that the treaties before the Civil War "were Treaties of Friendship and Alliance" and that the Cherokee Nation placed "itself under the protection of the United States and no other Sovereign whatever," with "the United States solemnly promising that Protection." Without a physical, military presence by the United States, Cherokees "were forced for the preservation of their country" to negotiate with the Confederate States.[21]

Not all Native American alliances received the right to advocate for their interests in the Confederate Congress: white bias created a racial ranking among Indigenous societies for what terms should be in play. Treaties with the Seneca, Shawnee, and Quapaw, in the words of one historian, "form a distinct class among the Pike treaties." These groups were held in lower esteem by white officials than the Five Nations. Their treaties did call on them to be parties at war and agree to furnish troops. "But this was neither an alliance nor a recognition of the nationality of these tribes," wrote Walter Lee Brown. "They were not, for instance, given delegates to Congress, nor control over their own trade."[22] Having a voice in governance with the Confederacy involved primarily the people who had been evicted from the Southeast in the 1830s.

The negotiations with Native Americans and Pike did not go entirely smoothly, revealing tensions among Indians. It was natural for some to side with the Confederacy because the Native people had come from the South and recognized slaveholding, which was guaranteed under the Southern government. However, the Confederates were some of the same people who had most strongly advocated for the forced removal of the citizens of the Nations. The memories of this tragedy had not waned. Also, it was not clear who would win the war between white people. It made sense to choose wisely, especially if—as ultimately happened—a Confederate alliance brought warfare into Indian Territory.

Cherokees led by John Ross at first rejected Southern overtures as they tried to maintain neutrality. It took Pike two attempts to reach a bargain. And although the tribe eventually joined an alliance in October 1861, it caused a segment to break off to maintain ties with the Union. Choctaw leaders also at first wished to avoid an alliance with Confederates, but the scales were tipped by the lobbying of Robert M. Jones, one of the wealthiest men in Indian Territory and a future delegate to the Confederate Congress. As for the Creek Nation, Pike timed his visit when the leadership opposing the Confederacy was away on other business. When these leaders returned after a treaty had been drafted, they rejected the pact and eventually mounted a bloody resistance under Chief Opothleyahola that resulted in refugees heading into Kansas.[23]

Even though the pacts awakened strong minority opposition among several tribes, the sum of the agreements was more than the Five Nations had enjoyed before the Civil War. Although Native American voting under the Confederacy was limited to tribes' selecting their own officials and not white political leaders, the alliance did not require them to abandon their traditions, lands, or sovereignty. True, there were some issues that had the potential to irk, such as whether white agents had the right to determine the logistics of elections.[24] Unlike provisions with the United States, however, the Nations received representation in the Confederate Congress, the possibility of a fairer judicial system in conflicts with whites, and autonomy in trade and lawmaking.[25]

Warfare did not allow the terms of the treaties to be fulfilled. The Civil War brought massive destruction that turned thousands of Southern-leaning refugees from their homes to seek safe harbor deeper within Indian Territory.

Amid this distress, the wheels of governance for Southern Cherokees continued to turn as Natives meshed their constitutional practices with Confederate policies while maintaining autonomy. Meanwhile, the Cherokee delegate made his way to Richmond, where his advocacy for the law regarding voting in Indian Territory revealed the contours of the Confederate-Indian alliance.

Elias Cornelius Boudinot represented a logical choice to serve as the Cherokee delegate to the Confederate Congress both because of his Native American lineage and because of his ability to move easily between two worlds. He was the son of Elias Boudinot, one of three Cherokee leaders murdered in 1839 by opponents outraged over supporting a treaty that ceded lands east of the Mississippi. Cornelius was sent to live with his deceased mother's family in New England, where he remained until adulthood. He returned to the West in the 1850s, settling in Arkansas, where he became an attorney and then an editor of two newspapers. His acumen and connections in working in a white political world propelled his rise to the chair of the Democratic State Central Committee and then to the position of secretary of the Arkansas Secession Convention.[26]

The Arkansas connections gave him friends in high places. Boudinot had the support of important white political figures—Senators Robert Ward Johnson and Charles Burton Mitchel, both from the state. Johnson especially exerted political clout as a former US congressman and senator; he was also the nephew of Richard Mentor Johnson, former vice president under Martin Van Buren. These networks, as well as the importance of Indian support for holding the Southern frontier, enabled Boudinot to contribute to the political history of the Confederacy.[27]

Southern defeat in the Battle of Pea Ridge in March 1862 and incursions by the Union later in the summer put Cherokees on the defensive and prompted a change in leadership. Union soldiers captured and then immediately paroled Chief John Ross, who left the territory in July and spent the rest of the war, for the most part, in Philadelphia. Kindred souls fled, too. Ross continued to comport himself as chief and, as noted, entered talks with the Lincoln administration. His supporters likewise considered him the rightful leader of the Cherokee Nation.

The situation required the Confederate Cherokees to reconstitute their government. During a mass meeting on August 21, 1862, they selected Stand Watie as the new principal chief. He was an uncle to Cornelius and the brother of the elder Boudinot slain in 1839 by men associated with Ross. Watie and Ross had been political foes for decades. At the same time, the assembly reaffirmed the constitution and laws of the Cherokee Nation, lending legitimacy to its organization as opposed to the faction under Ross. This became the government that aligned itself with the Confederacy.[28]

The body that performed this task was not the usual governing apparatus. The Cherokee had a two-branch legislature consisting of the National Committee and the Council, together referred to as the National Council. But Southern Cherokees met in August 1862 as a general convention, an appropriate mechanism for authorizing a constitution. Boudinot himself referred to this governing body during wartime as a "Convention," and Watie used the phrases "general mass convention" and "Cherokee National Convention." It persisted in meeting episodically in the capacity of a legislature for perhaps more than a year—the record is not clear on this point. It seemed to function like the Southern secession conventions that continued to handle legislative functions until new elections could be held.[29] Because some members of this body also served in the Confederate army, they performed double duty as both lawmakers and soldiers, with the principal chief often conducting official, executive business for his constituency while under arms in the field.

Even after this meeting, rival governments operated. Although Ross had left the territory, followers maintained a separate legislature from the Watie faction. The Ross supporters used the same constitution, organizational structure, and terminology as their political opponents. Consequently, in late 1864 Lewis Downing, acting principal chief for the Ross Cherokees, sent a request to an officer of the Union Indian brigade to allow thirty members of the National Committee and the Council to attend the annual meeting of the legislative body. Although this did not include the Native Americans who supported the Confederacy, the request showed the parallel structures that existed and the obstacles that faced lawmakers who tried to hold sessions while serving on the front lines of military action.[30]

Battles, raids, and skirmishes could disrupt legislative business. If the war enabled Ross supporters to follow their constitution, the thirty members of the National Council who served in the Union Indian ranks represented 75 percent of the legislative body. Cherokees voted for a total of forty representatives: electors from eight districts chose two for the National Committee and three for the Council. (Choctaws also elected forty members to their General Council.) The circumstances suggest that public officials on both sides of the Nation—unlike Anglo congressmen—either did not receive exemptions from military service or did not apply for them. The Cherokee National Council, according to the constitution, had to meet only annually, which undoubtedly helped matters: the representatives did not need the longer, multiple sessions employed by the Confederate Congress. But for either the Ross or the Watie government, the demands of war could tie down representatives in military service, complicating the timing for handling legislative affairs.[31]

When Boudinot showed up in Richmond as a delegate for the Watie government, a delay occurred in his seating that indicated the procedures between the two societies had not yet meshed. Nor had Southern legislators thought through the extent of participation for a delegate from the Five Tribes. On October 7, 1862, Representative Felix I. Batson of Arkansas welcomed someone he undoubtedly knew well from Democratic politics at home and moved that Boudinot be afforded the privileges of a member on the floor. However, Representative Henry S. Foote of Tennessee rose to amend the motion. He did not mind allowing Boudinot a seat, but he wished to refer "the question of privilege to the Committee on Indian Affairs." Boudinot could watch what unfolded, but it remained to be determined if he could raise as much as a hand for recognition, much less his voice.[32]

Committee members on Indian Affairs quickly resolved that Boudinot was "entitled to a seat on the floor of the House as a delegate from the Cherokee nation." This recommendation came without further explanation on October 9, or two days after he appeared. It enabled him to step forward to the Speaker's desk to swear an oath of loyalty to the Confederate States of America. At age twenty-seven, he became one of the two youngest people in the House.[33] His biographer suggests that the members of the committee had to define the participation afforded nonvoting delegates: "the question of privilege" raised by Foote. That makes sense, since representatives had more on their plates with mobilizing for war than defining the rights of an Indian delegate—until someone showed up to force the issue.[34] But subsequent action by legislators suggested that they also had in mind how to certify these new elections so that delegates arrived with the credentials for their seating.

The solution for this problem came via a Native American leaving his imprint on Confederate legislation. At a new session of the Confederate Congress on April 1, 1863, Boudinot proposed the bill that became "An Act to Provide Certain Regulations for Holding Elections for Delegates to the Congress of the Confederate States in Certain Indian Nations." That he could introduce the legislation showed the trust he enjoyed from lawmakers, which enabled him to creep close to serving as a full-fledged member. This represented a change from his initial status: prior to this, he had to lean on another member to present a memorial on his behalf. The privilege to introduce the election bill on his own came "under suspension of the rule," indicating it was out of the ordinary. Even this exception to procedures, however, did not allow him to vote.[35]

The law enacted on May 1, 1863, fused Native American with Southern white electoral practices, underscoring the alliance between the two societies. The Confederacy reaffirmed the autonomy of the Nations by allowing elections to proceed "according to the mode prescribed by the laws of the several Nations." In other words, Native rules and practices prevailed. Additionally, the law placed the governor (in the case of the Choctaw and Chickasaw) or the principal chief in the position of certifying the results, both from citizens who voted at home and from those voting absentee if they served in the Confederate army. Successful delegates received a certificate attesting to their victory. Elections were to occur every two years on the first Monday in September. To vote, electors had to swear loyalty to the Confederate States and could not have deserted to the enemy or sought protection from the US government. The law standardized participation by Native Americans in a white national legislature and provided for certification of the winners that eased the seating of delegates from Indian Territory.[36]

Even before the law was in place, the importance of credentials became clear during the acceptance of Robert M. Jones as a delegate-elect of the Choctaw and Chickasaw Nations. The electoral rules of the Choctaw Nation had dictated the method of his selection, which had occurred on October 7, 1861. Unlike Boudinot, Jones's welcome on January 17, 1863, went uneventfully. The *Journal of the Congress of the Confederate States* entry stated matter-of-factly, "Mr. Jones came forward, was duly qualified, and proceeded to take his seat." What made the difference between Jones's experience and the delay that Boudinot had faced? Jones had produced a document signed by Indian agent Douglas H. Cooper certifying that he had received the "greatest number of votes cast" as delegate to Congress for the Choctaw and Chickasaw. This made him "duly qualified."[37]

Jones left a light impression on the Confederate Congress. He tried to petition for supplies for Choctaws without making sufficient headway. One achievement came in his resolution for the distribution to the tribes within the Confederate States of 200 additional copies of the report of the commissioner of Indian Affairs. But he apparently believed that the Confederacy had broken its promise to give the Nations a true voice in governance. Jones was used to having his opinions heeded. He owned six plantations, more than twenty trading stores, and more than 200 enslaved people, and his lobbying had tipped the scales for the Choctaw to join the Confederate alliance. According to one study, Jones became disgusted with the lack of progress in the

House—especially in getting necessary supplies to Indian Territory—and resigned in June 1864, leaving his seat vacant for the rest of the war.[38]

Meanwhile, Boudinot showed what a delegate from Indian Territory could accomplish with white political connections that predated the war. Beyond the election bill, and another one for organizing Confederate courts in Indian Territory that he put forward on the same day, he continued to introduce legislation, achieving arguably his greatest visibility during lobbying for money for the Cherokee.

Choosing to go with the Confederacy shut off the flow of funds to Indians from the United States, and although the Confederacy endorsed paying the interest on annuities, it took time to sort through the situation and appropriate the amounts. Boudinot understood the potential that existed. As he told Watie in January 1863, "A good deal of money is due us and I suggest that the convention assemble and adopt the accompanying resolution authorizing me to receive such moneys." He added that if the convention "will pass this ordinance I am satisfied I can get the money, and with a full treasury you know what a new life will be infused into our infant government."[39]

After receiving the authorization from the convention to accept the money, Boudinot worked with increasing energy on finding aid as the fortunes of Southern Cherokees declined.[40] Military action had destroyed crops and dwellings, with refugees pushed south of the Arkansas River and into lands near Texas. The situation was so grim that in November 1863 Boudinot told his uncle he had borrowed "on my own responsibility $10,000 for the use of our refugees." He hoped within a couple of months to secure another loan of $40,000 from sources in Louisiana.[41]

What followed highlighted the importance to Confederate leaders for courting the continued loyalty of Indian tribes to protect the trans-Mississippi frontier. Boudinot on December 13, 1863, once again introduced a bill, this time for the Confederate government to provide $100,000 as a no-interest loan that would be paid back in full at the end of the war. If the Cherokee Nation defaulted, the amount owed could be deducted from future annuity payments. Once again showing the unusual privilege that he held, Boudinot stood up in the House to explain the rationale behind the measure. He was not simply proposing a bill; he now held the floor to address his colleagues on the appropriation, which he called "an act of plain justice."[42]

Boudinot knew how to play to the racism of the white legislators. After receiving the unanimous consent of the House to continue his remarks, he made a passionate plea for the appropriation based on the patriotism of Southern Cherokees to the Confederacy. They had resolved, he said, to "see their homes in ashes sooner than leave them to the invader." He reminded lawmakers of the progress Cherokees had made in leaving behind "aboriginal" ways while embracing "civilization." He said they no longer fit the image of "cigar-shop statuary, from which the popular conception of the Indian character were taken." A little more than a month later, the bill became law with only one dissenting vote. Whether he referred to the kind of plea he made concerning Cherokee advancement or voiced the frustration of most legislators, he told Watie, "No one unacquainted with legislative delays will appreciate the embarrassment under which I have labored."[43]

Watie reported on his nephew's accomplishment in an address in July 1864 to the traditional governing body of the Cherokee—the National Council. The principal chief had tried to hold a legislative session in April 1863 that was postponed because of action by Federal troops—the problem of having legislators also serving as soldiers. The next month he did hold a session that addressed needs for recruitment, refugees, and schools. For the 1864 session, he reminded representatives that the convention of 1862 had established the government, reaffirming the constitution and laws in operation. That was done, he said, "by that intelligent portion of the Cherokee people who could not be infected with the deliberate treachery of their principal rulers," a dig at Ross and his supporters. If they wished, Watie continued, the representatives could amend or add to the laws. However, he warned them to act quickly because military action could interrupt the session at any time. The chief urged the assembly to deliberate only "upon the most material subjects of legislative action affecting the immediate welfare of your constituents."[44]

He left little doubt over what should command their priorities. Watie said that the "destitute condition of the people" had been communicated to the Confederate government and that arrangements had been made to deliver army rations through an agent. Then he touted the achievement of his nephew who over the prior winter had obtained the appropriation for $100,000 from the government "to supply the most pressing necessities of the indigent Cherokees." Watie said that $45,000 of the money had been received by the commissioner for the Cherokee Nation, who used it to purchase articles to fill the most urgent needs. He told the Nation's lawmakers they now had to decide how to distribute goods to the people most deserving.[45]

Not everything Boudinot proposed met with the approval of his constituency. He concocted an unpopular scheme to promote white colonization in Indian Territory to boost recruitment for Native American units in the Confederate army. Under his plan, white Southerners who enlisted in Indian units—serving under Native officers—were to receive a 160-acre plot of land within the Cherokee Nation once the war ended. Boudinot hoped to settle the immigrants on Cherokee lands in the western portion of the territory. The implications were that these settlers would earn the rights of citizens in the Nation. Native Americans could receive the same land grants if they, too, mustered into service, with a maximum of 1,000 people eligible for the offer no matter the background of the person. The plan was supposed to go before voters as a referendum, but no record indicates that it went forward.[46]

If Confederates did not want Indians to have the possibility of gaining citizenship, Cherokees felt similarly strongly about an influx of white people making claims on Native rights. Reactions in the Nation against the proposal, according to one historian, were "swift and negative."[47] The acting assistant chief, president of the convention, and member of the executive council wrote Jefferson Davis a stern rebuke of the proposal. Because of hints that the plan could bring additional military appointments for Native Americans, they considered Boudinot's scheme one that surrendered "our nationality, lands, and homes" in exchange for "one brigadier general, one more colonel, a few favorite positions in office, and a ruined people." They added, "We have no longer any confidence in our delegate, and take this means of expressing to you our disapprobation of his course and the propositions made in convention upon his return." To them, Boudinot's plan would result in the wrong kind of people residing in the territory, making the Cherokee "a stranger at his home and in his own country."[48]

The repercussions from this and other positions taken by the Cherokee delegate created unhappiness with him among some constituents that festered throughout 1864. In January, Boudinot told his uncle that a judge had come to Richmond from the territory whom he suspected of bearing dispatches from a "secret caucus" that declared "I had lost the confidence of the Cherokee people, which they would testify to by electing another delegate, Bah!" He added that he laughed "at all such plots." However, he was more concerned in October when another person said he stood no chance for reelection. "I have done all and will yet do all I can for the Cherokees," he told Watie, "if they give me no credit at all with it." To help his cause, he asked his uncle to read an address by him to the Cherokees on dress parade to convey what he had done for the Nation. He had also angered others when he took a hard stand to make resistance to conscription in the territory punishable by loss of property and Native citizenship. Had the Confederacy survived beyond September 1865, Boudinot possibly could have been voted out of office through the very legislation that he had introduced.[49]

In one area, the goals of opponents overlapped with Boudinot and many others in Indian Territory. They hoped to see the creation of a separate military department from the Trans-Mississippi. Native Americans, including Watie and Boudinot, pushed for such an organizational change, which enhanced the independence of Indians and provided leadership they trusted.[50]

As part of the effort, Boudinot helped secure the appointment of his uncle as the first Native American brigadier general in the Confederate army. He took obvious pleasure in informing Watie of the appointment when it went to the Senate in early May 1864. The old Arkansas political connections had come in handy. Arkansas senators Johnson and Mitchel wrote a joint letter to President Davis on Watie's behalf, which certainly helped the cause. Yet Boudinot could not resist taking most of the credit as he boasted to his brother William, "I procured the appt. of Uncle Stand as Brig. Genl."[51]

Despite his detractors, Boudinot accomplished a great deal beyond what can be related here. In December 1863, his efforts earned him appointment as a corresponding member of the Committee on Indian Affairs. Although this came without the privilege of voting, he was the only one of the Native American delegates to win this assignment. He also worked on legislation to establish judicial courts in Indian Territory, introduced a bill to fill vacancies of delegates in Congress, and sought to have the claims answered for families of deceased Indian officers and soldiers. Additionally, he worked with a new collaborator. A third delegate from Indian Territory finally arrived in May 1864. Samuel B. Callahan, who represented the Creek and Seminole Nations, worked with Boudinot to protect the financial interests of the Nations. Confederate money had suffered from rampant inflation, and the two won the ability for Native Americans to redeem old notes on favorable terms.[52]

Boudinot never quit trying to secure relief for the destitute and payment of funds owed by the Confederate government to the Nations. Before leaving Congress in March 1865, he successfully sought for payment of annuities in cotton rather than in Confederate paper money. Nearly a month after Robert E. Lee had surrendered his army at Appomattox, Boudinot traveled near Shreveport, Louisiana, to convey the law to Gen. Edmund Kirby Smith, who agreed to consult with a Treasury agent about delivering the cotton. Boudinot knew he had to export the bales quickly to Mexico, to earn what he could before what he called "the general crash" came, which he expected by the summer. The effort went for naught. Smith surrendered his army in the trans-Mississippi before the transactions could take place.[53] Boudinot turned himself over to Federal authorities on May 26, 1865. His uncle became the last Confederate general to surrender on June 23.

Cherokees had suffered terribly for choosing the Southern side of the war. Historian Morris L. Wardell used a census of 1863 that revealed that one-third of adult Cherokee women were widows and one-fourth of the children orphans. The losses among families undoubtedly had worsened by the end of the war. Guerrilla warfare had devastated the country. Hundreds of thousands of cattle had been stolen through the complicity of Union soldiers. And tensions between the factions in the Cherokee Nation intensified. Raiders under Stand Watie had burned down Rose Cottage, the home of Chief Ross, and destroyed the plantation.[54] The war also ended slavery in Indian Territory, opening ongoing struggles among freedpeople for standing as citizens within the Nation and especially for claims on lands.[55]

What does this story say about Native American contributions to Confederate history? Should the actions in the Confederate Congress by Indian delegates change how we consider the Southern past?

Historians of the Confederacy have overlooked that Native Americans participated in shaping the legislative history of the South. Delegates from the Five Tribes did not just show up in Richmond. Boudinot was a significant advocate who also expanded the privileges of members from the Nations. He created legislation that tried to mesh the political practices of the Anglo government with Native procedures. On a number of occasions, he introduced bills and addressed fellow representatives. Callahan joined him in pushing through legislation to help funnel economic support to Indian Territory. That the effort fell short attests to the disruption by Union forces, along with their Indian allies, that impeded communications with the trans-Mississippi. These legislative efforts rarely show up in the histories of the Confederate Congress. Nor have historians considered Confederate Cherokees or members of the other tribes as contributing to Southern political history. Although not put into motion, the law determining voting in the Indian Territory outlined how these two societies conceived of the rights and political procedures of Native Americans under a protectorate.

That this relationship existed at all—and that Native Americans served in the Congress—also points to a hole in the diplomatic histories of the Confederacy. Foreign policy typically has meant describing the outreach by Southern envoys to Europe for possible recognition. Ever since Frank Owsley published his seminal work on King Cotton diplomacy in 1931, Southern ventures in this realm have generally been described as a failure by people blinded by hubris that caused them to overestimate the importance of their economic influence in the Atlantic World.[56] Yet diplomatic histories have ignored the treaties formed with Native Americans, which count among the achievements of the Southern government. That the promises between the two societies were even made reveals another dimension of the multiple ways the Confederacy tried to carve out its place in the world and how its leaders envisioned both the Confederate frontier and the lands to the southwest as a linchpin for the unrealized expansion of the Southern states.

NOTES

1. James M. Matthews, ed., *Statutes at Large of the Confederates States of America: Passed at the Third Session of the First Congress, 1863* (Richmond: R. M. Smith, 1863), 155–56. Also see the *Richmond Examiner*, June 19, 1863. Electronic searches of newspaper databases and a hunt for election returns in the Cherokee Papers at the University of Oklahoma turned up no signs of the election being held in Indian Territory in 1863.

2. *Richmond Whig*, November 8, 1864. For Boudinot introducing the bill for voting in Indian Territory, see *Journal of the Congress of the Confederate States of America*, 7 vols. (Washington, DC: Government Printing Office, 1904–5), 6:276. His speech may be found in the *Richmond Whig*, December 22, 1863.

3. Morris L. Wardell, *A Political History of the Cherokee Nation, 1838–1907* (1938; new ed., Norman: University of Oklahoma Press, 1977), 141; Jeffrey L. Fortney, "Serving the Choctaw Cause: Robert M. Jones, Sovereignty, and Pragmatic Diplomacy during the American Civil War," *American Nineteenth Century History* 17, no. 2 (2016): 220. For an example, see the treaty for the Cherokee Nation in US War Department, *The War of the Rebellion: A Compilation of the Official Records of the Union and Confederate Armies*, 127 vols., index, and atlas (Washington, DC: Government Printing Office, 1880–1901) (hereafter *OR*), ser. 4, 1:669–88.

4. *Message of the President, and Report of Albert Pike, Commissioner of the Confederate States to the Indian Nations West of Arkansas, of the Results of His Mission* (Richmond: Enquirer Book and Job Press, 1861), 18–19. The explanation for why a majority of the members of the Five Nations aligned with the Confederacy has changed over the years. Early works, as described recently by historian Fay A. Yarbrough, tended to focus on external factors such as pressure by Texans and Arkansans, non-native residents with Southern leanings, trade-economic pressures, and fears of Union actions to abolish slavery. More recently, historians have begun to expose the internal factors that favored an Indian alignment with the Confederacy. These include cultural affinities of the Nations with the South, familial ties, geographic connections, power struggles within Native groups that could benefit from the supplies and support being promised by the Confederates, and the need to protect themselves once the Union abandoned the region early in the war. For an overview, see Yarbrough, *Choctaw Confederates: The American Civil War in Indian Country* (Chapel Hill: University of North Carolina Press, 2021), 108–12. Similarly, Clarissa W. Confer has argued that Native Americans made decisions based on what seemed at the time to protect their sovereignty and "control over their own destiny." And Alaina E. Roberts has stressed that Native Americans fought for their own causes: to maintain autonomy, prevent incursions by US citizens, and maintain

annuity payments. See Confer, *The Cherokee Nation in the Civil War* (Norman: University of Oklahoma Press, 2007), 5; and Roberts, *"I've Been Here All the While": Black Freedom on Native Land* (Philadelphia: University of Pennsylvania Press, 2021), 30.

5. Scholars have known about the representation of Native Americans within the Confederate Congress and have highlighted the concessions gained by selected tribes in their treaties. Voting by Indigenous people for delegates to the Confederacy has not been foregrounded. Nor has the literature represented the issues involving protectorates or shown how governance by Native Americans had to adapt to changing circumstances in Indian Territory. The best book on the evolution of Native American political practices remains Wardell, *Political History of the Cherokee Nation*.

6. James W. Parins, *Elias Cornelius Boudinot: A Life on the Cherokee Border* (Lincoln: University of Nebraska Press, 2006), 48.

7. Kenny Arthur Franks, "Confederate Relations with the Five Civilized Tribes" (master's thesis, Oklahoma State University, 1971), 1–2, 7; Edward Everett Dale and Gaston Litton, *Cherokee Cavaliers: Forty Years of Cherokee History as Told in the Correspondence of the Ridge-Watie-Boudinot Family*, foreword by James W. Parins (1939; new ed., Norman: University of Oklahoma Press, 1995), 98; Zachery S. Cowsert, "The Civil War in Indian Territory, 1861–1865" (PhD diss., West Virginia University, 2020), 36–37.

8. On the goals for expansion into the Southwest, see Kevin Waite, "Jefferson Davis and Proslavery Visions of Empire in the Far West," *Journal of the Civil War Era* 6, no. 4 (December 2016): 536–65; Ray C. Colton, *The Civil War in the Western Territories: Arizona, Colorado, New Mexico, and Utah* (Norman: University of Oklahoma Press, 1959); Steven Hahn, *A Nation without Borders: The United States and Its World in an Age of Civil Wars, 1830–1910* (New York: Viking, 2016), 234–37; Andrew E. Masich, *Civil War in the Southwest Borderlands, 1861–1867* (Norman: University of Oklahoma Press, 2017), 57; Megan Kate Nelson, *The Three-Cornered War: The Union, the Confederacy, and Native Peoples in the Fight for the West* (New York: Scribner, 2020), xiii–xx; Troy Smith, "Nations Colliding: The Civil War in Indian Territory," *Civil War History* 59, no. 3 (September 2013): 282–83; and Annie Heloise Abel, "The Indians in the Civil War," *American Historical Review* 15, no. 2 (January 1910): 283–84.

9. Cowsert, "Civil War in Indian Territory," 251–52.

10. Walter Lee Brown, *A Life of Albert Pike* (Fayetteville: University of Arkansas Press, 1997), 355; *Report of Albert Pike*, 12–13, 15–16 (quotation).

11. *OR*, ser. 4, 1:669 (preamble); *Report of Albert Pike*, 18–19. For an early study that featured the term "protectorate" in the treaties, see Ohland Morton, "Confederate Government Relations with the Five Civilized Tribes: Part II," *Chronicles of Oklahoma* 31, no. 3 (1953): 304n28. Since then, few studies refer to the agreement as a protectorate. For Marshal's ruling, see *Cherokee Nation v. Georgia*, 30 US 1 (1831). The influence of the Cherokee Nation cases can be seen in the definition of Cherokees as dependent allies and "alien nationalities" in Coleman Phillipson, *Wheaton's Elements of International Law*, 5th English ed. (London: Stevens and Sons, LTD, 1916), 66–68. On the attractiveness of the treaties for Native interests, see Yarbrough, *Choctaw Confederates*, 111–12; Roberts, *"I've Been Here All the While,"* 30; and Smith, "Nations Colliding," 296.

12. *Statutes at Large of the United States of America, Volume VII* (Boston: Charles C. Little and James Brown, 1848), 31. Also see the Treaty of Holston (1798) in *Statutes at Large*, 62–64.

For an overview of treaties with Native Americans, see Francis Paul Prucha, *American Indian Treaties: The History of a Political Anomaly* (Berkeley: University of California Press, 1994).

13. Although the Cherokee Nation in August 2019 nominated Kimberly Teehee to serve as its delegate to the US House based on the Treaty of New Echota, as of this writing her seating had not been confirmed.

14. Adrian Brettle, *Colossal Ambitions: Confederate Planning for a Post–Civil War World* (Charlottesville: University of Virginia Press, 2020), 65–66.

15. James M. Matthews, ed., *The Statutes at Large of the Provisional Government of the Confederate States of America, from the Institution of the Government, February 8, 1861, to its Termination, February 18, 1862* (Richmond: R. M. Smith, Printer to Congress, 1864), 318.

16. *OR*, ser. 4, 1:679. Also see Franks, "Confederate Relations with the Five Civilized Tribes," 31.

17. *OR*, ser. 4, 1:785.

18. *OR*, ser. 4, 1:687.

19. A strain throughout the literature blames William Henry Seward for giving Native Americans a motivation for breaking treaties with the United States. The scholarship repeats a mistaken interpretation of Seward's speech in Chicago on October 3, 1860. Scholars accurately quote him: "The Indian territory, also, south of Kansas, must be vacated by the Indians." But the quotation has been taken out of context. Seward was talking about the designs of slaveholders in Kansas, not of the politicians in the Republican Party. The fuller quotation goes, "Kansas comes and asks or demands to be admitted to the Union. The Indian territory, also, south of Kansas, must be vacated by the Indians, and here at once the slave holders present the question as they will also do in the case of New Mexico." He was, however, misquoted in newspapers as a means of spreading the false idea that abolitionists in the Republican Party wanted Native American lands. For the relevant section of the speech, see "The National Idea; Its Perils and Triumphs," in *Works of William H. Seward, Volume 4* (Boston: Houghton Mifflin, 1861), 363. For insight into the misinformation campaign, see Grace Steele Woodward, *The Cherokees* (1963; new ed., Norman: University of Oklahoma Press, 1988), 254.

20. *Daily National Intelligencer*, April 2, 1861.

21. John Ross to President Lincoln, September 16, 1862, Abraham Lincoln Papers, Library of Congress, Washington, DC.

22. Brown, *Life of Albert Pike*, 370.

23. J. Ross, Principal Chief, to Lt. Col. J. R. Kannady, May 17, 1861, box 167, folder 6867, Cherokee Nation Papers, Western History Collection, University of Oklahoma (hereafter CNP); Dale and Litton, *Cherokee Cavaliers*, 102; Parins, *Elias Cornelius Boudinot*, 51. For a more negative view of the treaties and the maneuvering of Pike, see Cowsert, "Civil War in Indian Territory," 45–46, 52–53, 57.

24. Yarbrough, *Choctaw Confederates*, 99–100.

25. Prucha, *American Indian Treaties*, 263.

26. Paul Thomas Fisher, "Confederate Empire and the Indian Treaties: Pike, McCulloch, and the Five Civilized Tribes, 1861–1862" (master's thesis, Baylor University, 2011), 20; Edward E. Dale, "Arkansas and the Cherokees," *Arkansas Historical Quarterly* 8, no. 2 (Summer 1949): 105–6. For the only comprehensive biography of Boudinot, see Parins, *Elias Cornelius Boudinot*.

27. James M. Woods, "Devotees and Dissenters: Arkansans in the Confederate Congress, 1861–1865," *Arkansas Historical Quarterly* 38, no. 3 (Autumn 1979): 227–47.

28. Wardell, *Political History of the Cherokee Nation*, 160.

29. Dale and Litton, *Cherokee Cavaliers*, 120, 130; *OR*, ser. 1, 41(2):1046. Also see the term "Cherokee National Convention," used by Stand Watie for a later meeting, in "Special Message of Stand Watie to Cherokee National Convention," n.d., box 119, folder 3978, CNP.

30. L. Downing to S. H. Wattles, October 7, 1864, box 167, folder 6887, CNP. For the two competing governments, see John Bartlett Meserve, "Chief Lewis Downing and Chief Charles Thompson (Oochalata)," *Chronicles of Oklahoma* 16, no. 3 (1938): 319.

31. *The Constitution and Laws of the Cherokee Nation Passed at Tahlequah, Cherokee Nation, 1839–51* (Tahlequah: Cherokee Nation, 1852), 6–9, 9–10, 39–42; Yarbrough, *Choctaw Confederates*, 40–41.

32. Rev. J. William Jones and R. A. Brock, *Southern Historical Society Papers*, 52 vols. (1876–1959; repr., with 3-vol. index, Wilmington, NC: Broadfoot, 1990–92), 47:69 (hereafter *SHSP*).

33. *SHSP*, 47:89; Thomas Burnell Colbert, "Prophet of Progress: The Life and Times of Elias Cornelius Boudinot" (PhD diss., Oklahoma State University, 1982), 99–100; Parins, *Elias Cornelius Boudinot*, 53; T. Paul Wilson, "Delegates of the Five Civilized Tribes to the Confederate Congress," *Chronicles of Oklahoma* 53, no. 3 (Fall 1975): 355–56.

34. Parins, *Elias Cornelius Boudinot*, 53. Also see Wilson, "Delegates of the Five Civilized Tribes," 354–56.

35. *SHSP*, 49:73; *Journal of the Congress of the Confederate States*, 6:125 (uses an intermediary), 276 (introduces bill); Colbert, "Prophet of Progress," 103.

36. *Journal of the Congress of the Confederate States*, 6:459–60. A printing of the law also appeared in the *Richmond Examiner*, June 19, 1863.

37. *Journal of the Congress of the Confederate States*, 6:26. For the certification by Cooper, see Annie Heloise Abel, *The American Indian as Participant in the Civil War* (Cleveland: Arthur H. Clark, 1919), 180n487.

38. Jeffrey Lee Fortney Jr., "Robert M. Jones and the Choctaw Nation: Indigenous Nationalism in the American South, 1820–1877" (PhD diss., University of Oklahoma, 2014), 237; Wilson, "Delegates of the Five Civilized Tribes," 364.

39. Dale and Litton, *Cherokee Cavaliers*, 119–20.

40. "An Ordinance Authorizing E. C. Boudinot to Receive Certain Moneys Due the Cherokee Nation," box 155, folder 6357, CNP.

41. Dale and Litton, *Cherokee Cavaliers*, 143–44; Parins, *Elias Cornelius Boudinot*, 55.

42. *Richmond Examiner*, December 19, 1863. Also see *Journal of the Congress of the Confederate States*, vi:543; and Colbert, "Prophet of Progress," 109–10.

43. *Richmond Whig*, December 19 and 22, 1863; Dale and Litton, *Cherokee Cavaliers*, 150.

44. Wardell, *Political History of the Cherokee Nation*, 162; *OR*, ser. 1, 41(2):1046–47.

45. *OR*, ser. 1, 41(2):1047. Also see Dale and Litton, *Cherokee Cavaliers*, 150–52; Kenny A. Franks, "The Implementation of the Confederate Treaties with the Five Civilized Tribes," *Chronicles of Oklahoma* 51 (Spring 1973): 31; and Parins, *Elias Cornelius Boudinot*, 55.

46. Wardell, *Political History of the Cherokee Nation*, 162–63; Wilson, "Delegates of the Five Civilized Tribes," 358–59.

47. Wilson, "Delegates of the Five Civilized Tribes," 358–59.

48. *OR*, ser. 1, 22(2):1120–21. Also see Parins, *Elias Cornelius Boudinot*, 52; and Wilson, "Delegates of the Five Civilized Tribes," 358–59.

49. Dale and Litton, *Cherokee Cavaliers*, 152, 195.

50. *OR*, ser. 1, 41(2):1101, 1121–22; *OR*, ser. 1, 53:920–21. Also see Parins, *Elias Cornelius Boudinot*, 55–56; and Wilson, "Delegates of the Five Civilized Tribes," 361–62.

51. Dale and Litton, *Cherokee Cavaliers*, 157–158, 166.

52. Parins, *Elias Cornelius Boudinot*, 54, 55, 57–58; Wilson, "Delegates of the Five Civilized Tribes," 361, 364–65.

53. Dale and Litton, *Cherokee Cavaliers*, 222–23; Parins, *Elias Cornelius Boudinot*, 62.

54. Wardell, *Political History of the Cherokee Nation*, 175–76; Smith Christie to John Ross, August 19, 1864, box 167, folder 6886, CNP.

55. Alaina E. Roberts, "A Different Forty Acres: Land, Kin, and Migration in the Late Nineteenth-Century West," *Journal of the Civil War Era* 10, no. 2 (June 2020): 213–32; Fay A. Yarbrough, "'Dis Land Which Jines Dat of Ole Master's': The Meaning of Citizenship for the Choctaw Freedpeople," in *Civil War Wests: Testing the Limits of the United States*, ed. Adam Arenson and Andrew R. Graybill (Oakland: University of California Press, 2015), 224–41.

56. Frank Lawrence Owsley, *King Cotton Diplomacy: Foreign Relations of the Confederate States of America* (Chicago: University of Chicago Press, 1931).

Apples and Oranges and Hardtack

On the Uses of Comparison in Civil War History

AARON SHEEHAN-DEAN

Despite routine self-deprecation about the number of studies on the US Civil War, books continue to breach the levees and swell the flood. An overwhelming number of books begets yet more books. In the midst of this profusion, one subfield remains curiously underrepresented: comparative histories of the war. This despite the fact that all historical thinking is implicitly comparative thinking. In order to assess change over time—a historian's central task—we must evaluate one era against another. This requires historians to establish meaningful boundaries between eras. "Before and after" is too crude a distinction to be widely used in print, but the concept structures all historical writing. Whatever our topic or our approach, we compare across time. This is especially true for histories of military conflict. The binary nature of wars demands comparative thinking from participants. Military and political leaders base their decisions on evaluations of their enemy's strength in relation to their own, which cements comparisons into primary sources. The result is that comparisons are ubiquitous and essential in writing about the conflict, even though few Civil War scholars pursue comparative history per se. Why is that? And what is missing by not adopting more explicitly comparative approaches?

Many historians regard comparative analysis with apprehension. We pride ourselves on identifying the particular, we respect contingency and chance, and we abjure the more structural research protocols of the social sciences in favor of deep immersion in primary sources. No models or theories for us; induction or nothing! The result of this mindset is that any comparison of historical events or processes across time or space runs afoul of our professional loyalty to context. Nonetheless, even with our instinctive aversion to typologies, the most comparison-averse historians often adopt implicit comparative analyses. Sometimes this approach produces insights, but I hope to demonstrate that explicit comparative framings can produce real gains and that implicit comparisons would benefit from an honest reckoning with their structure.

Civil War historians are familiar with comparative history *within* the Civil War, where we juxtapose North and South or Union and Confederate, and *between* the Civil War era and the preceding and succeeding periods. Despite our familiarity with the method of comparative analysis (which I argue is more common than we usually appreciate), Civil War scholars rarely use this method across more extended geographical or chronological boundaries. My goals in this essay are to assess the ways in which comparison implicitly structures much contemporary writing and to offer suggestions for how comparison might be used more explicitly by building on the best models of that approach.[1] I also hope to convince Civil War historians that comparative thinking involves a familiar way of thinking and can play an important role in future scholarship. In his book *Metaphor*, the scholar Denis Donoghue argues, "To see a likeness in things that are essentially different requires an act of judgment."[2] Because comparisons require historians to identify likeness, they function as another form of interpretation, a way of making new meaning out of the past.

Phrases such as "multivariate analysis" and "macro-phenomena," which appear throughout the work of first-generation comparativists, might explain why Civil War historians rarely pursue comparisons. Marc Bloch's insistence on the "scientific" character of comparison may taint the method for some historians today. Even William Sewell, who did much to elaborate and refine Bloch's approach, adopted this tendency, writing about "hypothesis testing" and "the experimental method." But just as quantitative and spatial history have recovered from the excesses of first-generation cliometricians, so current comparativists take a more humanistic and less mechanistic approach than their predecessors. Part of Civil War historians' hesitation may also come from our preference for narrative rather than for the purely analytical approaches most comparisons assume. Wars—with their reassuring beginning-middle-end shape (once they are sufficiently far in the past)—take well to narrative. In his famous discussions about the liabilities of narrative, Hayden White characterized the balance of narrative and analysis in rather stark terms: "The amount of narrative will be greatest in accounts designed to tell a story, least in those intended to provide an analysis of the events of which it treats."[3] Civil War readers are fond of stories, and even academic historians respond to that pressure at some level. The volume of sources on the conflict enables historians to reconstruct a level of detail that few other fields can match, but that tendency can crowd out space for analysis. Third, comparative history, which even when well done has a tendency to abstract or blur our vision of historical actors, seems at odds with the granularity of social history, which has been the reigning approach among Civil War historians of the last three decades. Last, Civil War historians' allergy to theory does not help because most comparative history relies in some measure on theoretical frameworks to enable cross-cultural comparison.

Is it also possible that Civil War scholars resist comparisons because of a lingering exceptionalism? Even as American historians generally have rejected the exceptionalist framework bequeathed by the consensus school, Civil War historians remain wedded to internal, domestic explanations. I think it is safe to say that those of us who have written in this vein did so not because we shared the motives of earlier generations of historians who perceived America's post–World War II brand of democratic capitalism as a historical inevitability. Rather, the sheer mass of the literature on the US Civil War creates its own gravity and draws scholars into orbit along well-established paths. Recent global and transnational analyses of the conflict have disrupted this system, and comparisons can accelerate this salutary trend.

Part of historians' antipathy to the practice no doubt also stems from what we might call unconscious or latent comparative thinking. For historians coming of age in the 1960s and 1970s, the Vietnam War compelled them to ask new questions about the Civil War. This produced a more honest confrontation with the war's violence, an appreciation for the experiences of common soldiers, and a cynicism about the use of war to accomplish social change.[4] Many of these changes strengthened the field, but comparisons, especially when implicit rather than explicit, can corrupt our thinking in the same way that hindsight distorts historical vision.[5] The legacy of the

Vietnam War, in particular the nature of fighting and the persistence of North Vietnamese military resistance, produced both new insights and false impressions about the nature of the Civil War.

In the 1970s, American veterans and journalists published a spate of excellent books about the war. Michael Herr's *Dispatches*, a wry, at times hallucinatory reporter's account, stood alongside the stories and memoirs of Tim O'Brien and Philip Caputo.[6] These works shared an honest appraisal of American actions in the war that shocked many readers. In explaining the "savagery" of Vietnam, in particular what "prompted so many American fighting men—the good, solid kids from Iowa farms—to kill civilians and prisoners," Caputo emphasized the debilitating nature of the conflict there. He singled out the "barbarous treatment the Viet Cong and ARNV often inflicted on their own people"; the combination of "the two most bitter forms of warfare, civil war and revolution, to which was added the ferocity of jungle war"; the American strategy of attrition, which encouraged killing rather than territorial conquest; and "the conditions imposed by the country and the climate." These factors combined to produce a bitterness in American soldiers returned in kind by Vietnamese ones. "Men who do not expect to receive mercy eventually lose their inclination to grant it."[7]

Michael Fellman's *Inside War*, one of the first and most influential studies of Civil War guerrillas, bears the imprint of Caputo's and O'Brien's work. His characterization of the unforgiving ferocity of irregulars in Missouri echoes many of their conclusions. "Normal expectations collapsed, to be replaced by bewildering personal and cultural chaos. The normal routes by which people solved problems and channeled behavior had been destroyed. The base for their prior values—their 'moral structure'—underwent frontal attack. Ordinary people, civilians as well as soldiers, were trapped by a guerrilla war in a social landscape in which almost nothing remained recognizable or secure."[8] Fellman's study is rich and thoughtful. Though not the first guerrilla study, the depth of the research and the sophistication of the argument compelled scholars to take account of a part of the war they had ignored.[9] Nonetheless, it is hard now not to see the influence of the Vietnam War and, in particular, the writing of former soldiers about their experience on Fellman's work.

The tenacity of North Vietnamese fighting, first against the French and then against Americans, to liberate the country from foreign influence cast a long shadow over historians writing about the Confederacy. Just a few years before Fellman published his study of irregular fighting, a group of scholars leaned even more explicitly on the Vietnam experience in *Why the South Lost the Civil War*.[10] Its authors concluded that "the Confederates did lack morale, and their morale was sapped by uncertainty about their war aims."[11] It is hard not to read that line in light of the uncertainty among Americans about their war aims in Vietnam. The active protests in the United States, to say nothing of the confusion among soldiers on the ground (which appears in many memoirs as well), is cited by many scholars as the key reason for American defeat.[12] The authors argue that Ulysses S. Grant's strategy of destructive war—which "aimed *only* to break up the Confederacy's main armies by severing the railroads that connected them to their supplies of food, shoes, uniforms, weapons, and ammunition"—"alone could not have won a war against a people sufficiently determined to maintain their independence."[13] The only way to make this claim—in the face of the obvious questions about how an army would function without food, clothing, arms, and ammunition, to say nothing of Southern civilians who experienced the same ill effects from Union destruction of public infrastructure—is in light of the Vietnamese resistance to French colonialism and American invasion over the decades from 1945 to 1975. The sometimes-tortured course of Civil War historiography after the Vietnam War should not invalidate comparison; rather, it should compel greater attention to latent influences on historical writing.

Regardless of the qualms some scholars may possess, comparative thinking is pervasive in Civil War history, often implicit rather than explicit. Consider James McPherson's *Battle Cry of Freedom*. Because the book primarily offers a history of the war years, the North-South division enables readers to easily distinguish the protagonists, but that same division shapes the book's deeper argument. McPherson posits "sectional conflict between North and South over the future of slavery" as "the greatest danger to American survival at midcentury."[14] With hindsight, few scholars deny the importance of regional divisions, but they do argue over the terms of that divide. McPherson's vision of a white South, defending a slave-based economy, hierarchical social order, and antidemocratic politics against the North's embrace of an egalitarian, free-labor future, projects a Whiggish vision onto nineteenth-century America. As Edward Ayers and others have identified, McPherson associates the North with modernity and casts the South as anti-modern.[15] The treatment of the Northern experience as the normative one mostly functions below the radar, shaping how readers understand the story without defending the logic of the choice. Making implicit comparisons explicit and treating the two sides equally and independently would better equip readers to assess an author's arguments.

In his classic essay on comparative history, Marc Bloch explained that many comparativists "make a parallel study of societies that are at once neighbouring and contemporary, exercising a constant mutual influence, exposed throughout their development to the action of the same broad causes."[16] It would be hard to beat that sentence as a description of North-South comparisons, which structure most antebellum and Civil War historiography. Nearly every study of the war implicitly or explicitly adopts a comparative perspective by weighing the relative strengths of each side. Civil War historians have evaluated the strengths and weaknesses of the United States and the Confederate States along a variety of axes. Historians consider material resources such as manpower, matériel, draft animals, food supply, infrastructure, and economic capacity more generally. Nearly every summary of the war tabulates the geographic and psychological advantages and disadvantages for each side.[17]

Although few historians today engage in the contest of generals (long a favorite pastime for Civil War scholars), assessments of military and political leadership during the conflict still tend toward a "on the one hand . . . on the other hand" format.[18] A rough consensus has emerged that recognizes the Confederacy's more effective generals took up commands in the eastern theater while the more competent Union commanders started in the western theater before moving east in 1864. Scholars are similarly united in rating Abraham Lincoln a better commander in chief than Jefferson Davis.[19] The Confederate Congress, staffed by many former US congressmen and senators (and a former US president), should have matched the US wartime Congresses. As it turns out, the Thirty-Seventh and Thirty-Eighth US Congresses achieved fame for their management of the war and forward-looking policies, while the Confederate Congress mired itself in infighting and obstructionism. Writing on state-level politics during the war invites easy comparisons, especially as a consensus emerges that Northern states cooperated with the Lincoln administration in the war's prosecution, while irascible governors like Georgia's Joseph Brown and North Carolina's Zebulon Vance obstructed Confederate efforts.[20]

Sectionalism is the closest thing Civil War historians have to gospel, and it is predicated on an analytical division that should enable comparison. Done the right way, sectional comparisons can teach us a great deal. Many recent studies of the border adopt a comparative geographic approach, usually singling out two counties or states for similar analysis.[21] The work of these historians has enriched and complicated easy assumptions about a fundamental difference between North and South. In doing so, they challenge an earlier comparative literature (which often contrasted the Deep South and New England) that essentialized sectional difference.[22]

Still other scholars enable readers to compare without making comparison itself the analytical framework. Gary Gallagher's work, though not explicitly comparative, provides readers with the opportunity to compare Union and Confederate experiences because he adopted the same goal in two books: explaining the sustaining motivations of each side. What compelled soldiers and citizens to continue fighting through four years of unimaginably bloody civil conflict? In the case of the Confederates, Gallagher was particularly concerned to respond to scholars who asserted that "political dissension, class strife, pitting the yeomanry against planters, doubts about the morality of slavery, fears that God favored the North, the absence of a shared sense of purpose, and other factors explain why the Confederate experiment in rebellion failed."[23] To the contrary, Gallagher shows that most white Southerners supported the Confederacy throughout the war, in particular the soldiers who developed a strong sense of national commitment as a result of their military experience.[24] Fourteen years later, Gallagher turned his attention to the Union experience, asking, in effect, what sustained Northern soldiers and citizens through their harrowing four years of war? The heart of his answer—that Northern soldiers fought for a Union they associated with democracy and regarded emancipation as a tool with which to accomplish that lofty aim—has generated as much productive debate as his earlier volume.[25] Considering these books as an extended exercise in comparative history demonstrates the value of differences exposed by a comparison. While James Oakes's response to Gallagher achieves an elegant balance by positioning antislavery Northerners against the proslavery Confederates, Gallagher's conclusion offers a more realistic asymmetry: some Northerners opposed slavery, some supported it, and a large middle expressed ambivalence.

Similarly, Michael Woods's recent study of the Democratic Party generates its heat from a comparison of the party's two greatest representatives in the late antebellum era: Stephen Douglas and Jefferson Davis. Woods emphasizes Douglas's and Davis's differences rather than similarities, but in doing so he shows how much there is to learn from taking two close subjects and analyzing them along the same lines. Woods's account shows how the divergence between the two men, not just over slavery and its fate but over the nature of democracy, presaged and propelled the Civil War itself.[26] Neither Gallagher nor Woods framed their studies as comparative history, but their work reveals the analytical gains from implicit comparisons between North and South.

If the Civil War demarcated America by space—and thus requires complementary analysis of each of its two sections—the war also ruptured time.

The result is that historians of the Civil War era also center another comparison, often latent, in their writing about the conflict: How did the antebellum era differ from the war years? As Peter Kolchin, one of the leading practitioners of comparative history, notes, "Just as the attempt to make variations over space explicit can turn noncomparative into comparative history, so too can a conscious attention to change over time."[27] This framing is the most effective way to grapple with the changed landscape of the war, especially for social historians seeking to understand how the war reshaped gender, race, or class relations. The hardship experienced by Southern civilians, both Black and white, offers the sharpest contrast with prewar life. Army confiscation, the disruption of transportation lines, the blockade, and the absence of nearly all adult white men from agricultural production exacerbated the ordinary scarcities experienced by enslaved people and poor whites across the region. These disruptions, in turn, upset the Southern social order. Women took on new jobs, both industrial and office-based, and they assumed greater authority over agricultural production.[28]

Historians of gender have adopted this approach to generate great insights into the nature of the war's changes for men and women. Nina Silber's study of Northern women and Stephanie McCurry's work on Southern women, among much other excellent work, enable robust comparisons of how the war reshaped the nature of gender in the United States.[29] In a recent study, Thavolia Glymph identifies the drawbacks with this approach, noting that "the story of women in the Civil War continues to be written largely along the lines of the regional divide imposed by slavery's geographical borders; lines that are assumed to correspond legibly to the political divides over the question of slavery. This approach favors the study of Northern and Southern women separately rather than in juxtaposition. It disfavors class analysis."[30] Instead, Glymph's approach, which takes up both sides of that border in sequence and then together, reveals how much context mattered to shaping the experience of women during the Civil War. For a variety of reasons, the war produced greater hardship for Southern women and, consequently, spurred a sharper internal conflict along class lines than it did for Northern women. In this case, the comparison helps throw into sharper relief the nature of the war experience. At the same time, Glymph's study also distinguishes white women's experience and Black women's experiences, as do many other studies. Rather than position the Black experience in implicit comparison to the white one, Glymph reverses the polarity, identifying Black women as the major drivers of historical change in the era as they sought freedom, undermined the Confederacy, and pursued economic power.

The same is true for historians of emancipation. Enslaved people also transformed the uncertainties of war into opportunities. Some fled plantations entirely. The mass movement of enslaved people to freedom behind Union lines represents the single starkest change between antebellum and wartime life.[31] A simple comparison of numbers of runaways—from hundreds per year before the war to half a million during it—suggests an unprecedented shift in scale.[32] From this perspective, the demarcation between these two periods is sharp and leads some historians to characterize the Civil War as the largest slave rebellion in American history.[33] But for most enslaved people, escape was impossible. For the three and a half million who remained in bondage to the war's end, the chaos on the Southern home front provided incremental (though hardly unimportant) chances to improve their lives. Wherever the Union army or the demands of the Confederacy disrupted the ability of white Southerners to policy slavery, enslaved people demanded greater autonomy.[34] In this same camp are historians who emphasize that the majority of slaveholders retained control of enslaved people through the war and sometimes even of freedpeople after the war.[35] The debate over continuity and change thus hinges on how (and even whether) historians frame their comparisons.

Where some scholars situate the Civil War in time by comparing the antebellum and wartime periods, other scholars compare the United States before and after the conflict. This practice accounts for our ability to distinguish the "Civil War" and "Reconstruction" as distinct periods in American history. It is easy to summarize the macro changes that resulted: the preservation of the Union and the repudiation of secession; the end of slavery; and an empowered federal government (and especially military). Any one of these transformations would qualify as momentous; all three together must surely mark an epochal shift in the nature of national life, a discrete "before and after." The characterization of the Civil War as a watershed in American life reigned for a long time in academic and popular history, but it has been challenged over the past two decades. Historians of emancipation now nearly always frame their stories across both eras, treating the war itself as a fundamental but not solely determinative factor.[36] For instance, Stephen Kantrowitz's study of Black activists in Boston shows how capacious we must be to truly understand the complex braid of change and stasis that inhered in this moment. By orienting ourselves away from Congress and toward Black people, Kantrowitz shows that "black activists did not consider their battle won with the end of slavery in 1865, nor even with the revolution of Reconstruction. Instead, they worked to shape and extend these victories."[37]

Kate Masur's study of the efforts of Black people to achieve meaningful equality in Washington, DC, begins in 1862 and concludes in 1878.[38] Another central concern of Civil War historians—the war's effect on state power—is also resistant to the easy demarcating of wartime and postwar. As Greg Downs has shown, the older framework of the Civil War birthing a "Yankee Leviathan" overstates the pace and degree of change.[39] In this case, the logic of comparative thinking led historians to exaggerate the differences between wartime and postwar. Challenging that framework has spurred a range of creative scholarship.

Civil War historians looking for a model of how to proceed have examples ready at hand. The well-established field of comparative slavery and emancipation offers scholarship relevant for both *what* we study and *how* we might study. Frank Tannenbaum's *Slave and Citizen* offered one of the earliest explicit comparisons of North and South American slavery.[40] Tannenbaum argued that the differences between Anglo slavery and Spanish slavery produced relatively better conditions for enslaved people in Central and South America: more generous manumission policies; more stable families; and less stigma associated with race itself. Tannenbaum's explanation emphasized the Roman legacy of slavery in the Iberian peninsula, which prioritized status over any inherent stigma that predisposed people to enslavement, and religion; Catholicism and the power wielded by the church generated a more fluid system in Latin America than did the Protestant regime in British North America. Carl Degler reached different conclusions; rather than credit the Spanish church or state, he emphasized the role of demography, geography, and economic developments.[41] At the same time, Degler was alert to the differences in racial attitudes in the two countries: "In Brazil the slave may have been feared, but the black man was not, whereas in the United States both the slave and the black were feared."[42] Historians of Spanish and Portuguese colonies have since disabused us about the supposed protections offered by the Catholic church. Slavery in South America was different but no less cruel than its northern counterpart.[43]

Nonetheless, Tannenbaum's work inspired later generations to adopt more rigorously comparative perspectives. Peter Kolchin's *Unfree Labor: American Slavery and Russian Serfdom* and Shearer Davis Bowman's *Masters and Lords: Mid-19th-Century U.S. Planters and Prussian Junkers*, published within a few years of each other, demonstrate the rich interpretive possibilities of explicit comparative history.[44] Kolchin emphasized the scarcity of labor as a key factor in North America and Russia. Both places evolved into societies with slaves, including the accompanying ideological justifications and class systems those require. In both countries, these systems were also reified in law, though Kolchin is attentive to how race and religion created profound differences between the two systems. The Russian one, as he characterized it, was fundamentally an economic system, and a rickety one at that. By midcentury, most people recognized the problems, and the *pomeshchik* acceded to the tsar's abolition of the system in 1861. In contrast, American slaveholders grounded both their social and political worlds in slavery and fought to preserve them in the Civil War.

Prospective comparativists and indeed all historians should take heart from the comparative slavery literature: those scholars were not scared off by both similarity and difference. The first chapter of Degler's foundational book is titled "The Challenge of the Contrast." As with the best comparative history, neither Kolchin nor Bowman offered easy equivalencies. For many years, one of the underexplored insights in Kolchin's study was his observation that Russian serfdom expanded as the state centralized and increased its reach.[45] Over the last decade, American historians have revised an older interpretation that juxtaposed state power and mastery; instead, historians have shown how masters depended on central authority and how effectively they manipulated that power for their own benefit.[46] Alongside comparative slavery, we might consider the value of comparative studies of race, as in John Cell's and George Frederickson's comparisons of the United States and South Africa. Although both these authors adopted longer time frames than is typical among Civil War scholars, their studies offered important insights into the nature of race in both places, an issue of crucial importance for Civil War era historians.[47]

More recently, comparative emancipation historians have stuck to this hemisphere. Although the prospect of mastering Russian or German no doubt discourages some US historians, one impetus to focus on the Caribbean comes from the primary sources. Nineteenth-century Americans followed the course of British and French emancipation in the West Indies carefully.[48] Slaveholders marshaled evidence from the post-emancipation experience of the islands as proof that ending slavery would impoverish both the nation and the people. Abolitionists drew the opposite lesson, celebrating the autonomy of the new freedpeople even as they critiqued British and French efforts to keep them bound to the land. Rebecca Scott has pioneered her own comparative trail through the history of Cuba and the Gulf states, especially Louisiana.[49] Some American historians have made glancing reference to Brazil, but its experience presents perhaps the most useful comparison. Because of its size and proximity to the United States, it served as an important part of antebellum slaveholders' vision of their global analogues (John C. Calhoun said of Brazil, "Between her and us there is a strict identity of interest on almost all subjects, without conflict, or even competition"). While the connection between American emancipation and Brazilian emancipation is important to elucidate, more forthright studies of the practice of slavery, as well as its end, have much to teach us.[50] Jeffrey Kerr-Ritchie's *Freedom's Seekers: Essays on Comparative Emancipation* shows how to expand this field beyond the bimodal approach favored by the first generation of scholars. Covering the experience of people of African descent across all of the Americas (regardless of imperial or national system under which enslaved people lived) and including brief forays into the Indian Ocean and Africa, Kerr-Ritchie "compares, contrasts, and connects" the strategies that enslaved people used to liberate themselves.[51] His book also offers a robust challenge to previous comparative studies that unintentionally reified an American exceptionalism built around its supposedly unique emancipation history. The lesson for Civil War historians is to make comparisons with close attention to historical actors and their contexts and also to the historiographical context within which we construct our arguments.

In addition to comparisons within the Civil War era itself, the deeper past provides opportunities for comparison. Participants in the conflict made frequent reference to the American Revolution.[52] Sometimes they affiliated themselves with the virtue of the founding generation; other times they used the earlier conflict as a way to assess what might happen in the contemporary one. Confederates thrilled to the example of an outnumbered and ill-equipped insurgent successfully defeating a global power, while Northerners trusted that the spirit of Washington and Jefferson to build a nation would help them win this second struggle over unity. Other participants reached back further still, citing the English Civil War as a model for how English-speaking people might conduct and perhaps survive a fratricidal conflict.

Military historians have made more effective use of comparative frameworks than many of their colleagues largely because of the applied nature of much military history. Mark Grimsley's justly lauded *Hard Hand of War*, which explains the escalation of Union military policy in the South, includes references to England's Hundred Years' War, the Thirty Years' War, and the wars of German unification.[53] Grimsley's balanced account accommodates both those elements that encouraged a harder war as well as those that were restraining factors. The latter emerges in sharp contrast with the behavior of European armies, especially before the eighteenth century and the rise of professional militaries.[54] Similarly, I have used brief comparisons with nineteenth-century conflicts—the Taiping Rebellion and the French Commune—to contextualize the relative restraint of American actions in the US Civil War.[55]

Nonetheless, the field of foreign comparative studies of the Civil War remains surprisingly small. One of the earliest such studies was written by David Potter in 1968, a consensus historian whose preceding work carefully analyzed the domestic politics that produced the Republican Party and secession.[56] In a reprint edition of the essay, Potter included a prologue that scolded historians for their failure to contextualize American history in relation to the rest of the world: "Some of our worst navel-gazing has occurred in connection with the Civil War."[57] Potter's brief essay assessed the impact of the Civil War on world history—appropriate for a volume dedicated to reconsidering American exceptionalism. He displayed more modesty than the exceptionalists; Potter regarded both the preservation of the Union and emancipation as processes that followed rather than led the mid-nineteenth-century world. "But for good or ill, here are two things which the Civil War did: first, it turned the tide which had been running against nationalism for forty years, or ever since Waterloo; and second, it forged a bond between nationalism and liberalism at a time when it appeared that the two might draw apart and move in opposite directions."[58] Potter rejected the inevitability that clouded midcentury analysis of these systems, insisting that the merger resulted from history, not destiny. Though the argument Potter made has yet to be tested in a more rigorous way, his essay demonstrates one of the great strengths of making comparisons explicit rather than implicit: it enables scholars to isolate analytical framework with precision. As Peter Kolchin explained more than thirty years ago, "Comparison enables one to weigh the impact of different variables and hence to distinguish the specific or incidental from the general or inherent."[59]

Enrico Dal Lago's comparative study of William Lloyd Garrison and Giuseppe Mazzini frames their parallel efforts to end American slavery and build an independent and democratic Italian nation as reflective of the broad movement toward liberal reform in the nineteenth century.[60] Abandoning the perspective of the American experience as singular, Dal Lago shows how it worked in tandem with radical change in other parts of the Western world. His study shows that Western reform movements in the mid-nineteenth century assumed different forms in different places but shared a hostility to arbitrary governance and unequal laws and an enthusiasm for universal liberty. Dal Lago's geographical comparison speaks to the problem that encouraged emancipation historians to dissolve the previously well-established wartime-postwar divide: the question of why reform stalled after the wars themselves. As Dal Lago shows, Garrison was content with emancipation (in a way other abolitionists like Wendell Phillips never were), but Mazzini recognized his own failure. The year 1861 created an Italian nation but one unified under a kingdom rather than a liberal republic. His study reveals the divergent fortunes of reform movements that succeed through war.

Dal Lago's most recent work, *Civil War and Agrarian Unrest: The Confederate South and Southern Italy*, through an even more classically structured comparative perspective, helps us reframe the Confederate experiment not within the usual confines of America's tragic past but as yet another instance of nineteenth-century nation building.[61] It would not be unfair to say that this perspective is impossible to obtain through traditional histories of the Confederacy, which, of necessity, root their story in native soil. We need those histories, and we also need Dal Lago's and others that could situate the Confederate experiment alongside the raft of new nations created in the nineteenth century. Dal Lago, borrowing from the historical sociologist Michael Hechter, uses the concepts of "unification nationalism" and "separatist or 'peripheral nationalism'" to frame the different efforts of the Union and Confederate governments, respectively.[62] These frameworks can enable Civil War scholars to more readily position the American experience in relation to others around the world at the same time. In his book, Dal Lago offers a more specific argument that interprets Southern resistance (mostly Black Southerners) as similar to that of southern Italian peasants, both part of a familiar agrarian demand for autonomy within the rapidly changing economic landscape of the industrializing nineteenth century, an interpretation that calls back W. E. B. Du Bois's framing of the Civil War as a "general strike." One might quarrel with his characterization of the significance of internal opposition in the Confederacy or of the scope of Black freedom during the conflict but still appreciate that the narrative brings us to reconsider a question that often remains inchoate in our narratives: What was the relationship between civil war and social revolution? Last, the ability of elites in both regions to reassert their dominance produced a strangely parallel process of mostly landless peasants, from the American South and southern Italy, moving to northern American cities in search of industrial jobs in the late nineteenth and early twentieth centuries.[63]

The work of historian Don Doyle merits an essay in itself. More than anyone in recent decades, Doyle has encouraged historians of the nineteenth century to think comparatively. He has done this in his own work, comparing the nature of sectionalism and nation building in Italy and the United States, and in a series of edited collections that brought together scholars from around the world.[64] These collections have not been explicitly comparative in terms of the methodologies adopted by contributors; most of the essays are written by area specialists who pursue explanations—of nationalism, secession, nation building, or war—according to the logic they uncover in the sources.[65] But the combined effect is to enable comparisons across a broad range of places and times. Doyle's contributors generally eschew the older social scientific approach to comparative history. Instead, many adopt a more explicitly transnational analysis, which identifies the connections among communities in a given era. Economic, diplomatic, and cultural networks bound people together in the mid-nineteenth century, vertically within the Americas and horizontally across the Atlantic basin. Among the many insights generated by this work is an appreciation that the US response to secessionist rhetoric and secession itself—a military response that consumed more than three-quarters of a million lives—was not the only possible route. The Spanish Empire, among other New World powers, reacted to challenges to its authority from colonial elites and enslaved people in a variety of ways. In Europe, Spain faced many of the same problems as the United States, including disputes over the nature and role of liberalism, the transition to a market economy, and the problem of slavery and the looming specter of emancipation. Mexico, similarly, faced insurgencies in the Yucatán Peninsula and from the French Empire, which sought to colonize the country in the midst of the US conflict.

Notwithstanding Greg Downs's recent book, which offers a compelling transnational analysis of the American and Spanish imperial experiences of the 1860s, all of these topics merit sustained attention.[66] Throughout the nineteenth century and much of the twentieth, Americans were reluctant to see any parallels between the US and Mexican experiences. Despite the rise of xenophobia in recent years, scholars today recognize they could learn a lot from comparing the nature of these two large, diverse republics during the formative nineteenth century. Similarly, much more comparative work on emancipation, especially between the United States, Cuba, and Brazil, remains to be done.[67]

The most intellectually ambitious recent work in this vein is David Armitage's *Civil Wars: A History in Ideas*, which tackles the protean nature of civil conflicts across a huge span of time.[68] Starting with Rome, Armitage situates how historical actors (mostly Western in this case) understood and used the idea of "civil" conflict. His account does not compare civil wars, in the traditional comparativist sense; instead, Armitage writes a "history *in* ideas" to explain the changes in how people have conceptualized what internal conflicts mean as forms of communal violence and politics. As Armitage characterizes the contested historical legacy of the term, it represented for many the worst conflict that mankind could conjure. Importantly for our field, Armitage positions the US Civil War as the moment during which "civil war came firmly under the authority of the lawyers."[69] By this he means policymakers like Francis Lieber, who defined civil conflict as akin to foreign conflicts in a way that reduced the total casualties by treating all participants as legitimate soldiers rather than one side treating the other as comprising traitors suitable only for death. More histories of the laws of war that adopt transnational framing or explicit comparisons among midcentury conflicts would subject this insight to more rigorous scrutiny.

The more materialist companion to Armitage's book is Stathis Kalyvas's *Logic of Violence in Civil War*.[70] Though the primary material in the study comes from the mid-twentieth-century Greek Civil War, the book gathers data from nearly every conflict of the twentieth century to establish laws and theories regarding the patterns of violence in civil conflicts. Because the book is written by a political scientist and includes not just tables and graphs but charts and figures that hypothesize and visualize the ramifications of internal conflicts, few historians use it. But Kalyvas's conclusions, like those of Armitage, hold real value for scholars of the US Civil War. Among these, he refers to the role played by external forces in civil wars (the Greek conflict began during World War II) and the social ramifications of collaboration by civilian and military actors.

Another promising opportunity is comparing the US Civil War with other nineteenth-century conflicts. Even without meaning to, domestic histories tend toward the exceptional even if they are not exceptionalist narratives. Until we treat the conflict as part of world history, as the war's participants did, we will not fully understand it. Recently, I have ventured comparisons between the American experience and the Indian, Polish, and Chinese rebellions that occurred alongside the Southern one.[71] The French Commune of 1871 has generated only one comparative study, and despite its strengths, there is surely more to learn here.[72] The French experience in the 1870s bears some similarity to the American one, as both empires sought to balance political reform, expansion, and a restive population. All of these topics deserve much more attention, especially from scholars with the linguistic skills to research primary sources on multiple continents.

As newspaper op-ed pages demonstrate, readers appreciate comparisons between the US Civil War and more recent conflicts. The corrupting influence of Vietnam as a latent comparison does not mean that more explicit framings of the two conflicts are without value. To the contrary, one of the only forthright comparisons of the wars, Eric Dean's *Shook over Hell: Post-traumatic Stress, Vietnam, and the Civil War*, inaugurated a new subfield for Civil War scholars exploring the psychological effects of warfare on soldiers.[73] Even as Dean used the new research into post-traumatic stress disorder to rethink the nature of Civil War soldiering, he respected the differences between these two eras. Dean wanted Civil War scholars to take greater stock of the psychological suffering of regular soldiers—though he rejected the notion "that they were all potential victims just waiting to break down"—and Vietnam scholars to appreciate the satisfaction that veterans maintained, even in the face of societal condemnation of the war.[74] By respecting the unique cultural context of the two eras, Dean's study avoided the problem of implicit comparison, in which the insights of one period are deployed to explain behavior in another.

Gaines Foster's less well known but valuable essay "Coming to Terms with Defeat" probes both the similarities and the differences between the Civil and Vietnam Wars.[75] In particular, Foster tracks the postwar contests over the treatment of veterans and competing interpretations of both conflicts. For instance, Foster notes that the rise of prowar interpretations in the 1980s formed an American analogue to Germany's World War I "stab-in-the-back thesis," though in this case writers have used it "to explain away American defeat. In that regard, the emerging defense of America's role in Vietnam resembles the South's interpretation of defeat in the Civil War. The South, too, insisted upon the morality, nobility, and heroism of its cause and so celebrated its efforts in the war that Southerners came to perceive their defeat almost as military victory. The same thing appears to be happening to Americans' views of Vietnam."[76] Although academic and popular interpretations of Vietnam have shifted yet again, Foster's essay reveals the dividends to be gained from a careful analysis of the two conflicts.

Because of historians' reluctance to offer predictions, Civil War era scholars remained relatively quiet during the wars of Afghanistan and Iraq. Edward Ayers offered a thoughtful assessment of Reconstruction in 2005, exactly as the United States mounted expensive, large-scale reconstruction projects in both nations, and concluded modestly that "any effort at reconstruction, our nation's history shows us, must be implemented not only with determination and might but also with humility and self-knowledge."[77] To my knowledge, no Civil War historians have offered a more precise comparison between Southern and Middle Eastern occupations. Conversely, scholars of military reconstruction often avoid the case study of the United States because it does not fit the parameters of foreign occupation.[78] This creates real opportunities for our field to step into the breach.

In addition to the opportunities articulated above to compare the Civil War to conflicts across time and space, scholars can also isolate elements of the conflict to compare separately, as historians of comparative emancipation do. Civil War guerrillas are almost always discussed in a vacuum, even though histories of irregular combat exist (which, it should be noted, often slight the American experience).[79] Public perception of the guerrilla changed significantly in the twentieth century, as World War II partisans yielded to Marxist freedom fighters in Asia or Latin America. These multiple contexts promise new insights into the mid-nineteenth century. Scholars of state formation in the late eighteenth century have leaned heavily on European precedents.[80] The same cannot be said for the otherwise excellent recent writing on American political development, which closely tracks change but almost always within a domestic framework.[81] What would this story look like if we included Meiji Japan in the story? Thomas Bender has suggested important parallels and disjunctures between the American and German nation-building experiences at midcentury, but these merit sustained attention, at least on the order of Don Doyle's comparisons of the United States and Italy.[82]

On the other hand, what about more comparative analysis of the fate of empires? The Ottoman Empire slowly collapsed—witness the Greek War for Independence in the 1820s and Bulgaria's also successful bid in 1878. The British, Russian, and Chinese Empires, which all faced proto-national or secessionist movements at midcentury, weathered them like the United States did. How do we account for the variety of outcomes here? The economics of war beg for more comparative work. Max Edling has explained the financing tools that Americans inherited from the Europeans and how creatively Americans put them to use.[83] What happened at midcentury? The independence movements suppressed by the British, Russians, and Chinese consumed huge resources; why and how did Americans exit their conflict in stronger fiscal condition than their peers?[84]

Global comparisons have also proved useful for an emerging field of what might be called comparative memory. Practitioners of this approach study not conflicts themselves but the aftermaths and the ways that participants process and adapt to new conditions. The framework of "Reconstruction," which emphasizes the experience of freedpeople, the political and partisan dynamics at the federal and state levels, and the fate of free labor, has generated valuable insights into the nature of race and democracy in the United States. At the same time, it partitions the South both geographically and topically from the rest of the national narrative, so that the issues of the Gilded Age rarely intersect with those of Reconstruction.[85] The field of memory studies has encouraged historians to think more capaciously and critically about the post–Civil War era.[86] In some framings, the consequences of the war extend well into the twentieth century. In nearly all memory studies, formal politics blends with cultural politics, and problems of sectionalism and development take shape from the ways historical actors interpreted and represented the Civil War. Still, memory studies, like Reconstruction studies, have generated their own grooves that draw historians into a debate over the relationship between Union veterans and emancipation.

In more recent years, historians of memory have adopted comparative framings that enable us to position the American experience alongside the other postwar environments. This allows us to see that reunion and reconciliation are not uniquely American problems and that they require societies to rebuild their racial and also ethnic, religious, geographic, and partisan alignments. Paul Escott's *Uncommonly Savage: Civil War and Remembrance in Spain and the United States* takes up two places divided by the legacy of their civil conflicts.[87] In particular, Escott traces the tenacity of conservatives—white Southerners in the United States and Catholic reactionaries in Spain—in deploying memories of their national conflicts to retain political power.[88] As Escott and others show, the structure of the postwar political order matters a great deal. In places like Spain or Rwanda in the 1990s, where one party held exclusive dominance in the postwar government, memory could be shaped more intentionally.[89] Northern Republicans may have dominated Reconstruction governments, but Southern Democrats did not disappear, and the relative openness of the US political system gave them space to shape memories of the war in a way rarely possible elsewhere. By positioning the American and Spanish experiences of reconciliation side by side, Escott shows that the general pace of social and cultural change determined the persistence of war interpretations more so than their political relevance. The Lost Cause held sway over a South that "changed very slowly over three or four generations, roughly a hundred years," while the pace of change since World War II has accelerated that process for Spain.[90]

Postwar comparisons necessarily require cross-temporal analysis, which inevitably generates both commonalities and dissimilarities. A recent edited collection brings together case studies across a wide geographic and chronological range, leaving the reader to see how many different paths are possible in the wake of civil wars.[91] Some of these alternatives suggest what might have happened in the postwar United States, while others remind us that the American experience was hardly unique. As Americans living with the racial legacy of the Civil War, we must continue to expose the concessions created through the Lost Cause and even the Union Cause, but a broader comparative lens reveals that true reconciliation—which demands recognizing all sides in a conflict as victims—is "an extraordinarily difficult task."[92] The fact that these are so rarely achieved after civil wars challenges historians of the US conflict to reframe their orientation toward memory away from the blaming posture inherent in critiquing white Northerners for failing to more vigorously defend emancipation as a war aim. An even more recent study, a comparison of popular memory in postwar Germany and the American South, suggests that our impact as historians in changing ideas about the past proceeds much more slowly than we might believe or desire. "For decades," Susan Neiman writes, "German historians had worked to provide a detailed reckoning with the Nazi period, but there were layers of popular consciousness that work had not reached."[93] The only way to break through that consciousness is with persistent and precise argument that exposes the history with full honesty. Neiman's argument that the German case presents object lessons in how a society confronts and absorbs painful lessons about its history should inspire modesty in our practices.

The long reach of the Lost Cause and recent public reckoning with the public memorial culture of the Civil War makes comparative memory even more difficult to practice in the American case because it requires what Wolfgang Schivelbusch calls "defeat empathy." For Americans in 2020, asking even empathy for the Confederacy is a tall order. But as Schivelbusch shows, in his comparative history of the US South, France, and Germany after military defeats, we can learn from these experiences. In fact, Schivelbusch quotes the German historian Reinhart Koselleck to argue that "'there is something to the hypothesis that being forced to draw new and difficult lessons from history yields insights of longer validity and thus greater explanatory power.'"[94] In order for this to be true, the defeated must have performed that hard work of introspection, a condition that was not necessarily met by defeated Confederates. Nonetheless, we hopefully possess the chronological and cultural distance from the war to more honestly assess what both victory and defeat mean.

Although religious historians have explored the ways that white Southern Christians assimilated defeat, Schivelbusch's comparison of the post–Civil War South with post-1871 France and post-1918 Germany helps explain the continuing appeal of the Lost Cause in a way that American historians, understandably focused on the toxic racial attitudes embodied in the Lost Cause, have not. Schivelbusch, in contrast, identifies a process by which vanquished nations claim redemption. "To see victory as a curse and defeat as moral purification and salvation is to combine the ancient idea of hubris with the Christian virtue of humility, catharsis with apocalypse." This cultural framework gives shape to the political responses of the defeated communities. By "understanding defeat as an act of purification, humility, and sacrifice," the three communities transformed "their philosophies of defeat into a moral bulwark for the protection of all humanity."[95] The New South effort to leverage Northern technologies and techniques while repudiating the Yankees' crass materialism, if not modernity itself, speaks to the ways that white Southerners did not simply persevere but refashioned an ethos of white supremacy into a supposedly noble model for the Western world.

Comparative history is not the perfect tool for every question.[96] It will never replace standard historical investigation. But it can illuminate the way we understand the US Civil War. As with global history or interdisciplinary approaches, the more we challenge ourselves, the better.[97] I also believe it is a more familiar tool than may be apparent at first glance. Historians continuously think about how the patterns and trajectories we identify might have been different. Considering a counterfactual example or visualizing a path not taken requires an act of imagination that compares multiple possibilities. Comparative history connects us to both humanists and scientists, for whom "likeness and similarity is one of the few foundational categories of thought."[98] In most cases, comparisons will not change the domestic or local explanations that historians have crafted to account for specific moments or aspects of the conflict. Instead, comparative history broadens the context within which we situate the US Civil War. Analyzing the war or aspects of the war, like emancipation, alongside other conflicts can spark insights. Many of the shorthand criteria we use to characterize the conflict—the bloodiest of the nineteenth century; the most consequential for the fate of liberalism or nationalism—look less persuasive when we compare the American conflict to other wars across time and space. The American experience—its causes, its nature, its memory—was not unique. The more we upset our conventional ways of studying the era, the richer our histories will be.

NOTES

1. I would like to thank Carrie Janney, Peter Carmichael, Enrico Dal Lago, and the anonymous reviewers for their helpful comments on earlier drafts of this essay. This essay is not the place for a full analysis of the methodology of comparative history, but defining terms will hopefully bring greater clarity to the conversation. Marc Bloch, one of the sharpest theorists of historical comparison, described the comparative approach as "a tool, in ordinary use, easy to manipulate, and yielding positive results." Marc Bloch, "A Contribution towards a Comparative History of European Societies," in *Land and Work in Medieval Europe: Selected Papers by Marc Bloch*, trans. J. E. Anderson (Berkeley: University of California Press, 1969), 44. Bloch identified "two conditions . . . necessary to make a comparison, historically speaking, possible: there must be a certain similarity between the facts observed—an obvious point—and a certain dissimilarity between the situations in which they have arisen" (44). Comparisons produce insights not through the process of always seeing similarity; sometimes insight is generated through exposing difference. As Shearer Davis Bowman, another comparativist, explained, "The principal benefit of the comparative method is that it both enables and encourages the historian to see past phenomena not only for what they were but also for what they were not." Shearer Davis Bowman, *Masters and Lords: Mid-19th-Century U.S. Planters and Prussian Junkers* (New York: Oxford University Press, 1993), 15–16. In this way, comparison allows us to appreciate deep contingency—how events could have turned out differently from what actually happened. Edward L. Ayers, *In the Presence of Mine Enemies: The Civil War in the Heart of America, 1859–1863* (New York: Norton, 2003), xix–xx, 275–76.

According to Theda Skocpol and Margaret Somers, "Practitioners of comparative history from Alexis de Tocqueville and Max Weber to Marc Bloch, Reinhard Bendix, and Barrington Moore Jr. have typically been concerned with understanding societal dynamics and epochal transformations of cultures and social structures." Theda Skocpol and Margaret Somers, "The Uses of Comparative History in Macrosocial Inquiry," *Comparative Studies in Society and History* 22 (April 1980): 174. Civil War historians manifest sympathy with these goals (emancipation must surely be counted as one of the epochal transformations of American life), but of the godfathers identified, only Barrington Moore studied the US Civil War and few scholars rely upon his work now. Barrington Moore, *Social Origins of Dictatorship and Democracy: Lord and Peasant in the Making of the Modern World* (Boston: Beacon Press, 1966). Skocpol and Somers identify three main approaches to comparison: "The Parallel comparativists seek above all to demonstrate that a theory similarly holds good from case to case; for them differences among the cases are primarily contextual particularities against which to highlight the generality of the processes with which their theories are basically concerned." In contrast, a second group makes "use of comparative history to bring out the unique features of each particular case . . . and to show how these unique features affect the working-out of putatively general social processes." Skocpol and Somers, "Uses of

Comparative History," 178. Both of these approaches bend toward the sociological and fail to enable the explanatory project at the heart of most contemporary historical practice. William Sewell, though a historian, identified this problem, writing, "*The comparative method is a set of rules which can be methodically and systematically applied in gathering and using evidence to test explanatory hypotheses. It does not supply us with explanations to be subjected to test: this is a task for the historical imagination.*" William H. Sewell Jr., "Marc Bloch and the Logic of Comparative History," *History and Theory* 6 (Spring 1967): 217 (italics in original). While Sewell is correct that "insight, sympathy, and intellectual power" (217) are essential attributes of any effective historian, it does not follow that we cannot compare explanations themselves. Sewell's logic assumes an independent hypothesis for each study, unique to each place being studied. But given a coherent analytical framework, we can compare different or similar outcomes in different places or at different times. In response to Sewell's concern, Skocpol and Somers identify an additional cohort of comparativists who pursue these sorts of causal comparisons. "This third variant of comparative history is, indeed, a kind of multivariate analysis to which scholars turn in order to validate causal statements about macro-phenomena for which, inherently, there are too many variables and not enough cases." Skocpol and Somers, "Uses of Comparative History," 182.

2. Denis Donoghue, *Metaphor* (Cambridge, MA: Harvard University Press, 2014), 65.

3. Hayden White, *The Content of the Form: Narrative Discourse and Historical Representation* (Baltimore: Johns Hopkins University Press, 1987), 27; Sewell, "Marc Bloch," 208–18. For a critique of the social scientific hypothesis-testing approach to comparative history, seek Skocpol and Somers, "Uses of Comparative History."

4. John S. Rosenberg, "Toward a New Civil War Revisionism," *American Scholar* 38 (Spring 1969): 250–72; Philip S. Paludan, "The American Civil War: Triumph through Tragedy," *Civil War History* 20 (September 1974): 239–50; John S. Rosenberg, "The American Civil War and the Problem of 'Presentism': A Reply to Philip S. Paludan," *Civil War History* 21 (September 1975): 242–53; and more recently, Yael A. Sternhell, "Revisionism Reinvented? The Antiwar Turn in Civil War Scholarship," *Journal of the Civil War Era* 3 (June 2013): 239–56.

5. Peter Kolchin, *A Sphinx on the American Land: The Nineteenth-Century South in Comparative Perspective* (Baton Rouge: Louisiana State University Press, 2003), 116.

6. Michael Herr, *Dispatches* (New York: Knopf, 1977); Tim O'Brien, *If I Die in a Combat Zone, Box Me Up and Ship Me Home* (New York: Delacorte, 1973), and *The Things They Carried* (New York: Houghton Mifflin, 1990).

7. Philip Caputo, *A Rumor of War* (New York: Holt, Rinehart, and Winston, 1977), xvii–xviii, 228–30.

8. Michael Fellman, *Inside War: The Guerrilla Conflict in Missouri during the American Civil War* (New York: Oxford University Press, 1989), xvi.

9. Barton Myers, "Guerrillas," in *A Companion to the U.S. Civil War*, ed. Aaron Sheehan-Dean (Malden, MA: Wiley and Sons, 2014), 1:154–77.

10. Richard E. Beringer, Herman Hattaway, Archer Jones, and William N. Still Jr., *Why the South Lost the Civil War* (Athens: University of Georgia Press, 1986).

11. Beringer et al., *Why the South Lost*, 425.

12. Andrew Mack, "Why Big Nations Lose Small Wars: The Politics of Asymmetric Conflict," *World Politics* 27 (January 1975): 175–200.

13. Beringer et al., *Why the South Lost*, 436.

14. James M. McPherson, *Battle Cry of Freedom: The Civil War Era* (New York: Oxford University Press, 1988), 7.

15. Edward L. Ayers, "Worrying about the Civil War," in *What Caused the Civil War? Reflections on the South and Southern History* (New York: Norton, 2005), 103–30; Frank Towers, "Partisans, New History, and Modernization: The Historiography of the Civil War's Causes, 1861–2011," *Journal of the Civil War Era* 1 (June 2011): 248.

16. Bloch, "Contribution," 47.

17. Though it must be said that, anxious to avoid the Lost Cause trap of explaining Union victory by recourse to the North's matériel predominance, historians often diminish these material factors and emphasize the importance of contingency to the war's outcome.

18. T. Harry Williams, "The Military Systems of the North and South," in *The Selected Essays of T. Harry Williams* (Baton Rouge: Louisiana State University Press, 1983), 149–72; T. Harry Williams, "The Military Leadership of North and South," in *Why the North Won the Civil War*, ed. David Donald (Baton Rouge: Louisiana State University Press, 1960), 38–57.

19. Though note that Brian Dirck's sensitive dual portrait assesses each man not against each other but in terms of a common standard—how they understood and promoted a vision of national community. Brian Dirck, *Lincoln and Davis: Imagining America, 1809–1865* (Lawrence: University Press of Kansas, 1991).

20. Recent studies of governors and Northern state politics create new opportunities for comparison across the sectional divide. See Stephen D. Engle, *Gathering to Save a Nation: Lincoln and the Union's War Governors* (Chapel Hill: University of North Carolina Press, 2016); and Jack Furniss, "States of the Union: The Rise and Fall of the Political Center in the Civil War North" (PhD diss., University of Virginia, 2018). Note that these broad studies also create new insights into the comparative nature of governance and experience within the North, something previously available only for Southern states.

21. Edward Pessen, "How Different from Each Other Were the Antebellum North and South?," *American Historical Review* 85, no. 5 (December 1980): 1119–49; John W. Quist, *Restless Visionaries: The Social Roots of Antebellum Reform in Alabama and Michigan* (Baton Rouge: Louisiana State University, 1998); Jonathan Dean Sarris, *A Separate Civil War: Communities in Conflict in the Mountain South* (Charlottesville: University of Virginia Press, 2006); Aaron Astor, *Rebels on the Border: Civil War, Emancipation and the Reconstruction of Kentucky and Missouri, 1860–1872* (Baton Rouge: Louisiana State University Press, 2012); Jonathan Earle and Dianne Mutti Burke, *Bleeding Kansas, Bleeding Missouri: The Long Civil War on the Border* (Lawrence: University Press of Kansas, 2013); Bridget Ford, *Bonds of Union: Religion, Race, and Politics in a Civil War Borderland* (Chapel Hill: University of North Carolina Press, 2016); Stephen I. Rockenbach, *War upon Our Border: Two Ohio Valley Communities Navigate the Civil War* (Charlottesville: University of Virginia Press, 2016); Michael Robinson, *A Union Indivisible: Secession and the Politics of Slavery in the Border South* (Chapel Hill: University of North Carolina Press, 2017).

22. William H. Pease and Jane Pease, *Web of Progress: Private Values and Public Styles in Boston and Charleston, 1828–1843* (New York: Oxford University Press, 1985); Lloyd Benson, "Planters and Hoosiers: The Development of Sectional Society in Antebellum Indiana and Mississippi" (PhD diss., University of Virginia, 1990); John Majewski, *A House Dividing:*

Economic Development in Pennsylvania and Virginia before the Civil War (Cambridge: Cambridge University Press, 2000).

23. Gary W. Gallagher, *The Confederate War: How Popular Will, Nationalism, and Military Strategy Could Not Stave Off Defeat* (Cambridge, MA: Harvard University Press, 1997), 17.

24. A conclusion supported by subsequent studies: Stephen V. Ash, *When the Yankees Came: Conflict and Chaos in the Occupied South, 1861–1865* (Chapel Hill: University of North Carolina Press, 1995); William A. Blair, *Virginia's Private War: Feeding Body and Soul in the Confederacy, 1861–1865* (New York: Oxford University Press, 1998); Anne Sarah Rubin, *A Shattered Nation: The Rise and Fall of the Confederacy, 1861–1868* (Chapel Hill: University of North Carolina Press, 2005); Aaron Sheehan-Dean, *Why Confederates Fought: Family and Nation in Civil War Virginia* (Chapel Hill: University of North Carolina Press, 2007); Michael T. Bernath, *Confederate Minds: The Struggle for Intellectual Independence in the Civil War South* (Chapel Hill: University of North Carolina Press, 2010). For competing readings of this process, see Mark A. Weitz, *A Higher Duty: Desertion among Georgia Troops during the Civil War* (Lincoln: University of Nebraska Press, 2000); David Williams, Teresa Crisp Williams, and David Carlson, *Plain Folk in a Rich Man's War: Class and Dissent in Confederate Georgia* (Gainesville: University Press of Florida, 2002); and David Williams, *Bitterly Divided: The South's Inner Civil War* (New York: New Press, 2008).

25. Gary W. Gallagher, *The Union War* (Cambridge, MA: Harvard University Press, 2011). A contrary reading of the importance of emancipation to the Northern cause is most clearly articulated in James Oakes, *Freedom National: The Destruction of Slavery in the United States, 1861–1865* (New York: Norton, 2013). Adam Smith's recent work offers something like a synthesis of these positions. Adam I. P. Smith, *The Stormy Present: Conservatism and the Problem of Slavery in Northern Politics, 1846–1865* (Chapel Hill: University of North Carolina Press, 2017).

26. Michael E. Woods, *Arguing until Doomsday: Stephen Douglas, Jefferson Davis, and the Struggle for American Democracy* (Chapel Hill: University of North Carolina Press, 2020).

27. Kolchin, *Sphinx on the American Land*, 41.

28. For a recent summary of the field, see Judith Giesberg, "Women," in *A Companion to the U.S. Civil War*, ed. Aaron Sheehan-Dean (Malden, MA: Wiley and Sons, 2014), 2:779–94. On farming, see the remarkable admission from a Florida Confederate to his wife: "You said that you thought that we would have near a hundred head of hogs to fatten this fall. That is doing well, aint it I think you are a better farmer than I am you have done exceedingly well since I left." Aaron Sheehan-Dean, "'If It Was Not for You I Would Be Willing to Die': The Civil War Correspondence of Michael and Sallie Raysor," *Florida Historical Quarterly*, Winter 2008, 390–405.

29. Nina Silber, *Daughters of the Union: Northern Women Fight the Civil War* (Cambridge, MA: Harvard University Press, 2005); Stephanie McCurry, *Confederate Reckoning: Power and Politics in the Civil War South* (Cambridge, MA: Harvard University Press, 2010), and *Women's War: Fighting and Surviving the American Civil War* (Cambridge, MA: Harvard University Press, 2019).

30. Thavolia Glymph, *The Women's Fight: The Civil War's Battles for Home, Freedom, and Nation* (Chapel Hill: University of North Carolina Press, 2020), 8. Judy Giesberg and Randall Miller's *Women and the American Civil War: North-South Counterpoints* (Kent, OH: Kent

State University Press, 2018) enables more precise sectional comparisons by pairing essays on the same topic in both regions.

31. Within the field of emancipation studies, exemplary recent works include Chandra Manning, *Troubled Refuge: Struggling for Freedom in the Civil War* (New York: Knopf, 2016); Amy Taylor, *Embattled Freedom: Journeys through the Civil War's Slave Refugee Camps* (Chapel Hill: University of North Carolina Press, 2018); and Joseph P. Reidy, *Illusions of Emancipation: The Pursuit of Freedom and Equality in the Twilight of Slavery* (Chapel Hill: University of North Carolina Press, 2019).

32. Eric Foner, *Gateway to Freedom: The Hidden History of the Underground Railroad* (New York: Norton, 2014); R. J. M. Blackett, *The Captive's Quest for Freedom: Fugitive Slaves, the 1850 Fugitive Slave Law, and the Politics of Slavery* (Cambridge: Cambridge University Press, 2018).

33. W. E. B. Du Bois, *Black Reconstruction in America, 1860–1880* (1935; repr., New York: Free Press, 1998); Steven Hahn, *The Political Worlds of Slavery and Freedom* (Cambridge, MA: Harvard University Press, 2009).

34. James Marten, "A Feeling of Restless Anxiety: Loyalty and Race in the Peninsula Campaign and Beyond," in *The Richmond Campaign*, ed. Gary W. Gallagher (Chapel Hill: University of North Carolina Press, 2000), 121–52; Glenn David Brasher, *The Peninsula Campaign and the Necessity of Emancipation: African Americans and the Fight for Freedom* (Chapel Hill: University of North Carolina Press, 2012).

35. Susan E. O'Donovan, *Becoming Free in the Cotton South* (Cambridge, MA: Harvard University Press, 2007); Jim Downs, *Sick from Freedom: African-American Illness and Suffering during the Civil War and Reconstruction* (New York: Oxford University Press, 2012); Reidy, *Illusions of Emancipation*.

36. Kate Masur, *An Example for All the Land: Emancipation and the Struggle over Equality in Washington, D.C.* (Chapel Hill: University of North Carolina Press, 2010); Greg Downs and Kate Masur, "Echoes of War: Rethinking Post–Civil War Governance and Politics," in *The World the Civil War Made*, ed. Greg Downs and Kate Masur (Chapel Hill: University of North Carolina Press, 2015), 1–21.

37. Stephen Kantrowitz, *More Than Freedom: Fighting for Black Citizenship in a White Republic, 1829–1889* (New York: Penguin, 2012), 4.

38. Masur, *Example for All the Land*.

39. Greg Downs, "The Civil War and the American State," in *Cambridge History of the American Civil War*, vol. 3, ed. Aaron Sheehan-Dean (Cambridge: Cambridge University Press, 2019), 350–71; Gary Gerstle, *Liberty and Coercion: The Paradox of American Government* (Princeton, NJ: Princeton University Press, 2015), 90–92. In another example of this sort of historiographical dispute, see the illuminating debate over how to characterize the nature of the war's end. Gregory P. Downs, *After Appomattox: Military Occupation and the Ends of War* (Cambridge, MA: Harvard University Press, 2015); William A. Blair, "Finding the Ending of America's Civil War," *American Historical Review* 120, no. 5 (December 2015): 1753–66; Andrew Lang, "Union Demobilization and the Boundaries of War and Peace," *Journal of the Civil War Era* 9 (June 2019): 178–95; David C. Williard, "Criminal Amnesty, State Courts, and the Reach of Reconstruction," *Journal of Southern History* 85 (February 2019): 105–36; Caroline E. Janney, *Ends of War: The Unfinished Fight of Lee's Army after Appomattox* (Chapel Hill: University of North Carolina Press, 2021).

40. Frank Tannenbaum, *Slave and Citizen: The Negro in the Americas* (New York: Knopf, 1947).

41. Carl N. Degler, *Neither Black nor White: Slavery and Race Relations in Brazil and the United States* (New York: Macmillan, 1971).

42. Degler, *Neither Black nor White*, 89.

43. Herbert S. Klein, *Slavery in the Americas: A Comparative Study of Cuba and Virginia* (Chicago: University of Chicago Press, 1967); Ada Ferrer, *Freedom's Mirror: Cuba and Haiti in the Age of Revolution* (Cambridge: Cambridge University Press, 2014).

44. Peter Kolchin, *Unfree Labor: American Slavery and Russian Serfdom* (Cambridge, MA: Harvard University Press, 1987); Bowman, *Masters and Lords*.

45. Kolchin, *Unfree Labor*, 4–5.

46. Adam Rothman, *Slave Country: American Expansion and the Origins of the Deep South* (Cambridge, MA: Harvard University Press, 2005); Robin Einhorn, *American Taxation, American Slavery* (Chicago: University of Chicago Press, 2006); Gautham Rao, *National Duties: Custom Houses and the Making of the American State* (Chicago: University of Chicago Press, 2016); Ryan Quintana, *Making a Slave State: Political Development in Early South Carolina* (Chapel Hill: University of North Carolina Press, 2018); Aaron R. Hall, "Public Slaves and State Engineers: Modern Statecraft on Louisiana's Waterways, 1833–1861," *Journal of Southern History* 85 (August 2019): 531–76.

47. George M. Frederickson, *White Supremacy: A Comparative Study in American and South African History* (New York: Oxford University Press, 1982); John Cell, *The Highest Stage of White Supremacy: The Origins of Segregation in South Africa and the American South* (Cambridge: Cambridge University Press, 1982).

48. Edward Bartlett Rugemer, *The Problem of Emancipation: The Caribbean Roots of the American Civil War* (Baton Rouge: Louisiana State University Press, 2009); Matthew Clavin, *Toussaint Louverture and the American Civil War: The Promise and Peril of a Second Haitian Revolution* (Philadelphia: University of Pennsylvania Press, 2011).

49. Rebecca Scott, Frederick Cooper, and Thomas C. Holt, *Beyond Slavery: Explorations of Race, Labor, and Citizenship in Postemancipation Societies* (Chapel Hill: University of North Carolina Press, 2000); Rebecca Scott, *Degrees of Freedom: Louisiana and Cuba after Slavery* (Cambridge, MA: Harvard University Press, 2005).

50. Vitor Izecksohn, Slavery and War in the Americas: Race, Citizenship, and State Building in the United States and Brazil, 1861–1870 (Charlottesville: University of Virginia Press, 2014); Gerald Horne, *The Deepest South: The United States, Brazil, and the African Slave Trade* (New York: New York University Press, 2007), 55.

51. Jeffrey R. Kerr-Ritchie, *Freedom's Seekers: Essays on Comparative Emancipation* (Baton Rouge: Louisiana State University Press, 2013).

52. Rubin, *Shattered Nation*, 14–25.

53. Mark Grimsley, *The Hard Hand of War: Union Military Policy toward Southern Civilians, 1861–1865* (Cambridge: Cambridge University Press, 1995), 190, 214.

54. David A. Bell, *The First Total War: Napoleon's Europe and the Birth of Warfare as We Know It* (Boston: Houghton Mifflin, 2007).

55. Aaron Sheehan-Dean, *The Calculus of Violence: How Americans Fought the Civil War* (Cambridge, MA: Harvard University Press, 2018).

56. David Potter, "The Civil War in the History of the Modern World: A Comparative View," in *The South and the Sectional Conflict* (Baton Rouge: Louisiana State University Press, 1968), 287–99, originally published in *The Comparative Approach to American History*, ed. C. Vann Woodward (New York: Basic, 1968).

57. Potter, "Civil War in the History of the Modern World," 287.

58. Potter, "Civil War in the History of the Modern World," 291, 298.

59. Kolchin, *Unfree Labor*, ix.

60. Enrico Dal Lago, *William Lloyd Garrison and Giuseppe Mazzini: Abolition, Democracy, and Radical Reform* (Baton Rouge: Louisiana State University Press, 2013).

61. Enrico Dal Lago, *Civil War and Agrarian Unrest: The Confederate South and Southern Italy* (Cambridge: Cambridge University Press, 2018).

62. Dal Lago, *Civil War and Agrarian Unrest*, 11–14.

63. Dal Lago, *Civil War and Agrarian Unrest*, 400–404.

64. Don H. Doyle, *Nations Divided: America, Italy, and the Southern Question* (Athens: University of Georgia Press, 2002).

65. Don H. Doyle and Marco Antonio Pamplona, eds., *Nationalism in the New World* (Athens: University of Georgia Press, 2006); Don H. Doyle, ed., *Secession as an International Phenomenon: From America's Civil War to Contemporary Separatist Movements* (Athens: University of Georgia Press, 2010); Don H. Doyle, ed., *American Civil Wars: The United States, Latin America, Europe, and the Crisis of the 1860s* (Chapel Hill: University of North Carolina Press, 2017).

66. Gregory P. Downs, *The Second American Revolution: The Civil War–Era Struggle over Cuba and the Rebirth of the American Republic* (Chapel Hill: University of North Carolina Press, 2019).

67. Matt D. Childs, "Cuba, the Atlantic Crisis of the 1860s, and the Road to Abolition," in Doyle, *American Civil Wars*, 204–21; Rafael Marquese, "The Civil War in the United States and the Crisis of Slavery in Brazil," in Doyle, *American Civil Wars*, 222–46; Christopher Schmidt-Nowara, *Empire and Antislavery: Spain, Cuba, and Puerto Rico, 1833–1872* (Pittsburgh: University of Pittsburgh Press, 1999).

68. David Armitage, *Civil Wars: A History in Ideas* (New Haven, CT: Yale University Press, 2017).

69. Armitage, *Civil Wars*, 193.

70. Stathis N. Kalyvas, *The Logic of Violence in Civil War* (Cambridge: Cambridge University Press, 2006).

71. Aaron Sheehan-Dean, *Reckoning with Rebellion: War and Sovereignty in the Nineteenth Century* (Gainesville: University Press of Florida, 2020).

72. Philip M. Katz, *From Appomattox to Montmartre: Americans and the Paris Commune* (Cambridge, MA: Harvard University Press, 1998).

73. Eric T. Dean, *Shook over Hell: Post-traumatic Stress, Vietnam, and the Civil War* (Cambridge, MA: Harvard University Press, 1997).

74. Dean, *Shook over Hell*, 90, 216–17.

75. Gaines M. Foster, "Coming to Terms with Defeat: Post-Vietnam America and the Post–Civil War South," *Virginia Quarterly Review* 66 (Winter 1990): 17–35.

76. Foster, "Coming to Terms," 27.

77. Edward L. Ayers, "Exporting Reconstruction," in *What Caused the Civil War?*, 145–66.

78. See the otherwise quite helpful David M. Edelstein, *Occupational Hazards: Success and Failure in Military Occupation* (Ithaca, NY: Cornell University Press, 2008).

79. Walter Lacquer, *Guerrilla Warfare: A Historical and Critical Study* (1976; New Brunswick, NJ: Transaction, 2010); Robert B. Asprey, *War in the Shadows: The Guerrilla in History* (New York: William Morrow, 1994); Max Boot, *Invisible Armies: An Epic History of Guerrilla Warfare from Ancient Times to the Present* (New York: Liveright, 2013).

80. Max Edling, *A Revolution in Favor of Government: Origins of the U.S. Constitution and the Making of the American State* (New York: Oxford University Press, 2003).

81. Richard John, *Spreading the News: The American Postal System from Franklin to Morse* (Cambridge, MA: Harvard University Press, 1998); Brian Balogh, *A Government Out of Sight: The Mystery of National Authority in Nineteenth-Century America* (Cambridge: Cambridge University Press, 2009); Rao, *National Duties*.

82. Thomas Bender, *A Nation among Nations: America's Place in World History* (New York: Hill and Wang, 2006).

83. Max Edling, *A Hercules in the Cradle: War, Money, and the American State, 1783–1867* (Chicago: University of Chicago Press, 2014).

84. Some of the answers to that query can be found in David K. Thomson, *Bonds of War: How Civil War Financial Agents Sold the World on the Union* (Chapel Hill: University of North Carolina Press, 2022).

85. This is changing as more scholars adopt Elliot West's call for a "Greater Reconstruction" that takes account of the experience in western states. "Reconstructing Race," *Western Historical Quarterly* 34, no. 1 (Spring 2003): 7–26; Heather Cox Richardson, *West from Appomattox: The Reconstruction of America after the Civil War* (New Haven, CT: Yale University Press, 2007). David Prior's *Between Freedom and Progress: The Lost World of Reconstruction Politics* (Baton Rouge: Louisiana State University Press, 2019) does not reorient around the West per se or adopt a comparative perspective, but his global framing is similarly liberating.

86. Gaines M. Foster, *Ghosts of the Confederacy: Defeat, the Lost Cause, and the Emergence of the New South, 1865–1913* (New York: Oxford University Press, 1987); David W. Blight, *Race and Reunion: The Civil War in American Memory* (Cambridge, MA: Harvard University Press, 2001); Caroline E. Janney, *Remembering the Civil War: Reunion and the Limits of Reconciliation* (Chapel Hill: University of North Carolina Press, 2013); John R. Neff, *Honoring the Civil War Dead: Commemoration and the Problem of Reconciliation* (Lawrence: University Press of Kansas, 2005).

87. Paul D. Escott, *Uncommonly Savage: Civil War and Remembrance in Spain and the United States* (Gainesville: University Press of Florida, 2014).

88. Escott, *Uncommonly Savage*, 162.

89. Escott, *Uncommonly Savage*; Joseph Sebarenzi, "Reconciliation Challenges in Post-Genocide Rwanda," in *Reconciliation after Civil Wars: Global Perspectives*, ed. Paul Quigley and James Hawdon (New York: Routledge, 2018), 17–34; Julius Ruiz, "Franco's Peace: Fighting the Spanish Civil War, 1939–1975," in Quigley and Hawdon, *Reconciliation after Civil Wars*, 84–85.

90. Escott, *Uncommonly Savage*, 215.

91. Quigley and Hawdon, *Reconciliation after Civil Wars*.

92. James Hawdon, "United We Heal, Divided We Reconcile: Group Solidarity and the Problem of Status after Civil Conflicts," in Quigley and Hawdon, *Reconciliation after Civil Wars*, 258.

93. Susan Neiman, *Learning from the Germans: Race and the Memory of Evil* (New York: Farrar, Straus and Giroux, 2019), 24.

94. Wolfgang Schivelbusch, *The Culture of Defeat: On National Trauma, Mourning, and Recovery*, trans. Jefferson Chase (New York: Picador, 2003), 3–4.

95. Schivelbusch, *Culture of Defeat*, 20, 31.

96. I have also not taken up here the many ways in which comparative studies shade into transnational ones. Dal Lago, *Willian Lloyd Garrison and Giuseppe Mazzini*, 10–14.

97. For an excellent and related call to broaden the field, see Michael E. Woods, "Interdisciplinary Studies of the Civil War Era: Recent Trends and Future Prospects," *Journal of American Studies* 51 (May 2017): 349–83.

98. Donoghue, *Metaphor*, 74.

The Confederacy's Use of Nationalism and Vice Versa

ANDRE M. FLECHE

In 1962, historian David M. Potter declared that "the rise of nationalism has been the major political development of modern times."¹ The wars and revolutions of the eighteenth and nineteenth centuries ensured that nation-states would become the dominant form of political organization around the world. The American Civil War contributed to emerging understandings of nationalism in more ways than one. While many accounts emphasize the role that Union victory played in preserving republican government in the New World, the rise and fall of the Confederate States of America also underscored the degree to which the establishment of nation-states had become essential to the pursuit of political power. In 1860 and 1861, secessionists responded to a policy dispute over the expansion of slavery by constructing a new nation. The Confederacy's founders wrote their own national constitution, elected their own president, and, in the words of Jefferson Davis, assumed a separate position "among the nations of the earth."² Under the pressures of war, Confederate politicians conferred upon their government far-reaching powers of conscription, the right to collect income taxes, the ability to impress slaves and goods, and the authority to operate factories and mines.[3] In short, the architects of the Confederacy created the strongest central government that had yet been seen in North America.

Confederate statesmen surely did not intend for their government to become, in the words of historian Emory M. Thomas, "more centralized, more nationalized than her Northern enemy." Still, the Confederacy's transformation "from a state rights confederation into a centralized, national state" was not carried out "unwittingly."[4] Global events of the late eighteenth and early nineteenth centuries convinced American statesmen in both the North and the South that the nation-state had become the most legitimate instrument with which to pursue policy goals. The American Revolution, the French Revolution, the Haitian Revolution, the wars of independence in Latin America, and the European revolutions of 1848 all asserted that aggrieved peoples had the right to self-government. In many of those cases, revolutionaries attempted to protect those presumed political rights by establishing national independence. Successful revolutionaries in the United States and Latin America erected governments that proved powerful enough to withstand military challengers, while failed movements in Ireland, Hungary, Poland, the German states, and elsewhere had witnessed embryonic polities collapse when confronted by strong armies. Thoughtful statesmen could take away at least one clear lesson: in the world of international politics, only strong national governments could successfully defend sovereignty and project power.

In 1861, a majority of white Southerners came to believe that they could best defend their interests by seceding from the United States and establishing a new nation. Alternative models of dissent existed. For much of the early republic, most Americans had accepted the proposition that competition between political parties could safely channel political disagreements.[5] The most effective way to influence policy would be to win elections to gain the right to lead the federal government. In fact, slaveholding politicians during the antebellum era had used their frequent control of Congress and the White House to support the army, develop the navy, and ultimately expand slavery.[6] When a Republican candidate won the presidency in 1860, however, many white Southerners concluded that the United States had become too ideologically, ethnically, and racially heterogeneous for electoral competition to work in protecting their vital interests. During the 1850s, many white Southerners, especially those serving in US embassies in Latin America, had become convinced that states with diverse populations and internal divisions would inevitably succumb to weakness and failure. What is more, Great Britain and other European empires stood poised to stamp out the independence of any New World nations whose unity of purpose faltered. Only strong and cohesive national governments, white Southerners believed, could protect American republicanism, which, in the words of historian Tom Chaffin, included "white-male suffrage, popular sovereignty, laissez-faire individualism (for whites), slavery, and territorial expansion."[7] The recent history of the Atlantic World demonstrated that a "family of nations" existed and that new powers might reasonably expect to join it. When the election of Abraham Lincoln threatened the future of slavery, Confederates sought to protect the institution the most effective way past precedent had offered them—by establishing an independent nation-state. In short, the Confederates did not construct a strong slaveholding nation accidentally; instead, it appeared to many white Southerners to be the only natural course Confederates could take to achieve their policy goals.

Despite the fact that secessionists deliberately created a new nation, many historians have questioned the extent and strength of Confederate nationalism. David Potter complained that in contemplating the matter, historians have too often allowed their own moral judgments to cloud their empirical analysis. Potter argued that historians often hesitate to recognize nations whose cause they disapprove of for fear of sanctioning their actions. "When the historian attributes nationality to any group," Potter explained, "he establishes a presumption in favor of any acts involving an exercise of autonomy that the group may commit; when he denies nationality he establishes a presumption against any exercise of autonomy."[8] As a consequence, Potter implied, many historians dismissed the existence of true Confederate nationalism because the Confederacy fought for slavery and fought against the maintenance of an existing nation—the United States.

The historiographical record offers many examples of scholars who have doubted the existence of a real Confederate national identity. Richard E. Beringer, Herman Hattaway, Archer Jones, and William N. Still Jr. supplied the most explicit articulation of the position when they argued that a lack of "will," "oneness," and "an adequately developed sense of nationalism" contributed substantially to Confederate defeat.[9] Other historians have pointed out that social divisions along the lines of class, gender, and race hampered Confederate unity. William Freehling posited that the Civil War actually pitted "the South versus the South" in what amounted to a struggle for regional power between planters, poor whites, and African Americans.[10] More recently, Stephanie McCurry has contended that the Confederacy's exclusion of women and slaves doomed the divided nation to failure.[11] Steven

Hahn goes so far as to eschew the use of the word "Confederacy," seeing the self-proclaimed slaveholding nation as a "rogue rather than a legitimate state because no other state power in the world ever recognized it." He likens what he calls the slaveholders' rebellion to acts of resistance to the federal government by Native Americans, Mormons, and Peace Democrats.[12]

There can be no doubt that Black Southerners rejected any attachment to Confederate national identity. It is also true that white Southerners' commitment to slavery deprived the Confederate state of the support of its Black population, which the US government eventually recruited as soldiers. Conceding these facts does not imply that the architects of the Confederacy had not created a nation, even though it was a nation founded on racism and white supremacy. One might argue that all nations are divided by race, class, and gender, including the United States. Gary W. Gallagher pointed out that the Confederacy demanded and received from its white citizens a level of sacrifice unprecedented in American history. He argued that "strong feelings of national identity" inspired white men and women to persist in the cause throughout the war.[13] A number of other historians have also taken the existence of Confederate nationalism seriously. Drew Gilpin Faust contended that in order to sustain support, white Southern patriots "created" a Confederate nationalism, which relied on patriotic sermons, songs, flags, and symbols.[14] Anne Sarah Rubin demonstrated that white Southerners remained attached to many of these symbols and identities well after their nation had met defeat.[15]

More recently, a number of scholars interested in Southern nationalism have discovered that contemporaneous trends in nineteenth-century world history provided powerful precedents from which Confederates drew as they constructed their nation. Don Doyle has noted similarities between Southern secession and other separatist movements around the world.[16] Doyle shows that Confederate diplomats cited a number of European nationalist movements as justification for their own war of independence.[17] I have argued that Confederates drew lessons and inspiration from some aspects of the European revolutions of 1848 in particular.[18] Paul Quigley reasons that white Southerners derived their sense of nationhood from long-standing engagement with the legacies of both the American Revolution and the revolutions of 1848.[19] Ann Tucker agrees that the wars and revolutions of the nineteenth century shaped ideas about Southern nationhood both before and after 1861.[20]

The works of these and other transnational historians have reframed the historiographical discussion over Southern nationalism. The field has moved beyond debates over the verity, extent, and strength of Confederate nationality and asked an evident question instead: Why did white Southerners' response to a political problem take a nationalist form? Why had Southern secessionists chosen to respond to the election of Lincoln by writing a constitution, forming a separate government, and dispatching diplomats abroad, steps that other rebel groups in other circumstances did not necessarily undertake? The work of transnational scholars answered that world events had trained the people of the era to understand that political power could best be achieved through the institution of the nation-state. Only strong nations could protect sovereignty and achieve policy goals, both at home and abroad.

Jefferson Davis certainly agreed. A close examination of his inaugural address reveals the extent to which the international developments of the nineteenth century had shaped his thinking about nationalism. In explaining the Confederacy's purpose to the world, Davis turned to Thomas Jefferson. He closely copied Jefferson's statement of intent from the Declaration of Independence but made one small but significant change. Whereas Jefferson had declared that the United States aspired to assume a separate position "among the *powers* of the earth," a formulation that assumed a world made up of a variety of polities that might include empires, federations, and smaller states, Davis contended that the Confederacy wished to assume a separate position "among the *nations* of the earth." By 1861, the nation-state seemed destined to become the prime vessel for effectively organizing sovereignty, and Davis concurred. He elaborated on what joining the world's family of nations might mean for the Confederacy. He asserted that the formation of a permanent government would endow the new Southern nation with strength. Consolidation of the seceding states under one central government, he explained, would offer the Confederacy "greater moral and physical power" than it might otherwise have. He then went on to describe the advantage that would accrue to strong states. Davis assumed that during the nineteenth century, competition between countries would continue to shape international relations. A unified government, he declared, would be "better able to combat with the many difficulties which arise from the conflicting interests of separate nations."[21]

In the years before the Civil War, white Southern politicians became very familiar with the differences that might arise among rival powers. Davis himself, while serving as US secretary of war, augmented the military in hopes of expanding American influence in the Western Hemisphere. Davis, of course, assumed that American interests included the expansion of slavery.[22] Those twin goals might be blocked not only by Free-Soilers working internally to redirect American state policy but also by European empires, whose presence and military capacity stood as a barrier to US expansion. The British Empire, in particular, which had already abolished slavery in its hemispheric possessions, vied with the United States for control of territory and trade routes in Central America and beyond. US policymakers, unwilling or unable to confront the British directly, realized that US interests depended on the maintenance of a number of independent nation-states in the region that had the strength, power, and capability to check European encroachments. US diplomats of all political persuasions urged the State Department to revive the Monroe Doctrine, which had asserted that the future of the Western Hemisphere belonged to independent nations organized on the principles of republican self-government. As historian Jay Sexton has shown, the Monroe Doctrine had lain dormant if not forgotten during the 1830s and 1840s. During the 1850s, however, it became a useful tool to employ in the effort to keep North and South America free of powers that might impede the commercial or territorial expansion of the United States.[23]

The many white Southerners serving in Latin America in the US foreign service proved to be as enthusiastic as any for the enforcement of the Monroe Doctrine. Only strong and independent nation-states could maintain sovereignty, protect interests, and project power, they believed. As long as the United States included the protection of slavery as one of its interests, these white Southerners could confidently serve it. Once their country became as strong a threat to slavery as European countries were, however, Confederates could apply many of the lessons learned from contemplation of the wider world in their efforts to protect their interests at home, efforts that eventually included Southern separatism, secession, and the establishment of the Confederate nation.

During the 1850s, Central America became a particularly illustrative flashpoint. Control of transit routes across the isthmus grew in importance after the United States conquered California in the Mexican-American War. Great Britain and the United States both hoped to dominate the region, and few strong powers stood in the way. In 1841, the Federal Republic of Central America had splintered into the smaller nations of Guatemala, Nicaragua, Honduras, Costa Rica, and El Salvador. American diplomats from both the North and the South worried that a vacuum of power would invite increased British meddling. These fears proved to be well founded. During the late 1840s, the British Empire solidified long-standing claims to Belize, the Bay Islands off of Honduras, and the "Mosquito Coast," a strip of land in Nicaragua and Honduras that was occupied by a Native American kingdom under the protection of Britain. Alexander Dimitry, an ambassador to Costa Rica and Nicaragua under James Buchanan and the future assistant postmaster general of the Confederacy, explained to Pedro Zeledón, Nicaraguan minister of foreign affairs, that Central American disunion had invited calamity. In a formulation that might be termed ironic given Dimitry's future support for the Confederacy, he dated the region's struggles "from the day, when the feuds and dissensions of States... first broke the bond of Union, which gave strength and dignity to their original compact."[24]

A succession of white Southerners in US service, many of whom defended Southern rights while at home, agreed that in Latin America the existence of strong nations would best protect US interests, which for them included the expansion of slavery. These diplomats feared that Great Britain would thwart US ambitions by taking advantage of feeble states in the region. Beverly L. Clarke, a Southern-rights Democrat from Kentucky who served as US minister to Guatemala and Honduras during the Buchanan administration, compared Central American states to slaves and the British to their masters. In 1859, he wrote from Guatemala City to Secretary of State Lewis Cass to complain that the British Empire "whips and drives" the nations of the region, backing up its claims with a "man-of-war" when needed. For Clarke, the lesson was obvious: weak nations invariably succumbed to great powers. In his letter to Cass, he explained that Great Britain also used "commercial advantages" to ensure that "the stronger power" gained "preponderating influence over the weaker." He accused the British of using the strongest state in the region, Guatemala, to exert influence over the others: "Guatemala is the most potent state in Central America, and is supposed to exercise a vast influence over all the rest: thus Guatemala became an almost indispensable auxiliary in accomplishing the ends of British intrigue and diplomacy."[25] Mirabeau B. Lamar, the Texas nationalist and US minister to Costa Rica and Nicaragua during the Buchanan administration, agreed with Clarke's assessments. In his own letter to Cass, he warned that "if these Republics are left to themselves they will inevitably become very little more than French and British Colonies."[26]

Lamar and others urged US policymakers to confront British power in the region by resurrecting the Monroe Doctrine. Hindsight imbues their position with irony. Historian Patrick Kelly and others have shown that the Confederate States of America would eventually renounce the Monroe Doctrine in the hopes of gaining European support for its own independence. The invocation of the doctrine by white Southerners during the 1850s, however, underscores the degree to which Southern nationalists equated the preservation of a vigorous national independence with the protection of hemispheric interests, including self-government and slavery.[27] Lamar wrote to Cass that in order to thwart British interests in Central America, "there is but one way to do it, and that is to unfurl the Monroe Banner at once." He lamented that "if we are afraid to do this, then let us revert back to our colonial condition, and pay the Tea-Tax without any further complaint."[28] Lamar later reported that, before leaving the country, he made the Monroe Doctrine the special topic of conversation in his last meeting with the Costa Rican president, Juan Rafael Mora.[29] During the interview, Lamar reminded Mora that the announcement of the Monroe Doctrine had acted to ensure the independence of Latin America. If the United States had not displayed the determination to protect national independence in the New World, he declared that Latin American nations "would have been resubjected to the power of Spain." Lamar asserted that "the stand then taken by the United States in favor of Spanish American liberty ... put an end to European despotism in this portion of the Continent; and confirmed to the inhabitants the right of Self-government."[30]

In the absence of direct US military intervention, concerned white Southern diplomats urged Latin Americans to counter British power by establishing strong unions of their own. In 1859, Dimitry pressed Pedro Zeledón to join with the statesmen of Central America to "win over their people to unite themselves in one brotherhood, for the sake of their interests, their freedom and their safety."[31] He recommended "the timely consolidation of now scattered powers, to avert the disasters, which obvious inducements to aggression and isolated means of defence must invite on single and, it may be, distracted States." He concluded by reminding Zeledón that "by this concentration of their powers, the United States have hitherto succeeded in guarding their political integrity and protecting their sovereign rights."[32] Though unionist sentiment might seem incongruous for future and sometimes concurrent defenders of Southern separatism, their contention that only strong nations could protect sovereignty explains why the slaveholders' rebellion took a nationalist form. Given that secession would only weaken the United States in the face of European powers, the Confederacy's founders would insist that their new nation become as strong as possible, a lesson Jefferson Davis clearly repeated in his inaugural address.

The convictions that white Southerners developed in contemplating the state of nationalism in the hemisphere offered ideological as well as utilitarian justifications for the creation of the Confederacy. Southern thinkers held that shared interests, which might include slavery, created an appropriate and obvious basis for sound nation building. Alexander Dimitry justified Central American independence with words that fewer than two years later could apply equally well to the Confederacy. He explained that he feared British intrusion because the governments of the Americas "by reason of their peculiar institutions ... have peculiar interests of their own."[33] He lamented that "in a contiguity of territory, covered by a people with an identity of language, customs and manners, pointing to an identity of social relations and political interests," the "aggregate powers of the people" were "now uselessly, if not mischievously, disseminated among individual and almost helpless States."[34] Mirabeau Lamar bluntly summed up the stakes of abandoning independent nationalism in the region for Latin America, the United States, and later the Confederacy: "I do not wish to see our jealous rivals engraft their institutions upon this country, and rear up, in our very front, a mighty bulwark of power against us."[35]

Southern diplomats in US service also believed that Mexico displayed the dangers that weak governments posed for the preservation of the rights of slavery and self-government. Although the United States had annexed vast expanses of Mexican territory as an outcome of the Mexican-American War, interest in additional acquisitions remained high, especially among Southerners. In 1854, Congress approved the purchase of a strip of territory in northern Mexico negotiated by James Gadsden, President Franklin Pierce's ambassador to that country. Gadsden hailed from South Carolina and professed deep devotion to the institution of slavery. In 1850, he had hoped that at least a portion of California would be opened to the peculiar institution, and he advocated the secession of his home state when the Compromise of 1850 blocked that possibility. His Gadsden Purchase promised to advance Southern interests by providing land for the construction of a transcontinental rail line on a deep southern route. Other US expansionists hoped to acquire Baja California and secure rights-of-way for a rail line across Tehuantepec, which would link the Pacific Ocean with the Gulf of Mexico.

Just as in Central America, the United States faced competitors for influence in Mexico. Great Britain and France in particular had made significant investments in the country and held large portions of its government's debt. American fear of European involvement in Mexico only grew during the Ayutla Revolution of 1854–55. In that conflict, Mexican liberals, led in part by Ignacio Comonfort and Benito Juárez, overthrew the conservative regime of Antonio López de Santa Anna. European powers, especially the French, backed the conservatives and would eventually offer them clandestine support in the War of the Reform that broke out between the two competing factions in 1857. As early as 1855, James Gadsden warned the US State Department of European "conspiracies" against the liberal government. Gadsden especially worried about the "weakness" of the new government, and particularly its "exhausted Treasury & Credit," which he predicted would force Mexico "into the clutches of the European designs antagonistical to America" and, by extension, the expansion of slavery.[36]

John Forsyth Jr., who replaced Gadsden as minister, shared Gadsden's concerns that Mexico's weak nation-state would invite disaster. Forsyth grew up in Georgia and became an important newspaper editor in Alabama's Democratic Party. He went on to become one of the first representatives of the Confederate States of America sent to treat with the US government before eventually becoming chief of staff in the Confederate Army of Tennessee. After his arrival in Mexico, he professed the belief that "whether Mexico maintains her nationality, or falls to pieces, we have a deep interest in her future."[37] Forsyth argued in a letter to Secretary of State William Marcy that only US intervention could ensure a "stable government" for Mexico. These convictions led Forsyth to develop a scheme for what he called the "regeneration of the Mexican Nation" several years before he played a key role in the creation of the Confederate States of America. He proposed offering "the powerful aid of the United States" in the form of a protectorate that would include a commercial treaty, loans, military assistance, and the promotion of emigration from the United States.[38] In a follow-up to Marcy's successor, Lewis Cass, he argued that if the United States did not step in, then Britain or France would. Such an event would prove disastrous for US ambitions in the hemisphere. "If it be Europe," he wrote, "I can foresee a multitude of contingencies that will make Mexico the battle ground for the maintenance of American supremacy in America; the theater for the practical illustration of the value and virtue of the Monroe doctrine."[39]

Forsyth's thinking clearly revealed that his interpretation of US interests dovetailed with the concerns of proslavery expansionists. Both the protection of slavery and the expansion of the United States depended on pitting powerful nation-states in North America and Mexico against European ambition. "I am of course a believer in what in the political nomenclature of the day is termed 'Manifest destiny,'" he explained. "In other words I believe in the teachings of experience and history, and that our race, I hope our institutions,—are to spread over this continent and that the hybrid races of the West, must succumb to, and fade away before the superior energies of the white man."[40] What he did not say at the time is that when he came to believe that the United States would no longer protect slavery, he would advocate for the construction of another powerful North American nation to protect it—the Confederacy.

The beginning of the War of the Reform in 1857 threatened to remove one potentially strong North American nation from opposing European encroachment. After fighting commenced, Forsyth ominously reported to Lewis Cass that the "[Mexican] State is in a condition of rapid disintegration & decay, & is tottering to its fall." He maintained that those Mexicans who favored "public order & tranquility" advocated for the establishment of a "strong Central Government." Though it might seem incongruous in a future supporter of the supposedly states' rights Confederacy, Forsyth agreed that "Mexico requires a master." Forsyth's reasoning offers insight into how he might later break from the United States and embrace Confederate nationalism. As long as the United States protected slavery, he supported the Union's maintenance as a force for power and order in the hemisphere. Once the US government no longer offered consensus on the issues of slavery, however, Forsyth would conclude that only a nation with a uniform interest in maintaining white supremacy and slavery could protect the peculiar institution. Mexico, he believed, demonstrated that nations that had become too ideologically and ethnically diverse could not long survive. In speaking of Mexico, but in a formulation he could later apply to the fracturing United States, he explained, "I cannot but look on a Federal, or Republican form of Govt. as a complete farce in a country where there is really no people, & where there are none of those habitudes of public spirit, loyalty, & patriotism, which are the essential conditions of self-government."[41]

In 1859, the Buchanan administration sent William M. Churchwell as a special agent to further investigate conditions in Mexico. Only two years later, Churchwell, unlike many citizens in his native East Tennessee, would join the secession movement and eventually the Confederate army. Upon his arrival in Mexico in 1859, he offered sentiments that agreed with Forsyth's. "A new phase in Mexican nationality is now a positive necessity," he declared in a prescription that he would later apply to the South.[42] As Southern nationalists would later insist in their own case, he explained that "Mexico must inevitably lose her nationality or become the prey of despotic rulers." Churchwell attributed Mexico's "pitiable condition" to the "incessant intestine commotion" the country had faced since independence.[43] His analysis can only be termed ironic given that Churchwell would soon be fighting in his own civil war. As with Forsyth, however, the key point is that he imagined a nationalist solution to Mexico's problems, as he eventually would for those of the Southern states. Churchwell believed that Mexico's governing Liberal

Party, though struggling to hold onto power, could eventually be led "upward to a point from which they will again loom up upon the path-way of nations, full of new life and national spirit," a faith he eventually embraced for his own Southern states.[44]

As the American Civil War grew closer, some of the most extreme fire-eaters in US service took care to offer interpretations of nationalism that might prove more congruous with states' rights and separatism. As in the cases above, however, their opinions always rested on the assumption that nation-states most properly embodied all political power, sovereignty, and legitimacy. In 1859, Benjamin Yancey, brother of the famous fire-eater William Lowndes Yancey, served far to the south as US ambassador to Argentina. As such, he found himself positioned to weigh in on a long-standing dispute between Buenos Aires and the Argentine Confederation. After the fall of Juan Manuel de Rosas, the province of Buenos Aires had attempted to assert independence from the rest of the country, a status it would tenuously defend throughout the 1850s. Yancey took an unambiguous view of the controversy: Buenos Aires held a right to a separate existence. "I hold that Buenos-Aires is neither a seceding nor a rebellious Province," he declared. Instead, he asserted that "she had the unquestionable sovereign right to decline to go into a new system of Gov't for these different Provinces, and to remain an independent State."[45] Yancey based his opinion on his interpretation of the criteria for viable nationhood. "Buenos-Aires is a de facto Govt," he reasoned, "& has maintained a separate & independent existence since Sept 1852. She has a Republican Constitution."[46] He fiercely defended Buenos Aires's "belligerent right." Perhaps with his brother's dream of a separate Southern nation in mind, he explained that "even granting, for the sake of argument, Buenos-Aires is only a revolted Province, wishing to overthrow lawful Gov't of the Confederation, & organize the Republic anew, as a Gov't de facto she is entitled to the rights of war against its enemy."[47]

White Southerners who served US interests in the Western Hemisphere during the 1850s took several lessons from their experiences. They remained convinced that peoples might claim a right to independence for a variety of reasons, including feelings of cultural distinctiveness, a commitment to republican government, or an attachment to slavery. Only well-organized nation-states, however, would hold the power and capacity to protect sovereignty. When, in the minds of many white Southerners, the United States replaced Great Britain as the greatest threat to the expansion of slavery and the commercial system it served, many of the Confederacy's advocates made similar arguments. Secession was justified because it would protect people committed to a uniform interest—slavery—but separatism would succeed only if it included the construction of a strong and viable nation-state. During the winter of 1860–61, seven states in the Deep South seceded from the United States in response to the election of Abraham Lincoln. Those states quickly erected a unified national government and sent representatives of their own abroad. White Southerners who supported the Confederacy no longer faced a pressing need to oppose Great Britain by supporting the creation of strong nations in the hemisphere; instead, they found themselves forced to construct a powerful enough polity to replace the United States as the most effective defender of slavery in the world. To do so, they would need to convince Great Britain and other European powers that Confederates had themselves created a viable nation-state that should be worthy of support.

In making their case to the world, the Confederacy's spokesmen made few secrets of their ambitions. The new Confederate state would take its place as a rising power among the nations of the earth. The newspaper the *Index*, established in England to influence British public opinion by the Confederate agent Henry Hotze, predicted that the American Civil War would give rise to "two great powers in the place of one." The editorial argued that the conflict should not be characterized as a "revolution" in which people took up arms against their government but as a war between sovereign "states."[48] The *Richmond Enquirer* agreed. The conflict in America was not a civil war, one editorialist maintained, but a war carried out according to "the law of nations." The paper declared that "we regard this war as one prevailing between opposite nations."[49] Some Confederate civilians felt the same way. A correspondent using the pen-name "Planter" wrote the *Richmond Enquirer* to assert that the stakes of the war involved "nothing less than . . . national life and death."[50] J. Quitman Moore declared that "a Revolution has been consummated, a people united, a Government established, and a vigorous young power, forced upon the perilous career of independent empire, has vindicated its nationality and assumed its position among the powers of the earth. . . . From this moment a Nation is born that will stand first among nations."[51]

The arguments put forth by the supporters of the Confederacy revealed a belief that a family of nations existed in the world and that the Confederate States of America should be welcomed into it. *DeBow's Review* declared that the "sentiment of nationality . . . is the basis of all that is great and glorious in the records of a people, and gives it . . . a place of high honor and influence among the powers of the earth."[52] Existing governments, the *Index* similarly argued, "should treat with friendship a new-born government, and greet her as a sister entering into the great society of nations." The article asked that Europeans apply to the Confederacy the same "rules" of "nations" that continental powers themselves had established. Those rules included "the right of sovereignty" and the "*absolute right*" to constitute a government.[53] The *Richmond Enquirer* agreed that recent world history had established that a "Free Nation" could be considered as such only if it enjoyed "*national independence*" and the exercise of "*autonomy*."[54]

As in Latin America, white Southerners explained that the benefit of establishing nationhood included, above all, strength and power. The *Index* argued that the Confederacy should be welcomed into the "family of nations" because it occupied a "dominion the size of twenty kingdoms," maintained an army of "more than 300,000 men," and enjoyed the support of "millions of people with a sacrifice, a devotion, and a unanimity rarely equaled in modern history."[55] Another article praised the Confederate government as a sublime creation, which "waged war upon a scale unprecedented even in this century of Napoleonic wars," "enjoys the obedience of a numerous and devoted population," and "commands a confidence which few nations in so short a space have won."[56] Another commentator marveled at "the spectacle of a whole nation rising as one man to a great and sustained effort."[57] If the world community doubted that the Confederacy had met the criteria for viable nationhood, one supporter concluded, it should remember that the Confederacy boasted greater "stability" and maintained "a stronger hold upon the affections and loyalty of its citizens" than the United States itself.[58]

Confederate spokesmen argued that because the Confederacy had attained a viable national existence, it deserved to be recognized by the world's powers. The *Index* claimed that because the Confederate States of America had fulfilled "the usual conditions of nationality," it should not be denied "a right which in no modern instance has been refused to any people," namely, national independence.[59] *DeBow's Review* asked the world for recognition because the Confederacy had "established a government de facto ... standing in the established line of precedents, within the spirit and letter of the laws of nations."[60] The Confederate press teemed with articles pointing out that Great Britain and other powers had recognized a succession of new nations during the nineteenth century, including the Latin American republics, Greece, Poland, the Republic of Texas, and Italy.[61] Confederates pointed out that all of those nations were smaller and militarily weaker than the Confederate States of America.[62] Evidence exists that more than a few European policymakers took notice.[63] During the summer of 1862, the British Parliament debated the possibility of recognizing the Confederacy, a matter that Prime Minister

Henry John Temple, third Viscount Palmerston, also gave serious attention to that year. One MP reminded lawmakers that Great Britain had "hitherto . . . constantly acted" on the "principle" of "acknowledging governments *de facto*."[64]

In order to convince the rest of the world to act on such sentiments, Confederates strove to establish what they understood to be the vital practices of legitimate nations. In addition to writing a constitution and establishing a government, they sent representatives abroad to make their case to the family of nations. In early April 1861, the Confederacy dispatched John Forsyth, fresh from his efforts to bolster Mexican nationality, along with Martin J. Crawford and A. B. Roman to treat with the government of the United States itself in hopes of future peaceful relations. In a letter to William H. Seward, US secretary of state, they explained that the Confederate people had "established a government of their own" and hoped that the United States of America and the Confederate States of America would avoid becoming "rival and hostile nations." The commissioners assured Seward that the Confederacy had the law of nations on its side. They asserted that "the people of the Confederate States have declared their independence with a full knowledge of all the responsibilities of that act, and with as firm a determination to maintain it."[65] The Confederate State Department sent James Mason to England with similar instructions. Mason's orders asked him not to claim to be the representative of rebellious or revolted provinces but to act as a representative of "Sovereign States" that had "established a Government." The Confederate people, Mason should explain, had taken up "arms in defense of their right to self-government, and, in the name of the sacred right, they have appealed to the nations of the earth."[66]

In making their appeals, white Southerners refused to respect the sovereignty of one of those nations—the United States as it had existed. Confederates also proved willing to abandon the hopes they had once held for Latin American nationalism. With the American Civil War raging in North America, several European powers sought to benefit from the situation by making moves to reestablish dominance in the hemisphere. In 1861, Spain re-annexed the Dominican Republic, and later that year, Spain and Great Britain joined France in invading Mexico, a development that had long been feared by US diplomats from the North and South alike. Although Great Britain and Spain abandoned the expedition, France eventually succeeded in installing a puppet regime in Mexico City, led by the Emperor Maximilian.[67] The resurgence of European empires in the Americas no longer seemed to many white Southerners to threaten slavery the way it had in the past. The protection of the peculiar institution now required the permanent severance of the United States, which the Confederacy could best ensure with European support. Consequently, Southern diplomats assured European statesmen that the Confederacy would make no attempts to enforce the Monroe Doctrine. In fact, Confederate representatives tacitly welcomed the French invasion of Mexico.[68] The Southern nationalist George Fitzhugh went so far as to encourage the French to take back Haiti as well.[69]

The Confederates who advocated these positions proved more consistent than it initially might seem. During the 1860s, Confederate observers believed they had found evidence of what many of their compatriots had long suspected: Latin American states had proved too disorganized, too racially diverse, and ultimately too weak to defend their nationhood in the face of aggression by greater powers. While many white Southerners had feared that outcome during the 1850s, the situation looked different after the election of 1860. While European empires once threatened the interests of slaveholders by blocking the expansion of the United States, a country that explicitly protected slavery, now the United States under Lincoln represented the most immediate threat to slavery's expansion. Under these new circumstances Europeans appeared more likely than the United States to "regenerate" Latin American nationalism. During the 1860s, many Confederates believed Old World empires promised to protect a racial hierarchy that might prove compatible with the sensibilities of what stood to become the hemisphere's most powerful slaveholding nation. George Fitzhugh welcomed a French reconquest of Haiti because he believed "the civilized world will not much longer permit the naturally paradisiacal isle of Hayti to remain a useless waste, infested by a horde of idle savages." An assertion of the Monroe Doctrine, he warned, would only tempt the "Yankees" to intervene, while France could "at once subjugate it, and set the negroes to work."[70]

The French, many Confederates came to believe, would also reestablish racial hierarchy in Mexico. The Confederate press argued that Mexican nationality had long been weakened by racial diversity. The *Richmond Examiner* called it a "declining" power, reminding readers that its leadership was made up of "many men who are not of pure Castilian blood, but almost pure Indians."[71] In similar fashion, the *Index* referred to "what is facetiously termed the Mexican Nation," asserting that it was made up of an unmanageable mixture of Europeans, Africans, and Native Americans. The paper argued that only by maintaining "the hierarchy of races" could "an orderly or prosperous government . . . [be] established." White Southern diplomats had once hoped that the United States might have led Mexico in that direction, but not under the United States' current leadership and condition. The South had once provided a "conservative check" to government in the United States, the *Index* asserted, but now "cut loose from its conservative partner," the North had already begun to decline "rapidly into anarchy." Some argued that the United States had lost its claim to nationality. As in Latin America, racial and ideological differences had weakened it. One supporter wrote, "To-day we know that the Federal Government did not represent a homogenous people or even a league of homogenous states, but ... nationalities ... distinct and irreconcilable."[72] If the North, the paper declared, had imposed on Mexico its "radical theories ... among a population so constituted ... the result must inevitably be what it has been in all the Central and South American Republics." As a result, the article held that "the establishment of monarchy in Mexico is, therefore, the beginning of a new, and we hope a better era in the history of the New World."[73] The *Richmond Enquirer* concurred, calling the French conquest of Mexico the "triumph of civilization and regular responsible government."[74] Only the Confederacy, the *Index* concluded, "basing its social fabric upon the principle of subordination of one race to the other, is capable of retaining republican forms and principles of government."[75]

Ultimately, the Confederacy did not succeed in establishing an independent nation-state. No foreign governments recognized the Confederate States of America before it collapsed. Still, Confederates had sought to pursue their policy goals the only way they believed they could—through the auspices of a formally organized nation-state. The experiences of white Southerners in Latin America and elsewhere had taught them the powerful uses of nationalism. In the nineteenth-century world, nations alone had the capacity to protect sovereignty, pursue objectives, and project power. Both before and after secession and in both North and South America, white Southerners had attempted to harness the considerable powers of the nation-state in order to protect the interests of slaveholders, even though their efforts ultimately failed.

NOTES

1. David M. Potter, "The Historian's Use of Nationalism and Vice Versa," *American Historical Review* 67, no. 4 (July 1962): 924.

2. "Jefferson Davis' First Inaugural Address," Papers of Jefferson Davis, Rice University—MS 215, Houston, TX, https://jeffersondavis.rice.edu/archives/documents/jefferson-davis-first-inaugural-address (accessed April 11, 2023).

3. Emory M. Thomas, *The Confederacy as a Revolutionary Experience* (Englewood Cliffs, NJ: Prentice Hall, 1971; Columbia: University of South Carolina Press, 1991), 62–71. Citations refer to the University of South Carolina Press edition.

4. Thomas, *Confederacy as a Revolutionary Experience*, 58–59.

5. Michael F. Holt, *The Political Crisis of the 1850s* (New York: John Wiley and Sons, 1978; New York: Norton, 1983), 17–38. Page references are to the Norton edition.

6. Matthew Karp, *This Vast Southern Empire: Slaveholders at the Helm of American Foreign Policy* (Cambridge, MA: Harvard University Press, 2016), 32–49, 199–225.

7. Tom Chaffin, *Fatal Glory: Narciso López and the First Clandestine U.S. War against Cuba* (Charlottesville: University of Virginia Press, 1996), 8.

8. Potter, "Historian's Use of Nationalism and Vice Versa," 930.

9. Richard E. Beringer, Herman Hattaway, Archer Jones, and William N. Still Jr., *Why the South Lost the Civil War* (Athens: University of Georgia Press, 1986), 64, 68.

10. William W. Freehling, *The South vs. the South: How Anti-Confederate Southerners Shaped the Course of the Civil War* (Oxford: Oxford University Press, 2002), xiii.

11. Stephanie McCurry, *Confederate Reckoning: Power and Politics in the Civil War South* (Cambridge, MA: Harvard University Press, 2010).

12. Steven Hahn, *A Nation without Borders: The United States and Its World in an Age of Civil Wars, 1830–1910* (New York: Viking, 2016), 4.

13. Gary W. Gallagher, *The Confederate War: How Popular Will, Nationalism, and Military Strategy Could Not Stave Off Defeat* (Cambridge, MA: Harvard University Press, 1997), 63.

14. Drew Gilpin Faust, *The Creation of Confederate Nationalism: Ideology and Identity in the Civil War South* (Baton Rouge: Louisiana State University Press, 1988).

15. Anne Sarah Rubin, *A Shattered Nation: The Rise and Fall of the Confederacy, 1861–1868* (Chapel Hill: University of North Carolina Press, 2005).

16. Don H. Doyle, *Nations Divided: America, Italy, and the Southern Question* (Athens: University of Georgia Press, 2002); Don H. Doyle, ed., *Secession as an International Phenomenon: From America's Civil War to Contemporary Separatist Movements* (Athens: University of Georgia Press, 2010); Don H. Doyle and Marco Antonio Pamplona, eds., *Nationalism in the New World* (Athens: University of Georgia Press, 2006).

17. Don H. Doyle, *The Cause of All Nations: An International History of the American Civil War* (New York: Basic Books, 2015).

18. Andre M. Fleche, *The Revolution of 1861: The American Civil War in the Age of Nationalist Conflict* (Chapel Hill: University of North Carolina Press, 2012), 80–106.

19. Paul Quigley, *Shifting Grounds: Nationalism and the American South, 1848–1865* (Oxford: Oxford University Press, 2011).

20. Ann L. Tucker, *Newest Born of Nations: European Nationalist Movements and the Making of the Confederacy* (Charlottesville: University of Virginia Press, 2020).

21. "Jefferson Davis' First Inaugural Address" (emphasis added).

22. Karp, *This Vast Southern Empire*, 199–225. For discussion of widespread interest among white Southerners to expand slavery into Latin America, see Matthew Pratt Guterl, *American Mediterranean: Southern Slaveholders in the Age of Emancipation* (Cambridge, MA: Harvard University Press, 2008); and Robert E. May, *The Southern Dream of a Caribbean Empire, 1854–1861* (Baton Rouge: Louisiana State University Press, 1973), and *Slavery, Race, and*

Conquest in the Tropics: Lincoln, Douglas, and the Future of Latin America (New York: Cambridge University Press, 2013).

23. Jay Sexton, *The Monroe Doctrine: Empire and Nation in Nineteenth-Century America* (New York: Hill and Wang, 2011), 85–121.

24. Alexander Dimitry to Pedro Zeledón, December 19, 1859, in *Diplomatic Correspondence of the United States: Inter-American Affairs*, ed. William R. Manning, 12 vols., (Washington, DC: Carnegie Endowment for International Peace, 1932–39), 4:833.

25. Beverly L. Clarke to Lewis Cass, October 15, 1859, in Manning, *Diplomatic Correspondence*, 4:783, 785.

26. Mirabeau B. Lamar to Lewis Cass, July 26, 1858, in Manning, *Diplomatic Correspondence*, 4:696.

27. Patrick J. Kelly, "The Cat's Paw: Confederate Ambitions in Latin America," in *American Civil Wars: The United States, Latin America, Europe, and the Crisis of the 1860s*, ed. Don H. Doyle (Chapel Hill: University of North Carolina Press, 2017), 58–81.

28. Lamar to Cass, July 26, 1858, in Manning, *Diplomatic Correspondence*, 4:696.

29. Lamar to Cass, December 22, 1858, in Manning, *Diplomatic Correspondence*, 4:724.

30. Lamar to Cass, December 22, 1858, in Manning, *Diplomatic Correspondence*, 4:725.

31. Dimitry to Zeledón, December 19, 1859, in Manning, *Diplomatic Correspondence*, 4:835.

32. Dimitry to Zeledón, December 19, 1859, in Manning, *Diplomatic Correspondence*, 4:834.

33. Dimitry to Zeledón, December 19, 1859, in Manning, *Diplomatic Correspondence*, 4:835.

34. Dimitry to Zeledón, December 19, 1859, in Manning, *Diplomatic Correspondence*, 4:834.

35. Lamar to Cass, July 26, 1858, in Manning, *Diplomatic Correspondence*, 4:696.

36. James Gadsden to William Marcy, November 26, 1855, in Manning, *Diplomatic Correspondence*, 9:799.

37. John Forsyth to Lewis Cass, April 4, 1857, in Manning, *Diplomatic Correspondence*, 9:907.

38. John Forsyth to William Marcy, November 8, 1856, in Manning, *Diplomatic Correspondence*, 9:854–56.

39. Forsyth to Cass, April 4, 1857, in Manning, *Diplomatic Correspondence*, 9:908.

40. Forsyth to Cass, April 4, 1857, in Manning, *Diplomatic Correspondence*, 9:908.

41. Forsyth to Cass, December 17, 1857, in Manning, *Diplomatic Correspondence*, 9:962.

42. William M. Churchwell to Lewis Cass, February 8, 1859, in Manning, *Diplomatic Correspondence*, 9:1027.

43. Churchwell to Cass, February 8, 1859, in Manning, *Diplomatic Correspondence*, 9:1025.

44. Churchwell to Cass, February 8, 1859, in Manning, *Diplomatic Correspondence*, 9:1027.

45. Benjamin Yancey to Lewis Cass, April 12, 1859, in Manning, *Diplomatic Correspondence*, 1:684.

46. Yancey to Cass, June 23, 1859, in Manning, *Diplomatic Correspondence*, 1:718.

47. Yancey to Cass, June 23, 1859, in Manning, *Diplomatic Correspondence*, 1:714, 719.

48. "Are the Confederates Rebels?," *Index*, June 26, 1862.

49. "Civil War," *Richmond Enquirer*, January 15, 1864.

50. Planter, "Look to the East for Light," *Richmond Enquirer*, November 6, 1863.

51. J. Quitman Moore, "The Belligerents," *DeBow's Review* 31, no. 1 (July 1861): 69–70.

52. "National Characteristics—The Issue of the Day," *DeBow's Review* 30, no. 1 (January 1861): 44.

53. "European Political Heresies," *Index*, May 29, 1862.
54. "Liberty," *Richmond Enquirer*, March 20, 1862.
55. "Our Object," *Index*, May 1, 1862.
56. "The Anomaly of the Age," *Index*, March 19, 1863.
57. "The South and Slavery," *Index*, November 6, 1862.
58. "The American Question in Parliament," *Index*, February 26, 1863.
59. "The War in America," *Index*, May 22, 1862.
60. "Our True Policy, Our True Position," *DeBow's Review* 31, nos. 4 and 5 (October–November 1861): 401.
61. See, for example, "Sympathy or No Sympathy?," *Richmond Enquirer*, November 11, 1863; "Confederacy and Europe," *Richmond Enquirer*, September 15, 1863; "Our Foreign Policy," *Charleston Mercury*, October 29, 1861; "The Want of a Policy," *Index*, October 23, 1862; "Recognition of the Republic of Texas," *Index*, January 15, 1863; and "The United States and the Doctrine of National Independence," *Index*, January 12, 1865. For in-depth discussion of this issue, see Doyle, *Cause of All Nations*, 27–49; Fleche, *Revolution of 1861*, 80–106; and Quigley, *Shifting Grounds*, 128–70.
62. *Richmond Examiner*, February 5, 1862.
63. See, for example, "England," *Index*, November 6, 1862; "Social and Political Aspects of the American Question," *Index*, January 29, 1863; "The Party Leaders on the American Question," *Index*, February 12, 1863; "Mr. Roebuck's Motion," *Index*, June 4, 1863; and "Mr. Roebuck's Notice," *Index*, June 11, 1863.
64. "The Debate on the War in America," *Index*, July 31, 1862.
65. John Forsyth, Martin J. Crawford, and A. B. Roman to William Henry Seward, April 9, 1861, in *A Compilation of the Messages and Papers of the Confederacy, Including the Diplomatic Correspondence, 1861–1865*, ed. James D. Richardson (Nashville: United States Publishing Co., 1905), 88–93.
66. *The Public Life and Diplomatic Correspondence of James M. Mason, with Some Personal History by His Daughter* (Roanoke, VA: Stone Printing and Manufacturing Co., 1903), 248–50.
67. For discussion of these episodes, see, for example, Alfred Jackson Hanna and Kathryn Abbey Hanna, *Napoleon III and Mexico: American Triumph over Monarchy* (Chapel Hill: University of North Carolina Press, 1971); Patrick J. Kelly, "The North American Crisis of the 1860s," *Journal of the Civil War Era* 2, no. 3 (September 2012): 337–68; Thomas Schoonover, *Dollars over Dominion: The Triumph of Liberalism in Mexican-American Relations, 1861–1867* (Baton Rouge: Louisiana State University Press), 140–77; Stève Sainlaude, *France and the American Civil War: A Diplomatic History* (Chapel Hill: University of North Carolina Press, 2019); Sainlaude, "France's Grand Design and the Confederacy," in Doyle, *American Civil Wars*, 107–24; Erika Pani, "Juárez vs. Maximiliano: Mexico's Experiment with Monarchy," in Doyle, *American Civil Wars*, 167–84; and Anne Eller, "Dominican Civil War, Slavery, and Spanish Annexation, 1844–1865," in Doyle, *American Civil Wars*, 147–66.
68. Kelly, "Cat's Paw," 58–81. See also Fleche, "Race and Revolution: The Confederacy, Mexico, and the Problem of Southern Nationalism," in *The Transnational Significance of the American Civil War*, ed. Jörg Nagler, Don H. Doyle, and Marcus Gräser (London: Palgrave, 2016), 189–204.

69. George Fitzhugh, "Hayti and the Monroe Doctrine," *DeBow's Review* 31, no. 2 (August 1861): 131–36.
70. Fitzhugh, "Hayti and the Monroe Doctrine," 131.
71. *Richmond Daily Examiner*, October 7, 1861.
72. "The Rightfulness of Southern Secession," *Index*, August 6, 1863.
73. "The Empire of Mexico," *Index*, August 13, 1863.
74. "France in Mexico," *Richmond Enquirer*, July 10, 1863.
75. "Empire of Mexico."

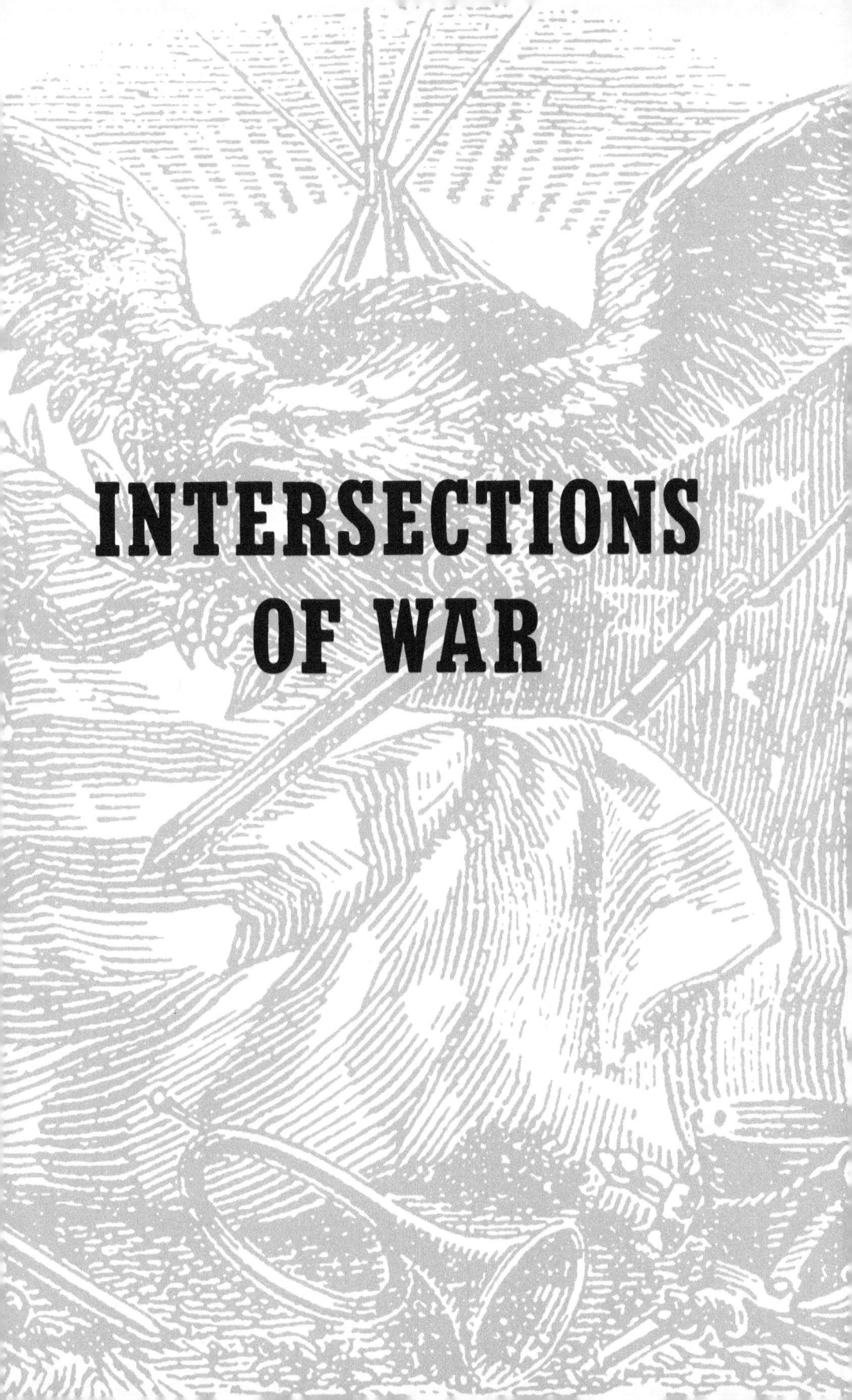

INTERSECTIONS OF WAR

Science and Daring

Robert E. Lee as Engineer, Soldier, and Modernizer

WAYNE WEI-SIANG HSIEH

Before Lost Cause mythology turned Robert E. Lee into an atavistic Christian paladin riding out of Sir Walter Scott's vision of the Middle Ages, he had graduated from antebellum America's premier engineering college and supervised federal improvements to navigation on the Mississippi River vital to a burgeoning market economy.[1] The army Lee served not only subdued Indian tribes on the frontier who resisted federal authority but also helped lay the groundwork for American industrialization via innovations in arms manufacturing and railroad management. During the Mexican War, Lee then distinguished himself at the vanguard of a modernizing army in Mexico that conquered a continental empire. Indeed, when taken in its entirety, Lee's military career provides us a window onto the actual unfolding of the rise of modernity itself, because nineteenth-century armies in both war and peace served as crucial constitutive institutions of the modern nation-state order. Nevertheless, even as they embodied all the ambitious pretense of modernity—bureaucratization, discipline, and social transformation through the blood and fire of industrialization's new machines—these military institutions also displayed modernity's internal contradictions and limits.

Armies remained imperfect enforcers of modernity, as they struggled to reconcile bureaucratic dreams of order and discipline with a disordered battlefield where chance, glory, fear, and soldiers' subversion of hierarchy frustrated rationalist aspirations. Even at the height of his martial reputation, Lee sometimes struggled to discipline his soldiers in the Army of Northern Virginia; he surrendered his army partly due to his fear of their disorderliness as potential guerrillas; and in his retirement he hoped to modernize a civilian college and depart the regimented world of West Point and a decades-long military career. Just as the two-faced Janus of ancient Rome presided over both war and peace, soldiers like Lee sought to impose order and discipline among strife and insubordination, and the new human and mechanical technologies that increased their disciplinary power contained within them hidden vulnerabilities to subversion. Lee could thus embody both state power and insurrection at the same time. Mid-nineteenth-century soldiers thus served as synecdoches for the self-conflicted nature of both modernity and state power.

The idea of modernity looms in the background of so much of our understanding of Civil War era America, but how to define the term remains vexatious. C. A. Bayly provides a useful working definition: the modern "encompassed the rise of the nation-state, demanding centralization of power or loyalty to an ethnic solidarity, alongside a massive expansion of global commercial and intellectual links.... The scope and scale of change broadened dramatically. Modernity, then, was not only a process, but also a *period* which began at the end of the eighteenth century and has continued up to the present day in various forms."[2] Not only did Lee stand at the center of so many of the phenomena that Bayly identifies as the core components of modernity, but the dynamics of his military career in many ways subvert those categories. Lee's switch in time from antebellum US Army modernizer to proponent of Confederate nation-state centralization and consolidation undermines the notion that the Union held an exclusive claim to the banner of modernity. Most importantly, Lee's military service also reveals how deep within "modern" armies—the supposed domain of bureaucratic technicians loyal to the nation-state and servants of war's new machines—prideful disobedience reminiscent of premodern warrior cultures such as Homeric Greece remained powerful and resilient.

In sum, academic historians' ignorance of war or its sublimation into "war and society" shibboleths will not free us from it and its associated forces of modernity. Lee's central position in this story as an engineer, modernizer, general, and state builder reveals that while Lincoln rightly called the Civil

War a "People's contest,"[3] it was also a clash of state institutions that embodied global trends within the ideological configuration of mid-nineteenth-century America. Both Americanists and global historians of the nineteenth century have mistakenly assumed that the military institutions connected to early modern state formation extended into the nineteenth century fully formed, and they have failed to follow the thread begun by scholars of the early modern world such as such as Geoffrey Parker, Michel Foucault, and Charles Tilly—a military historian, a critical theorist, and a historical sociologist all bound together by both an interest in military institutions and the shadow of Max Weber.[4] Indeed, despite historians' criticism of political science as overreliant on static models, it is a political scientist, Janice E. Thomson, who has argued that the state's monopoly on violence took centuries to achieve and nonstate violence was not delegitimated until the nineteenth century.[5]

The early modern locus of this prior literature, however, has led nineteenth-century historians to take states and armies as established institutions in the Western world. Controversies might rage over phenomena such as nationalism or empire or whatever other "ism" exercises scholarly attention, but while there might be a struggle for control of the state, the state and its army remain in much of the literature as a looming but fully formed player, as opposed to a contingent force that continues to evolve in profound and significant ways. Foucault thus located one source of the "political anatomy" of "discipline" in the military institutions of the eighteenth century, stretching from Frederick II, "the meticulous king of small machines, well-trained regiments and long exercises," to an interpretation of Napoleon as a figure that "wished to arrange around him a mechanism of power that would enable him to see the smallest event that occurred in the state he governed; he intended, by means of the rigorous discipline that he imposed, 'to embrace the whole of this vast machine without the slightest detail escaping his attention.'"[6] While soldiers play an important role in this vision of modernity's development, it recedes from view as the prison and the psychiatrist emerge, even if "in this central and centralized humanity ... we must hear the distant roar of battle."[7] Nevertheless, at least Foucault recognized the deep connection between armies and modernity, even if he did not fully comprehend the dynamics of the relationship.

Noted global historians of the nineteenth century C. A. Bayly and Jürgen Osterhammel in contrast present a flawed treatment of American armies and state building, despite their great erudition and herculean synthesis of a vast monographic literature. Following the early work of Stephen Skowronek, Bayly associates state building in the United States with the very end of the nineteenth century and the rise of an overseas American empire that required greater state capacity.[8] Osterhammel perceptively notes that the "prevailing ideology of statelessness, which in many ways harked back to old English conceptions of law, conflicted with reality on a number of points."[9] He even highlights the relative strength of the American state on the frontier, where Lee himself served as an agent of state authority, and describes the American Civil War as "the first total war," because it involved mass mobilization and "its bureaucratic organization within the framework of the state monopoly of force."[10] However, as is unavoidable in such global work of synthesis, Osterhammel provides little granular detail on the particular American processes of military mobilization and their intersection with the forces of modernity.

In a significant (if small enough for Bayly and Osterhammel to have not fully absorbed) body of work, historians have mostly exploded the notion of a "weak" American state in the nineteenth century. Nevertheless, aside from Samuel Watson's and Robert Wooster's important monographs on the US Army,[11] such scholarship usually skims over armies and military institutions, despite their obvious association with state power,[12] and other ambiguities of Civil War era America that require greater explication. While military historians such as William Skelton,[13] Watson, and I have argued that the antebellum US Army professionalized in the antebellum period when it came to the development of educational institutions and a shared body of practical expertise, that process obviously did not preclude the secession of professionalized officers such as Lee himself. And while Richard Franklin Bensel has rightly pointed out that the Confederacy over the course of the war sought to consolidate centralized power beyond what Federal power attempted in the loyal states,[14] both the Union and the Confederacy opened the war with localized methods of military recruitment that belied a Weberian model of modernity and state development. Even though in its broad sweep the nineteenth century mostly bears out the Weberian analysis, with mass armies utilizing the material and organizational resources we commonly associate with the modern world, the fracturing of the US Army officer corps along mostly sectional lines clashes directly with Weber's famous dictum that "a state is a human community that (successfully) claims the *monopoly of the legitimate use of physical force* within a given territory."[15]

Historians have certainly paid ample attention to the question of the American Civil War and modernity writ large, with James McPherson and Edward L. Ayers representing different historiographic poles—the former seeing the industrializing North as a modern Weberian state in conflict with an atavistic Confederacy, and the latter highlighting the Confederacy's compatibility with modernity even as it fought to preserve slavery.[16] Much of this literature focuses on slavery and its relationship to nationalism, capitalism, and other supposedly characteristic constituent pieces of modernity.[17] While slavery and other labor regimes obviously had profound effects on modernity's progress,[18] armies cut across political borders and labor regimes extending far beyond slavery and the Western Hemisphere, while serving as the most important component of the state's monopoly on violence.[19] Historians (or theorists of various stripes) should not attempt to distill as complex a phenomenon as modernity into the history of military institutions, but neither should they view armies as indecipherable black boxes[20]—a sometimes influential but inexplicable background force in history, akin to geography and climate. Academic historians can and do with great skill chronicle the effects of war, but their reluctance to examine the bloody internal machinery that drives armies speaks ill of the larger profession. Opening that block box shows that even "modern" armies were much more than they seem at first glance. Lee was many things—American, Virginian, Unionist, Confederate, Christian, enslaver, and teacher—but most importantly he was a soldier. And in his career, we can see the collision of the world of the modern state, with its material machines and bureaucratic analogues demanding discipline, and the prerogatives of the world of honor, with its embrace of pride and disorder.

Lee's effectiveness as a soldier stemmed in part from his ability to straddle these contradictory impulses. He proved as adept as any of his contemporaries in the development and management of the new material and human devices of the era's new military machines. The professionalization of armies went far beyond state-appointed officers drilling musket-armed infantrymen in close order drill, with both groups drawing their pay from a common state authority. The new modern state armies demanded soldiers and officers conform their behavior to the technical capabilities of their weapons and the new bureaucratic machines that made those weapons possible. For example, in an antebellum manual, West Point graduate Cadmus Wilcox (who later served as one of Lee's division commanders during the Civil War) described "the moral condition attributed to cannoneers, whose proverbial *sang froid* in the presence of the enemy is said to be due to the occupation that the pointing or aiming of the piece gives."[21] But the problem with a purely materialist analysis of military organizations in this period is that while the new machines made military organizations more lethal (as measured by the bloody criteria of the butcher's bill), such success frequently required the physical demise of individual soldiers among "successful" armies. In fact, acceptance of or even a degree of enthusiasm for actions that frequently led to self-destruction constituted an important part of military effectiveness. This was as true of military elites as it was of the rank and file—as seen in the famous Lee-to-the-rear episodes of the Overland Campaign.[22] Moreover, historians should not overstate the efficacy of armies' disciplinary structures. The chaos of battle, the wide distribution of weapons, and the inherent fractiousness of soldiers opened the door to evasion of orders, malingering or flight in battles, and outright desertion. Effective military organizations frequently used harsh disciplinary measures, but fighting power could not be extracted by pure coercion.[23] It would be a mistake to confuse current notions of consent and volition with the complicated question of unit cohesion, but acquiescence and even pride in self-sacrifice was an indispensable part of any effective military organization.

Pride, courage, honor, self-sacrifice—these are all the seemingly atavistic martial virtues found as much in the world of Homeric Greece as in the increasingly technicist military professions of the nineteenth century that embraced machines as part of their mental models. Even Weber, who saw discipline as originating in modern war and an enemy of individualistic charisma, still believed that "military leadership uses emotional means of all sorts—just as the most sophisticated techniques of religious discipline, the *exercitia spiritualia* of Ignatius Loyola, do in their own way."[24] The fact that these martial values could in fact clash with and subvert the needs of bureaucratic discipline added further complexity to the issue. Machinelike efficiency required prompt obedience to lawful superiors, but honor-driven officers also saw shared elite status as a counterweight to the disciplined hierarchy of armies organized as bureaucratic machines.[25]

Hidden in the gauzy haze of Lee's aristocratic origins is how his family bloodlines remained channeled through West Point's modernizing disciplinary machine. Lee's famous lineage helped him obtain the necessary nomination for a place at the academy, but Lee also fully embraced the institution's technical culture and curriculum, where his mathematical aptitude proved useful. For example, Lee's wide range of recreational reading at West Point included scientific volumes on navigation, astronomy, and algebra.[26] Unlike the presumptively modern William T. Sherman, who supported ending the Corps of Engineers' control of West Point after the war and who could not be bothered to lower his demerit total to be eligible for graduation into that self-styled elite, Lee graduated as an engineer and even returned to serve as a superintendent in the 1850s.[27] Furthermore, while Lee's long service in the engineers before he transferred to the cavalry branch insulated him from much of the rough-and-tumble nature of frontier service, he could hardly be ignorant or unaware of the larger institution's problems with violence, drinking, desertion, and general disorder.[28] Like other regular officers, Lee saw enlisted soldiers (and even some officers) as potential forces of anarchy if not properly disciplined by men such as himself.

Nevertheless, even at West Point, one finds deep and profound resistance to discipline. Foucault himself reserved a measure of individual human agency to the self in its relations with disciplinary machinery—that "at the very heart of the power relationship, and constantly provoking it, are the recalcitrance of the will and the intransigence of freedom."[29] Ulysses S. Grant went on to fame and glory by conquering model cadet Robert E. Lee, despite the former's indifference at West Point, his droll distaste for its strict regimen, and possible struggles with alcohol in garrison that led to post–Mexican War resignation.[30] Indeed, even within the confines of West Point, cadet culture in many respects consciously (and at times, violently) rebelled against the regime, and its second most-famous Union general product after Grant, Sherman, also thought little of its regimentation—and had the record of demerits to prove it.[31] In contrast, among Grant, Sherman, and Lee— the traditional triumvirate of great Civil War captains—it was Cadet Lee who conformed most to the disciplinary ideals of the institution, although General Lee would prove to be more akin to the impetuous Achilles than to the scientific Vauban.

Lee and other West Point alumni did not learn this or that specific detail in class that then affected their decisions as Civil War generals, but the entire cadet experience and subsequent life in the regular army molded them into modernizing military bureaucrats. While a cantankerous cadet subculture percolated underneath the surface and periodically asserted itself in episodes such as the infamous "eggnog riot" of 1826,[32] West Point's educational and disciplinary regime strictly regulated the lives of cadets and converted their character, conduct, and talents into a single quantifiable metric—the academy's order of merit—an innovation whose origins in eighteenth-century France Foucault made much of in his account of the rise of "docile bodies."[33] West Point in many ways represented the most "legible" part of the antebellum American state, to use James Scott's analytical framework for modern governance based on simplified and standardized forms of measurement amenable to bureaucratic control.[34] For example, Scott has highlighted the significance of surnames to the state's modern need to make its population legible,[35] and it is telling that Grant, the institution's most important alumnus from this period, had his very name transformed by the American state's insistence on bureaucratically rigorous legibility.

Christened Hiram Ulysses Grant, the future general went by his middle name as a child. Grant's congressman thus knew Grant by his preferred name, Ulysses, but did not know his middle name and used Simpson (Grant's mother's maiden name) in his nomination paperwork. When Grant arrived at West Point, the US Army bureaucracy insisted on the primacy of Grant's "legible" documentation. As Grant put it later, "I tried on entering West Point to correct this mistake but failing, after I received my Diploma and Commission, with the 'S' inserted, adopted it and have so signed my name ever since."[36] The future president thus found his identity recast—first by West Pont's modernizing and disciplining bureaucracy, then by the nickname give to him by his fellow cadets ("Sam," a play on Grant's new initials, "U. S."), and finally by a Northern press that rendered his government-given initials "Unconditional Surrender" after his triumph at Fort Donelson during the Civil War.[37] While the state might have been the first mover in this sequence, its authority was not complete.

Students of Foucault such as Gilles Deleuze also perceive a profound characteristic in the metonymic signature and the disciplinary society's "two poles: the signature that designates the *individual*, and the number or administrative numeration that indicates his or her position within a *mass*."[38] The signature embodied the state's power to name and discipline mass populations—and that power extended from Grant's bureaucratic transformation to the renaming of enslaved people freed from the African slave trade "with names fit for American-given freedom" to post–Civil War attempts to rename American Indians for the sake of land title registration and census data collection.[39] While not formally cited or fully digested, the malignant power of discipline looms above recent scholarly interest in nineteenth-century American empire, the links between slavery and capitalist production, Indian removal, squalid "contraband" camps of freedmen and freedwomen, and prisoner-of-war camps where captured Union and Confederate soldiers wasted away in miserable conditions.[40]

As a member of the Corps of Engineers, Lee began his career more concerned with the disciplining of nature via science than with unruly troops and at a time when the branch had its most significant direct influence on the railroad industry. While those managerial links subsided after Congress restricted federal assistance to railroads, leading in turn to the resignation of large numbers of West Point–trained engineers and the Corps of Engineers' committing itself to a more overtly military conception of professionalism, the US Army's technical and bureaucratic organizations remained an important model for the corporate practices and culture of early American railroads.[41]

Through its influence on both railroad management and manufacturing—in the latter via the Ordnance Bureau–supported modernization of firearms production with interchangeable parts—the US Army played an important role in American industrialization as an early and influential model of technical and bureaucratic expertise.[42]

Lee's engineering career did not expose him in a serious way to railroads (although he became an investor in railroad bonds in the 1850s),[43] but his most important pre–Mexican War assignment focused on navigational improvements on the Mississippi River in the vicinity of St. Louis. Military historians of the Civil War have debated Lee's preferred focus on the Virginia theater during the Civil War, but his antebellum military service included ample experience in the West. In 1837 Lee arrived in St. Louis and embarked on a years-long project to improve the Mississippi's navigation and to protect St. Louis's harbor from being obstructed by silt and sand. At the start of his work, Lee used a canal and a steamboat (other exemplary examples of American "internal improvements") to travel from Virginia to the West, and he was accompanied by 2nd Lt. Montgomery C. Meigs, the talented engineer and West Point graduate who would later do so much to supply the Union war effort as its quartermaster general. In addition to the technical aspects of his assignment, Lee also had to navigate both local and federal politics in an exemplary case of the Old Army's intersection with antebellum economic development and state building. At the close of his posting, and despite being hamstrung by a penurious Congress and political controversies in St. Louis, Lee's efforts proved mostly successful and provided a foundation for later navigational improvements on the Mississippi.[44] Even before his wartime service in Mexico, Lee thus played his own small role in helping make the Mississippi a navigable waterway for the expanding antebellum republic—a waterway that would eventually become an avenue of invasion into the nascent Confederacy.

In his first wartime campaign during the Mexican War, Lee served as an engineer on Brig. Gen. John E. Wool's staff, and he increased the "legibility" of Mexico to the US Army via devices such as mapmaking that in turn facilitated military logistics and fortification. Such cartographic skills came not from Lee's quasi-aristocratic family background but from West Point's academic instruction and his practical service as an engineer before the Mexican War.[45] Even during his initial campaign with Wool where he saw no combat, however, Lee's services as an engineer went beyond the simply cognitive. As an engineering officer, he helped supervise the creation and improvement of roads that allowed Wool to move his men and matériel through the space that he had earlier made legible via mapmaking.[46] Much to his chagrin, Union armies during the Civil War would also build their own roads to facilitate the assertion of Federal authority in the Confederacy, as seen in such notable examples as Herman Haupt's management of Federal military railroads and Sherman's road building during the Carolinas Campaign in the last year of the war. Haupt was another West Point–trained engineer who had resigned to go into the railroad business, while Sherman for a brief time had been head of a railroad in St. Louis—the same city whose economic development Lee's engineering work had facilitated and where the conqueror of Atlanta would be buried after the war.[47]

During the Civil War, Lee's position as an army commander meant he himself no longer produced maps, but their larger importance remained. Maj. Gen. Thomas J. "Stonewall" Jackson, for example, famously used Jedediah Hotchkiss's maps of the Shenandoah Valley to great effect, including detailed tables that allowed Jackson to know the distance between important points in his area of responsibility.[48] Even the US government valued Hotchkiss's cartographic skills so highly that it utilized his maps in the atlas that accompanied the official War Department compilation of wartime records.[49] While not a West Pointer, Hotchkiss had taught himself mapmaking and engineering amid a successful career as a schoolmaster in antebellum Virginia. Like Lee during the Mexican War, he also proved to be a talented scout and diviner of terrain, which further assisted his military superiors.[50] Unfortunately for the Confederates, Union generals also used such tools to make Confederate territory more legible. For example, while planning for the possibility of needing "to subsist on the chance food which the country was known to contain" during the Atlanta campaign, Sherman "obtained not only the United States census-tables of 1860, but a compilation made by the Controller of the State of Georgia for the purpose of taxation, containing in considerable detail the 'population and statistics' of every county in Georgia."[51] Sherman would put that knowledge to use for his army during the March to the Sea.

After serving with Wool's staff in northern Mexico, Lee saw more than his fair share of combat during the climactic Vera Cruz campaign, where he earned well-known laurels on Maj. Gen. Winfield Scott's staff as a closely trusted aide. Just as he had scouted and helped build a road for Wool's army, Lee now performed similar services for the American flanking movement at Cerro Gordo, but under significantly more dangerous circumstances. During a crucial reconnaissance to find a practicable path to turn the Mexican left, a surprised Lee had to hide from Mexican troops for a whole day while concealed under a log near a spring—an echo of the premodern tradition of martial cunning and bravery recounted in Odysseus's nighttime raid during the Trojan War.[52] Most importantly, Lee's bold reconnaissance helped Scott find a path for a crucial flanking movement, which he himself helped direct as a guide attached to Brig. Gen. David Twigg's division.[53] Lee at the very least duplicated and even surpassed these feats during the Battles of Contreras and Churubusco later in the campaign, where he once again served as scout, road builder, mapmaker, and guide in challenging combat conditions.[54] In his official report, Scott singled out Lee for praise, describing him "as distinguished for felicitous execution as for science and daring." Indeed, Scott associated science with "generals and other officers," while he gave thanks "to the gallantry and prowess of all—the rank and file included."[55] One officer who also helped Lee with the acquisition of topographical information was none other than Grant.[56] Lee's wartime service in the Mexican War thus looked forward to a modern world of the state imposing its will with armies utilizing new tools of epistemological and material conquest and backward to the warrior who achieved glory and fame with individual courage and guile.

After US forces captured Mexico City, Lee remained in its environs along with the rest of the army, waiting for peace negotiations to conclude. During this period, guerrillas continued to vex the US Army, and by the end of 1847, roughly a quarter of Scott's troops focused on protecting supply lines that were being harassed by Mexican irregulars. Compounding the complexity of the situation, civil war broke out among Mexico's own inhabitants, with the most serious revolt occurring among Indigenous peasants in the Yucatán in opposition to Mexican elites. This internal crisis helped further along peace negotiations with the United States, and the truce agreement that followed the initial negotiation of the Treaty of Guadalupe Hidalgo even committed US military forces to fight any anti-regime forces it might encounter. The US Army also transferred arms and ammunition to Mexican government forces at a discounted price in order to help create a stable enough situation to allow American forces to withdraw.[57] Lee seems to have played little direct role in the Mexican denouement, but after transferring to a cavalry regiment, he would have his own experience fighting irregulars in Texas as he fruitlessly searched for hostile Comanches and attempted to engage in frontier diplomacy.[58] Like other regulars, Lee had ample firsthand experience with the chaotic world of soldiers fighting outside disciplinary institutions, whether they be hostile guerrillas or one's own troops. In one letter he commented that "it is difficult for a general to maintain discipline in an army, composed as this is, in a foreign country, where temptations to disorders are so great, and the chance of detection so slight."[59] Indeed, Lee's last significant duty in the US Army was to suppress the insurgents of John Brown's failed raid on Harpers Ferry.[60]

Lee referred to Brown's raiders with terms such as "banditti" and "robbers"—the same terms later used in the Union army's wartime Lieber Code to demarcate illegitimate from legitimate combatants.[61] Like the former US Army colleagues he later fought on the battlefield, Lee feared the disorder of guerrillas. He supported the Confederacy in large part because he believed individuals such as himself—scientifically trained and disciplined officers—would lead its military forces. Professional military expertise associated itself with the modernist pretentions of the nation-state and its creation of an identity that claimed to transcend other types of human loyalty such as family, sect, or tribe. Armies also created a transnational identity based around approved patterns of conflict with other armies, whose reciprocal violence served as a form of mutual legitimation that in turn used nonstate actors as foils. The aforementioned willingness of the US Army to assist the Mexican government in its suppression of Yucatán insurgents at the end of the Mexican War was one example of how nation-state armies might loathe internal enemies more than foreign foes, as was Lee's own support for a formal demobilization and surrender of his troops at Appomattox.

Even as they defined themselves in opposition to foreign and domestic nonstate rivals, nation-state armies remained in obvious conflict with one another. They reconciled their desire to both battle and recognize each other's legitimacy by adopting laws of war that focused on procedural practice as opposed to moral intent. Following the eighteenth-century legal authority Emmerich de Vattel, who defined moral conduct in war as more a question of following certain procedures than a war's larger political rationale,[62] American professionals also created a sense of duty that emphasized procedure and regulation as opposed to final purposes. As a pragmatic matter, all laws of war (defined as combatants' willingness to accept any sort of restraints on violence) depended on the combatants believing and acting on the belief that soldiers' moral value could not be reduced to their larger political causes. In this conception, while one party may even have had God on its side, honorable soldiers could still be found on both sides and were thus worthy of protections such as a prohibition on mutilating bodies, the right to surrender under certain conditions,[63] medical treatment after active hostilities ceased, and the like. These procedural and symbolic rituals reinforced the notion that mortal foes on the battlefield still shared a common humanity and even common martial virtues, which belligerents acknowledged may be used in the service of an unjust cause.

For military professionals, however, this notion of shared humanity also required a willing subordination of their individual moral judgments to the prerogatives of the state. The secession crisis revealed some of the ambiguities inherent in the Weberian monopoly on violence, and other mid-nineteenth-century crises of legitimacy could be found in far-off climes such as Taiping China or Germany and Italy. While Lee had himself been a model of obedience to the antebellum US Army bureaucracy, when the secession winter arrived, he transferred his allegiance to the Confederacy despite the unwavering Unionism of many of his relatives and respected professional peers in the US Army.[64] Winfield Scott—another scion of Virginia and Lee's staunchly Unionist mentor in the Old Army—disagreed with Lee's choice to back secession, but he also accepted Lee's legal right to resign from the US Army to avoid unwelcome orders.[65] Scott believed Lee chose wrongly and, according to one of his staff officers, "mourned as for the loss of a son,"[66] but the officer corps as a whole accepted the right to resignation—a separate issue from secession's legality.[67] Lee himself recognized that others might choose differently—when writing about his momentous decision to a Unionist cousin in the Old Army who eventually chose otherwise, Lee held back his counsel and simply remarked, "I merely tell you what I have done that you may do better."[68]

While Union commanders believed secession illegal and unjust according to the domestic principles of the American constitutional order, they also believed that Confederate military personnel remained lawful belligerents according to the law of nations that governed warfare writ large. For practical reasons, Union military authorities, by declaring a naval blockade and approving a cartel to conduct prisoner exchanges, conceded to some degree the Confederacy's claim to being a government. Confederate authorities in turn fulfilled most of the legal obligations associated with belligerency, with the important exception of refusing to acknowledge African American soldiers as lawful combatants.[69] As Aaron Sheehan-Dean has put it, "In the Union and the Confederacy central governments set limits on violence. Because both states curried the favor of international observers, they professed adherence to the laws of war, which sanctioned lethal violence only against combatants."[70] Whether Unionist or secessionist, US Army officers during the secession winter saw themselves not as machines blindly obeying orders or as conscripts fighting due to legal compulsion but as moral agents free to choose their allegiance—for better or for ill.[71]

Indeed, even these new model "professionals" could and did react with violence against superiors whom they perceived to encroach upon their treasured equality of status as honorable gentlemen. The nation-state ritualization of war not only made no attempt to banish violence from the political sphere but also struggled to restrain the passions of honor-driven soldiers. Two famous examples of violent insubordination by professional military officers during the Civil War were not in the supposedly premodern Confederacy but in the Union army—Brig. Gen. Thomas Sweeny's pugilistic altercation with his corps commander, Maj. Gen. Grenville Dodge, and Brig. Gen. Jefferson Davis's murder of his corps commander, Maj. Gen. William Nelson.[72] The West Point–trained and arch-professional Sherman frowned on Davis's misdeed, but he also wrote his wife, "I cannot justify the act, but do not condemn it."[73] Davis's de facto promotion to corps commander by the end of the war by Sherman casts doubt on any oversimplified visions of Civil War armies as rationalized and modernizing bureaucracies. Sherman also proved to be less than enthusiastic in disciplining Sweeny for his less spectacular (but still serious) outburst of insubordination.[74] Both Sweeny and Davis showed the resilience of the aristocratic practice of dueling in a nominally republican army organized according to a modernizing disciplinary regime, despite a general decline in the practice among US Army officers before the Civil War.[75] Indeed, dueling and sensitivity to insults—what the anthropologist Frank Stewart describes as "reflexive honor"—actually became more prevalent in the Western world after the Renaissance,[76] although Ayers has argued that ritualized dueling in the post–Civil War South declined due to elites' loss of confidence in their rituals following the Confederacy's defeat.[77] In the world of military professionals, it was unsurprising that as warfare became increasingly influenced by the leveling tendencies of machines, dueling among military professionals survived as a somewhat forlorn attempt to retain aristocratic and elite status. Returning to antebellum America, as Samuel Watson puts it, "ultimately, the army's personnel policies toward officers were still based on the model of the independent gentleman asserting his rights in an eighteenth-century language of personal honor rather than that of an officeholder in a routinized bureaucratic hierarchy."[78]

Like any other Civil War army commander, Lee had to balance martial notions of honor with the prerogatives of a functioning military bureaucracy. He had to manage, for example, Jackson's mercurial dealings with subordinates while encouraging the former's famed aggressiveness.[79] In sum, like any successful commander of armies, Lee encouraged the indispensable influence of certain martial virtues—willingness to sacrifice oneself for the group, endurance, aggressiveness, a desire for martial glory, cunning, and so on. Both sides of the Civil War acknowledged the cultural authority of these traits even as they slaughtered one another over political differences. And whatever his faults, Lee built and led an organization in the Army of Northern Virginia that possessed the martial virtues listed above in spades. Those virtues harked back to an era before the rise of armies drilled on the parade ground to fight and die like windup machines in battle. As Col. Charles Marshall put it in recounting the moment of Lee's greatest martial triumph at Chancellorsville,

> The fierce soldiers, with their faces blackened with the smoke of battle; the wounded, crawling with feeble limbs from the fury of the devouring flames, all seemed possessed with a common impulse. One long, unbroken cheer, in which the feeble cry of those who lay helpless on the earth blended with the strong voices of those who still fought, rose high above the roar of battle and hailed the presence of the victorious chief. He sat in the full realisation of all that soldiers dream of—triumph; and as I looked upon him in the complete fruition of the success which his genius, courage and confidence in his army had won, I thought that it must have been from some such scene that men in ancient days ascended to the dignity of the gods.[80]

Postwar Lost Cause hagiography of a pious Christian Lee elided this vaguely pagan pre-Christian Lee.[81] The "cruel old Chief," to use the sobriquet of one of Lee's long-suffering aides, struggled with controlling his rage, but as with the half-divine Achilles, his fury was part and parcel of his aggressive prowess in battle. And most of Lee's aides remained respectful of their general, even after suffering through his periodic outbursts.[82] The scientific discipline of West Point coexisted with atavistic forces rooted in martial cultures of honor. On the battlefield, that aggressiveness might lead to errors in judgment such as Pickett's Charge, and off the battlefield, Lee proved unable to master his own temper when misruling his slaves. Lee may even have flogged his slaves with his own hand[83]—a far cry from the kindly Lee of Lost Cause civil religion, but explicable in a profession where violent domination determined status. Lost Cause hagiography obscured Lee's wrath, but it highlighted his military success on the battlefield and closely linked it to the Confederacy's vision of a slaveholding republic based on racial domination and led by a patrician aristocracy. The Confederacy's eventual defeat, however, posed an existential crisis for Confederate nationalism, and with material victory made unobtainable, Lee himself began a narrative by which

Confederate virtue had simply been overwhelmed by the malignant power of modern industrialization—or, to use his own words, "overwhelming numbers and resources."[84]

Lost Cause apologists' special pleading for Lee's supposedly archaic virtues also aimed to deny such moral qualities to the Union army. Later historians indifferent or hostile to the Lost Cause discarded such moralizing, but they remained impressed by the Union army's mobilization of military power, and many linked the Civil War to the world wars of the twentieth century. Historians such as Bruce Catton thus reversed the moral calculus associated with modernity and the Lost Cause—now it was Grant as the moral apostle of progress and Lee serving as his atavistic and outdated foil who "might have ridden down from the old age of chivalry, lance in hand, silken banner fluttering over his head."[85] John Keegan, in comparing both Lee and Jackson unfavorably with Grant, argued that the Confederate duo "proved men of limited imagination. Neither found means of forcing the North to fight on their terms, as they might have done had they tempted the Northern armies to enter the vast spaces of the South and manoeuvre out of touch with their railroad and river lines of supply."[86] Both of these interpretations neglected Lee's deeply modern career, which extended far beyond the exigencies of field army command during the Civil War and included his antebellum service.

Lee's admittedly audacious generalship also should not obscure the enduring influence of his engineering training. From his early Confederate service defending the Carolina and Georgia coasts, Lee gained a strong sense of the limitations of fortifications in the face of Federal sea power. Lee's first antebellum assignment in the Corps of Engineers had been to construct fortifications at Cockspur Island to defend Savannah, whose Fort Pulaski fell shortly after he left the Carolinas for Richmond, and he later helped besiege and reduce fortifications at Vera Cruz in Mexico by siting naval guns manned by his own brother.[87] Lee's deep-seated fear of a US siege of Richmond, where Union superiority in weight of ordnance would overwhelm trapped Confederate defenders, had roots in his firsthand knowledge of military engineering and fortification. Indeed, shortly after taking command of the Army of Northern Virginia, Lee immediately set his troops to work digging entrenchments to reposition his forces for the coming Seven Days' offensive.[88] The war's end in Virginia, where Lee's forces gradually wasted away in their trench lines before being eventually flanked by a powerful combined cavalry-infantry force led by Maj. Gen. Philip Sheridan, vindicated this fear. His preoccupation with fighting a war of maneuver north of Richmond stemmed not from an obsession with supposedly obsolete Napoleonic tactics but from a recognition that US material superiority made a siege of Richmond and Petersburg a foregone conclusion. Lee thus hoped to neutralize Federal industrial strength in the new modern machines of war by attacking loyal public opinion through offensive operations in the North—an eminently modern strategy, as Gary Gallagher has pointed out.[89]

Lee's surrender of the Army of Northern Virginia at Appomattox also highlighted the limitations of the modern state's disciplinary reach even within its foundational institution. Looming over Lee's concerns about the demoralization of his troops into dangerous guerrillas was his own constant struggle during the war to discipline the Army of Northern Virginia, whose men had chronic problems with plundering civilians (including fellow Confederates), looting, straggling, and general disorderliness.[90] He had seen firsthand over the course of a decades-long military career how the barracks—that originating institution of Foucault's notions of discipline and modernity—could not fully control the chaotic social world of soldiers. Indeed, as Caroline E. Janney has shown, due to desertions, straggling, or a desire to avoid the formal process of paroling due to continued defiance of Federal authority, at least 20,000 of Lee's troops did not even surrender in conformity to their commander's orders at Appomattox.[91]

Nevertheless, both sides in the Civil War subscribed to a notion of mutually legitimate belligerency, with the pragmatic effect that the war did not escalate into something like the Taiping Civil War or the violence used by white settlers in wars against American Indians. The Confederate slaughter of uniformed African American troops unmasked the racial tinge of the law of war, but while nation-state rituals to constrain battlefield violence flexed, they did not break. Civil War era white Americans slaughtered each other on the battlefield over secession and slavery, but they also recognized that belligerents could self-consciously separate political and ideological differences from shared martial values reflecting a common humanity. And while it is obviously true that that these restraints helped protect military and political elites, especially in a defeated state like the Confederacy, restraint in wartime has an inherent moral value that historians should not easily dismiss. And one beneficial product of such notions of limits and restraints on violence in warfare is that they help wars end by giving combatants a plausible path to accepting defeat on the battlefield—which is precisely what Lee did by surrendering his army.

In his last act as a general, Lee dissolved his army rather than risk its soldiers become an undisciplined rabble, but at the end of his life, Lee the university president expressed some ambivalence regarding the rigors of martial discipline. Even as superintendent at West Point, Lee had enforced the school's famously severe disciplinary standards with some hesitancy; as the postwar head of Washington College, Lee conveyed regret at having been educated at a military school and even refused to keep time with the drum when walking with the head of the neighboring Virginia Military Institute during ceremonial occasions.[92] No one could know more than Lee the importance of marching in time.[93] One of Lee's biographers, Emory Thomas, has also noted Lee's independent-minded streak in his curricular reforms at Washington College and his flirtatious correspondence with young women.[94] As both a West Point superintendent and a commander of troops in the field, Lee certainly would have also seen more than his fair share of soldierly resistance to discipline—that was, after all, an important part of his decision to surrender his troops as an organized body. More darkly, however, Lee's use of supposedly premodern forms of punishment such as flogging against his own slaves before the war while playing the role of the disciplined and modernizing military bureaucrat shows that Foucault's demarcations between modernity and its predecessors overstate the disjunction between the two.[95]

Nation-state armies march with all of modernity's most macabre instruments—new machines of death and destruction enabled by forms of discipline that harness the human soul to the optimization of machines. But hope survives for freedom, in part because those machines by themselves do not guarantee victory. Lee might have been a modernizer, but his vision of modernity had to compete with that of rivals, and it was the Union's vision that emerged victorious. Furthermore, when we peer inside the dark recesses of both the Union and Confederate military machines, we find that humanity could remain defiant and ill-disciplined, because beyond the inherently chaotic nature of the battlefield, success in war still depended to some degree on the irrational forces of fighting spirit and morale that could slip beyond the control of the military machine's bureaucracy. Like the armies of the French Revolution, Civil War armies showed that overdisciplined military machines also robbed armies of an indispensable fighting spirit. In the end, soldiers might decide to advance and fight and die more or less willingly, or they could desert or straggle beyond the control of the machine. And Lee, who had chosen to fight for the Confederacy as a modernizer and defender of its racial order built on slavery, could later hope to exchange slavery's survival as an institution for Confederate independence by recruiting African Americans into the Confederate army—but found that option repudiated by the freedmen themselves, who chose abstention, resistance, or even military service in the Union army instead. Faced with the grim logic of the Union's modern military machines at Appomattox, Lee then dismantled his dread apparatus, retiring to a different vision of modernity at yet another disciplinary institution—Washington College—only to march out of step with the drummer's cadence that had so dominated his entire adult life.

Most of us insist on our modernity (or perhaps the postmodern variant); as Bayly puts it, "The nineteenth century was the age of modernity precisely because a considerable number of the thinkers, statesmen, and scientists who dominated the ordering of society believed it to be so."[96] Bayly left soldiers out of this list, even though they marched, killed, and sometimes died at the sharp edge of history—skilled technicians in the service of bureaucratic and material machines. Nevertheless, they coexisted with supposedly atavistic phenomena such as the charismatic authority of Weber's warlord and the Army of Northern Virginia's notorious slave raiding in Pennsylvania—both apostles of modernity and successors to the centurion in the Gospel of Matthew, but under a new authority.[97] No one should hope to learn from Lee's life and career the discredited lessons of Lost Cause hagiography, but neither should it become a straightforward parable of our own era's triumph over backwardness—of history bending toward progress. It is beyond the scope of this essay to say what we ought to learn from the history of the Civil War for the sake of our fraught present and uncertain future, but no credible lessons can evade the somber drums beating retreat and tattoo.

NOTES

Many thanks go to the volume editors' suggestions and guidance, close readings from J. E. Lendon and Edward L. Ayers, and an anonymous reader's report. All errors and misperceptions remain, of course, my responsibility.

1. On the army and internal improvements, see Robert Wooster, *The United States Army and the Making of America: From Confederation to Empire, 1775–1903* (Lawrence: University Press of Kansas, 2021), 107–8.

2. C. A. Bayly, *The Birth of the Modern World, 1780–1914: Global Connections and Comparisons* (Malden, MA: Blackwell, 2004), 11.

3. Abraham Lincoln, *The Collected Works of Abraham Lincoln: The Abraham Lincoln Association, Springfield, Illinois*, ed. Roy P. Basler (New Brunswick, NJ: Rutgers University Press, 1953), 4:438.

4. Geoffrey Parker, *The Military Revolution: Military Innovation and the Rise of the West, 1500–1800*, 2nd ed. (Cambridge: Cambridge University Press, 1996), 1–5, 156; Michel Foucault, *Discipline and Punish: The Birth of the Prison*, 2nd ed., trans. Alan Sheridan (New York:

Vintage Books, 1995), 135–36, 168–69; Michel Foucault, *"Society Must Be Defended": Lectures at the Collège de France, 1975–1976*, ed. Mauro Bertani, Alessandro Fontana, and François Ewald, trans. David Macey (New York: Picador, 2003), 267. On French theory's interest in military metaphors, see Anders Engberg-Pedersen, *Empire of Chance: The Napoleonic Wars and the Disorder of Things* (Cambridge, MA: Harvard University Press, 2015), 250–51. For premonitions of all these preceding ideas, see Max Weber, *From Max Weber: Essays in Sociology*, trans. H. H. Gerth and C. Wright Mills (New York: Oxford University Press, 1958), 254, 260, 221–23, 77–78.

5. Janice E. Thomson, *Mercenaries, Pirates, and Sovereigns: State-Building and Extraterritorial Violence in Early Modern Europe* (Princeton, NJ: Princeton University Press, 1994), 143.

6. Foucault, *Discipline and Punish*, 136–41.

7. Foucault, *Discipline and Punish*, 308. For a critique of Foucault's analysis as applied to eighteenth-century France, see Christy Pichichero, *The Military Enlightenment: War and Culture in the French Empire from Louis XIV to Napoleon* (Ithaca, NY: Cornell University Press, 2017), 116–17.

8. Bayly, *Birth of the Modern World*, 251–52; Stephen Skowronek, "Present at the Creation: The State in Early American Political History," *Journal of the Early Republic* 38, no. 1 (2018): 98.

9. Jürgen Osterhammel, *The Transformation of the World: A Global History of the Nineteenth Century*, trans. Patrick Camiller (Princeton, NJ: Princeton University Press, 2014), 605. Also see Osterhammel's treatment of post-Reconstruction state retrenchment, 614. For an expansive view of state power via the US Army in Reconstruction, see Gregory P. Downs, *After Appomattox: Military Occupation and the Ends of War* (Cambridge, MA: Harvard University Press, 2015), 6–7.

10. Osterhammel, *Transformation of the World*, 490.

11. Samuel J. Watson, *Peacekeepers and Conquerors: The Army Officer Corps on the American Frontier, 1821–1846* (Lawrence: University Press of Kansas, 2013), 429; Wooster, *United States Army and the Making of America*, 3.

12. William J. Novak, "The Myth of the 'Weak' American State," *American Historical Review* 113, no. 3 (2008): 758, 760, 763, 766. While these references are not entirely incidental, as a whole the piece treats the US Army as a niche institution.

13. William B. Skelton, *An American Profession of Arms: The Army Officer Corps, 1784–1861* (Lawrence: University Press of Kansas, 1992), xiii–xiv.

14. Richard Franklin Bensel, *Yankee Leviathan: The Origins of Central State Authority in America, 1859–1877* (Cambridge: Cambridge University Press, 1990), 95–98, 153–54. Lee also became an advocate of state support for manufacturing during the war. See Adrian Brettle, *Colossal Ambitions: Confederate Planning for a Post–Civil War World* (Charlottesville: University of Virginia Press, 2020), 198.

15. Weber, *Essays in Sociology*, 78.

16. James M. McPherson, "Antebellum Southern Exceptionalism: A New Look at an Old Question," *Civil War History* 50, no. 4 (2004): 418–33; Edward L. Ayers, "Worrying about the Civil War," in *What Caused the Civil War? Reflections on the South and Southern History* (New York: Norton, 2005), 127. For a direct rebuttal of Ayers, see Michael F. Conlin, "The Dangerous Isms and the Fanatical Ists: Antebellum Conservatives in the South and the North Confront the Modernity Conspiracy," *Journal of the Civil War Era* 4, no. 2 (2014): 206.

17. Bayly, *Birth of the Modern World*, 161–63; Osterhammel, *Transformation of the World*, 845–48. Americanist historians of a transnational persuasion such as Don H. Doyle and Stephanie McCurry pay close attention to the American Civil War's place in a larger hemispheric struggle over slavery. See Don H. Doyle, *The Cause of All Nations: An International History of the American Civil War* (New York: Basic Books, 2015), 10; and Stephanie McCurry, *Confederate Reckoning: Power and Politics in the Civil War South* (Cambridge, MA: Harvard University Press, 2010), 2. For a recent discussion on the contentious scholarship surrounding slavery and capitalism, see Christopher Morris, "With 'the Economics-of-Slavery Culture Wars,' It's Déjà Vu All Over Again," *Journal of the Civil War Era* 10, no. 4 (2020): 524–57.

18. Sven Beckert, *Empire of Cotton: A Global History* (New York: Knopf, 2014), xv–xvii. Note that despite Beckert's analytic framing of "war capitalism," he assumes the existence of military institutions and their coercive apparatus. See, for example, his chapter on the American Civil War (pp. 242–73).

19. On antebellum proslavery attempts to build state power in foreign and military policy, see Matthew Karp, *This Vast Southern Empire: Slaveholders at the Helm of American Foreign Policy* (Cambridge, MA: Harvard University Press, 2016), 4–8.

20. For the idea of the "black box" as a metaphor for an absence of sources "that mercifully conceals from us the horrendous experience of massed close quarter combat" in antiquity, see Philip Sabin, *Lost Battles: Reconstructing the Great Clashes of the Ancient World* (London: Hambledon Continuum, 2007), xv. For a more frustrated reaction to the same problem, see Jon E. Lendon, "Battle Description in the Ancient Historians, Part I: Structure, Array, and Fighting," *Greece and Rome* 64, no. 1 (2017): 51. Nineteenth-century Americanists, in contrast, have far more ample source material than these scholars. On the metaphor of the black box in relation to technology and automation, also see Dennis E. Showalter, *Railroads and Rifles: Soldiers, Technology, and the Unification of Germany* (Hamden, CT: Archon Books, 1975), 13. On the metaphor of the black box among historians of technology, see Rosalind Williams, "Opening the Big Box," *Technology and Culture* 48, no. 1 (2007): 104–7.

21. Cadmus M. Wilcox, *Rifles and Rifle Practice: An Elementary Treatise upon the Theory of Rifle Firing, Explaining the Causes of Inaccuracy of Fire, and the Manner of Correcting It* (New York: D. Van Nostrand, 1859), 238. Also see Robert L. O'Connell, *Of Arms and Men: A History of War, Weapons, and Aggression* (New York: Oxford University Press, 1989), 155–60.

22. Gordon C. Rhea, *The Battles for Spotsylvania Court House and the Road to Yellow Tavern, May 7–12, 1864* (Baton Rouge: Louisiana State University Press, 1997), 250, 320–21; Douglas Southall Freeman, *Lee's Lieutenants: A Study in Command* (New York: Charles Scribner's Sons, 1944), 3:357–58.

23. Peter S. Carmichael, *The War for the Common Soldier: How Men Thought, Fought, and Survived in Civil War Armies* (Chapel Hill: University of North Carolina Press, 2018), 133–34.

24. Weber, *Essays in Sociology*, 254.

25. On the continued survival of dueling in the Union army, see Lorien Foote, *The Gentlemen and the Roughs: Violence, Honor, and Manhood in the Union Army* (New York: New York University Press, 2010), 93–118.

26. Douglas Southall Freeman, *R. E. Lee: A Biography* (1934; repr., New York: Charles Scribner's Sons, 1943), 1:38–42, 50, 69–82.

27. John F. Marszalek, *Sherman: A Soldier's Passion for Order* (New York: Free Press, 1993), 27–28, 441; Freeman, *R. E. Lee*, 1:317.

28. On the regular army's problems with discipline, see Edward M. Coffman, *The Old Army: A Portrait of the American Army in Peacetime, 1784–1898* (New York: Oxford University Press, 1986), 192–200, 63–64.

29. Michel Foucault, "The Subject and Power," *Critical Inquiry* 8, no. 4 (1982): 790.

30. Brooks D. Simpson, *Ulysses S. Grant: Triumph over Adversity, 1822–1865* (Boston: Houghton Mifflin, 2000; repr., Minneapolis: Zenith Press, 2014), 14, 17, 61.

31. Marszalek, *Sherman*, 27–28.

32. Theodore J. Crackel, *West Point: A Bicentennial History* (Lawrence: University Press of Kansas, 2002), 88.

33. Foucault, *Discipline and Punish*, 145–47. Sylvanus Thayer, a military engineer and reformer, created the post–War of 1812 educational system at West Point by modeling it on the French École Polytechnique, which he had visited after the War of 1812. See Wayne Wei-siang Hsieh, *West Pointers and the Civil War: The Old Army in War and Peace* (Chapel Hill: University of North Carolina Press, 2009), 24.

34. James C. Scott, *Seeing Like a State: How Certain Schemes to Improve the Human Condition Have Failed* (1998; repr., New Haven, CT: Yale University Press, 2020), 33–45. On the importance of censuses—which were mandated in the US Constitution—to larger nineteenth-century processes of state building, see Osterhammel, *Transformation of the World*, 26–27.

35. Scott, *Seeing Like a State*, 64–71.

36. Simpson, *Ulysses S. Grant*, 11–12; Ulysses S. Grant, *The Papers of Ulysses S. Grant*, ed. John Y. Simon et al., 32 vols. (Carbondale: Southern Illinois University Press, 1967–2012), 11:122.

37. Joan Waugh, *U. S. Grant: American Hero, American Myth* (Chapel Hill: University of North Carolina Press, 2009), 21, 54.

38. Gilles Deleuze, "Postscript on the Societies of Control," *October* 59 (1992): 5.

39. Ted Maris-Wolf, "'Of Blood and Treasure': Receptive Africans and the Politics of Slave Trade Suppression," *Journal of the Civil War Era* 4, no. 1 (2014): 75–76; Daniel F. Littlefield Jr. and Lonnie E. Underhill, "Renaming the American Indian: 1890–1913," *American Studies* 12, no. 2 (1971): 33–45.

40. Amy Murrell Taylor, *Embattled Freedom: Journeys through the Civil War's Slave Refugee Camps* (Chapel Hill: University of North Carolina Press, 2018), 8–18.

41. Robert G. Angevine, *The Railroad and the State: War, Politics, and Technology in Nineteenth-Century America* (Stanford, CA: Stanford University Press, 2004), 66–67, 87–107. On early Prussian military thinking on railroads, including the idea that railroad and military organizations were natural analogues, see Showalter, *Railroads and Rifles*, 28–31.

42. Wooster, *United States Army and the Making of America*, 159–60.

43. Emory M. Thomas, *Robert E. Lee: A Biography* (New York: Norton, 1995), 159.

44. Thomas, *Robert E. Lee*, 86–100.

45. For a comparison of how Washington's colonial military service intersected with his early career as a surveyor and the road building of British troops during the Seven Years' War, see W. W. Abbot, "George Washington, the West, and the Union," in *George Washington Reconsidered*, ed. Don Higginbotham (Charlottesville: University Press of Virginia, 2001), 199–201. On mapmaking and the rationalization of the American landscape to a square grid, see Osterhammel, *Transformation of the World*, 105; and Scott, *Seeing Like a State*, 49–52.

46. Freeman, *R. E. Lee*, 1:210–11.

47. Angevine, *Railroad and the State*, 134–37; Marszalek, *Sherman*, 140–43, 319–20, 498–99.

48. Freeman, *Lee's Lieutenants*, 1:321–22, 481–82. Tracking distances between points on a military map goes back to Roman practice. See Engberg-Pedersen, *Empire of Chance*, 148.

49. Edward L. Ayers, *The Thin Light of Freedom: The Civil War and Emancipation in the Heart of America* (New York: Norton, 2017), 483.

50. Jedediah Hotchkiss, *Make Me a Map of the Valley: The Civil War Journal of Stonewall Jackson's Topographer*, ed. Archie P. McDonald (Dallas: Southern Methodist University Press, 1973), xvii, x–xi.

51. William T. Sherman, *Memoirs of General William T. Sherman*, 2nd ed. (New York: D. Appleton, 1886), 2:31–32.

52. Thomas, *Robert E. Lee*, 125–26; Freeman, *R. E. Lee*, 1:238–41. On military reconnaissance and the absence of maps in Roman military practice, see A. C. Bertrand, "Stumbling through Gaul: Maps, Intelligence, and Caesar's Bellum Gallicum," *Ancient History Bulletin* 11, no. 4 (1997): 107–22. For Odysseus's night raid, see *Iliad*, bk. 10.

53. Freeman, *R. E. Lee*, 1:244–47.

54. Thomas, *Robert E. Lee*, 130–33.

55. S. Ex. Doc. No. 8, 30th Cong., 1st Sess. (1848), Serial 515, *Message from the President of the United States to the Two Houses of Congress at the Comments of the First Session of the Thirtieth Congress* (Washington, DC: Wendell and Van Benthuysen, 1848), 315, 313.

56. John Keegan, *The Mask of Command* (New York: Viking, 1987), 212–13.

57. Irving W. Levinson, "A New Paradigm for an Old Conflict: The Mexico–United States War," *Journal of Military History* 73, no. 2 (2009): 403, 410–15. Also see Peter Guardino, *The Dead March: A History of the Mexican-American War* (Cambridge, MA: Harvard University Press, 2017), 340–42.

58. Thomas, *Robert E. Lee*, 139, 165–68.

59. J. William Jones, *Life and Letters of Robert Edward Lee: Soldier and Man* (New York: Neale, 1906), 56–57.

60. Thomas, *Robert E. Lee*, 180–83.

61. Jones, *Life and Letters of Robert Edward Lee*, 105; "General Orders No. 100: The Lieber Code," para. 47, 52, 82, https://avalon.law.yale.edu/19th_century/lieber.asp (accessed May 5, 2021). On the Lieber Code in general, see D. H. Dilbeck, *A More Civil War: How the Union Waged a Just War* (Chapel Hill: University of North Carolina Press, 2016), 87–97.

62. Carl Schmitt, *The Nomos of the Earth in the International Law of the Jus Publicum Europaeum*, trans. G. L. Ulmen (Candor, NY: Telos Press, 2006), 165–67.

63. David Silkenat, *Raising the White Flag: How Surrender Defined the American Civil War* (Chapel Hill: University of North Carolina Press, 2019), 1–4.

64. Elizabeth Brown Pryor, "'Thou Knowest Not the Time of Thy Visitation': A Newly Discovered Letter Reveals Robert E. Lee's Lonely Struggle with Disunion," *Virginia Magazine of History and Biography* 119, no. 3 (2011): 287–88. On the strength of Lee's Southern white slaveholding identity, also see Gary W. Gallagher, *Becoming Confederates: Paths to a New National Loyalty* (Athens: University of Georgia Press, 2013), 17.

65. Pryor, "'Thou Knowest Not,'" 281, 283.

66. Pryor, "'Thou Knowest Not,'" 291.

67. On the issue of when resignations could and could not occur in compliance with US Army Regulations, see Wayne Wei-siang Hsieh, "'I Owe Virginia Little, My Country Much': Robert E. Lee, the United States Regular Army, and Unconditional Unionism," in *Crucible of the Civil War*, ed. Edward L. Ayers, Gary W. Gallagher, and Andrew J. Torget (Charlottesville: University of Virginia Press, 2006), 45; and Hsieh, *West Pointers and the Civil War*, 109–11. The timing of Lee's resignation pushed the envelope of propriety, although the principle of resignation was accepted by the army's larger institutional culture. Outside of the initial post–West Point service obligation, officers of this era served at will (unlike enlisted soldiers), although they frowned upon resignation in order to evade imminent duty or the abdication of trusted responsibilities. Also see Wooster, *United States Army and the Making of America*, 113–14.

68. Quoted in Pryor, "'Thou Knowest Not,'" 281.

69. Silkenat, *Raising the White Flag*, 168–81.

70. Aaron Sheehan-Dean, *The Calculus of Violence: How Americans Fought the Civil War* (Cambridge, MA: Harvard University Press, 2018), 3.

71. The idea that the honorable warrior freely chooses either the right or the wrong path in a moment of crisis is deeply embedded in Western military history: "to make, like Achilles in the *Iliad*, the heroic choice of an heroic death." See J. E. Lendon, *Song of Wrath: The Peloponnesian War Begins* (New York: Basic Books, 2010), 274–75.

72. Jack Morgan, *Through American and Irish Wars: The Life and Times of Thomas W. Sweeny, 1820–1892* (Dublin: Irish Academic Press, 2005), 102–4; Nathaniel Cheairs Hughes Jr., and Gordon D. Whitney, *Jefferson Davis in Blue: The Life of Sherman's Relentless Warrior* (Baton Rouge: Louisiana State University Press, 2002), 100–126.

73. William T. Sherman, *Sherman's Civil War: Selected Correspondence of William T. Sherman, 1860–1865*, ed. Brooks D. Simpson and Jean V. Berlin (Chapel Hill: University of North Carolina Press, 1999), 314.

74. Morgan, *Through American and Irish Wars*, 103.

75. Skelton, *American Profession of Arms*, 196. On the lingering importance of dueling into even twentieth-century armies, see Frank Henderson Stewart, *Honor* (Chicago: University of Chicago Press, 1994), 69n15. On dueling and other forms of extralegal violence in Congress, see Joanne B. Freeman, *The Field of Blood: Violence in Congress and the Road to Civil War* (New York: Farrar, Straus and Giroux, 2018), 234–41.

76. Stewart, *Honor*, 67–71. Dueling also first spread to America through English and French military officers during the Revolutionary era. See Edward L. Ayers, *Vengeance and Justice: Crime and Punishment in the 19th-Century American South* (New York: Oxford University Press, 1984), 15–16.

77. Ayers, *Vengeance and Justice*, 270–71.

78. Watson, *Peacekeepers and Conquerors*, 231.

79. Lee had to frequently calm matters in Jackson's command due to the latter's tendency to arrest and discipline high-ranking subordinates—the most important being an altercation between him and A. P. Hill. Lee's general strategy to deal with such problems was a mixture of diplomacy and misdirection to, in the words of his biographer Douglas Southall Freeman, trust "to time what he could not himself settle." See Freeman, *Lee's Lieutenants*, 2:243–47, quote on p. 246. For a more recent scholarly overview of the Jackson-Hill imbroglio, see Christian B. Keller, *The Great Partnership: Robert E. Lee, Stonewall Jackson,*

and the Fate of the Confederacy (New York: Pegasus Books, 2019), 285–86n13. The general fractiousness of Civil War generals, Union and Confederate, is as a general phenomenon well known to Civil War military historians, although it deserves more sustained and systematic analytical attention.

80. "Tributes to General Lee," *Southern Magazine* 8 (January 1871): 29.

81. On the continued potency of this image, see Ty Seidule, *Robert E. Lee and Me: A Southerner's Reckoning with the Myth of the Lost Cause* (New York: St. Martin's Press, 2020), 19–21.

82. Elizabeth Brown Pryor, *Reading the Man: A Portrait of Robert E. Lee through His Private Letters* (New York: Viking, 2007), 323–24, 353, 407.

83. Pryor, *Reading the Man*, 270–73.

84. Gary W. Gallagher, "Shaping Public Memory of the Civil War: Robert E. Lee, Jubal A. Early, and Douglas Southall Freeman," in *Lee and His Army in Confederate History* (Chapel Hill: University of North Carolina Press, 2001), 256; Robert E. Lee, *The Wartime Papers of Robert E. Lee*, ed. Clifford Dowdey, Louis H. Manarin, and Samuel Bryant (Boston: Little, Brown, 1961; repr., New York: Da Capo Press, 1987), 934.

85. Bruce Catton, "Grant and Lee: A Study in Contrasts," in *The American Story: The Age of Exploration to the Age of the Atom*, ed. Earl Schenck Miers (Great Neck, NY: Channel Press, 1956), 204. Among military historians, the question of the Civil War's modernity also involved the legacy of World War I and how B. H. Liddell Hart and J. F. C. Fuller interpreted the American Civil War in light of their own service with the British army on the Western Front. See Wayne Wei-siang Hsieh, "Total War and the American Civil War Reconsidered: The End of an Outdated 'Master Narrative,'" *Journal of the Civil War Era* 1, no. 3 (2011): 402.

86. Keegan, *Mask of Command*, 197.

87. Thomas, *Robert E. Lee*, 57, 122, 212–17.

88. Hsieh, *West Pointers and the Civil War*, 155–56.

89. Gary W. Gallagher, "An Old-Fashioned Soldier in a Modern War: Lee's Confederate Generalship," in *Lee and His Army in Confederate History* (Chapel Hill: University of North Carolina Press, 2001), 181–82.

90. Hsieh, *West Pointers and the Civil War*, 1–2; Joseph T. Glatthaar, *General Lee's Army: From Victory to Collapse* (New York: Free Press, 2008), 176–85, 437–38.

91. Caroline E. Janney, "We Were Not Paroled: The Surrenders of Lee's Men beyond Appomattox Court House," in *Petersburg to Appomattox: The End of the War in Virginia*, ed. Caroline E. Janney (Chapel Hill: University of North Carolina Press, 2018), 193.

92. Thomas, *Robert E. Lee*, 156–57, 396.

93. Also see William H. McNeill, *Keeping Together in Time: Dance and Drill in Human History* (Cambridge, MA: Harvard University Press, 1995), 131.

94. Thomas, *Robert E. Lee*, 18–19, 399–401.

95. Note that Foucault linked nineteenth-century ideas of race to the exterminatory powers of the state, but that analysis applies more to Western imperialism at the end of the nineteenth century than to Civil War–era America. See Foucault, *"Society Must Be Defended,"* 254–58.

96. Bayly, *Birth of the Modern World*, 10.

97. David G. Smith, "Race and Retaliation: The Capture of African Americans during the Gettysburg Campaign," in *Virginia's Civil War*, ed. Peter Wallenstein and Bertram Wyatt-Brown (Charlottesville: University of Virginia Press, 2005), 137.

Guerrillas, Vengeance, and Mercy after Appomattox

The Trial of John W. McCue

CAROLINE E. JANNEY

Late in the evening on Tuesday, April 4, 1865, a courier galloped into a Union post in Maryland. Dismounting his horse, he asked to speak with the provost marshal, Capt. George H. Curry. The young courier breathlessly explained that the previous night three men had tried to rob Coffron's store in Prince George's County. Two of the bandits had escaped. The locals, however, had managed to capture a third, but not before the robber fired his pistol, injuring two men, including Richard N. Ryan, a Union detective. Immediately, Captain Curry mounted his horse for the five-mile ride to the village of Croom, where he found a crowd standing guard over a wounded civilian, a dead Union detective, and a prisoner, John W. McCue. Dressed in the full uniform of a rebel soldier, the nineteen-year-old informed the captain he was a member of John S. Mosby's Forty-Third Virginia Battalion serving under the command of Lt. Col. William H. Chapman. He and his comrades were under orders to raid the post office at Coffron's store when they were ambushed. His companions had managed to escape, but McCue, outnumbered and injured, fought back before being overpowered. Curry needed no more explanation. He bound the Rebel's wrists and started for the district headquarters in Annapolis.[1]

McCue assumed that he would be treated as a prisoner of war, cloaked with the label of soldier, and therefore excused from the charge of murder. The worst that awaited him, he believed, was a Northern prison camp, the fate that had befallen most others captured from Mosby's command. But he soon learned otherwise. Even as other members of the Forty-Third Virginia Battalion were paroled by Union forces and released from Northern prisons, McCue stood trial before a military commission as a guerrilla. In July, the commission found him guilty of murdering a Union detective and sentenced him to hard labor for life. Shocked by the outcome, his friends, family, and neighbors in the months that followed organized petitions and lobbied government officials for his pardon. Only upon General-in-Chief Ulysses S. Grant's intervention with President Andrew Johnson in the fall of 1865 would McCue be released.

While the focus of the Union military was always on defeating regular Confederate armies on the battlefield, irregular warfare had posed a threat to the Union war effort across theaters throughout the war. Central to the problem was the very definition of guerrilla warfare, which encompassed a vast range of tactics and personnel, from small groups of marauders to organized and sanctioned partisans.[2] In Virginia, John S. Mosby and his rangers had proved especially difficult to defeat. Exploiting the ambiguity of who and what counted as an irregular, in 1864 Secretary of War Edwin Stanton and Judge Advocate General Joseph Holt turned to military commissions, hoping to convict Mosby's men as guerrillas who stood outside of the protections afforded by the laws of war. When the trials failed to curtail Mosby, they ceased. But in the aftermath of Lincoln's assassination, Federals turned once more to a military commission for McCue's case. Although most soon agreed that the war had ended, following through with trials of so-called guerrillas might help maintain order in a conquered but not vanquished South.[3]

In the spring of 1865, John Willis McCue (known by his family as Johnnie) had seen less than a year of service in the Confederate army. A native of Nelson County, Virginia, he was the eldest son of the lawyer John Howard McCue and Signora C. E. Willis McCue. His father volunteered in the spring of 1861, serving as a captain in the commissary department of the Fifty-First Virginia before joining the staff of his cousin General John Imboden in 1863. But fifteen-year-old Johnnie remained at the family home of Pleasant Grove with his mother and six siblings. Whether he hoped to avoid conscription as he approached eighteen or merely longed to be part of the action is unclear. Whatever his motivation, in August 1863 Johnnie enrolled at the Virginia Military Academy. His time as a cadet, however, proved short-lived. In late March 1864, the academy dismissed him for "general neglect of duties," and he returned briefly to Pleasant Grove until the Confederate army conscripted him later that spring.[4]

Unlike almost every other conscript, Johnnie found an ally at the mustering post of Camp Lee in Richmond when he arrived in early June 1864: his father. The elder McCue had been appointed to the Conscript Bureau the previous December, and it seems likely that he had a hand in his son's appointment to the Eighteenth Virginia Cavalry, a unit in Imboden's Brigade—that of his old commander and relative.[5] During Johnnie's first few weeks in the Shenandoah Valley, his commanders took note of his "intelligence and fine character," which quickly earned the new soldier a position as Brig. Gen. John C. Vaughn's acting inspector for the brigade. When Vaughn was ordered to East Tennessee, McCue requested a transfer to Col. John S. Mosby's Forty-Third Virginia Battalion sometime in late July. McCue was soon riding with the famed—or some might say infamous—partisan rangers.[6]

By the spring of 1863 twenty-nine-year-old John Singleton Mosby had risen to prominence as the commander of the Forty-Third Battalion of the Virginia Cavalry, a partisan unit that was sanctioned by the Confederate government but operated independently of Robert E. Lee's Army of Northern Virginia. Most of Mosby's men hailed from Fauquier, Loudoun, Fairfax, and Prince William Counties in northern Virginia, where they engaged in raids of Union lines close to their homes. When their missions were complete, they dispersed, fading back into the countryside. The rangers' repeated and very successful raids on Union camps and supply lines in northern Virginia, in the Shenandoah Valley, and even into southern Maryland had brought much public attention from both Unionists and Confederates.[7]

Even before Mosby's rise to prominence, irregular warfare had thwarted Union efforts from Missouri to Virginia. As early as August 1862, General-in-Chief Henry Halleck had asked jurist Francis Lieber for his thoughts on the matter of guerrilla war. Halleck explained that rebel leaders had claimed the right to send men dressed in civilian clothing to attack Union troops, burn bridges, and destroy property and then demanded that they be treated as ordinary belligerents when captured. Were these men protected by the laws of war and thus entitled to be taken as prisoners of war (and therefore not subject to punishment for their fighting), he wondered?[8] Lieber replied that guerrillas were irregular bands of armed men, self-constituted to carry out irregular war without sanction of a government, who received no regular pay from the army and who might disband and regroup at any time.[9]

By contrast, partisans were legally obligated to the Confederate nation even as they acted independently. They had a clear command structure, and the men had enlisted in the Confederate armies. According to Lieber, the partisan's objective was "to injure the enemy by action separate from that of his own main army; the partisan acts chiefly upon the enemy's lines of connection and communication, and outside of or beyond the lines of operation of his own army, in the rear and on the flanks of the enemy." Perhaps most importantly, Lieber observed that the partisan was "part and parcel of the army, and as such, considered entitled to the privileges of the law of war, so long as he does not transgress it." Guerrillas, on the other hand, were not legitimate belligerents and deserved no such protections. Lieber expanded upon this discussion in General Orders No. 100 (otherwise known as the Lieber Code), stating that "partisans are soldiers armed and wearing the uniform of the army." If captured, they were "entitled to all the privileges of the prisoner of war."[10]

One of the chief questions for Union officials regarding Mosby and the men of his Forty-Third Virginia Battalion was how to define them. Were they partisans as outlined by Lieber? Or were they guerrillas? Unlike the marauding bands that murdered and pillaged from Missouri to Virginia, Mosby's men had been authorized by the Confederate government under the 1862 Partisan Rangers Act. But they employed irregular tactics such as donning civilian clothing and blending back into civilian populations after raids. Section 82 of the Lieber Code held that men who intermittently returned "to their homes . . . divesting themselves of the character or appearance of soldiers" were "not entitled to the privileges of prisoners of war but shall be treated summarily as highway robbers or pirates." Indeed, Northern newspapers routinely failed to differentiate between raiding expeditions conducted by Confederate cavalry and attacks by guerrillas. As historian Aaron Sheehan-Dean observes, few people in either the Union or the Confederacy could readily distinguish between guerrillas and partisans.[11]

By the winter of 1863–64, Secretary of War Edwin Stanton and Judge Advocate General Joseph Holt had decided to harness this legal ambiguity against Mosby. Rather than wage a war with guns, they would deploy the weapons of military justice. They knew the Lieber Code recognized Confederate partisans as legal and entitled to the privileges of prisoners of war. They likewise knew convicting Confederate irregulars by military commission had proved challenging because defendants could successfully argue they had committed the acts as Confederate soldiers. But when the Bureau of Military Justice found a deserter from Mosby's command willing to testify that the unit served only as a gang dedicated to plunder, Holt pounced. Men captured from Mosby's unit would face a military commission and be charged as guerrillas.[12]

Whereas courts-martial tried Union soldiers accused of breaking army regulations and the laws of war, commissions allowed the military (rather than civil courts) to try civilians under the laws of war. Composed of army officers, commissions had the discretion to examine, decide, and sentence. Defendants were allowed counsel, but only the defendant could question witnesses or address the court by statement. Beginning in 1862 and expanding in the wake of the Lieber Code in 1863, the US Army used military commissions to prosecute individuals for a wide range of crimes, including bridge burning, property destruction, robbery, spying, murder, and waging guerrilla warfare. As one jurist has noted, "The trials appear to be a legal arm of the war effort and were being used to wage a counterinsurgency effort," targeting individuals who were "actively at arms against the U.S. government." By war's end, the army had conducted between 3,300 and 5,460 hearings in which nearly 85 percent of the defendants proved to be noncombatants and guerrillas. More than half of the trials occurred in the border states of Missouri, Kentucky, and Maryland.[13]

With deserter Charles Binns serving as the government's chief witness, military commissions began trying some of Mosby's men in early 1864. The first was Philip Trammell. Union forces had captured the twenty-two-year-old Trammell in November 1863 and charged him with carrying on guerrilla warfare by robbing from citizens. Binns testified that he was never formally mustered into Mosby's command and that the men drew no pay but received only spoils. He admitted that when raids ended, the men dispersed to private homes. And when pressed if Mosby's men were required to assemble for the next raid, he replied no: "They were under no obligation to meet [Mosby] but if they did they shared the proceeds if anything was captured." Trammell attempted to defend himself against the armed robbery charge. But as historian James A. Ramage observes, he failed to realize the case hinged on Binns's testimony regarding the legality of Mosby's command. The commission affirmed that Trammell was one of Mosby's "guerrilla force," which was "not a regularly organized military force." The court found him guilty and sentenced him to be shot.[14]

Reviewing the case, Holt concurred that Mosby's men were illegal guerrillas, setting a standard by which three more members of the Forty-Third would be tried that summer. Although President Lincoln agreed to commute several of the sentences to ten years in the Albany penitentiary, the Confederate government insisted that Mosby's was a sanctioned partisan unit. These debates would continue through the war (indeed, they continue in the literature today). But such arguments miss the key point: the malleable definitions of irregulars provided a strategy for the US military to utilize the laws of war and wage battle by another means.[15]

Holt's attempts to try Mosby's men as guerrillas proved short-lived. In late July, Robert M. Harrover of Washington, DC, faced the commission charged with avoiding conscription and joining Mosby's "irregular and unlawful band of Guerrillas." Harrover called as one of his witnesses a Union colonel who had been held as a prisoner by Mosby for seven days. The colonel testified that his son was a member of Mosby's command who had been mustered into service like all the rangers. He likewise confirmed that they were paid just like all Virginia cavalrymen. His testimony swayed several members of the commission who noted that the judge advocate had "failed to prove Mosby's band an irregular organization as charged."[16] Even though Harrover was found guilty on the charge of draft evasion, Holt's legal argument regarding the status of Mosby's unit appeared to be unraveling.

Moreover, the guilty verdicts and the execution of one of his men by a commission failed to dissuade Mosby. Indeed, his command continued to harass and frustrate Union troops with great effect.[17] Upon taking command of the new Army of the Shenandoah in August 1864, Maj. Gen. Philip Sheridan ordered his army to rid the Shenandoah Valley and northern Virginia of as many of Mosby's gang as possible. Despite Sheridan's determined efforts, including creating a special force under Capt. Richard Blazer tasked solely with capturing or killing Mosby and his men, the raids continued. Grant, who had been bedeviled by guerrillas and partisans during his time in Missouri, proved equally as frustrated as Sheridan. If the combination of cavalry patrols and military commissions had failed to deter them, Grant suggested the Union should deploy even harsher methods. "The families of most of Mosby's men are known, and can be collected," he instructed. "I think they should be taken and kept at Fort McHenry, or some secure place, as hostages for the good conduct of Mosby and his men. Where any of Mosby's men are caught *hang them without trial.*" Grant tempered his instructions in a second letter to

Sheridan ordering him instead to arrest all men under fifty and hold them as prisoners. But his message was clear: Mosby's men needed to be stopped.[18]

Perhaps some members of Sheridan's command had not received the second message. Or perhaps their anger could not be contained. On October 4, cavalry general William H. Powell had two "bushwhackers" shot to death in retaliation for the murder of a Union soldier who had been found with his throat slashed from ear to ear. A week later, upon learning of the "willful and cold-blooded murder" of another Union soldier by two members of Mosby's "gang of cut-throats and robbers," Powell ordered the execution of one of Mosby's men whom he had captured. Strung from a tree, he died with a placard upon his breast reading "A. C. Willis, member of Company C, Mosby's command, hanged by the neck in retaliation for the murder of a U.S. soldier."[19]

By November, the situation reached a fevered pitch when Maj. Gen. George A. Custer ordered six of Mosby's men hanged in Front Royal, Virginia, after they killed several Union prisoners of war. Bloody retaliation spawned an even bloodier counterretaliation, with Mosby selecting seven prisoners from Custer's command to execute in return. Although only four of the Federals died, the cycle of retaliation continued. Sheridan would take the war to Mosby's home territory, burning hundreds of barns and outbuildings as well as seizing hundreds of cattle and horses in a mere week. "The task was not a pleasant one," a Union cavalry captain admitted, "for many innocents were made to suffer with the guilty, but something was necessary to clear the country of the bands of Guerrillas that were becoming so formidable."[20]

Amid the escalating retaliations, the trials of Mosby's men had ended. Perhaps the testimony in Harrover's case regarding the legitimacy of Mosby's men had discouraged the commissions. Perhaps it was because the military's star witness, Charles Binns, had been arrested for murder in November and awaited a trial of his own. Or maybe it was because the trials not only failed to deter Mosby but may have motivated him. (In September, the Confederate agent of exchange, Robert Ould, had warned that "prompt and efficient measures of retaliation will be taken" if those convicted by the commission were not released.)[21] Whatever the reason, by March 1865, the Federal government held more than 180 members of the Forty-Third Virginia Battalion as prisoners of war treated not unlike other Confederate soldiers.[22] Not until McCue's capture would the Union again attempt to fight Mosby's men in the halls of military justice rather than on the field of battle.

On the night of March 25, 1865, McCue and several others from the command slipped across the Potomac River from Westmoreland County,

Virginia, into St. Mary's County, Maryland, in what he would later claim was a scouting expedition with instructions to raid the post office. From there, they stole several horses before heading northwest into Prince George's County, not far from Washington, DC, where three of the party deserted. Late in the evening on April 3, the three remaining men agreed to seize any mail they could find at the US Post Office located inside John Coffron's store in the small village of Croom. Placing a pistol at Coffron's temple, they demanded his money before ransacking the store. Moments later, Coffron's brother, Jeremiah, alongside Richard N. Ryan, a Union army detective in the area to arrest draft resisters, burst through the door and commenced firing. At the first volley, McCue's comrades fled into the woods. Unable to escape, McCue fired his cavalry pistol, hitting Jeremiah Coffron in the shoulder and leveling a mortal shot to Ryan's stomach. By the morning of April 5, McCue found himself in a Baltimore jail, where he was charged with murder and operating as a guerrilla.[23]

Four days later, Lee surrendered his army to Grant at Appomattox Court House. The terms Grant offered Lee were intended to be pragmatic and bring about a swift end to the war. Officially prisoners of war, officers and men of the Army of Northern Virginia would be allowed to return to their homes "not to be disturbed by U.S. authority so long as they observe their paroles and the laws in force where they may reside." When Secretary Stanton asked Grant the following day whether the terms applied to all of Lee's army or only to those with him at Appomattox, the general responded that he believed they should extend to "all the fragments of the Army of Northern Virginia."[24] If it meant ending the war sooner rather than later, Grant would be as generous as possible.

In the days and weeks that followed, Union provost marshals paroled thousands of those who had served in detached units, fallen out of the lines during the retreat, or escaped the surrender site.[25] But there was an exception: John S. Mosby. Stanton had initially instructed commanders in the field that "the guerrilla chief Mosby will under no consideration be paroled."[26] When Stanton consulted Grant about this decision on the afternoon of April 10, however, the general-in-chief had other thoughts. Recognizing the potential threat that Confederate irregulars still posed, Grant informed Stanton that Mosby should be offered the same terms of surrender and parole.[27]

Grant's position could hardly have been more different from his stance the previous August when he had ordered Sheridan to execute Mosby's men without trial (later retracted). But with Lee's capitulation, Grant hoped that all rebels, including the partisan rangers, would soon lay down their guns.

No Union general had been able to eliminate the partisan threat in Virginia. If the cycles of retaliation continued with Mosby and other guerrillas, even with the surrender of the main armies the war might never end. Indeed, earlier that day Union officials reported that some of Mosby's men had crossed the Blue Ridge with intentions of capturing and plundering Union wagon trains south of Winchester, another company had been sent to Maryland on a raid, while yet another battalion had attempted to steal US horses and mules in Fairfax County. This continued threat necessitated that Mosby and his men be compelled to surrender as quickly as possible.[28]

Grant's fears were not unfounded. Fleeing Richmond in early April, Confederate president Jefferson Davis had suggested that the struggle might enter "a new phase" that resembled partisan warfare. Although Lee repeatedly dismissed the idea out of hand, even some regular Confederate soldiers insisted that they might continue the fight by any means necessary. Cavalry officers Thomas Rosser and Thomas Munford, both of whom had escaped the Union cordon at Appomattox on April 9 and refused to capitulate, offered to lead their men onward despite Lee's surrender. "If we are true to ourselves and to honor," Rosser proclaimed only days later, "we can never abandon a cause we have so nobly sustained for the last four years."[29] The threat of irregular, partisan war had not ended at Appomattox.

On April 12, even as Lee's regular infantry prepared for the formal surrender ceremony at Appomattox, in Baltimore Brig. Gen. William W. Morris, who had been particularly incensed by the number of returning Confederates sailing into the harbor each day, ordered charges brought against John McCue "as soon as possible." He conveyed no sense that Lee's capitulation marked the end of the war.[30] Two weeks later, a military commission led by Col. S. M. Bowman, former commander of the Eighty-Fourth Pennsylvania, convened in Baltimore to try McCue. The US government charged McCue, "a guerrilla of the so-called Southern Confederacy," with three counts: (1) the murder of US Detective Richard Ryan with malice aforethought and the assault and attempted murder of a citizen, Jeremiah Coffron; (2) violating paragraph 86 of General Orders No. 100 in passing within the lines of the US Army in Maryland "for the purpose of robbing and plundering loyal and peaceful citizens"; and (3) violating paragraph 83 of General Orders No. 100 by robbing and plundering the store of John W. Coffron with a loaded pistol (an action clearly outside the bounds of the laws of war). McCue pleaded not guilty to all three counts.[31]

While McCue awaited his fate in a Baltimore jail, Mosby decided to disband rather than surrender his rangers.[32] On April 21, he summoned his men to an open field just north of Salem, Virginia, where he released them from their duty. While a handful elected to travel with their colonel south in hopes of continuing the war, the great majority of his men rode northwest to the Union garrison at Winchester. By the evening of April 22, at least 380 rangers and most of the officers had been paroled, including Mosby's second in command (and McCue's commanding officer), Lt. Col. William H. Chapman.[33]

Five days later, the commission proceedings against McCue opened in Baltimore. He would have been hard-pressed to find a city where the Union command, led by Maj. Gen. Lew Wallace, proved more hostile to rebels. The three weeks since his arrest had witnessed an unimaginable tide of events and emotions. Only a week after Unionists had reveled in the news of Lee's capitulation and rejoiced that peace might finally arrive, the actor John Wilkes Booth had assassinated President Lincoln, leading to calls for vengeance. Not only was Baltimore home to Booth (a noncombatant who had acted instead of donning a uniform), but the outpouring of Confederate sympathies had led the Republican Wallace to seek out any rebel who dared enter the city. Grant had helped slow the tide by forbidding former Confederates, including those who had been paroled, from passing through loyal states and ordering those who failed to comply to be detained. By late April, Wallace had implemented the orders with enthusiasm. Hundreds and possibly thousands of paroled Confederates passing through the region had been detained in local jails. Moreover, loyal civilians took matters into their own hands. Hoping to purge their communities of traitors, groups of Unionists in counties throughout eastern Maryland formed committees of vigilance and safety, pledging to arrest any returning rebel soldiers and turn them over to the authorities.[34]

Meeting amid this atmosphere, the military commission had two issues before it. The first was jurisdiction. Did it have the right to try McCue by military commission? If so, then the question became the substantive charge of murder. The judge advocate pressed witnesses, including John Coffron and Captain Curry, to recall whether McCue had acted alone, stolen horses, pilfered goods from the store, fired the first shot, and confessed to killing Detective Ryan. All agreed that he had.[35]

McCue never denied that he killed Ryan but argued that the commission did not have jurisdiction (although he never used the legal term) to try him. If he was acting under the orders of his superior officers, "no matter what occurred, no matter who he may have killed or what difficulty may have arisen," he was protected by the laws of war and could not be found guilty of murder. (Conversely, even a legitimate soldier could commit murder if he did so without orders.) He might be held as a prisoner of war, but as a legitimate soldier, he could not be tried by a military commission. In his cross-examination of the prosecution's witnesses, therefore, he pressed them to admit that he had consistently declared himself one of Mosby's men who wore a "rebel gray" uniform, which they did.[36]

Not convinced that he had made his point decisively, after the prosecution closed, McCue and his counsel submitted a request to secure the testimony of witnesses on his behalf. Chief among them was Chapman, Mosby's second in command who could affirm that McCue was a member of the unit acting under his authority. Also called from the Forty-Third were Lt. John Russell, commander of McCue's company who had been paroled alongside Chapman on April 23; Boyd Smith, most likely not paroled but who had been serving in the vicinity of the raid; and Abraham Wilson, a member of McCue's company and possibly one of the men who had been with McCue at Croom. He asked that his father, John H. McCue, a prisoner of war at Fort Delaware, be summoned. McCue insisted that each could testify that he was regularly enlisted in the Confederate army. Finally, he requested the presence of Nicholas J. (N. J.) Watkins, a Maryland resident and Confederate deserter now imprisoned in Baltimore.[37]

The commission agreed to consider McCue's request. As one member observed, if McCue succeeded in establishing that he was acting under orders, "then no matter what resistance he met with . . . it is now one of the principles of Military Law that he had a right to resist it." This was the crucial point: if McCue had been one of Mosby's men *and* acting under orders, the commission would not have jurisdiction and would have to drop the charges and release him.[38]

As the nation turned its attention to the trial of the Lincoln conspirators, which began in Washington on May 10, McCue waited for his witnesses to prove he was in fact carrying out orders as a soldier. Despite a summons from Gen. Winfield Scott Hancock in command at Winchester, William Chapman and the other members of the Forty-Third Virginia Battalion failed to appear. Such an absence is both noteworthy and curious. After all, it had been Chapman, Mosby's second in command, who had met with Hancock to discuss terms of a potential surrender of Mosby's command. After Mosby elected to disband his unit on April 21 rather than surrender it, Chapman had ridden with more than 300 other rangers to Winchester, where he again met with Hancock and secured paroles for his men. There he informed the provost marshal that he was headed toward Fauquier County, where his wife resided (although he may have returned to his father's home in Page County). He was most likely somewhere in northern Virginia in May as McCue's trial began, but Hancock could not locate him. He may have been keeping a low profile as Mosby remained a fugitive with a bounty on his head. Perhaps he feared that he would be become embroiled in the manhunt for his former commander. Neither did Russell, Smith, or Wilson show.[39]

Without their testimony, Johnnie McCue relied on that of his family. Arriving from his cell at Fort Delaware and questioned by his son on May 10, the senior McCue affirmed his son's account of conscription into the Eighteenth Virginia Cavalry and subsequent service with Mosby, explaining that the Forty-Third Virginia Battalion was "always regarded as a portion of the Army of Northern Virginia directly under the command of Gen'l Lee."[40] But upon cross-examination, the judge advocate asked why his son had never secured proper transfer papers to Mosby's command and what inducements had led his son to join the rangers. The senior McCue admitted that Mosby's men were not subject to the same rigid military discipline as regular units. "They were mounted men which to the Southern youth has always been a great desideration," he noted. "In addition to that the proceeds of whatever was captured from the Federal troops was[,] as has already appeared, divided among them, I understood." When asked if Mosby's command occupied a different footing from those in the regular service, he conceded that in those respects, it did.[41]

There was one more witness whom Johnnie McCue had called who failed to testify—one who could have easily appeared if the commission had so desired: N. J. Watkins. Even as McCue's commission closed its proceedings on May 12, Watkins remained in a Baltimore jail awaiting his own trial. Federal pickets had captured Watkins on April 6. Brought to the same Captain Curry who had arrested McCue just days prior, Watkins was charged with rendering aid to enemies of the United States by accompanying several "soldiers in the said Confederate army disguised and not in uniform" across the Potomac River on the night of March 30 and murdering Ryan "in conjunction with John W. McCue." Although General Wallace ordered a commission established to try Watkins in mid-May, the trial did not begin until June 6, just as the Lincoln conspirators' trial was concluding (with Wallace serving on the commission), and more significantly after McCue's trial.

Whatever the reason for the delay, during Watkins's trial the commission focused much of its attention on McCue. Watkins admitted crossing the Potomac with McCue and two or three other rebel soldiers (whom, like McCue, he never named). But he denied he was a member of Mosby's command or had participated in Ryan's murder. If the commission was hoping to find evidence of McCue's accomplices or proof that he did *not* belong to Mosby's command, they were disappointed. Instead, a witness testified that McCue had indicated the party was composed of "Chapman's men" who had been "sent up on a raid." On June 8 the commission found Watkins not guilty of all charges and released him from jail.[42]

Most other Confederate prisoners soon followed. On June 6, President Andrew Johnson followed Grant's advice and ordered the discharge of rebel prisoners of war. All enlisted men and officers not exceeding the rank of captain would be released upon taking the oath of allegiance—including all of Mosby's men. Only those standing trial for Lincoln's assassination, captured with Jefferson Davis, or who had broken their paroles were to be detained.[43] On June 16, the senior McCue took the oath of loyalty at Fort Delaware and boarded a steamer bound for Virginia.[44] Even as his father headed home, the young McCue still awaited his fate from the confines of a Baltimore city jail. Johnson's order did not apply to those facing military commissions for murder—especially alleged guerrillas.

Finally, on July 11, nearly two months after McCue's trial concluded, he learned the verdict in his case: guilty on all three counts, with the exception that malice aforethought had been dropped in the murder charge. The commission sentenced him to imprisonment and hard labor for life. His sentence confirmed by General Wallace, McCue boarded a steamer bound for Clinton Prison in New York.[45]

McCue was not the only alleged guerrilla to face a military commission in the weeks and months after Lee's surrender. Between April and October 1865, at least fifty-eight other individuals from Kentucky to Mississippi were tried by military commissions as guerrillas, most charged with murder. Of those, forty-four were found guilty. As with McCue, the commissions sentenced most of these men to hard labor. Seventeen, however, received death sentences. Ten were fortunate to have their sentences commuted, a common practice by commissions during the war. Still, seven were executed for their crimes.[46] Most famous among them was Champ Ferguson, a Kentucky native whose most atrocious killing occurred at Saltville, Virginia, in October 1864, when his band scoured the field after the battle executing wounded Union soldiers, especially African Americans. Captured in May, his trial received much national attention, as did his execution in October. But others also died for their barbaric tactics, including Cyrus Chappel, executed by firing squad at Little Rock on April 21; Henry Turner, hanged at Louisville on July 21; and John Bishop, hanged in Lexington, Kentucky, on August 18.[47]

Most of these men, however, either had been especially notorious characters, such as Ferguson, or had committed their crimes *after* Appomattox.

McCue, however, was an unknown nineteen-year-old. He had committed murder but prior to what most observed as the close of the war. Why had the commission remained so intent on charging McCue, finding him guilty, and sentencing him to life when the war seemed to be ending? He had not learned the verdict until early July, by which time Johnson had issued his amnesty proclamation pardoning most Confederates and ordered Northern prisons cleared, which included hundreds of McCue's comrades in the Forty-Third Virginia Battalion. Even Mosby had surrendered and received a parole in June. Only rebels who had committed crimes *after* being paroled, Confederate government officials (the vice president, cabinet secretaries, and governors), and those who had aided Jefferson Davis's escape remained imprisoned by Union authorities in July.

It appears that McCue was decidedly unfortunate in the location and timing of his apprehension. As already noted, the high command of Baltimore remained determined to quash all rebel sentiment in Maryland even weeks after Appomattox. Moreover, McCue could not have predicted Lincoln's assassination or the role it might play in his own case. McCue would serve as an example for Radical Republicans like Wallace and Holt who insisted that rebels pay for their crimes, especially those whose legitimacy as belligerents might be called into question. If most Confederates would escape punishment for their experiment in rebellion, following through on the punishment for wartime crimes might send a stern message to any not ready to fully capitulate.[48]

Throughout the summer, McCue and his family insisted that he was a member of Mosby's command and, as such, a regular Confederate soldier who should be released like most other prisoners of war. Having returned from prison, on July 13 the senior John McCue picked up his pen to write Robert E. Lee (who had been indicted by a grand jury in early June for treason at the insistence of President Johnson). Making much the same case as had his son during the trial, he explained that it was "important that I show what the military status of Col. Mosby and his command was." Because former Confederates lacked access to any records to prove the case, he believed a statement from Lee might convince Union authorities that Mosby's men were indeed legitimate soldiers who should be afforded the protections of the laws of war. "You will please state," he asked, "under and by virtue of what authority his [Mosby's] command, was organized? Was it a part of the Army of Northern Virginia and thus subject to your order?"[49] Within two weeks, he received Lee's reply. The general had not heard about McCue's situation, but he confirmed that Mosby's regiment was "regularly organized under the laws of the Confederate Congress" and governed by the same laws as every other unit in his army. Given these facts and Johnson's recent decision to release all rebel prisoners confined by sentence of military commissions, McCue's son might soon return home.[50]

Convinced that Grant might prove a more productive ally, Signora McCue wrote to the general-in-chief a few days later. Flattering the general for his "proverbial kindness and humanity to the soldiers of the late Confederate States, and great liberality to all, whether citizens or soldiers," she asked him to help secure a pardon for her son. After relaying the details of his capture, she explained that her son was a soldier who had been following orders when he killed Ryan. Wasn't the war over, she asked? Were not other Confederates being released from Northern prisons? Invoking maternal devotion, she asked Grant whether her "beloved and noble son may like wise have his shackles broken, and permitted once more to enjoy the blessings of liberty... and return to the bosom of an almost crushed and heart broken mother, whose sacred honor is pledged that henceforth he shall be an upright and law abiding citizen." Although Grant received the letter, there is no evidence that he responded.[51]

Even as his parents rushed off letters to Lee and Grant, their friends and family began lobbying President Johnson to pardon young McCue. In late July, residents of Lynchburg as well as Nelson and Augusta Counties signed petitions testifying to the character of both McCue and his family and echoing the common refrain of the legitimacy of Mosby's command. Whatever Union forces might have thought of the Forty-Third Battalion, Mosby's men "were recognized here as a regularly constituted military organization, having all the sanction as belligerents that could be given by the Confederate Government." The Nelson County residents reminded Johnson that as a member of the battalion, McCue "was acting under the command of officers who had the power to punish him, and whose orders he was bound to obey." If the war still raged, the US government might deny belligerent rights to suppress a command such as Mosby's. But the petitioners pointed out that most everyone agreed that the war was over and that most of Mosby's command had been granted paroles and many had availed themselves of the amnesty and pardon offered by the president. They had been fully pardoned and restored to all their social and political rights. Even Mosby had been paroled as a prisoner of war and claimed the benefits of amnesty. But having only followed orders, McCue faced a life sentence. "The officer who commanded those men who accompanied McCue on the expedition for which he is now punished have all been covered by the broad mantle of Executive clemency," the petition observed, "while he remains a convicted felon, a youth of eighteen years condemned to a life-long imprisonment." By late summer, more than 2,000 had affixed their names to the mass-produced petitions.[52]

In his continued efforts to secure his son's release, the senior McCue headed to Baltimore and Washington in late September, where he hoped to find any who might assist him. Well into October, he met with a variety of individuals and dashed off letters to loyal Unionists as well as ex-Confederates asking for their support. He convinced prominent Virginians such as William C. Rives, John B. Baldwin, and Alexander Rives to write the president beseeching a pardon. Even several Virginia Unionists, including John Minor Botts, B. Johnson Barbour, and Alexander H. H. Stuart, composed letters to Johnson on his son's behalf.[53]

Had Johnnie McCue not been so well connected, he likely would not have received such support. But more importantly, his advocates clearly did not find his act of killing Ryan a crime. Not only did most insist that as one of Mosby's men he was a regular Confederate soldier, but even the Unionists who supported him at least implied that they believed Mosby's command had been composed of legitimate soldiers. These Unionists understood that punishing such soldiers (beyond the egregious examples such as Champ Ferguson) after the surrender of Confederate armies was politically unwise and potentially detrimental to the cause of reunion.[54]

Seemingly exhausting his options, the elder McCue turned to his cousin and former general, John Imboden, asking him to reach out to the president of the commission that had tried his son, Col. S. M. Bowman. Traveling to New York in mid-October, Imboden, who had practiced law before the war, met with Bowman to ascertain his willingness to assist in McCue's case. Bowman agreed that the sentence had been harsh and indicated he would write a letter that McCue's father could present to President Johnson.

In his letter, Bowman raised the matter of jurisdiction, expressing his "grave doubts" about the "justice and policy" of trying McCue by military commission. The colonel believed McCue had received a fair trial, so far as it was possible "before a court composed of chiefly young officers not one of whom (except myself) had ever read a law book and knew but little about any system of jurisprudence, had never set [sic] on a jury, and probably never witnessed the trial of a case in court." Most important, he pointed out that McCue's trial had taken place just after Lincoln's assassination. "The temper of the country was averse to anything like leniency," he observed. "His principal crime," Bowman declared, "was that which pertains to a rebel."[55]

What Bowman argued was just as important as what he failed to address: McCue's status as a soldier. His missive to Johnson said nothing about

Mosby's command. Bowman had described Johnnie as a "daredevil boy" (much to Imboden's chagrin), but he had not explicitly engaged in the debate as to whether the young man was a guerrilla. Instead, he had focused on the atmosphere of the hour and the justice conferred by a commission composed of military officers rather than jurists. Indeed, Bowman recommended that the proceedings should be set aside and McCue remanded to the civil authorities in Maryland for a trial.[56] Military commissions had been a useful tool to be deployed against enemy belligerents during war, but in the aftermath of surrender they might not prove politically expedient.

Upon receipt of Bowman's letter, the senior McCue promptly took it to Grant at the War Department. His wife had written the general-in-chief back in July but had received no response. Now, Grant read Bowman's statement and nodded in agreement. Folding the letter, he affixed his endorsement: "I do not doubt that during the heat of the War much has been done under excitement, that would not otherwise have occurred. I deem it advisable to clear our prisons so far as possible of prisoners for mil[itary] Offenses, and if deemed advisable would recommend clemency in this case."[57] Like Bowman, Grant refused to engage the question of whether McCue had been a legitimate soldier protected by the laws of war.

With Grant's endorsement, John H. McCue forwarded Bowman's statement to President Johnson. In a separate letter, McCue recounted the details of the case and the sentence before reminding the president of the long list of prominent Virginians who had written in support of his son's character. And then he picked up the argument deployed by Bowman and Grant—the passions and vitriol following Lincoln's assassination had led to an unfair trial. The only reference to his son's status as a soldier appeared in a line referring to a separate letter from Imboden to the president.[58] Arguing that his son was not a guerrilla had proved unsuccessful—now he hoped to rely on the spirit of magnanimity and peace to assure the younger McCue's release.

Johnson was not convinced and forwarded the application to Judge Advocate General Holt for consideration. Not surprisingly, on October 24, the same day Grant offered his endorsement, Holt rejected the petition. Trying Mosby's men as guerrillas by military commissions had been his strategy in 1864. Once more, he argued that "Mosby's Corps" was "no regular organization, that is members were never mustered into it, but joined in and absented themselves from it at pleasure, receiving no pay, but living on the plunder obtained from wagon trains, by horse stealing, and robbing peaceful citizens." McCue had been assigned to the Eighteenth Virginia Cavalry, Holt observed, but "by refusing to join a regularly organized regiment, the man refused to become a regular soldier, and by his choice becoming a guerrilla, should be regarded in no different light from any other member of that lawless band, with which he seems proud to claim connection." Even if he was a member of this "highway band," there was no evidence that McCue had been under orders when he murdered Ryan. Not hesitating to get in a parting shot at the general-in-chief who had proven magnanimous toward the rebels since the surrender, Holt quipped that "the endorsement of Grant was probably obtained by the gross misrepresentations, and unexampled audacity, in which the whole case abounds." The court had already been lenient. McCue, Holt insisted, had no claim to clemency.[59]

By early November 1865, the great multitude of Confederates had reclaimed their status as citizens of the United States. Most had been pardoned by Johnson's May 29 amnesty act, and thousands more had been granted individual pardons. Most returned to the daily grind of work, even as Southern whites turned their attentions toward implementing new laws such as Black Codes that would ensure white social and political dominance in the wake of emancipation. Nevertheless, Johnnie McCue remained imprisoned. And still his father sought his release. Virginia Unionist John Minor Botts again wrote to Johnson pointing out the absurdity of the case. Others far guiltier than McCue, including governors, state legislators, and members of Congress, were enjoying the "rewards of the multitude," he observed. "Why then should this young soldier, acting in obedience to the orders of his superiors, & in the discharge of his duties which he felt himself to obey, be [subjected to] this harsh & cruel sentence?" he asked.[60] In one last effort, Grant agreed to accompany McCue's parents to visit Johnson, allegedly telling the president he would not leave until a pardon had been signed. Once more, Grant would defend his lenient choice on not punishing traitors in the name of reunion.[61] On November 8, Johnson complied. Johnnie McCue would head home.[62]

Throughout the summer and fall of 1865, the McCues had enlisted a prestigious roster of individuals to petition for their son's release. Lee, Grant, prominent Virginia Unionists, more than 2,000 petitioners, and even the president of the military commission that convicted McCue had asked Johnson to pardon the convicted rebel. Yet John S. Mosby and his officers were never forced to testify. By midsummer, both Mosby and Chapman were residing in Fauquier County. And Union officials were aware of Mosby's whereabouts after he appeared in Alexandria in August, causing quite the local stir.[63] But no one appeared to want or seek Mosby's help.

Perhaps that was for the best. After all, John W. McCue was freed not because the United States finally recognized that he was a regular soldier (as opposed to a guerrilla) who would be excused for killing and looting if under orders from a superior officer. Nor was he freed on a legal decision regarding whether the commission had jurisdiction in the case. Instead, his release had been secured solely because of Grant's intercession. The Union army had attempted to harness military justice in 1864 to curtail Mosby, but with the threat of guerrilla warfare abated, Grant was looking toward the future rather than to the past when he pressed for McCue's release. In the name of ending the war (and no doubt stopping the flood of pleas from McCue's friends and family), Grant would be magnanimous once more.

The case of John W. McCue was not an aberration but part of a larger, albeit ineffective, strategy aimed at fighting partisans through the system of military justice. His trial and conviction and the subsequent petitions for his release underscored the ways in which the military, politics, and the law all shaped one another throughout the war. Most importantly, his case illustrated how Union authorities strategically deployed both the specter of punishment through military commissions and magnanimity when appropriate, all in the name of ending the war.

NOTES

I would like to thank Cynthia Nicoletti, Peter Carmichael, Kathryn Shively, and Aaron Sheehan-Dean for their helpful comments on earlier drafts of this essay.

1. Provost Marshal Curry, Capt. 4th Delaware Vol., to Col. F. D. Sewall [?], Commanding Milt. Dist. of Annapolis, April 5, 1865, John W. McCue Compiled Service Record, National Archives and Record Administration, Washington, DC, accessed through Fold3.com (hereafter CSR); John W. McCue to Col. and Mrs. Sepps, September 1866, Papers of the McCue Family, MSS 4406, box 1, Small Special Collections, University of Virginia, Charlottesville (hereafter UVA); Testimony of McCue Commission in McCue and Martin Family Papers, MSS 6806-d, UVA. A slightly different account of events appeared in the *Evening Star* (Washington, DC), April 6, 1865. I would like to thank Nau Center intern Lilly Snodgrass for transcribing the commission trial.

2. As Gary Gallagher has noted, "Guerrillas did not play a major role in shaping the military outcome of the Civil War," but their "activities should not be ignored." Gary W. Gallagher, *The Enduring Civil War: Reflections on the Great American Crisis* (Baton Rouge: Louisiana State University Press, 2020), 34–35. His reflection comes in response to a growing body of literature that argues that the totality of the war cannot be understood without exploring guerrilla warfare. See, for example, Daniel E. Sutherland, *A Savage Conflict: The Decisive Role of Guerrillas in the American Civil War* (Chapel Hill: University of North Carolina Press, 2009); Mark Grimsley, *The Hard Hand of War: Union Military Policy toward Southern Civilians, 1861–1865* (Cambridge: Cambridge University Press, 1995); Michael Fellman, *Inside War: The Guerrilla Conflict in Missouri during the American Civil War* (New York: Oxford University Press, 1989); Barton A. Myers, *Executing Daniel Bright: Race, Loyalty, and Guerrilla*

Violence in a Coastal Carolina Community, 1861–1865 (Baton Rouge: Louisiana State University Press, 2009); Clay Mountcastle, *Punitive War: Confederate Guerrillas and Union Reprisals* (Lawrence: University Press of Kansas, 2009); Matthew M. Stith, *Extreme Civil War: Guerrilla Warfare, Environment, and Race on the Trans-Mississippi Frontier* (Baton Rouge: Louisiana State University Press, 2016); and Aaron Sheehan-Dean, *The Calculus of Violence: How Americans Fought the Civil War* (Cambridge, MA: Harvard University Press, 2018).

3. On the notion of the South as conquered but not vanquished, see Caroline E. Janney, *Ends of War: The Unfinished Fight of Lee's Army after Appomattox* (Chapel Hill: University of North Carolina Press, 2021).

4. Virginia Military Institute Archives Historical Rosters for John Willis McCue, Roster ID 2955, Virginia Military Institute, Lexington; Otelia McCue to Father (John H. McCue), October 14, 1865, Papers of the McCue Family, MSS 4406, box 5, UVA.

5. Confederate Citizens file for John W. McCue, accessed through Fold3.com; John H. McCue, CSR.

6. John Imboden to John H. McCue, November 1, 1865, Papers of the McCue, Martin, and Perry Families, MSS 6806-b, box 2, UVA; McCue Courts-Martial Files, MM2302, entry 15, Record Group (hereafter RG) 153, National Archives and Record Administration, Washington, DC (hereafter NARA); John W. McCue, CSR.

7. Sutherland, *Savage Conflict*, 166, 238–39, 242–45.

8. The Lieber Code deals with prisoners of war in section 3. For scholarly discussions, see John Fabian Witt, *Lincoln's Code: The Laws of War in American History* (New York: Free Press, 2012), 4, 13–14, 232; and Stephen C. Neff, *Justice in Blue and Gray: A Legal History of the Civil War* (Cambridge, MA: Harvard University Press, 2010), 22, 82–86. On the laws of war, see Cynthia Nicoletti, *Secession on Trial: The Treason Prosecution of Jefferson Davis* (New York: Cambridge University Press, 2017).

9. US War Department, *The War of the Rebellion: A Compilation of the Official Records of the Union and Confederate Armies*, 127 vols., index, and atlas (Washington, DC: Government Printing Office, 1880–1901) (hereafter *OR*), ser. 3, 2:301–9.

10. *OR*, ser. 3, 2:304; Sheehan-Dean, *Calculus of Violence*, 183–84. Articles 81 and 82 of the Lieber Code deal with partisans.

11. Sheehan-Dean, *Calculus of Violence*, 73–77; Witt, *Lincoln's Code*, 385.

12. James A. Ramage, *Gray Ghost: The Life of Col. John Singleton Mosby* (Lexington: University Press of Kentucky, 1999), 252–53. For more on Holt and military commissions, see Mark E. Neely Jr., *The Fate of Liberty: Abraham Lincoln and Civil Liberties* (New York: Oxford University Press, 1991), 162–75.

13. William Winthrop, *Military Law and Precedents*, 2nd ed. (Washington, DC: W. H. Morrison, 1920), 49, 54, 103–4, 165–66; Gideon M. Hart, "Military Commissions and the Lieber Code: Toward a New Understanding of the Jurisdictional Foundations of Military Commissions," in *Military Law Review* 203 (Spring 2010): 15–17; Neff, *Justice*, 158–59; Sheehan-Dean, *Calculus of Violence*, 244, 416n33; Witt, *Lincoln's Code*, 267–68; Neely, *Fate of Liberty*, 168.

14. Ramage, *Gray Ghost*, 254–56, quotes on pp. 254, 255. In July, Lincoln commuted Trammell's sentence to ten years in prison, as he did the subsequent cases.

15. Ramage, *Gray Ghost*, 254–56, quotes on pp. 254, 255. Ramage, for example, agrees that Mosby's men "were illegal guerrillas." The other rangers convicted included John H. "Jack" Barnes, Robert M. Harrover, and Charles F. Beavers.

16. Ramage, *Gray Ghost*, 257. Harrover was still found guilty on the charge of violating his draft registration and sentenced to be shot, although he escaped Old Capitol Prison.

17. Bruce Catton, *A Stillness at Appomattox* (Garden City, NY: Doubleday, 1953), 57, 282–83. The need to guard against Mosby meant that Sheridan frequently diverted troops from the Union army in the Valley. Ramage, *Gray Ghost*, 186.

18. Neely, *Fate of Liberty*, 79; *OR*, ser. 1, 43(1):811; Ramage, *Gray Ghost*, 186–93, 223–24 (emphasis added).

19. *OR*, ser. 1, 43(1):508–10; Ramage, *Gray Ghost*, 212. For more on how Union and Confederate armies approached retaliation, see Sheehan-Dean, *Calculus of Violence*; and Lorien Foote, *Rites of Retaliation: Civilization, Soldiers, and Campaigns in the American Civil War* (Chapel Hill: University of North Carolina Press, 2021).

20. Sutherland, *Savage Conflict*, 242–45; Ramage, *Gray Ghost*, 185–200.

21. *Baltimore Sun*, November 15, 1864; *OR*, ser. 2, 7:792–93.

22. Ramage, *Gray Ghost*, 232–42, 259–61. Ramage suggests that the Federals often refused to exchange Mosby's men (*Gray Ghost*, 259). But Confederate agent of exchange Ould suggested otherwise as late as March 25, 1865 (*OR*, ser. 2, 8:432).

23. John W. McCue, CSR; John W. McCue to Col. and Mrs. Sepps, September 1866, John W. McCue Papers, MSS 4406, box 1, UVA; *Baltimore Sun*, April 6, 1865. McCue described the Baltimore jail as a "negro jail."

24. Ulysses S. Grant, *The Papers of Ulysses S. Grant*, ed. John Y. Simon et al., 32 vols. (Carbondale: Southern Illinois University Press, 1967–2012), 14:380; *OR*, ser. 1, 46(3):665, 685–86.

25. For more on those who had not been at Appomattox, see Caroline E. Janney, "We Were Not Paroled: The Surrenders of Lee's Men beyond Appomattox Court House," in *Petersburg to Appomattox: The End of the War in Virginia*, ed. Caroline E. Janney (Chapel Hill: University of North Carolina Press, 2018), 192–219.

26. *OR*, ser. 1, 46(3):699.

27. *OR*, ser. 1, 46(3):685.

28. *OR*, ser. 1, 46(3):701.

29. Thomas Rosser to Veterans of the Old Dominion, broadside, April 12, 1865, Scrapbook of Betty Winston Rosser, Papers of Thomas L. Rosser and the Rosser, Gordon, and Winston Families, MSS 1171, box 2, UVA; Millard Kessler Bushong and Dean McKoin Bushong, *Fightin' Tom Rosser, C.S.A.* (Shippensburg, PA: Beidel Printing House), 182–83; Thomas L. Rosser, *Riding with Rosser*, ed. S. Roger Keller (Shippensburg, PA: Burd Street Press, 1997), 73–74; Jedediah Hotchkiss, *Make Me a Map of the Valley: The Civil War Journal of Stonewall Jackson's Topographer*, ed. Archie P. McDonald (Dallas: Southern Methodist University Press, 1973), 265 (diary entry April 10, 1865).

30. John W. McCue, CSR; Janney, *Ends of War*, 95.

31. McCue Courts-Martial Files, MM2302, entry 15, RG 153, NARA. Malice aforethought is "premeditation" or the intention to kill or harm, used to distinguish murder from unlawful killing.

32. For more on the negotiations between Mosby and Union forces requesting the surrender of his command, see Janney, *Ends of War*.

33. *OR*, ser. 1, 46(3): 897; Ramage, *Gray Ghost*, 266.

34. Witt, *Lincoln's Code*, 302. On response of Confederates returning to loyal states such as Maryland, see Janney, *Ends of War*.

35. Testimony of McCue Commission in McCue and Martin Family Papers, MSS 6806-d, folder 4, UVA. When McCue cross-examined the witnesses, he repeatedly asked whether in his confession he had insisted the pistol had fired accidentally. Most agreed that he had.

36. On jurisdiction of courts-martials and commissions, see Winthrop, *Military Law*, 81–109.

37. Testimony of McCue Commission in McCue and Martin Family Papers, MSS 6806-d, folder 4, UVA; N. J. Watkins Courts-Martial Files, MM2190, entry 15, RG 153, NARA. Milton Whitney and John Wills served as his counsel. McCue referred to Watkins as "Ellis" rather than "N. J." Watkins's trial began June 6. Watkins had been a member of the First Battery Maryland Artillery. N. J. Watkins, CSR.

38. Testimony of McCue Commission in McCue and Martin Family Papers, MSS 6806-d, folder 4, UVA.

39. Testimony of McCue Commission in McCue and Martin Family Papers, MSS 6806-d, folder 4, UVA; William H. Chapman, CSR; Peter A. Brown, *Mosby's Fighting Parson: The Life and Times of Sam Chapman* (Westminster, MD: Willow Bend Books, 2001), 235–36.

40. Testimony of McCue Commission in McCue and Martin Family Papers, MSS 6806-d, folder 4, UVA; Confederate Citizen file for John W. McCue, Fold3.com. A member of the Reserve Forces of Virginia, the forty-one-year-old had been captured by Maj. Gen. Philip Sheridan's forces at Waynesboro on March 2, 1865. Unfiled Papers and Slips Belonging in Confederate Compiled Service Records, John H. McCue, CSR. His first cousin Don P. Halsey provided similar testimony.

41. Testimony of McCue Commission in McCue and Martin Family Papers, MSS 6806-d, folder 4, UVA.

42. Watkins Courts-Martial Files, MM2190, entry 15, RG 153, NARA. He had deserted from the First Battery Maryland Artillery.

43. General Orders, No. 109, War Department, June 6, 1865, U.S. War Department, *Index of General Orders*; Charles W. Sanders, *While in the Hands of the Enemy: Military Prisons of the Civil War* (Baton Rouge: Louisiana State University, 2005), 289. The orders also included the release of those in the rebel navy not exceeding the rank of lieutenant.

44. John H. McCue, CSR.

45. McCue Courts-Martial Files, MM2302, entry 15, RG 153, NARA.

46. Tom Lowry database of courts-martial compiled from RG 153, NARA (supplied to the author by Lowry). Military commissions had sentenced more than 400 citizens to death during the war. Yet as historian Aaron Sheehan-Dean points out, less than half of those convicted found their sentences carried out. Most of those initially condemned to death had their verdicts upheld but their sentences reduced to a term of imprisonment at hard labor for five to ten years. Sheehan-Dean, *Calculus of Violence*, 244–45. Sutherland observes that "executions became rarer once the armies surrendered." Sutherland, *Savage Conflict*, 275.

47. Sutherland, *Savage Conflict*, 82–83, 229–30, 273; *New York Times*, October 24 and 25, 1865; Lowry database. George O'Bannon, a member of Mosby's command who had been paroled in May 1865, was found guilty by a military commission on June 1 for shooting a Union man in West Virginia. He was sentenced to three years' hard labor but pardoned by Johnson in 1866.

48. Neely describes a series of trials by military commissions in Louisville in April 1865 that tried men for being guerrillas but offers no analysis as to their rationale. Neely, *Fate of Liberty*, 177.

49. S. E. McCue to Lee, July 13, 1865, Papers of the McCue, Martin, and Perry Families s, MSS 6806-b, box 2, UVA. The folder indicates this letter was written by Signora McCue, but the letter references being imprisoned at Fort Delaware. Perhaps Signora drafted the letter for her husband. It is likewise unclear whether it was ever sent.

50. Robert E. Lee to John H. McCue, July 27, 1865, McCue Courts-Martial Files, MM2302, entry 15, RG 153, NARA.

51. Grant, *Papers of Ulysses S. Grant*, 15:604–5.

52. Petition from the Citizens of Nelson County, McCue Courts-Martial Files, MM2302, entry 15, RG 153, NARA; John H. McCue to Andrew Johnson, October 20, 1865, Papers of the McCue, Martin, and Perry Families, MSS 6806-b, box 2, UVA.

53. S. C. E. McCue to husband, October 5, 1865, Papers of the McCue Family, MSS 4406, box 6, UVA; McCue Courts-Martial Files, MM2302, entry 15, RG 153, NARA.

54. For a comparable example, see Matthew Christopher Hulbert's discussion of the postwar trials and acquittals of Frank James. Hulbert, "Guerrilla Veteranhood and the Double Edge of Wartime Notoriety," in *The War Went On: Reconsidering the Lives of Civil War Veterans*, ed. Brian Matthew Jordan and Evan C. Rothera (Baton Rouge: Louisiana State University Press, 2020), 81–100.

55. John Imboden, New York, to John [McCue], October 21, 1865, and S. M. Bowman to Andrew Johnson, October 20, 1865, Papers of the McCue, Martin, and Perry Families, MSS 6806-b, box 2, UVA. Bowman would not endorse a pardon for fear of the political fallout and requested the letter be certified by a notary public in case anyone tried to use his words against him.

56. *Baltimore Sun*, May 23, 1865.

57. Grant, *Papers of Ulysses S. Grant*, 15:604.

58. John H. McCue to Andrew Johnson, October 20, 1865, McCue Courts-Martial Files, MM2302, entry 15, RG 153, NARA. I'm not convinced the date is correct on this letter. Imboden met with Bowman on the night of October 19, and Grant offered his endorsement on October 24.

59. McCue Courts-Martial Files, MM2302, entry 15, RG 153, NARA.

60. John Minor Botts to Andrew Johnson, November 3, 1865, Papers of the McCue, Martin, and Perry Families, MSS 6806-b, box 2, UVA.

61. Peter A. Brown, ed., *Taking Sides with the Truth: The Postwar Letters of John Singleton Mosby to Samuel F. Chapman* (Lexington: University Press of Kentucky, 2007), 91–92. Mosby recounts this story in his memoir but never mentions McCue by name. John S. Mosby, *The Memoirs of Colonel John S. Mosby*, ed. Charles Wells Russell (Boston: Little, Brown, 1917), 389–90.

62. John H. McCue Diary entry, November 8, 1865, McCue and Martin Family Papers, MSS 6806-d, folder 2, UVA.

63. *Alexandria Gazette*, August 11, 1865.

Robert Smalls's Tax Title and the Endurance of Land Redistribution in Port Royal, South Carolina

CYNTHIA NICOLETTI

In *DeTreville v. Smalls*, an 1879 case from Port Royal, South Carolina, the Supreme Court declared that titles to land that had been sold in "insurrectionary districts" for federal tax delinquency during the Civil War would be considered presumptively valid.[1] This meant that former landowners who had lost their land for tax noncompliance would generally be unable to regain possession of that land by challenging the tax sales in court. Even if the wartime tax sales had been irregular (and they very much had been), the Court declared in *DeTreville* that it would not wrench the land back from the new purchasers: the former owners' only remedy would be (potentially) in the form of financial restitution from the government, which would have to be authorized by Congress.

On its face, the subject of the durability of tax titles might attract very little interest from Civil War historians, even from those among us who are interested in legal history. *DeTreville*, about the routine law of everyday life (tax payments and land conveyances) rather than the higher-profile topics of civil rights and the meaning of the Fourteenth Amendment, does not fit comfortably into our larger historical narrative about how the law transformed American life in the late nineteenth century. But the fate of tax titles was extremely important not only in the Port Royal area, where nearly all of the land in Beaufort County had been sold for tax delinquency, but also across the postwar South, because they were the sole legal mechanism undergirding wartime land redistribution that still remained in place by 1867. Land transfers from white plantation owners to formerly enslaved people that rested on tax sales survived the counterrevolution of Presidential Reconstruction. The durability of Black landownership secured through tax titles represented a small victory in a sea of disappointed hopes—and illustrates the crucial role of legal design, as well as waning political commitment, in explaining the ultimate demise of land redistribution in the United States.

As I have explained elsewhere, lawyers for the planter class in South Carolina worked tirelessly throughout the summer and fall of 1865 and 1866 to roll back land redistribution in the Carolina lowcountry.[2] Mobilized, organized, and ruthless, they negotiated with both the president and with members of Congress to ensure that land in government hands—and promised to the freedmen—went back to the original owners. This included the land "set aside" for Black settlement in forty-acre plots under the terms of General William T. Sherman's Special Field Orders No. 15, issued on his march through Georgia and the Carolinas in January 1865.[3] Most of the land available for freedpeople's settlement (turned over to the control of the Freedmen's Bureau by the terms of the first Freedmen's Bureau Act) had been seized from the planter class because of its designation as "abandoned property," which state executive agent William Henry Trescot believed to be an extremely flimsy legal foundation. Trescot, along with other South Carolina lawyers who acted on behalf of the state's lowcountry planters, made sure it was so. They used backroom influence with both President Andrew Johnson and select congressmen to contend that the presidential pardon, which removed the possibility of ex-Confederates' criminal liability for treason, also erased the legal basis for land seizure under the Captured and Abandoned Property Act.[4] The campaign, conducted informally through lobbying rather than litigation, was extremely successful.

By early 1867, only one type of property was still in the hands of either the federal government or the freedpeople themselves: land that had been sold for taxes owed under the federal Direct Tax Act of 1862.[5] Land sold under the terms of the Direct Tax Act was distinct from the other land transfers that Trescot and his crew were able to unwind with relative ease. The parcels had been *sold*, which marked these transfers as different in kind, because legal title had actually changed hands from seller to buyer.[6] While attacking the government's land redistribution policies through his 1865–66 lobbying campaign, Trescot had put the tax titles on the back burner because "the questions involved were of so grave and complicated a character that immediate relief was scarcely to be expected." It would take litigation rather than mere negotiation in order to challenge the legitimacy of transfers predicated on tax sales, which would be difficult. But although the transfer via sale had the veneer of legality, it was still vulnerable in a court of law. The "legislation under which this property has been sold cannot be sustained," Trescot said.[7]

Trescot turned out to be wrong, but not for want of trying. The planters' lawyers spent a decade and a half attacking the tax titles in court through a relentless and cleverly managed litigation campaign, which culminated in failure in *DeTreville v. Smalls*. The Supreme Court ultimately valued the stability of title more than anything else, refusing to entertain either constitutional objections to the Direct Tax Act (of which there were many) or complaints about the irregularity of the tax's administration (which were also legion). The case had real, tangible significance in Port Royal—where "every inch" of the occupied territory had been sold—and in a few other pockets of the South where tax sales had been conducted less systematically.[8] And once the land itself was sure to remain in the hands of Black purchasers, the planters' lawyers spent another decade trying to wrangle compensatory payments for their loss out of the hands of the federal government. Their eventual partial success in this endeavor came, ironically, due to the intervention of Congressman Robert Smalls, the leading Black politician in the state and the triumphant defendant in the *DeTreville v. Smalls* suit.[9] With the land titles (including his own) secure, Smalls did what he could to indemnify his white constituents.

In telling the story of land redistribution during the Civil War, historians have tended to characterize its failure as both quick and entirely inevitable. As Eric Foner tells us, of the 850,000 acres of Southern land held by the Freedmen's Bureau in 1865, and thus available for redistribution to Black settlers in small plots, "half" was "restored to its former owners [by mid-1866], and more was returned in subsequent years," although some restorations were "delayed by court challenges into the 1870s."[10] Much of the historiography on this topic has emphasized that land redistribution unraveled quickly because of a waning national political commitment to the utopian idea of endowing

Black Americans with land as partial recompense for their enslavement. As the Republican Congress (and the feckless President Johnson) became less and less interested in investing the freedmen with economic security and the ability to exert some negotiating power with their former enslavers in the postwar labor market, they reneged on their promises to provide quality land to freedpeople.[11]

Compounding the inevitability problem is the lack of precision with which this story is told. Historians are (understandably) much more interested in the consequences of land redistribution for Black potential recipients than for white plantation owners whose land was stripped, which has led them to ignore the legal mechanisms undergirding the transfers. It consisted of two parts: the government seizure from white landholders, and its subsequent grant of that property to landless Blacks. Legal form mattered immensely here, because only grants that could be traced back to a tax sale withstood legal challenge. The government's promises were ultimately only as secure as the legal foundation that undergirded the government's ability to terminate the previous owner's property interests. But by focusing solely on the government's default on its promises, rather than on the tug that came from legal challenges to the various bases of the land's seizure in the first place, it is very difficult to get a full picture of why and how it is that the government's promises to freedmen evaporated.

This nebulous tale of bureaucratic betrayal misses the drivers in the story: the lawyers who worked on the land issue from the end of the Civil War into the 1890s—and who approached it like lawyers. Their regressive politics meant that they opposed the idea of endowing former slaves with land, but their primary objective was to ensure the land's return to its former owners. If they accomplished that, there would be no land left for the government to grant. And they used the lawyer's toolbox to make that happen, by seeking to understand the laws that undergirded the land's seizure, sorting it into legally relevant categories, and systematically attacking where they saw vulnerabilities. They very much differentiated between land that was confiscated, abandoned, or sold for taxes, focusing on the grounds for seizure, and were thus able to shrink the pool of available land from which the government could bestow grants. Their success ran out in the *DeTreville v. Smalls* case, in which the Supreme Court upheld land transfers that were grounded in tax sales. The purchasers' victory was small, as the tax titles represented only a fraction (about one-sixth)[12] of the land initially within the control of the Freedmen's Bureau, but it was not insignificant. The tax sales had staying power.

In the early days of 1879, Representative Robert Smalls received word that he had won his case on the durability of his South Carolina tax title in the US Supreme Court. The news came just from across town, as Smalls was a lame-duck congressman, in Washington for a final few months before his replacement would be installed in his seat. Smalls, a Republican, was one of a very few Black congressmen—and he represented Port Royal, a district in the Sea Islands with a majority Black population. He was set to be replaced by a white Democrat, George Tillman, and although Smalls later won back his seat, he was dogged for the remainder of his political career by hardscrabble fights in which his opponents lobbed corruption charges at him while they themselves suppressed the Black vote through intimidation.[13]

His case was emblematic of his home region, as indeed his life was. Smalls had grown up in Port Royal, and the land at issue in *DeTreville v. Smalls* had been his boyhood home. It was a modest city house in the town of Beaufort, and Smalls had been enslaved by its previous owner, Henry McKee, who sold the house to William DeTreville sometime before the war. After a childhood spent in Port Royal, Smalls had relocated to Charleston, where McKee had hired him out and Smalls had worked as a longshoreman and boat pilot. Smalls's mastery of these seafaring skills had enabled him to seize command of the CSS *Planter* in May 1862 and sail it from Charleston into Port Royal and into Union hands—to much national acclaim. He had then served in the Union navy for the rest of the war, and he was able to parlay his wartime heroism into a successful postwar political career. By 1864, Smalls had been able to purchase the house on Prince Street for $600 from the federal government. The government's ownership had come via tax sale a year earlier, when DeTreville's $16 tax delinquency had caused the house to be sold at auction.

Smalls's fame made him exceptional, but the fact that his land title was derived from a tax sale was the norm in Port Royal. Port Royal was nearly unique in this respect, due to the region's singular position as Union-held territory during the Civil War. Crucially, it had also been devoid of Confederate civilians, who had fled the area before the arrival of the Union navy in November 1861. Port Royal was ground zero for the nation's "experiment" with freedom, creating a colony of freedpeople in the heart of the Confederacy, and it also was the staging point for accompanying wartime efforts to redistribute land from former slaveholders to former slaves.[14] To do this, the federal government had sent several tax commissioners to administer the Direct Tax Act of 1862, along with a bevy of other officials and private philanthropists to help Black Sea Islanders transition from slaves into free men, and thus to demonstrate to the skeptics of the world that such a transformation was possible.[15] Landownership was an essential part of this mission, and the direct tax was the tool by which this goal could be achieved.

The Direct Tax Act of 1862 was an amendment to the Revenue Act of the previous year, which had imposed a $20,000,000 tax on land throughout the United States. The Constitution required that direct taxes, such as those on land, be "apportioned by state, according to population," which meant that each state's citizens owed a specified amount of tax to the federal government.[16] Because the tax had not been collected in the "insurrectionary states," the 1862 act, which was aimed only at the states in rebellion, imposed a penalty for noncompliance and specified that property would be sold at auction after providing ninety days' notice of the delinquency to the taxpayer, which could be accomplished through newspaper advertisement.[17] Nominally a complicated enforcement mechanism for the logistically difficult task of collecting a federal property tax in hostile Confederate territory, the statute had been intentionally designed not to raise revenue but to ensure noncompliance and, thus, land forfeiture.[18] And so the success of the statute depended on an absent white population. There was no one to pay the tax in Port Royal because the property owners had fled. The US military was determined to keep them from coming back for the duration of the war in order to ensure the survival of the Port Royal experiment with freedom.

The South Carolina Sea Islands were not the only place where the US Direct Tax commissioners seized land for nonpayment of taxes. Indeed, the most famous instance of a tax sale was in Arlington, Virginia, where Mary Anna Custis Lee's estate was occupied and later sold for delinquent taxes to the US government, becoming the burial site for Union dead we now know as Arlington National Cemetery. Lee's noncompliance came about because she had attempted to pay her tax through a third party, but the government refused to accept it because it had not been tendered by the taxpayer directly.[19] The government was determined to ensure that Mrs. Lee (and later her son Custis) would never regain ownership of the estate, despite the Lee family's numerous legal challenges and legislative petitions to establish the illegitimacy of the forfeiture.[20] Despite the notoriety of the Arlington case, however, the Sea Islands were the site of the vast majority of tax sales conducted under the auspices of the Direct Tax Act. Tax sales occurred only sporadically in many Confederate states, as their administration required not just secure federal military control but also the creation of a robust bureaucratic apparatus in the form of tax commissioners, assessors, and surveyors. And in hostile Confederate territory, there were very few places that maintained a stable Union military presence for long enough to support a tax office.

The Direct Tax Act was remarkably effective at disgorging land from white plantation owners, but it was less so at placing the land at issue in the hands of freedpeople. In part, this was because the act was ultimately, and perhaps unfortunately, a revenue measure. Using land sales that arose out of tax noncompliance to endow impoverished people with property was at odds with the idea of raising revenue through the mechanism of taxes. Revenue officers struggled with the idea that they could not sell the land to the highest bidder at auction if they meant it to wind up in the hands of freedpeople. As a result, the tax commissioners proceeded with sales haltingly, in fits and starts, sometimes allowing land to pass into the hands of Northern land speculators, who promised, vaguely, to hold it for the benefit of the freedmen who worked it. At other times, the government itself purchased the property, with the idea of reselling it at a later date to deserving Black purchasers. Finally, some of the land did make it into the hands of former slaves, whose bids were preferred over other potential purchasers or who were allowed to pay in installments.[21]

Resales (both by private parties and the government), missed installment payments, and poor recordkeeping compounded the confusion about where legal title resided in Port Royal after the war. As one clerk of the Direct Tax Commission put it in 1871, "The unsettled condition of matters pertaining to property in Beaufort" required that "some [legislative] action be taken" to provide some stability to land titles "at an early date."[22] It was not forthcoming. All in all, the state of landownership as a result of the tax sales remained a mess for decades, despite numerous attempts to sort it out through the appointment of auditors, commissioners, and surveyors.

Sloppy administration was an issue, but the Direct Tax Act was also constitutionally suspect. Grounding the seizure of Confederates' property on the nonpayment of taxes was ingenious, avoiding many of the problems associated with land confiscation schemes based on criminal punishment for treason or the classification of Confederates as alien enemies whose property could arguably be seized under the law of war.[23] But it was hardly a foolproof alternative, because the act looked more like a confiscation measure than the tax it purported to be. Historian J. G. Randall complained that "it is difficult to see how these sweeping forfeitures can be defended on the basis of 'tax sales.'"[24] Its uneven administration was also a problem of constitutional dimensions because of the requirement that direct taxes be laid proportionally according to population. In South Carolina, the whole tax owed statewide had been collected in just one locality, without accounting for the relative amount for which the remainder of the state should have been responsible. Randall's opinion about the dubious legality of the policy was not just the product of backward-looking historical analysis; it was shared by the population of dispossessed delinquent taxpayers (primarily from Virginia and South Carolina) and their lawyers. As the governor of South Carolina once complained, the Port Royal area direct tax sales constituted "punish[ment] by lottery."[25]

Legal challenges to the tax sales began once the war ended, although not immediately. William Henry Trescot's successful lobbying mission in 1865 and 1866 to restore abandoned land to its former owners came first. Because the tax titles rested on a more regular legal foundation—a broadly applicable tax that was not, on its face, aimed specifically at traitors—and because the land transfers had been effectuated by the formality of sale, they would have to be attacked through litigation.[26] This campaign began in earnest in the late 1860s.

Initially, a number of high-profile national lawyers (including no fewer than three former US attorneys general) were attracted to the tax litigation, either because of the promise of a decent-sized return or because of the specter of notoriety. Robert E. Lee contacted Reverdy Johnson for help with Arlington, and South Carolina governor James Orr secured money from the state legislature (later disallowed by the state's military governor)[27] to hire Jeremiah Black, who in turn recruited Representative James Garfield, a former Union general who had previously endorsed wide-scale Confederate land confiscation on the floor of Congress.[28] Black and Garfield were set to reprise the association that had served them well in arguing *Ex parte Milligan*, and Garfield, a relative newbie, was flattered enough by the prominent older lawyer's desire to work with him that he conveniently ignored his views on the merits of land confiscation.[29] Caleb Cushing also got involved (for a contingency fee of one-quarter of the acreage recovered) on behalf of a number of private clients, who were simply bewildered by the varying legal grounds for government property seizure in the Sea Islands. The first round of litigation was aimed at fast-tracking the issue to the Supreme Court. As Cushing said, the rulings in the lower courts were "of secondary consequence." He was "confident of success."[30]

The goal of the first phase of the litigation was to take a big swing at the Direct Tax Act by challenging its constitutionality in the Supreme Court. But in the first three cases to reach the Supreme Court—*Cooley v. O'Connor*, *Bennett v. Hunter*, and *Tacey v. Irwin*, which originated in South Carolina and Virginia—the Court was very cautious.[31] It did not weigh in on the ultimate constitutionality of the act but decided the cases based on technical compliance with the mechanics of the tax sale. In *Cooley*, the Court decided that the sufficiency of a certificate signed by only two of three tax commissioners and the notice given by a vague description of the land in question were matters that could go to a jury for resolution. In *Bennett v. Hunter*, the Court decided that the commissioners had acted illegally in requiring tender of a tax payment in person by a delinquent landowner seeking to redeem the land prior to sale. In *Tacey*, the Court expanded *Hunter*'s holding to invalidate a sale where the owner's agent, a relative, had tendered the payment instead of the owner himself. The first round of litigation produced a bit of a mixed record, in the sense that the Court had been willing to invalidate the sales in two of the cases and allowed a jury to decide on the sufficiency of the government's compliance with the statute in the other. The land titles bestowed by the tax sales were thus not entirely secure, but neither was it clear that delinquent taxpayers were likely to prevail if they sued to eject the new owners. Two themes united the cases: the Court was willing to scrutinize the particular facts of each case and thus render the sales vulnerable to legal challenge, and it was avoiding the larger constitutional attacks against the Direct Tax Act.

While the nationally prominent lawyers sought to bring constitutional challenges to the direct tax sales, the local bar in Beaufort County pursued a subtler strategy. Richard DeTreville, a longtime local real estate lawyer in Port Royal, had, like many other attorneys in the area, a personal stake in the tax sales. His father's city home in Beaufort had been sold for taxes during the war and wound up in Robert Smalls's hands. He was determined to get the land back for both his father and for the many (formerly wealthy) white planter families that he represented. This was, in a sense, a continuation of his antebellum law practice, as he had worked on inheritance matters and land transactions in the Port Royal community. It was also a crusade, and he endeavored to restore the property of the prominent Elliott family for many years in spite of their inability to pay his retainer.[32]

Around 1870, DeTreville published an anonymous pamphlet, *Sea Island Lands: St. Helena Parish and Its Citizens*, which railed against "the course of wrong and oppression" that had been visited on the Sea Island planters "so foully despoiled and robbed of their lands and goods." Wartime abolitionists had sought to upend the culture of the Sea Islands by installing a "Yankee" community of Black landowners and "New England school-marms" in Port Royal, and they had done this by disguising "an act of confiscation and forfeiture of the most odious kind—a bill of attainder, intended to punish without trial all who owned property in an insurrectionary district," as an innocuous tax act. There had been no rhyme or reason to the valuation or land surveying done, no effort made to ensure that landowners were notified of taxes owed or forfeiture sales, and in the last extremity, tax commissioners had simply refused to accept payment when it had been proffered. Another indignity was the unevenness of the tax's application. The Constitution had sought to ensure that direct taxes were levied proportionally across the United States, but instead, "the single parish of St. Helena has thus been made to pay ... taxes to ten times the amount exacted of the whole state of South Carolina."[33] For DeTreville, the tax sales represented nothing more than government thievery gilded, insultingly, with a thin veneer of pseudo-constitutional gloss.

The pamphlet laid bare DeTreville's grievances, but he was more circumspect in court. There, he was guided more by stealth than by bluster. Rather than seeking to resolve constitutional difficulties in the federal courts, DeTreville quietly filed about fifty trespass cases in Beaufort County's local court of common pleas in 1869, shortly after it reopened for the first time since the end of the war. His aim was not to attract the attention of the US attorney or other federal officials but instead to secure default judgments against erroneous defendants—which a sheriff would then execute by removing the real occupant from the land in favor of DeTreville's client. In one emblematic suit, *Ellis v. Barnet*, DeTreville sued a defendant whom he knew was not actually in possession of the land. When no one showed up in court to defend the suit, DeTreville won by default, which was made possible through the complicity of the local judge. Once the deception was revealed, jury foreman John Conant signed a statement "certify[ing]" that "when I signed the verdict as foreman, I did it under protest because the facts stated in said verdict were known to me to be false. ... I signed only under the threat of the Hon. Court that I would be fined for contempt if I did not sign it."[34]

The lawsuits had the effect DeTreville had intended: they made the holders of tax titles uneasy about the durability of their land claims. It was an expensive and intimidating proposition for an impoverished freedman to have to hire a lawyer to defend his landownership, especially given DeTreville's underhanded tactics. If DeTreville could enforce default judgments he had won by suing the wrong defendant with the help of a corrupt judge, then the actual occupant of the property could be summarily ejected by the sheriff without any prior notice—and have to take legal action to regain possession. And because the suits were trespass actions of one private party against another, the US attorney was under no obligation to defend the validity of the land claims in court. The defendants were on their own. Laura Towne, a

Northern transplant who came to the Sea Islands as a wartime schoolteacher, reported in her diary that a "Mr. Duval, whose title was perfectly good, but who was threatened with a suit, paid the rebel a few hundred dollars not to bother him," and the plaintiff gladly settled. The Black community was worried enough about the lawsuits to hold public meetings to make plans to hire counsel and combat the suits. It was a certainty, they understood, that the planter class would continue to pursue the suits relentlessly.[35]

The purchasers were not defenseless, however. The planters had not confined their attacks to the most vulnerable members of the community; they had additionally "commenced [suits] against some of the large owners—white men," who would certainly fight back. There were also a number of powerful Black men in Port Royal, such as Robert Smalls, who were deeply invested in local economic affairs. And because the tax sales had been so ubiquitous, almost everyone in Port Royal had a personal stake in defending the tax titles. Towne noted that the juries in the trespass suits were "composed mostly of colored men who own land held by this same title," and indeed, the John Conant who, as jury foreman, had protested the default verdict in the *Ellis* case was himself a defendant in a different suit.[36] Another suit targeted William Whipper, one of the first Black attorneys admitted to the state bar, who later worked briefly on the *DeTreville* case before it went to the Supreme Court. W. M. French, who went on to become the editor of the local paper, was the defendant in yet another case.

Besides their relative power in the community, the purchasers also sought to rely on an implicit promise of validity that, they argued, necessarily accompanied a government land sale. Laura Towne asserted, with much more certainty than was warranted, that "there [was] no danger" of her purchase being invalidated. "As it was sold for non-payment of taxes, there is nothing of confiscation about it, and the sale was legal."[37] Towne's insistence on the inviolability of the tax sales rested on her assumption that the government's action in formally transferring the title from seller to purchaser—via sale—carried an imprimatur of legal legitimacy. This was not the ephemera of wartime property seizure. A series of editorials in the *Beaufort Tribune* made the same point: the tax titles were, effectively, a promise of warranty made by the US government to purchasers at these sales. The "legal fraternity" might "hold that the documents [the government had issued] are mere conditional titles," but such a flimsy promise was a betrayal of the trust of the average purchaser. The government got money, the writer in the *Tribune* said, so "what, in the name of common sense, did the purchasers get for *their money*?" It had to be more than nothing.[38]

The "legal fraternity" of the Beaufort bar followed DeTreville's lead in filing trespass suits in local court for more than a year before the Justice Department and the Internal Revenue Commission intervened to protect the purchasers. Complaints from both the planters and the purchasers had made their way to Congress, and the Treasury Department sent an inspector to South Carolina before recommending any legislative course of action. The inspection revealed that a "'Ring' of the Legal Fraternity has been formed to get ahold of these cases," which was actively attempting to disrupt title by suing private plaintiffs—and thereby drumming up business for itself.[39] The US attorney, David T. Corbin, had been asleep at the switch, noticing DeTreville's volume of lawsuits in local court only after final judgment had been rendered and the sheriff had sought to foreclose on the property. When he was made aware of the situation, he declined to get directly involved. He was "willing to accept a retainer" to act on behalf of private clients who desired his services as a lawyer, but "in [his] official capacity [as US attorney he] could not serve them" unless ordered to do so by officials in Washington.[40]

By 1872, the situation in Port Royal was alarming enough that Attorney General George Williams did order Corbin to defend the tax titles of private landowners in federal court. Corbin was to seek relief for the purchasers in the local court of common pleas by asking that court to set its problematic default judgments in *Ellis* and the other suits aside. If the court balked, Corbin was to remove all the cases to federal court and seek an injunction there to prevent the execution of the state court order.[41]

Corbin's direct involvement came about because the US government now had an important financial interest at stake in the lawsuits. In 1872, Congress had responded to petitions from those affected by the tax sales and sought to guard against the dislocations brought about by the onslaught of litigation in local courts. In cases where planters prevailed, Congress authorized payments to indemnify purchasers for the amount they had paid for the land, as well as for improvements they had made since taking possession. But Congress also worried about lawyers like DeTreville taking advantage of corrupt practices in local courts in order to intimidate defendants or grift indemnification money out of the federal treasury by facilitating "collusion" between plaintiffs and defendants. The legislation put safeguards in place. The new statutes sought to funnel litigation into the more reliable federal courts, refusing to pay promised indemnities when a litigant relied on a state court writ "to order money out of the [federal] Treasury."[42] The legislation also sought to dissuade bogus filings by requiring that plaintiffs reclaiming land pay the amount of tax originally owed before the lawsuits could commence.[43]

Corbin succeeded in getting Judge George S. Bryan of the federal district court to take up the tax cases, but he managed something even more important: an agreement with the planters' attorneys that they would drop their harassment litigation and focus their efforts on one "test case." This case would seek to settle, once and for all, the lingering questions about the legitimacy of the tax sales that the Supreme Court's previous narrow decisions had not answered. The case selected was an emblematic one: *DeTreville v. Smalls*.[44] The case was personal for Richard DeTreville, of course, because he was representing his father, but it was likely selected primarily because the defendant, Robert Smalls, was the most famous man in Port Royal.

By the time his suit was selected as a test case, Smalls had already been involved in efforts to broker a compromise between the planters and the purchasers on the matter of the tax titles. It was an ever-present issue for Port Royal politicians, who sought to represent a district where the durability of the tax titles mattered a great deal to almost all of their constituents. To a large extent, Smalls had built his political career on attempting to bridge the gap between white and Black, native-born and Northern transplant, capitalist and worker, in the Sea Islands. Smalls was very much dedicated to economic boosterism in Port Royal, believing that the whole community would benefit from attracting money and investment to the region.

Smalls's political efforts to achieve a fair outcome on the tax title issue started in 1871, when Congress began debating legislation that would provide relief to Port Royal—and that eventually passed the following year. Smalls, then a member of the South Carolina Senate, sent a long letter arguing for targeted federal help for his region to the Commissioner of Internal Revenue, who then passed it on to John Sherman, the head of the powerful Senate Finance Committee.[45] Throughout the letter, Smalls urged two points: the importance of providing stability for the region by confirming the tax titles of the new owners, and a recognition of the unfairness that had been visited on the planters who had lost their land through the wartime direct tax sales.

Smalls stressed the uniqueness of the situation in Port Royal. He agreed with his antagonist DeTreville on a key issue: Port Royal had been unfairly singled out, and the tax titles were a never-ending source of strife and economic hardship in the region. As a result, he was beset "almost every day" by constituents inquiring about the availability of land and the security of land titles in Beaufort.[46] Because the ownership of property in the Sea Islands was so uncertain, "the energies of the people are paralyzed [and] every branch of industry languishes," he said. The misery of uncertain title affected all segments of society: "not only those who have recently acquired their freedom and the privileges of citizenship, and the ownership of a portion of these lands," but also white transplants and even the "original owners of these lands," who were now "settled among us."[47]

Smalls was magnanimous enough to admit that since the government had largely chosen not to punish former Confederates, it was not "equitable ... that the inhabitants of one small Parish should have a burden that the government lays upon [no] others." Still, it was clear that the unfairness visited upon the planters was outweighed by the property rights of "those who have always been loyal, and who have acquired the property by legal means." Those who had purchased property at tax sales "should be guaranteed its quiet and peaceable possession." What Smalls's plan required was a baseline acknowledgment that the tax titles would be upheld as valid. If that could be established, he could be freehanded when it came to other adjustments. The government could sell the land that it still held itself and divide the proceeds among the former owners once their tax debts had been satisfied, Smalls suggested.[48]

In spite of the evenhandedness of the plan, it was not easy to persuade the planters of its wisdom. Smalls reported that they refused the "relinquishment of claims, and abandonment of suits etc.," determined to "suffer all the evils and waste of delay" of constant litigation. And no wonder. To those of the planter class, the loss of their land was not just an economic issue but also a moral affront. Planter Daniel Huger Smith's pitiless assessment of the situation was emblematic of the enmity Smalls faced. According to Smith, the radical wartime policy of providing for former slaves out of the land of their former enslavers was a form of legalized theft. The government had "provid[ed] for the negro by bestowing on each applicant forty acres of someone else's property."[49]

The precariousness of land tenure in Port Royal, brought on by the onslaught of litigation, was extremely dispiriting for the Black community. When *DeTreville* came up for trial in the federal court in 1875, Laura Towne reported that the Black community in Port Royal privately had a "little fright," thinking that the "rebs would get their land back and that there was to be a war in consequence." Initially, she said, "we supposed that the court had decided against the legality of the tax sales and that the people here would be ejected from their little homesteads. . . . I believe they WOULD have a war if this thing should be done." When the news came instead that Smalls had prevailed, there was rejoicing that "one Yankee lawyer, Mr. Corbin, had got the better of eight rebel lawyers, and that the lands were safe."[50]

The Supreme Court confirmed the validity of tax titles in 1879, thus closing the door to litigation that sought to eject the new purchasers. In so doing, the Court subtly changed course from its earlier direct tax opinions, without explicitly acknowledging that it was doing so. The Court abruptly cut off the kind of scrutiny for compliance with tax code technicalities that it had previously applied in *Cooley, Bennett,* and *Tacey*, a shift that likely prompted Justice Stephen Field's solo dissent, which did not produce a written opinion. In *DeTreville*, the Court declared that Smalls's certificate of purchase constituted prima facie evidence not only "of the *regularity* of sale" but also—per the statute—"of its *validity* and of the *title* of the purchaser." In other words, a former owner like DeTreville was permitted to challenge the sale only on very limited grounds: by establishing that the property had not been subject to taxes, that the taxes had already been paid, or that the property had been redeemed prior to sale.[51] Allowing challenges on any other grounds would negate Congress's intent in crafting the 1862 Direct Tax Act and its subsequent amendments. Congress had meant to create a strong presumption of a tax title's validity and had sought to ensure that the purchaser's possession could not be disrupted by claimants attacking various aspects of the government sale after the fact, Justice William Strong said in his majority opinion.[52]

The passage of time—and in fairness, a lack of mainstream historical interest in direct taxes or the technicalities of tax titles—has obscured just how unusual the *DeTreville* holding was when it was handed down. It was, indeed, a surprising decision. This was because tax titles were notoriously flimsy legal instruments. In general, they carried no guarantee of the durability of ownership, and they could nearly always be challenged in court by a former owner alleging that irregularities had marred the sale. This was not simply a design flaw; as one scholar has argued, the kinds of challenges seen in nineteenth-century tax title litigation provided the foundation for the emergent understanding of the constitutional limitations on government police powers.[53] *Blackwell on Tax Titles*, the leading treatise on the topic (and one of the most respected legal treatises of the time),[54] stated that "the presumption is, in fact, against their validity" and that out of a thousand tax title cases in American courts, "not twenty of them have been found legal and regular."[55] Taking a tax title was essentially a gamble, and as a result, the price of land sold at a tax sale was nearly always heavily discounted. This was the general rule of tax sales, but as a prominent legal scholar put it in 1889, this foundational view was "apparently controverted by a recent decision of the United States Supreme Court" in *DeTreville*.[56]

A terse paragraph at the end of the *DeTreville* opinion also swept aside the constitutional objections the planters had raised against the idea of disguising a punitive confiscatory measure as a mere tax, which left the planters with the sole option of pursuing partial monetary recompense from Congress. Robert Smalls had proposed such a solution years before, and the day after *DeTreville* came down, he presented himself in William Henry Trescot's office to discuss it again. Trescot's advocacy on the planters' behalf had been a daily task through 1865 and 1866, but the work had slowed to a trickle as the years passed. He had not taken part in the grunt work of litigating individual trespass suits, which often involved the patient assembly of family documents like wills and deeds. Trescot was back in the diplomatic service in the Hayes administration, about to embark on a mission to China to negotiate a treaty that would impose limits on Chinese immigration, and Smalls called on him in Washington. Trescot was open to the alliance—and intrigued by Smalls's suggestions about how the relief could be pitched. If Trescot could draft a bill that outlined some equitable form of compensation overnight, "he [Smalls] wished to introduce [it] tomorrow" in the House of Representatives. What the two of them hammered out in rough form in Trescot's office on January 26 looked remarkably like the pitch Smalls had made to the Internal Revenue Commissioner eight years earlier.[57]

Time was of the essence, as Smalls was set to be replaced in Congress by a white Democrat in about a month and a half. This was an opportunity for Trescot to work across the aisle with a powerful Republican. "I am inclined to think that [Smalls] could induce the Republicans to support a Bill which he introduced," Trescot said. He was skeptical that such a bill could pass Congress, "but [Smalls] thinks otherwise and ought to know better than I do." Smalls laid out his view that the surplus that the government had gained from the sales beyond the amount of tax owed rightfully should be paid to the former landowners. He explained it to Trescot using his own tax purchase as an example.[58] A $16 tax had been levied on DeTreville's land, and the government had itself purchased it at the initial tax sale in 1863 for something close to the amount of the taxes and penalties owed on it, as was routine practice for the South Carolina direct tax commission. Smalls had then purchased it at a government resale for $600 a year later. In fairness, Smalls told Trescot, "the difference between 16 and 600 should be paid to [De]Treville."[59]

This insight seemed right to Trescot, but it did not offer a full solution to the problem of calibrating the economic loss visited on the former landowners as a result of the tax sales. DeTreville's land had been resold at $600, but what if another similarly situated plot had been resold for $3,000? Would DeTreville be entitled to $584 in recompense and the other owner $2,984? Not all land had been resold, although most of it had, and the amounts realized at resales differed mightily. Simply "to give the owner the difference [between tax and the amount realized upon resale after the government took ownership at the initial sale] would make it impossible to equalize the overtax among all the tax payers," Trescot said. "The truth is it will be no easy matter to draw any bill" that would distribute the money equitably, or at least, he could "not frame one tonight." He had to think about how it could be done.[60]

Trescot did not draft the bill overnight, but he almost did. Smalls had approached him on January 26, and on February 8, Smalls introduced the bill in the House. It directed the secretary of the Treasury to "refund" the persons whose "property was sold for the satisfaction of the quota of direct tax" levied upon South Carolina. One crucial detail was filled in: the refund was to consist of the amount collected from sales in South Carolina over and above the money the state had owed back in 1861.[61] "The balance of surplus remaining in the treasury" was to be repaid to Port Royal's former landowners. The bill was a scant two pages long, and it was short on specifics. It simply stated that the refunds would be made based on a "pro rata proportion" of the surplus held by the Treasury Department.[62]

Smalls also reached out, as he had years earlier, to the commissioner of Internal Revenue. He apprised the commissioner, Green B. Raum, of the broad outlines of the bill and asked for the Treasury Department's support. Smalls emphasized that "the titles to the property so sold have been declared valid" by the Supreme Court, and so it was time to try to offset the harms suffered by the original landholders of the lowcountry. Providing compensation for them was "but an act of justice and humanity," Smalls said. The "unfortunate inhabitants" of Port Royal ("that fractional part of the state") were entitled to receive "the balance as remains over after paying the whole quota of South Carolina's Direct Tax."[63]

Smalls's bill went to the Committee on Ways and Means, where it was not acted upon in the Forty-Third Congress. A version of it eventually passed (and was signed into law by President Benjamin Harrison) in 1891, after being championed this time by Democrat William Elliott, the replacement for Smalls (who had been elected again in 1882).[64] Elliott, who had represented a number of the planters in court as they challenged the tax titles and later sought compensation for their losses in the court of claims, came from a prominent family that had itself been dispossessed. By the time that the compensation bill for the Port Royal tax sales became law, it was a measure that cut across party lines, and there was widespread agreement that the wrong visited on the planters during the war should be remedied.

Robert Smalls's choice to push for compensation for the lost land of the slaveholding class in Port Royal might strike us as surprising, particularly given that the land at issue was virtually the only land in the United States that made its way into the hands of former slaves during the Civil War. This was land, that, in the eyes of many, belonged rightfully—if not legally—to Black Sea Islanders, by virtue of "the sweat and blood of those who toiled there."[65] But only the clunky mechanism of the poorly constructed, ill-fitting, and badly mismanaged Direct Tax Act of 1862 made their ownership a reality—and then only partially so. What this episode, detailing Smalls's alliance with the planters and their lawyers, makes clear is how limited Smalls's options were in postwar South Carolina and how he was able to maneuver within those constraints.

Smalls was open to alliances with his white constituents, convinced that cross-racial coalitions were the only way to boost the fortunes of Port Royal. Smalls's actions accorded with the realities of Black political life in postwar South Carolina. His political survival depended on his willingness to appear moderate and to build bridges with white Democrats where he could, and yet he could also expect his character to be maligned and his overtures to be rebuffed frequently.[66] But Smalls did not compromise on the most important thing, which was the inviolability of title granted to purchasers at tax sales. He went to the Supreme Court to ensure that litigants would not be able to challenge the legality of those purchases after the fact. There Smalls had secured his own title and those of other Black wartime purchasers, but there would be no further federal efforts to provide freedmen with land in his home state.[67] After returning home to South Carolina in 1879 in the wake of the *DeTreville* case and his electoral defeat, Smalls went "to Arizona to look at lands, with a view to emigration—not to himself, but of such as will go somewhere."[68] He was aware that what he had won in the Supreme Court was only a morsel.

NOTES

1. DeTreville v. Smalls, 98 US 517 (1878).

2. Cynthia Nicoletti, "William Henry Trescot, Pardon Broker," *Journal of the Civil War Era* 11, no. 4 (December 2021): 478.

3. Special Field Orders No. 15, January 16, 1865, in US War Department, *The War of the Rebellion: A Compilation of the Official Records of the Union and Confederate Armies*, 127 vols., index, and atlas (Washington, DC: Government Printing Office, 1880–1901), ser. 3, 1:60–62.

4. 13 Stat. 375 (1864).

5. See Freedmen's Bureau Act of 1866, 14 Stat. 173, sec. 7, 9, 11.

6. See Rufus Waples, *A Treatise on Proceedings in Rem* (Chicago: Callaghan and Company, 1882), 176, on the effect of sale. Besides regular, voluntary sales, which were not at issue in land redistribution controversies, the other land that had been sold was land confiscated

under the Confiscation Act of 1862 (12 Stat. 589), which was to be sold at a sheriff's sale after a determination of the guilt of its owner (for treason) in a federal court proceeding. This act went largely unenforced, though, so this is a category without content. For more information, see John Syrett, *The Confiscation Acts* (New York: Fordham University Press, 2006).

7. William Henry Trescot to Benjamin Perry, October 13, 1865, Governor's Papers, South Carolina Department of Archives and History, Columbia (hereafter SCDAH).

8. Richard DeTreville, *Sea Island Lands: St. Helena Parish and Its Citizens* (n.p., ca. 1870).

9. See Act of March 2, 1891, ch. 496, 26 Stat. 422.

10. Eric Foner, *Reconstruction: America's Unfinished Revolution, 1863–1877* (New York: Harper and Row, 1988), 161.

11. Historiography on this topic includes Rene Hayden et al., eds., *Freedom: A Documentary History of Emancipation, 1866–67*, ser. 3, vol. 2 (Chapel Hill: University of North Carolina Press, 2013), 1–60, 211–25; Julie Saville, *The Work of Reconstruction* (New York: Cambridge University Press, 1994); Edward Magdol, *A Right to the Land: Essays on the Freedmen's Community* (Westport, CT: Greenwood Press, 1977); and William McFeely, *Yankee Stepfather: O. O. Howard and the Freedmen* (New York: Norton, 1968). See Claude Oubre, *Forty Acres and a Mule: The Freedmen's Bureau and Black Land Ownership* (Baton Rouge: Louisiana State University Press, 1978); and Carol Rothrock Bleser, *The Promised Land* (Columbia: University of South Carolina Press, 1969).

12. See Oubre, *Forty Acres and a Mule*, 37.

13. See Okon E. Uya, *From Slavery to Public Service: Robert Smalls, 1839–1915* (New York: Oxford University Press, 1971); Thomas Holt, *Black over White: Negro Political Leadership in South Carolina during Reconstruction* (Urbana: University of Illinois Press, 1977); and W. E. B. Du Bois, *Black Reconstruction in America, 1860–1880* (New York: Free Press, 1998), 381–430.

14. See Willie Lee Rose, *Rehearsal for Reconstruction: The Port Royal Experiment* (New York: Oxford University Press, 1964).

15. See Rose, *Rehearsal for Reconstruction*.

16. South Carolina owed $363,570.67.

17. See US Constitution, art. 1, sec. 10; Revenue Act of 1861, sec. 8, 12 Stat. 292; Act of June 7, 1862, 12 Stat. 422; Hylton v. United States, 3 US 171 (1796) (on direct taxes); Charles F. Dunbar, "The Direct Tax of 1861," *Quarterly Journal of Economics* 3, no. 4 (July 1889): 436; Robin Einhorn, *American Taxation, American Slavery* (Chicago: University of Chicago Press, 2006); and Irwin Unger, *The Greenback Era: A Social and Political History of American Finance, 1865–1879* (Princeton, NJ: Princeton University Press, 1964).

18. See A. D. Smith to Salmon P. Chase, August 6, 1862 (conveying Senator Doolittle's views on the purpose of the bill), General Correspondence, South Carolina Direct Tax Commission Records, Record Group 58, National Archives, College Park, MD (hereafter SCDTCR).

19. On this issue, see the discussion of Bennett v. Hunter, 76 US 326 (1869), and Tacey v. Irwin, 85 US 549 (1873), later in the chapter.

20. Even in the midst of discussions about returning property to former owners, there were carve-outs for land "on which there is a national cemetery." See Cong. Globe, 42nd Cong., 2nd Sess. 2455 (1872); and Act of June 8, 1872, 17 Stat. 330, sec. 7. See also Robert M. Poole, *On Hallowed Ground: The Story of Arlington National Cemetery* (New York: Walker and Co., 2009); Anthony J. Gaughan, *The Last Battle of the Civil War: United States versus*

Lee, 1861–1883 (Baton Rouge: Louisiana State University Press, 2011); and Memorial of G. W. Custis Lee, S. Misc. Doc. 96, 43rd Cong., 1st Sess. (1874).

21. See Rose, *Rehearsal for Reconstruction*, chaps. 7–10; and Ruth Dunley, *The Lost President: A. D. Smith and the Hidden History of Radical Democracy in Civil War America* (Athens: University of Georgia Press, 2019).

22. L. S. Emery to Commissioner of Internal Revenue, October 1, 1871, box 4, SCDTCR.

23. Constitutionally, seizure of property required a prior court proceeding, and under the law of war, property on land was generally exempt from seizure by an invading army. See Henry Halleck, *Elements of International Law* (Philadelphia: J. B. Lippincott, 1866), 209.

24. J. G. Randall, *Constitutional Problems under Lincoln* (New York: D. Appleton, 1926), 319, 320.

25. James L. Orr to Andrew Johnson, January 24, 1866 (broadside), 5, Lehigh University digital collections, https://digitalcollections.lib.lehigh.edu/islandora/object/digitalcollections:rare-book_2243#page/1/mode/1up.

26. William Henry Trescot to Benjamin Perry, October 24, 1865, Governor's Papers, SCDAH.

27. Daniel Sickles to James Orr, August 26, 1868, box 9, folder 40, Governor's Papers, SCDAH.

28. Robert E. Lee to Reverdy Johnson, January 27, 1866, Reverdy Johnson Papers, Library of Congress, Washington, DC; James Orr to Whaley, Mitchell, and Clancy, February 20, 1867, reel 23, Jeremiah Black Papers, Library of Congress; Whaley, Mitchell, and Clancy to Orr, February 22, 1867, and J. J. Pope to Orr, February 26, 1867, Governor's Papers, SCDAH; J. J. Pope Circular, January 3 1867, and Orr to Whaley, Mitchell, and Clancy, February 20, 1867, Whaley, Mitchell, and Clancy Papers, South Carolina Historical Society, Charleston; James Garfield, Confiscation of the Property of the Rebels, Speech Delivered in the House of Representatives, January 28, 1864, in *Works of James A. Garfield*, 2 vols. (Boston: James Osgood and Co., 1882), 1:1–18. See James Garfield Papers, vol. 2, Library of Congress, for Garfield's notes on the litigation.

29. See Allan Peskin, *Garfield* (Kent, OH: Kent State University Press, 1978), 270–72; and Dorothea Abbott, "President and Mrs. James A. Garfield and Judge Jeremiah S. Black: Their Land in Arlington County," *Arlington Historical Magazine* 8 (October 1985): 4–11.

30. Randell Croft to Caleb Cushing, October 19, 1867, Cushing to Croft, November 13, 1867, and Cushing to Robert Chisholm, December 4, 1867, box 306, Caleb Cushing Papers, Library of Congress.

31. 79 US 391 (1870); 76 US 326 (1869); 85 US 549 (1873).

32. See Richard DeTreville to Thomas Legare, March 11, 1867, South Caroliniana Library, University of South Carolina, Columbia; and Richard DeTreville to Ann Elliott, August 6, 1873, box 6, Elliott and Gonzales Family Papers, Southern Historical Collection, University of North Carolina Library, Chapel Hill.

33. DeTreville, *Sea Island Lands*, 10.

34. W. R. Cloutman to J. H. Douglass, June 22, 1872, box 2, SCDTCR. The larger story here is spelled out in a series of letters that Cloutman wrote, along with underlying filings. I also found the filings in the fifty suits DeTreville initiated in the microfilm records of the Beaufort County Clerk's office, Beaufort, SC.

35. Laura M. Towne, *Letters and Diary of Laura M. Towne* (Cambridge: Riverside Press, 1912), 207.

36. Towne, *Diary*, 214; list of trespass actions in David T. Corbin Papers, South Carolina Historical Society. The 1870 census confirms that Conant was a white transplant, and the Direct Tax records at the National Archives reveal that he worked for the commission.

37. Towne, *Diary*, 215. Here her claim ironically echoed DeTreville's *Sea Island Lands* pamphlet, although DeTreville turned the argument on its head by characterizing the tax scheme as merely confiscation in disguise.

38. *Beaufort Tribune*, January 14, 1875.

39. C. H. Wright to Lyman S. Emery, June 21, 1871, box 2, SCDTCR.

40. D. T. Corbin to William Wording, April 3, 1869, box 2, SCDTCR.

41. George Williams to D. T. Corbin, July 29, 1872, box 2, SCDTCR. This (a post–final judgment removal from state to federal court) was an extraordinary procedural maneuver, arguably permitted by the Habeas Corpus Acts of 1863 and 1866 but probably violative of the Seventh Amendment as interpreted by the Supreme Court in Justices v. Murray, 76 US 274 (1869). My full book manuscript will have more to say on nifty civil procedure oddities in this litigation.

42. Cong. Globe, 42nd Cong., 2nd Sess., 2526 (April 18, 1872). These were stopgap measures before Congress, and the courts could work out a more permanent solution.

43. 17 Stat. 89; 17 Stat. 330 (1872).

44. D. T. Corbin to J. W. Douglass (IRS Commissioner), April 20, 1875, box 2, SCDTCR.

45. George Waterhouse (and other petitioners, including Robert Smalls) to Commissioner of Internal Revenue, March 13, 1871, box 3, SCDTR (notation on the back).

46. Alfred Thomas to Robert Smalls, December 9, 1875, Direct Tax Commission Records, box 2, SCDTCR.

47. George Waterhouse (and other petitioners, including Robert Smalls) to Commissioner of Internal Revenue, March 13, 1871, box 3, SCDTR.

48. George Waterhouse (and other petitioners, including Robert Smalls) to Commissioner of Internal Revenue.

49. D. E. Huger Smith, *A Charlestonian's Recollections, 1826–1913* (Charleston: Carolina Art Association, 1950), 130.

50. Towne, *Diary*, 239, 240.

51. This did not overrule the previous decisions; it just declared that the Court would allow no further expansion of the grounds for challenging the tax sales. In the end, the government found other means of cutting off litigation that came under those previous rulings, such as the sovereign immunity doctrine. See Gaughan, *Last Battle of the Civil War*, which discusses further litigation about in-person tender of the tax in United States v. Lee, 106 US 196 (1882), as well as other cases.

52. *DeTreville*, 98 US at 521, 522.

53. See Howard Jay Graham, "'Prophet Unhonored': Robert S. Blackwell, Tax Titles, and the 'Substantive Revolution' in Due Process and Equal Protection," in *Everyman's Constitution* (Madison: State Historical Society of Wisconsin, 1968). See also Robert P. Swierenga, "The Odious Tax Title: A Study in Nineteenth Century Legal History," *American Journal of Legal History* 15, no. 2 (1971): 124–39.

54. See "Recent Publications," *Central Law Journal* 28 (April 26, 1889): 385, for discussion of Blackwell's place among the exalted company of "Washburn, Story, and Greenleaf."

55. Robert Blackwell, *A Practical Treatise on the Power to Sell Land for the Non-payment of Taxes* (Boston: Little Brown, 1869), 71.

56. Henry Campbell Black, *A Treatise on the Law of Tax Titles* (St. Louis: William H. Stephenson, 1889), 335n1. See also Waples, *Treatise on Proceedings in Rem*, 346–51, in which Waples twice characterized the Direct Tax Act and the Supreme Court's failure to invalidate it as "monstrous."

57. William Henry Trescot to James Campbell, January 26, 1879, James Butler Campbell Papers, South Carolina Historical Society.

58. William Henry Trescot to James Campbell, January 26, 1879.

59. DeTreville v. Smalls Case File, Case 7686, Record Group G 267, National Archives and Records Administration, Washington, DC; William Henry Trescot to James Campbell, January 26, 1879.

60. William Henry Trescot to James Campbell, January 26, 1879, James Butler Campbell Papers, South Carolina Historical Society.

61. There was dispute about whether there was any such surplus amount at all. Communication between commission and Treasury officials in the Direct Tax records shows that they attempted to deny that there was surplus. See D. T. Corbin to J. W. Douglass, April 29, 1875, SCDTCR. Litigants complained repeatedly about the problem of getting real accounting numbers from the Direct Tax Commission.

62. H.R. 6375, 43rd Cong., 3rd Sess., February 8, 1879.

63. Robert Smalls to Green Raum, February 15, 1879, box 4, SCDTCR.

64. Act of March 2, 1891, ch. 496, 26 Stat. 422 (1891).

65. Cong. Globe, 39th Cong., 1st Sess., 652 (February 5, 1866) (Representative Grinnell, IA).

66. See Thomas Holt, *Black over White*; and Julie Saville, *Work of Reconstruction*, 166–75, for more analysis on Black South Carolina politicians.

67. See Bleser, *Promised Land*, on the failed state effort to provide homesteads to poor South Carolinians. The Southern Homestead Act of 1866, which sought to replicate homesteading in the West, did not provide any land for settlement in South Carolina, and in other Southern states the available land was of poor quality. Paul W. Gates, "Federal Land Policy in the South, 1866–1888," *Journal of Southern History* 6 (August 1940): 303–30.

68. Towne, *Diary*, 294.

CONSTRUCTING THE PAST

We Cannot Believe Americans Can Do These Things

Erasing Violence from the Civil War Record

PETER S. CARMICHAEL

After an afternoon of scrutinizing the tax books of Sussex County, Virginia, I gathered my notes and headed for the door, having identified fifteen homes destroyed by Federal troops during the Hicksford Raid in 1864. Before I left the reading room, I noticed the county seal for notarizing official documents, which was roughly the size of a half-dollar, made of pure silver, and hanging next to a framed letter from a Union veteran named Joseph Murphy. Murphy had pocketed the seal during the raid while some of his comrades desecrated or destroyed nearly all the records of the county, located some thirty miles south of Petersburg. Murphy explained in a 1901 letter that "I accidentally moved the handle of the press and the seal fell out, which I return with pleasure and I might add I have thought of returning it for some years past."[1] I took a photo of the seal and letter before heading outside. I walked across the courthouse square, stopping briefly at the Confederate monument in the center, but then a country store, with a sign above the door that read

"T. E. Thornton" in bright yellow letters, caught my attention. I immediately recognized the name as that of a slaveholding family whose home had been torched by the Federals. Inside the dimly lit store, the old wooden floors creaked with every step. I tried to befriend the store cat, who found me unworthy, before I interrupted a lively conversation among some locals. I announced that I was from out of town—an admission that shocked no one—and that I was searching for any Civil War era homes or ruins. I had hoped a descendant of the Thorntons would regale me with family tales and take me to the site where the Yankees had burned their plantation. Instead, I was met with silence; no one could think of a single site or relate a story. One man, probably in his early sixties, bluntly stated the Civil War had bypassed Sussex County. When I mentioned the 1864 Hicksford Raid (also referred to as the Sussex Raid or Stony Creek Raid) that had run through the heart of his community, he insisted in a firm but friendly manner that I should go to Petersburg, where history actually happened during the Civil War.

How could this man deny Sussex County's traumatic past when the wartime clerk's office, a rare survivor of the 1864 Union raid, stood next door to Thornton's store? Inside that small brick building, Union soldiers had covered the wall with obscene graffiti still visible today. I walked out of the store and onto Main Street, devoid of residences and businesses, except for a small branch of the BB&T bank. It was not hard to imagine why some people believe their community has no past, when the world they inhabit appears so desolate. Just as I was getting into my car, a man asked me if I was a lawyer in town, since court was in session. As much as I wanted to pretend to be Matlock for the day, I confessed that I was a historian and that I had been in the courthouse researching the Civil War. He introduced himself as Bill Jenkins, the general registrar of voting in Sussex and a native of the county. I asked Bill if he knew of any Civil War era structures that had survived. He did, and so I followed his car down a series of back roads zigzagging through densely forested flatlands until we came to an impassable muddy road. A quarter-mile walk awaited us, and the red Virginia mud would likely claim my dress shoes, but as long as Bill wasn't a serial killer, I couldn't possibly turn away from a chance to see a surviving vestige of Civil War Sussex. While walking we chatted about Sussex today, where small farmers once thrived but have now all but disappeared. We arrived at the house, a once-stately dwelling now abandoned, falling into disrepair, and surrounded by scrub vegetation, the unmistakable sign of human neglect. Bill told me that the home had been moved from its original location, but he didn't know from where in the county or anything about its antebellum owners, who were certainly slaveholders, given the size of the dwelling. The house looked entirely out of place, like a shipwreck that had landed on a foreign shore. There was nothing more to see there, and as we headed back to our cars, I felt no closer to Sussex's Civil War history.

Along the way back Bill told me that his grandmother had loved the history of Sussex and Surry Counties, as well as the Civil War sites around Petersburg. She took him on many trips and shared her interest in the past. I asked Bill what his grandmother had to say of the 1864 Hicksford Raid, led by Gouverneur K. Warren from December 7 to December 13. He was only vaguely familiar with the expedition, so I offered him a fuller account of the event with all the grisly details. Nearly 22,000 Federal soldiers had left the Petersburg trenches to destroy the Weldon Railroad, one of Robert E. Lee's remaining supply lines. Along the way, hundreds, if not thousands, of Union soldiers raided stills of applejack from neighboring farms. Scores of men collapsed along the roadside, ridiculously drunk and left by their more sober comrades, who had no choice but continue to march toward the Weldon line. Once they wrecked tracks, I explained to Bill, the Federals returning to Sussex Court House found a few Union stragglers slashed from ear to ear, stripped naked, and their bodies desecrated. In one instance, a severed penis had been stuffed in a corpse's mouth. Outraged, Warren's men wanted revenge at all costs. They forced Southern women and children out of their houses in bitter weather and took all the valuables they could either carry or pack on their wagons before torching their homes. When I finished with my explanation, Bill looked stunned. "If I had heard any of this as a kid," he said, "I would have said, 'Damn Yankee this' and 'Damn Yankee that,' but I never did."

Before Bill and I said goodbye, he gave me his email address and promised to reach out to African Americans in the area who might have an interest in the local history. Hundreds of their ancestors had found opportunity in the upheaval and had flocked to the Union armies during the Hicksford Raid. I got in my car and followed Gouverneur Warren's 1864 route to Petersburg. Nothing about the contemporary route hinted of the past violence inflicted by Union soldiers. Trailers and modular homes were scattered like jacks across acres of endless pine trees. I stopped at the Nottoway River, put my blinkers on, and ran to the middle of the bridge for a few quick pictures. The river was calm, but the water ran high; a full moon reached above the trees lining the Nottoway, where Warren's soldiers had ended their expedition exhausted, miserably cold, still embittered. Not far from where I stood, some Union soldiers had strung up a Sussex plantation owner, believing that this man had ordered guerrillas to viciously murder their comrades. He had swayed from a tree along the banks of the river, his plantation in flames off in the distance, his family dispossessed. In that moment, I added the Nottoway to the long list of Southern rivers where unspeakable acts of violence have vanished from the historical record.

Although Bill and the man I met in Thornton's store possessed a strong sense of the past, I was mystified by how stories of civilians murdering enemy soldiers, of Federals torching homes and sending women and children adrift in the night, and of slaves running for freedom failed to register in their historical consciousness. Maybe I happened to stumble upon two locals who lived in a state of historical denial. Yet even if this were the case, their silences cannot be dismissed as an anomaly or as a gaping hole in the historical record. Rather, their silences originated within a landscape where history seems lost in time. The things of which memories of the Civil War are made do not exist in Sussex. There are no cannon, no battle monuments, no trenches, and no state historical markers that might summon images of the savage war unleashed in that county in 1864. Anyone who visits Sussex has come too late. Even the charred ruins left by Warren's vengeful soldiers have vanished, giving the countryside a sense of placelessness, where history's physical indentations have withered away.

The historical silences in Sussex's Civil War past may appear as an inevitable outcome of time's passage. But silences are not simply handed down from one generation to the next. Some silences are eventually retrieved as facts in time while other facts become silenced. What is permitted and what is discarded in the creation of a historical narrative emerged as the pressing question in my study of the Hicksford Raid, but how to pursue the creation of silence eluded me until I read Michel-Rolph Trouillot's *Silencing the Past: Power and the Production of History*, which shows the way. The act of silencing, Trouillot writes, is "an active and transitive process: one 'silences' a fact or an individual as a silencer silences a gun."[2] These silences, as Trouillot reminds us, express the power wielded in the production of historical accounts. Deconstructing silences is also important in revealing why certain narratives become accepted as truth.

In the case of the Hicksford Raid, the correspondence written during the raid and the official reports that immediately followed from Union and Confederate officers softened or entirely sidestepped the war crimes committed by their adversaries. Such omissions make little sense on the surface and seemingly defy explanation when both sides freely propagandized the violent excesses of their enemies. Although Union and Confederate officers in official correspondence did not entirely ignore the uncontrollable violence that erupted in Sussex, they veered away from evidence that showed men fighting savagely while their officers refused to interfere. Union communiqués and reports as well as Confederate dispatches (official reports from the Confederates are virtually nonexistent for the Hicksford Raid, given that guerrilla operatives never recorded their movements) stressed the military bearing and discipline of their own troops in their separate claims of having achieved victory in Sussex.

The first Confederate accounts published in Richmond newspapers minimized the threat posed by the Warren expedition. The editors utilized the trope of Yankee cowardice to defang the Federal advance, and their language mocked the Yankees as vandals who preyed upon the innocent until the sight of Lee's veterans sent them scurrying back to Petersburg. Additionally, Confederate military officials and Southern correspondents kept rumors of sexual violence against the Sussex women from the papers. And no editor thought the flight of Sussex slaves to Warren's column marked the beginning of a slave uprising in the tradition of Saint-Domingue. Any Southern reader who learned of the Hicksford Raid from Richmond papers must have drawn comfort from the news that Warren's raid was short-lived because Confederate troops had restored order and stability to the countryside.

Reassuring news also reached the Northern people from Warren and his subordinates, whose communiqués and reports celebrated the Hicksford Raid as a decisive Union victory. This fact, however, was not beyond reproach. The frenzy of looting and burning, if widely publicized, would have called into question the claim that the Sussex expedition was a great triumph achieved through controlled violence. Warren himself was particularly important in directing the public's attention away from the atrocities of Sussex. In his congratulatory orders and reports, he applauded his troops for their discipline, praising their hard marching as some the finest he had ever witnessed. However, in extolling the soldierly qualities of the rank and file, Warren downplayed evidence of excessive straggling and extreme drinking. He also devoted little attention to the murderous acts of Confederate guerrillas, even suggesting that the killing spree that targeted stragglers was mostly based on rumor, not fact. Why Warren minimized the presence of Confederate guerrillas in his narrative is mystifying, when the private letters from the rank and file tell a very different story. The men confessed that some of their comrades were ruthlessly cruel to women and children. The excesses were regrettable, soldiers admitted, but the vile killing of Union stragglers justified harsh retaliation.

All in all, the first narratives of the Hicksford Raid reveal that the military officers and newspaper editors held a monopoly of power in the earliest productions of historical narrative. Neither side merely reported facts or chronicled the movements of armies but rather constructed interpretive narratives by retrieving some facts as truth and silencing others. Making the silences in the first Hicksford Raid speak is critical to making the "distinction between what happened and that which is said to have happened."[3]

However, before I delve into the construction of the first histories of the Hicksford Raid, a more detailed narrative of the raid's basic events must be established. On December 6, 1864, Gen. George Gordon Meade, in consultation with Gen. Ulysses S. Grant, ordered Fifth Corps commander Gouverneur K. Warren to leave Petersburg with his three divisions as well as Gershom Mott's division from the Second Corps and David Gregg's cavalry division. The column moved south to the Weldon Railroad with orders to destroy the line from the Stony Creek Depot to Hicksford, a Virginia town eleven miles from the North Carolina border. In all, 22,000 infantry and 4,200 troopers broke camp during the early morning hours of December 7. As a mixture of sleet and snow fell to the ground, Gregg's horsemen led the way, screening Warren's marching column from the west. Not long into the march, men started to drop out of the ranks, a breakdown in discipline that grew worse with every passing hour. Warren had to detail cavalry companies to round up the stragglers and return them to Petersburg, while the rest of his command pressed forward, pushing deep into the heart of Sussex County.

At the close of the day, Warren's forces were stretched along seven miles of narrow roads, dangerously separated by the Nottoway River and vulnerable to Confederate attack. Fortunately for Warren, Confederate general Ambrose Powell (A. P.) Hill did not strike the advancing blue column. He did mobilize two infantry divisions, pulling them from the Petersburg trenches and inching them toward the Weldon line while dispatching Gen. Wade Hampton's cavalry to cut off the head of the Union column at Hicksford. The next day, December 8, the last of Warren's command passed through Sussex Court House, which consisted of a brick courthouse, a clerk's office, and a dilapidated jail and tavern. Straggling continued to plague Warren's column. Many were perfectly fit; they excused themselves from the ranks to plunder and steal from the locals. Of all the goods confiscated, nothing brought more joy to Warren's men than the discovery of applejack, a hard cider boiled down to a potent alcoholic mixture containing 30 percent alcohol, or 60 proof. Some of the men who imbibed the drink, according to a Maine soldier, "lost the power of locomotion and fell by the wayside, stupefied. We had to leave them, of course, and this was the last seen of them alive."⁴ The sober soldiered on, reaching the Weldon Railroad by late afternoon. The demolition started immediately, with the men ripping up the rails first before placing them on the piles of burning ties. When the track became sufficiently pliable, the Federals twisted the rails into unusable hunks of iron. Throughout the evening new bonfires sprang up along miles of the Weldon line, sending a streak of light into country darkness and illuminating the sky above to enable the men to keep working past midnight.⁵ Exhausted from the hard labor as well as the hard marching, Warren's veterans unrolled their blankets just as a piercing wind swept across the flatlands of Sussex County. Men huddled close to their bonfires, desperate to stay warm, especially those who had tossed away their overcoats earlier in the day.

On December 9, with the first rays of light, Warren's wrecking crews returned to the tracks, prying rails apart and burning ties from Jarratt's Station to Bellfield, leaving the Weldon inoperative for some seventeen miles. A portion of Gregg's cavalry continued to screen Warren's infantry to the west, allowing the foot soldiers to tear up the rails in peace. The rest of Gregg's command advanced to the south, meeting light resistance until they reached the Meherrin River, where a few hundred Confederates, mostly North Carolina home guard, waited behind freshly dug trenches. One of Gregg's regiments mounted a charge, but the assault was more of a reconnaissance than a concerted attack. With the repulse of the cavalrymen, Warren worried about the strength of the Confederate line, the ominous weather looming to the west, and rations that were running low. He could pack up his command and return to Petersburg and declare mission accomplished.

Meanwhile, Confederate infantry under General Hill were pressing from the west, threatening to turn Warren's right flank and cut his forces off from their base at Petersburg, approximately twenty miles to the north. If the Confederates reached Sussex Court House first, the Federal line of retreat to the north would be severed. On December 10, Warren began withdrawing from his advance position, but a wintry storm during the night foiled his plans for an efficient retreat. The narrow roads turned into a slop of ice and mud, horses balked, and men floundered. Icicles loaded down the trees, occasionally breaking and slashing the men. Many of the soldiers marched barefoot, their shoes having given out during the long march. Squads of runaway slaves raced to the column, an encumbrance that did not trouble all the Federals. One Union officer wished that everyone in the North could see slaves of all ages "running to the road to join our moving column." "They were all either very thinly or very poorly clad," the officer observed, but "on pushed these contrabands," trudging through the mud and ice, buoyed by the promise of "liberty and freedom."[6]

The weather conditions, as dreadful as they were, did not pose the most serious impediment to marching order. The imbibing of applejack continued, becoming more than a minor hindrance to marching efficiency.[7] A countless number of weary veterans guzzled down the home brew. "The boys that went out got liquors of one kind & another," a member of the famed Iron Brigade noted in his diary, "viz. peach Brandy & apple brandy & applejack &c. All the best of liquors & some have used them rather too freely." "A number of the boys are so drunk," he added, "they can scarcely walk & some dead drunk."[8] What Warren's men couldn't drink, they poured on the frozen ground or into their canteens for the return trip to Petersburg. The Provost Guard also destroyed countless barrels of applejack.

By the evening of December 10, Warren's force, though reunited, was in a tight spot just south of Sussex Court House. Grant and Meade were understandably worried that Warren might not escape the converging Confederates shadowing the Federal column from the west and south. Rear-guard actions erupted throughout the day, but the skirmishing never escalated into a major Southern attack. By noon, portions of Warren's command had recrossed the Nottoway River on pontoon bridges. The safe haven of the Petersburg lines was within reach.

The retreat nearly unraveled when word spread through the Federal column that local civilians or guerrillas had murdered Union stragglers, stripped them naked, and desecrated their bodies. Very few Federals, it appears, actually saw the mutilated corpses of their comrades, and how many Union stragglers were executed is impossible to determine. Warren insisted in his official report that only a few stragglers fell into the hands of the guerrillas. Just three days after the end of the raid, the general informed Meade that "it is not believed the enemy picked up any prisoners from straggling, except a few who became drunk to complete prostration on apple jack found on the way."[9] Warren dodged the pressing question as to whether Union soldiers had been murdered in cold blood. He was certain that the rumor of the killing had incited his soldiers to retaliate. "It is reported," he wrote, "[that] some of our men were found dead along the route: in one instance, with throat cut. Whether this was true or not, it soon became the belief of all the men in the command, and in retaliation almost every house was set on fire."[10]

Warren's conclusions were not in alignment with the wartime testimony of his own high-ranking subordinates. Many of them saw the mutilated bodies, and they did not hesitate to report the atrocities in their official correspondence. Gen. Robert McAllister, a divisional commander in the Second Corps, informed his wife that soon after the march started on December 10, "I was informed that the bodies of six or seven of our murdered soldiers lay close together in the woods not far from the spot. It was a sad sight. From the appearances they had been stripped of all their clothing and, when in the act of kneeling in a circle, they were shot in the head—murdered in cold blood by the would-be Chivalry of the South."[11] A Maine soldier recorded a separate atrocity, writing to his sister that "when we started to come back we found some of our men with their throats cut from ear to ear & a stake sharpened & drove through their necks into the ground. We found a number with their throats cut on our way back."[12] Numerous letters offer similar descriptions of dead men who were likely tortured during their last moments of life. It is, however, difficult to determine whether the authors of these letters actually saw the bodies or were just repeating stories that had circulated in the ranks.[13]

From the swamps and woods, the Confederate guerrillas watched the enemy force their wives and children from their homes, sending them into the bitter cold as refugees, before setting fire to their homes, barns, and outbuildings. Women were left to fend for themselves in a dangerous environment of sexual violence. Insults and threats were likely hurled from a mob of enraged men looking to settle the score by violating a woman's body. There is strong evidence to suggest that some women were raped, possibly with their husbands and fathers seeing this unfold from their hideouts in the woods. Gen. Joshua Chamberlain of Little Round Top fame confessed that "our men on our return *burnt almost every house on the road.* This was a hard night. Our men got very much exasperated & one day when I brought up the rear, I saw sad work in protecting helpless women & children from outrage. . . . I invariably gave them the protection which every man of honor will give any woman as long as she is a woman."[14] What Chamberlain meant by protecting any woman "as long as she is a woman" is impossible to say. Did enslaved women qualify as women worthy of protection? Did a woman harboring guerrillas lose the right to be defended? Or did poor white women exist outside the bounds of respectability?

Chamberlain's use of the word "outrage" is also vague. Civil War Americans often used the term to describe rape, but Chamberlain identified both women and children as targets of outrage. More conclusive evidence of rape comes from Pvt. John Haley of the Seventeenth Maine, who recorded in his diary on December 10 that "during the night, Colonel Byles, of the 99th Pennsylvania, and his adjutant were perpetrating one of the foulest outrages upon two defenseless women whose house was within our lines. These women were compelled to submit to their infamous proposals or have their house burned down and themselves turned out into the bleak December. Had this been the work of privates, said privates would have suffered death. The nearest tree would have been requisitioned, and it would have been just punishment, but old Byles is an officer, and was drunk, as is his custom."[15] No record at the National Archives exists of a general court-martial of Byles or for any other soldier charged for committing rape or any other act of sexual violence during the Hicksford Raid.

If any Federal soldier questioned the legality of burning Sussex to the ground, a rumor spread that Warren had authorized the firing of all the buildings, giving "sanction" to the rank and file to loot and destroy with impunity. Not all the buildings were leveled in the rampage. The brick courthouse survived, and the interior did not suffer any fire damage. Once inside the courthouse, the men tossed tax records on the lawn, stole ledgers as trophies of war, and slashed deed books with their sabers. The clerk's office, a brick structure, also avoided destruction, but inside the cramped office the soldiers covered the walls with autographs and obscene graffiti. One Federal sketched a solder having intercourse with a cow and accompanied it with the inscription "John Bull, looks pretty full."

The obscene doodles appear as child's play in comparison to what was happening on the outskirts of the village. An enslaved man informed some Maine soldiers that his owner had overseen the savage killing of some Union stragglers, in which irregular Confederates slit the throats of the Federals, stripped bodies naked, and drove sharpened stakes through their necks and into the ground. "There was a Darkey," Luther Gerrish of the Seventeenth Maine informed his sister, "[who] told me that he saw his master take two of our fellows out & tell his men to kill them. So, they did." The slave jumped at the chance to hunt down his runaway owner. He led the Maine soldiers straight to his plantation, where they discovered and captured his owner. The master of a grand estate was now a prisoner. He stood helpless, watching his captors steal or destroy his prized possessions before his home was devoured in flames. "He had a splendid house. We burnt that flat & every house we came to," Gerrish bluntly stated. "I had a good horse to ride & I would go ahead & go into every house on the road & take everything I could get. I got some nice dishes & chears [sic]. O Net I wish you could have some of the pianos I saw destroyed. Here I will stop. When I get home [I] will tell you all about such times for I cannot seem to write what I want in regard to what I have seen." But Gerrish had no trouble in disclosing how veterans meted out justice to suspected guerrillas. The men from the Seventeenth Maine marched their civilian prisoner to the Nottoway River, where the troops of Warren's entire army were crossing on their return to Petersburg. From a sturdy branch, they hung the man without ceremony and presumably without approval from their superiors. "We took him along with us as far as the river," the same Maine soldier stated, "then strung him up to a tree."[16] This unnamed Sussex resident was likely the only retaliatory execution. Although there were rumors that Warren's men hung suspected civilians around the courthouse square, the evidence is too thin to support such a claim.

On December 11, when the last elements of Warren's command recrossed the Nottoway River, at least fifteen houses were torched. Barns, smokehouses, stables, slave cabins, and mills were either gutted or destroyed. What possession or foodstuffs could not be demolished, the soldiers carried off. They returned to Petersburg with a caravan full of fine furniture, dishes, trunks, chairs, and other personal valuables—irrefutable evidence that discipline had collapsed in Warren's command. The sight of newly freed Black people clinging to the marching column told every observer in powerful visual language that life as people in Sussex had once known it was no more. In taking the first step to freedom, Sussex's enslaved population began a harrowing journey into an unknown world.

In the earliest documentation of the raid, the story of the freedpeople did not surface in what can be described as the chronicling phase of the Hicksford Raid, when the participants did not know the outcome of the expedition. They sent dispatches to their superiors in real time, informing them of their own movements, checking on the enemy's whereabouts, and generally assessing the situation as it unfolded. The dispatches were intended to be more directive than descriptive, and the sources read like the play-by-play of a sporting event. When Warren composed his dispatches, his decisions to retrieve certain facts were not entirely of his own making. He, like all professional military men, adhered to accepted practices in writing a professional report. Significantly, the very form and practice of military communications permitted certain facts to be mentioned and others to be discarded. Dispatches were primarily intended to provide immediate intelligence about the flow of military movements—not to explain how soldiers could turn into a drunken mob bent on destruction. Details of soldiers' misconduct would have appeared superfluous to most professional Civil War officers. Quite simply, the rules of military communication could not help but silence key, but also disturbing, facts from dispatches written in the field.

Warren's communications with Meade followed army protocol. He informed his superior of his progress, acknowledging the loss of 800 stragglers, who were eventually returned to Petersburg by Union cavalry.[17] Otherwise, Warren played it close to the vest. He did not mention the applejack, the murderous attacks from Confederate guerillas, or the destruction of Sussex. On December 11, his retreating force started to cross the Nottoway River. When he wrote the following note to Meade, it should be noted, great plumes of smoke and flame were shooting in the sky above Sussex:

> I have completely destroyed the railroad track from the Nottoway to Hicksford, and my command is all at the crossing of the Nottoway. Time did not allow me to go in between the Nottoway and Stony Creek, but that can be done at any time. I have met but trifling opposition or annoyance, but the marching and working night and day has been very fatiguing, and the weather very uncomfortable. The men, however, stood it all in good spirit, and we have made the best marching I have ever seen. The roads are now in a very bad condition. I propose to return tomorrow.[18]

The silences in Warren's report are telling, suggesting that he struggled with the truth. To just conclude that Warren lied falls short in understanding Warren's decisions as a writer. Warren understandably wanted his superiors to see the Hicksford Raid as an unmitigated success, and he intentionally projected the expedition as a triumph.[19] He needed his superiors to see the Hicksford campaign in a favorable light or he might face removal from command, given his stormy relationship with Meade and Grant. While in Sussex, Warren had managed to make things worse by failing to communicate regularly with headquarters. Meade was furious, and Grant demanded a full report from Warren as soon as operations ended, a highly unusual request when most Civil War officers took months to complete their official reports.[20]

On December 13, the day the raid ended, Warren issued a congratulatory address in General Orders No. 65, the first published narrative of the Hicksford Raid. He commended his men for "accomplishing successfully" their "mission—the destruction of the Weldon railroad as far as Hicksford, making forced marches during six days and nights in the most inclement weather."[21] In this address Warren had lifted two key and interrelated facts from the morass of information about the raid: the endurance of the soldiers and their destruction of the Weldon line, which crowned the expedition as a stunning success. General Orders No. 65 was widely distributed in Warren's command, and it set the tone for the official reports that followed.

Whether the officers under Warren followed the talking points from General Orders No. 65 is difficult to say. It is quite possible that Civil War officers, by the latter stages of the war, avoided controversy in official reports, believing that the army's dirty laundry should not be aired in public. Whatever might have been the case, the veteran officers of the Hicksford Raid retrieved the same facts of the raid and repeated the same silences found in Warren's general order. In the thirty-five reports related to the expedition that the War Department ultimately published in the *Official Records*, every officer proclaimed that the Hicksford Raid had delivered a devastating blow against Lee's Weldon line. The expedition's success, as noted by virtually every officer, would have been in doubt without the iron discipline of the rank and file. Gen. Samuel Crawford was far from alone when he expressed his heartfelt admiration for his men: "I regard the marching of this division, its cheerful obedience to orders, and the anxiety that was manifested by officers and men to do what in them lay to contribute to the success of the expedition, as worthy of all praise." A similar opinion came from Warren's assistant medical officer, who declared, "During the whole time the troops were absent, exposed to great vicissitudes of weather and enduring great fatigue and hardship, I have rarely seen men work with better spirits or march better closed up."[22] Several officers did admit that their men had straggled, but they discounted the problem as isolated incidents involving a few rookie soldiers. Even though the stealing and imbibing of applejack had contributed to excessive straggling and had incapacitated a countless number of men who were ultimately murdered while in a drunken stupor, only three officers—Warren, his chief of artillery, and his assistant medical officer—mentioned the pervasive drinking of hard cider. Division, brigade, and regimental officers all considered the drinking of applejack a fact to be discarded in constructing their historical narratives of the campaign.

Of all the omissions in the Hicksford reports, the virtual silencing of Confederate guerrillas defiling the Union dead is the most deafening. Gen. Robert McAllister, whose letter to his wife describes the desecration of Union bodies in excruciating detail, failed to mention Southern atrocities or Federal reprisals in his official report. He outlined his command's operations without commentary or description, his report a simple recording of daily movements that resemble the thirty other official narratives submitted to Warren. Only five officers reference the outrages committed by Confederate guerrillas, and only three of them offer any detail.[23]

Explaining these absences as a cover-up among Warren's subordinates is too conspiratorial and not entirely persuasive. Moreover, such a theory misses how the formalized protocol for writing official reports helped determine which facts were worthy of being mentioned and which were unimportant.

Even though Warren's subordinates penned reports that are woefully incomplete and downright misleading, their narratives work from the assumption that the facts could be recovered and that a realistic past could be retrieved. Yet an officer's understandable need to protect his own reputation as well as the reputations of his men do help explain the active silencing of controversy in the Hicksford narratives.

The logic of military reporting did not produce perfectly uniform narratives. The uncontrollable destruction unleashed by Confederate guerrillas seeped into the official writings of three officers, Warren being one of them. The three reports contained only a passing mention of the atrocities. Details were still sparse, but all three officers stressed the trope of soldierly sacrifice, even as they acknowledged that scores of soldiers had turned into a destructive mob, rabid with revenge, and defiant of their officers' authority.[24] In a report submitted just one day after the raid had ended, Warren lauded the men for their physical sacrifice during an operation that lasted some six days, covered more than 100 miles, and had been executed under hostile weather: "The men marched and behaved most praise-worthily during this tiring expedition." He did acknowledge that some men had straggled, and among the laggards a few became "drunk to prostration" thanks to the applejack discovered "in almost every house." During the return to Petersburg, Warren learned that "some of our men were found dead along the route: in one instance, with throat cut." He had his doubts as to the veracity of the account. "Whether this was true or not, it soon became the belief of all the men in the command, and in retaliation almost every house was set on fire. Every effort was made by the officers to stop this incendiarism (which most likely punished the innocent), and with partial success."[25] In contrast to his subordinates, Warren addressed the bloody work of the guerrillas and the subsequent destruction of Sussex. He must have realized that Meade and Grant would eventually learn that the Sussex raid had unraveled in the final two days of the march. Yet, Warren devoted only ten lines to the controversial topic in a report that was nearly four pages long. For the sake of his professional standing and the reputation of his men, Warren downplayed the incident. He wanted his superiors to know that the violence had arisen spontaneously and that no officer could rein in the men aroused by rumors of Confederate atrocities.

By minimizing the presence of Confederate guerrillas and awarding significance to the soldiers destroying the Weldon line, Warren and his subordinates relegated the atrocities of Sussex to the periphery of the emerging historical narrative. Did their correspondence during the chronicling phase of the Sussex expedition as well as their official reports establish a factual and interpretive plotline followed by Northern journalists? With the Hicksford expedition, as with any military operation, it is difficult to trace the flow of information from the field to a particular correspondent. Newspapermen often created the impression that they were embedded with the troops, but often they were a comfortable distance behind the lines. Whatever was the case, newspapers announced the start of the Hicksford expedition on December 10, three days after the Federals broke camp.[26] Even though speculation swirled around the destination of the Federals, the *New York Times* assured its readers that Warren's men were in "high spirits" and would deliver a crushing blow to Lee's army. On December 13, Washington, DC's *Evening Star* ran a banner headline proclaiming Warren's raid as a great success: "Important from the Front. Success of Warren's Expedition." S. W. D. McGregor, correspondent of the Associated Press, trained his readers' eyes on the expedition's movements without delving into any of the raid's controversies. He described the guerrillas as more of a nuisance than a threat, noting the rumor that one guerrilla might have been hung by the Federal soldiers.[27] McGregor, for the most part, wrote a heroic account of Warren's expedition. His position behind the lines likely explains his detached perspective. McGregor wrote not what he had seen firsthand but what he had learned from official communications and other sources at headquarters in the Petersburg and Richmond siege lines.

The portrayal of Warren's men as conquering heroes defined subsequent narratives of the Hicksford Raid through the rest of December 1864.[28] Even as news correspondents detailed the operational aspects of the raid, the public narrative of the campaign became more layered and expansive once the accounts from Warren's veterans surfaced in print. On the night of December 11, a correspondent for the *Philadelphia Inquirer*, possibly Gen. Robert McAllister, described the raid from the perspective of a person experiencing it at the ground level of war. He informed his readers that during the return trip to Sussex, the troops discovered the "naked bodies" of stragglers who were "placed in ostentatious bravado upon the roadside just beyond the town." "The site sealed the fate of Sussex Court House," the writer observed. "Our army giving its dastardly citizens such a lesson in retribution as they will not soon forget. The town was fired, and we staid long enough to make sure that it would not in the future give shelter to cowardly murderers."[29]

Depicting retaliation as a just and moral act of war was foundational to the author's portrait of Warren's command as an army of liberators who were remaking the despotic South into a land of freedom. The political and moral stakes of this expedition, as the author understood them, explain his elevation of runaway slaves as a significant fact in the Hicksford expedition. The correspondent used redemptive language to describe their flight to Union armies. Through the smoky haze arising from the "smoldering ruins of Sussex," the author saw the "starry flag of freedom streaming for a day over those benighted counties of Virginia," and "the negroes flocked beneath its folds and followed it as the Israelites followed the pillar of fire, and the clouds that led them from their bondage to their promised land of liberty."[30]

In subsequent newspaper accounts written by insiders with the Army of the Potomac, facts were retrieved or silenced to frame the Hicksford Raid as a moment of redemption. The writers did not attempt to hide the brutality of the guerrillas or to mask the vengeful acts of Warren's veterans.[31] Yet the emergence of the redemptive narrative brought new silences. The moral misgivings about waging hard war against civilians, which some of Warren's men expressed in letters home, vanished in published accounts. Many veterans had told family members that plenty of men had straggled to plunder private homes and that they were likely killed in the act of stealing. Newspaper accounts, however, did not mention any criminal activity committed by Warren's veterans. Such thievery and wanton destruction weighed on the consciences of some men, including Maine's Joshua L. Chamberlain. He considered the Hicksford Raid a "sad business." "I am willing to fight men in arms, but not *babes in arms*." He could not shake off the guilt, writing in a subsequent letter that he considered the burning of homes "a sad sight & showed war in its most disagreeable aspect; for my part." "I had rather charge lines of battle," he grimly concluded.[32] The print culture depicting the Hicksford campaign also distanced Warren's men from their acts of unrestrained violence. In *Frank Leslie's Illustrated Newspaper*, the artist G. F. Williams drew bridges, depots, and stores engulfed in flames, while orderly work parties went about their business with proficient military discipline. The sketch reinforced the public's perception of Union armies as unstoppable military machines rolling over the Southern countryside and gutting the logistical networks sustaining the Confederacy.[33]

The illustrations, like the accompanying newspaper accounts, stripped Sussex County of a civilian presence, including the guerrillas. By making the enemy invisible, the illustrations also removed Confederate women from the Sussex narrative. They disappear as political actors and are reduced to the role of helpless bystanders, as has almost always been the case in the depictions of women during a time of war. But Warren's men, like any Northern soldiers who spent time in the Confederacy, knew that white Southern women were not passive onlookers. In their letters home, Union soldiers repeatedly charged Sussex women with hiding weapons and harboring guerrillas. They were cagey and deceptive, and Union soldiers came to see them not as innocent bystanders but as political adversaries whose tactics could cost a Union soldier his life—an essential fact deemed unworthy to publish in Hicksford newspaper accounts.[34] Northern correspondents also ignored the sexual violence unleashed during the Union retaliation. It is inconceivable that the Sussex County women could have escaped a drunken mob of soldiers without enduring sexual insults and other indignities. The crime of rape, though not extensively documented during Warren's expedition, was registered in a credible wartime letter from a Maine soldier. No Northern paper would deem such news as suitable for print, however.

While it is hardly surprising that Northern papers silenced the crime of rape, the Richmond editors also kept any reference to sexual violence in Sussex out of the papers. The *Richmond Enquirer, Richmond Dispatch, Richmond Daily Dispatch, Richmond Daily Examiner,* and *Richmond Sentinel* silenced the evidence of local guerrillas murdering Union soldiers as well as the assault on women by Warren's men as retaliation. Richmond editors created an alternative narrative by trivializing Warren's raid through the trope of Yankee vandalism, a reassuring and understandable depiction of Union soldiers as nothing more than a band of ragamuffins who broke into chicken coops and burned barns. Why did Richmond editors, when presented with a propaganda opportunity to damn Yankees as rapists, drain their accounts of sexual violence? Reporting the news of Yankees physically assaulting women would have enraged Lee's veterans, who were stuck in the Petersburg trenches and unable to stop the enemy from raping their wives. Exposing the sexual crimes of Sussex could have driven Confederates to desert.

Silencing the crime of rape was not new in Richmond papers. On June 20, 1864, William Johnson, a member of the Twenty-Third US Colored Troops, faced the hangman for the crime of rape. The Federals displayed William Johnson's body from the gallows in front of thousands of Confederates along the Petersburg front. During a truce the Confederates learned that Johnson had raped a white woman outside Richmond. Photographers took multiple images of Johnson's hanging corpse. Woodcuts were made and then printed in the *New York Times* on a full page. Yet this national story in the North was intentionally buried in the Confederacy. Only two brief references surfaced in a single Richmond paper during the summer of 1864.[35] Even then the editors minimized Johnson's story in the miscellaneous column, and the copy came directly from Northern papers. Confederate discourse, like all discourse, was riddled with tensions and inconsistencies. The fear of a slave insurrection had been a staple in the South's rhetorical war against the North.[36] Jefferson Davis's denouncement of the preliminary emancipation in 1862 rested upon an imagined race war in which white women would fall prey to rebellious slaves. When credible news of a sexual crime was committed by a Black soldier against a white woman, the Confederate ruling class kept the information away from the public, even though there was overwhelming evidence—both written and visual—coming from the enemy. Their calculating decision is a reminder that political solidarity in the Confederacy did not simply rely upon the call for white solidarity. To be sure, racial ideas forged a powerful sense of unity in the South, but they also had the potential to divide. Southern newspaper editors, politicians, and generals understood the risk of reporting the rape of a white woman when they silenced the news of Johnson's execution.

All in all, neither North nor South could accept the events of the Sussex raid as they had occurred. Men on both sides actively created silences to advance political goals, to adhere to moral imperatives, and to fit facts into people's understanding of the world. To simply conclude that both sides falsified the past misses an opportunity to explain the process of historical production. The first narratives of the Hicksford Raid affirm Michel-Rolph Trouillot's observation that silences and mentions are "active dialectical counterparts" of which history is the synthesis.[37] When Northerners retrieved the fact that Confederate guerrillas had savagely murdered their comrades, they also had to silence their own violent excesses, including rape, or their narrative would have contradicted their view of themselves as disciplined soldiers who were responsible for the successful Hicksford Raid. The first Sussex narratives also reveal the tremendous power that military officers wielded in the first stages of historical production. They selected facts, assigned significance to them, and decided what to silence, creating plotlines in the process that structured the first newspaper accounts. The under-reporting of violence in official documents and in newspapers suggests that the violence in the American Civil War was far more lethal and unrestrained than what some scholars have maintained. But the private voices of the individual soldier did not remain buried for long. Letters from the rank and file, with their graphic descriptions of guerrilla violence and retaliation, appeared widely in newspapers. Still, their revelations, no matter how shocking to Northern audiences, did not change popular perceptions of Warren's Weldon raid as anything but a success.

The initial historical narrative of the Hicksford Raid was not fixed but open-ended, fluid, and contested. In the postwar period, the narrative went from dark to light, taking a sharp turn toward nostalgia when Union veterans started referring to the Hicksford Raid as the Applejack Raid. Facts depicting their drunken behavior in a humorous light had a stronger presence in the historical narrative, while facts about the war crimes in Sussex disappeared almost entirely. The silences have accumulated since then, offering clues as to why the historical memory of the Hicksford Raid has lost its hold on the very people who reside there today. Forgetting, however, is not an inevitable consequence of time passing. While the lack of ruins has always made it possible for people to visualize a Civil War free of apocalyptic violence, it is too reductionist to blame historical forgetfulness on the loss of a cultural resource. The silences that I heard during my Sussex visit can be neither dismissed as the product of nostalgia nor blamed on the wearing of Lost Cause blinders. Silences are more complicated and dynamic, and they are always taking new shapes and forms as the physical world changes.

Understanding why Bill Jenkins was not familiar with the war crimes of Warren's raid begins with his personal history, but the inquiry cannot end there. It is common for historians to refer to legacies of the past as responsible for silences. The use of legacies as an explanatory device can be limiting because it is so sweepingly ambiguous. Legacies can suggest an unthinking acceptance of historical traditions, which tends to skim over the highly public battles over the control of historical narrative.

One of the key takeaways from the study of the Hicksford Raid is that we must look more closely at the creation and revision of historical narratives. We must examine the production of history and its relationship to who wields power in a place like Sussex County, where the largest employer today is the Virginia Department of Corrections followed by the Chinese-owned Smithfield Farms. Small farmers have called it quits, jobs are scarce, and 16 percent of the population lives below the poverty line.[38] Nearly 60 percent of the population is African American, and the county's population, which grew faster in the 1990s because of two new prisons, is currently declining.[39] Sussex is caught in the maelstrom of global capitalism. Whatever crimes might be occurring behind the prison walls or whatever poisonous waste is being dumped by factory farms, the Hicksford Raid reminds us that silences don't remain silent forever in the historical record.

NOTES

1. Quoted from Christopher Calkins, "Action in the Petersburg Campaign: The Beefsteak Raid and Apple Jack Raid," *Blue and Gray Magazine*, Summer 2005, 62.

2. Michel-Rolph Trouillot, *Silencing the Past: Power and the Production of History* (Boston: Beacon Press, 1995), 48.

3. Trouillot, *Silencing the Past*, 3.

4. John W. Haley, *The Rebel Yell and the Yankee Hurrah: The Civil War Journal of a Maine Volunteer*, ed. Ruth L. Silliker (Camden, ME: Down East Books, 1985), 225.

5. Robert McAllister to Ellen McAllister, December 8, 1864, in *The Civil War Letters of General Robert McAllister*, ed. James I. Robertson Jr. (New Brunswick, NJ: Rutgers University Press, 1965), 554.

6. Robert McAllister to Ellen McAllister, December 14, 1864, in *Civil War Letters of General Robert McAllister*, 552, 553.

7. Warren Report, in US War Department, *The War of the Rebellion: A Compilation of the Official Records of the Union and Confederate Armies*, 127 vols., index, and atlas (Washington, DC: Government Printing Office, 1880–1901) (hereafter *OR*), ser. 1, 42(1): 445.

8. William Ray, *Four Years with the Iron Brigade: The Civil War Journal of William Ray, Company F, Seventh Wisconsin Volunteers*, ed. Lance Herdegen and Sherry Murphy (Cambridge: Da Capo, 2002), 342, 343.

9. Warren Report, in *OR* 42(1):445

10. Warren Report, in *OR* 42(1):445–46

11. Robert McAllister to his wife, December 11, 1864, in *Civil War Letters of General Robert McAllister*, 558.

12. Luther M. Gerrish to His Sister Nettie, December 14, 1864, Accession #15713, Small Special Collections, University of Virginia, Charlottesville (hereafter UVA).

13. *Four Brothers in Blue; or, Sunshine and Shadows of the War of the Rebellion: A Story of the Great Civil War from Bull Run to Appomattox*, ed. Robert Goldthwaite Carter (Austin: University of Texas Press, 1979), 496; James B. Thomas to his father, December 12, 1864, in *The Civil War Letters of First Lieutenant James B. Thomas*, ed. Mary Warner Thomas and Richard A. Sauers (Baltimore: Butternut and Blue, 1995), 264.

14. Joshua Chamberlain to My Dear Sae, December 14, 1864, in *Through Blood and Fire: Selected Civil War Papers of Major General Joshua Chamberlain*, ed. Mark Nesbitt (Mechanicsburg, PA: Stackpole Books, 1996), 144–45.

15. Haley, *Rebel Yell and the Yankee Hurrah*, 226–27.

16. Luther M. Gerrish to His Sister Nettie, December 14, 1864, Accession #15713, UVA.

17. Charles K. Winne, December 16, 1864, in *OR* 42(1):453.

18. G. K. Warren to George G. Meade, December 11, 1864, *OR* 42(3):951.

19. On Warren's well-documented problems with Meade and Grant, see David M. Jordan, *"Happiness Is Not My Companion": The Life of General G. K. Warren* (Bloomington: Indiana University Press, 2001).

20. U. S. Grant to George G. Meade, December 13, 1863; Meade to G. K. Warren, December 13, 1864, *OR* 42(2):985.

21. G. K. Warren, "General Orders No. 65," December 13, 1864, *OR* 42(1):447.

22. Samuel W. Crawford, December 19, 1864, *OR* 42(1):496; Charles K. Winne, December 16, 1864, *OR* 42(1):454.

23. Robert McAllister, December 15, 1864, report, *OR* 42(1):339–400. For additional Union reports that overlook Confederate guerrilla activities and Federal retaliation, see the

thirty-five reports of the Fifth Corps and of the Third Division in the Second Corps in *OR* 42(1).

24. Lorenzo Barber, December 16, 1864, *OR* 42(1):356–57.

25. G. K. Warren to George G. Meade, December 14, 1864, *OR* 42(1):445–46.

26. "An Important Movement on Foot. The Second and Fifth Corps March on Stony Creek," *New York Times*, December 10, 1864.

27. "Extra, Important from the Front. Success of Warren's Expedition. He Goes to Hicksford, on the Weldon Road," *Evening Star* (Washington, DC), December 13, 1864.

28. "Warren's Operations," *New York Times*, December 18, 1864.

29. Correspondent for the *Philadelphia Inquirer*, "Gen. Grant's Army. Heavy Firing on the James River. Warren's Corps Back in the Old Position," printed in *New York Times*, December 15, 1864.

30. Correspondent for the *Philadelphia Inquirer*, "Gen. Grant's Army."

31. On the Union army's design to redeem the South, see Elizabeth R. Varon, *Armies of Deliverance: A New History of the Civil War* (New York: Oxford University Press, 2019).

32. Joshua Chamberlain to My Dear Sae, December 14, 1864, and Chamberlain to John, December 19, 1864, in *Through Blood and Fire*, 145, 146.

33. "Burning the Weldon Railroad Bridge," *Frank Leslie's Illustrated Newspaper*, December 31, 1864.

34. "The News," *Daily Richmond Enquirer*, December 14, 1864; "Return of the Raiders," *Daily Richmond Enquirer*, December 14, 1864; "The Enemy on the Weldon Railroad—They Are Repu[l]sed at Bellfield," *Richmond Daily Dispatch*, December 12, 1864; "The South Side," *Richmond Daily Examiner*, December 14, 1864; "The War News," *Richmond Daily Dispatch*, December 15, 1864.

35. "Miscellaneous," *Richmond Daily Dispatch*, June 28 and 29, 1864.

36. Robert F. Berkhoffer Jr., *Beyond the Great Story: A History as Text and Discourse* (Cambridge, MA: Belknap Press of Harvard University Press, 1995), 203–5.

37. Trouillot, *Silencing the Past*, 48.

38. "Top Employers," Sussex County, Virginia, website www.sussexcountyva.gov/page/top-employers (accessed May 16, 2019).

39. "Sussex County, Virginia," Wikipedia, https://en.wikipedia.org/wiki/Sussex_County,_Virginia (accessed May 16, 2019).

Jubal A. Early, Lee Commemoration, and the Consolidation of Confederate History, 1870-1890

KATHRYN J. SHIVELY

September 28, 1870, was a punishing day for the residents of Lexington, Virginia.[1] One of the severest floods the Shenandoah Valley had ever seen killed dozens and swept "large houses, bridges, mills & every sort of lumber" down the Maury River. The same day, Washington College president and former Confederate general-in-chief, Robert E. Lee, suffered a debilitating stroke. John Esten Cooke, belletrist and onetime Confederate staff officer, thought the stroke a "symptom of... the depression produced by the sufferings of the Southern people." It had been five years since US victors toppled the Confederacy, and now its foremost general's life dimmed. A nigh-biblical flood that swept the land clear coupled with Lee's imminent demise portended an erasure of the Confederate past. The loss of Lee would mean the loss of a definitive military history of the Confederacy, which Lee had contemplated writing but had not yet committed to paper. The question was: Who would take up the mantle?[2]

Lee died two weeks later on October 12, 1870. His funeral offered little pageantry for the Confederacy and seemed to betoken its symbolic end. In Washington College's Grace Episcopal Church his body lay attired in a plain black suit, bearing no reminders of his recent military service. Lee had remarked to a former Washington College president, David McConaughy, a year earlier, "I think it wiser . . . not to keep open the sores of war, but . . . to commit to oblivion the feelings [the war] engendered." In respect of these wishes, Lee's coffin was buried beneath the Washington College chapel draped only in evergreen and flowers. The South's most celebrated military leader since George Washington passed from the scene with the equivalence of a whisper.[3]

Lee's legacy to the South appeared a show of peaceful reconciliation, as did his public comments before his death. Privately, however, he had worked steadfastly to promote a martial, pro-Confederate history. In his famous General Orders No. 9 on April 10, 1865, he laid the framework for this narrative by claiming that the Confederates had lost only because of long odds, not inferior military skills or a deficient cause. Hoping to follow up this thesis with a written history of the Army of Northern Virginia, his field army and the Confederacy's preeminent institution, Lee felt his lack of documentary evidence prevented him. Therefore, while Lee had presented the appearance of a statesman to the public, refusing to dwell on the past, in private he had tenaciously defended the Confederacy. Indeed, before his death, he invested heavily in an unlikely historian to carry the message, one who demonstrated unqualified loyalty to Lee, his army, and the long odds thesis: Jubal Anderson Early.[4]

Despite a previous rupture in their acquaintance, when Lee had dismissed Early from the Confederate army for losing the Shenandoah Valley in March 1865, their mutual historical ambitions had sparked a close intellectual partnership immediately postwar. Between 1865 and 1869 Early won Lee's trust when Early produced the first postwar memoir of a general on either side, along with a second unpublished memoir and several high-profile articles on the Army of Northern Virginia. In each document, Early eagerly adopted Lee's odds thesis, which also helped to justify Early's own loss to Union general Philip Sheridan in the Shenandoah. As a skilled lawyer, Early's facility with evidence prompted his embrace of emerging scientific-historical methods, lending credibility to his account. Marshaling numbers, primary sources, and citations, he catapulted the odds thesis to believability. In turn,

Lee provided peer review and urged an objective tone, understanding that dispassionate analysis would prove the point better than emotionally charged invective. While the former did not come naturally to the famously quarrelsome Early, he dutifully tried to confine his rancor to footnotes in these initial writings—at least while Lee lived. All told, these techniques—impartial tone, emphasis on data, documented source use, and peer review—shrouded Early and Lee's special pleading. Thus, a fierce Confederate apologia masqueraded as objective history. Clad in the noble garb of truth, this highly partisan valorization of the Confederacy would serve as the starting point for much of American historical writing about the Civil War.[5]

Though Early helped to frame and disseminate Lee's nascent history in the late 1860s, the two did diverge in some respects. While Lee felt "the South require[d] the presence of all her sons" to rebuild after the war, Early opted instead to avoid Reconstruction under the foes he despised and enter voluntary exile. When Early returned to Virginia in 1869, his writing edged away from an objective tone; he began to use historical writing as an overt conservative tool instead of directly participating in political campaigning. Moreover, he attacked historical narratives that questioned the odds thesis or scientific methods as a form of outsider rule, just as white Southern politicians opposed Yankee carpetbaggers. Effective at doing so, he became a feared critic and public personality. While Lee did not agree with all of Early's tactics, their historical union remained beneficial; Lee could maintain a reputation as a peaceful, Christian gentleman, while his acrimonious lieutenant welcomed the controversy his historical writings attracted. Thus, when Lee died, Early stood ready to ascend as chief historian of the Confederacy with Lee's blessing.[6]

What happened next, however, caught Early by surprise. Lee's death prompted a spate of competitors to memorialize the chieftain in contrasting ways, challenging Early's historical dominance, which largely had depended on his proximity to Lee. Early coveted control of Lee's image both to authenticate his claim to being chief historian and to serve as a rallying point for his Army of Northern Virginia–centric narrative. Unfortunately for Early, while he was skilled with deploying evidence, he had little experience with monuments, public celebrations, and oration necessary to commemoration. More provoking still to the resolutely elitist Early, commemoration was democratic. Even white women and Black people could construct historical memory in the public sphere, whereas the scientific-historical writing that had stoked Early's fame could use emerging professional standards and qualifications to exclude troublesome groups.[7]

Reacting to these challenges to his authority and put off by the unruly commemorative sphere, Early attempted numerous tactics to discipline and eradicate rivals. Ultimately, it was his use of apparently dispassionate historical methods, combined with a concerted effort to construct documentary archives, that proved most durable; this approach concealed his special pleading under a mountain of statistics and facts, minimizing the emotionalism that surrounded monument dedication. Early's history advanced well beyond the tactics and ideas he and Lee had discussed in Lee's lifetime. Thus, in terms of historical influence, the lieutenant far exceeded the commander.[8]

In the waning days of 1870 after Lee's death, events unfolded rapidly, threatening Early's historical authority and forcing him into the commemorative sphere. First, Early missed Lee's funeral because of pervasive regional flooding and obligations at Franklin County court, where Early practiced law; yet it was essential to his personal reputation that he demonstrate his close connection to Lee and succeed his commander in historical leadership. Second, Lee's funeral had gone all wrong for Early's purposes, de-emphasizing Lee's martial, rebellious ties to the Confederacy and centering, instead, Lee's public, reconciliationist overtures. Third, and most alarming to Early, two squabbling groups sought to inter and memorialize Lee, underscoring the pressing need to use symbols and celebrations to popularize Early's preferred historical narrative.[9]

The first of the Lee memorial groups to emerge, on the very day of Lee's passing, was the Washington College–based Lee Memorial Association, whose members hoped to retain the general's remains in Lexington and erect a statue there, emphasizing Lee's postwar career and overtures toward sectional harmony. Several days later, the Ladies' Lee Monument Committee, composed of members of the Hollywood Memorial Association, sought to continue its work of burying and honoring the dead in Richmond's most prominent Confederate cemetery by linking it with the Confederacy's greatest general. While Early had trailblazed Confederate historical writing, he was quickly outshone in the realm of public commemoration.[10]

Scrambling on October 25, 1870, to assert his threatened authority over Lee's image, Early announced his own Lee Monument Association via an article in the *Lynchburg Daily Virginian*, a friendly forum. Early aimed to inter and commemorate Lee the rebel general, the primary martial symbol for his historical narrative, in the capital of the former Confederacy to emphasize his narrative's centralizing power. As Early explained in the news article, Lee's fame belonged to "the world and to history," not to a trivial locality, such as Lexington, nor to the women of the Ladies' Lee Monument Committee or other memorial associations, whose proper sphere was the home rather than the masculine domains of war and history. Though Early boldly laid forth his credentials as the obvious head of any attempt to set Confederate history in bronze—"being, as I believe, the senior in rank of all the officers of the Army of Northern Virginia now living in the state"—he also recognized the need to build consensus around his leadership. As a famous curmudgeon, he would never be well liked, but Lee's appeal, and Stonewall Jackson's for that matter, was universal. Thus did Early insist that "we owe it to our fallen comrades, to ourselves, and to posterity to manifest to the world for all time to come, that we were not unworthy to be led by our immortal chief, and that we are not now ashamed of the principles for which LEE fought and JACKSON died." These words also emphasized his narrative's requirement of continued, unwavering loyalty to the Confederate nation—or at least, the limited nation he styled in historical writing. Finally, while his competitors appealed to mere regional interest groups, he "respectfully" invited all surviving Confederate officers, sailors, and marines to convene at a meeting on November 3 in Richmond.[11]

With his plan laid, Early now sorely needed prominent supporters and entrée into commemorative activities. Marylander Bradley T. Johnson, a well-regarded Confederate general who had served under Jackson and Early, offered prompt fidelity and promising opportunities. Writing on the very day of the article's appearance, Johnson not only backed Early's Lee memorial initiative but also invited Early to head a new veterans' organization, the Association of the Army of Northern Virginia (AANVA). Johnson confessed that the organizers had preferred Lee before his death but deemed Early, who had already achieved a formidable reputation for defending Lee's army, the obvious successor. For Early, AANVA leadership presented an opportunity to consolidate control over what he viewed as the most important Confederate institution, the Army of Northern Virginia, and encourage his former comrades to collect primary sources and disseminate Confederate history. Johnson also recognized kindred impulses in Early's October 25 article to de-emphasize reconciliation by focusing on the war, to curtail the Ladies' Lee Monument Committee's influence, and to fuse regional veterans' initiatives into one powerful, central entity. Thus did they add an additional Richmond meeting to inaugurate the AANVA on November 4, 1870, with Early now poised to accept two major leadership roles and give two very public commemorative speeches.[12]

During the orations of November 3 and 4, Early advanced several tactics to unite Lee commemoration with his historical work. To the AANVA audience members, Early legitimized his historical leadership by reading out two letters from Lee to Early. One affirmed Lee's faith in Early's "high intelligence, sagacity and bravery, and untiring devotion to the cause," and the other praised Early for his skillful use of numbers-based history. Then, designating the AANVA as a vehicle for historical production, Early invited his comrades to begin collecting primary documents for the cause. Additionally, to both audiences, Early declared Virginia the epicenter of Confederate history, better positioning himself, as the senior-most Army of Northern Virginia veteran, to control its narrative. Specifically, he insisted that the primary Lee statue should be in Richmond, "as the Confederate capital was so prominently a feature in General Lee's military career"; likewise would the AANVA be headquartered "in the State of Virginia, for reasons too obvious to require enumeration." Finally, on the topic of his Lee Monument Association, Early promised to have the Virginia state legislature incorporate it, thereby underscoring its principal legitimacy in the face of competitors. Regarding commemorative opponents, he claimed he would hinder neither "the proposal of the ladies" nor "the plan of a memorial ... at Lexington"; however, he publicly asserted irreconcilable goals, including reinterring Lee in Richmond against his widow's wishes and counter to the Lexington memorial plan. Early then proceeded to antagonize both groups, manifesting a particularly ferocious vendetta against the Ladies' Lee Monument Committee.[13]

The twenty-year conflict between Early and the Ladies over a Richmond-based Lee equestrian statue, well documented by historian Caroline E. Janney, exposed Early's determination to exclude women from historical production because of its political nature. Janney argues that Early, along with Bradley Johnson, sought to reclaim Confederate memorialization from women, who had led such efforts in a period of Virginia Reconstruction during which veterans had their rights restricted and, incidentally, when Early had been in voluntary exile. Ladies' Memorial Associations saw themselves as "the [rightful] guardians of Confederate memory," using their status as alleged apolitical beings to obscure partisan messages. While Early had praised the Ladies for burying the dead during his absence and had even given them the proceeds from his first memoir, he now saw their commemorative enterprises as rival attempts to shape Confederate history, a political—and to Early, exclusively masculine—enterprise. The threat to Early's dominance compounded because the Ladies had more organizational and fundraising experience and quickly outpaced Early's group in raising money and attention through a hired agent. When the Ladies suggested to Early that they unite the two Richmond efforts, they were met with shocking bitterness and spite. Early disavowed them in the newspapers in March 1871, attempted to undermine their fundraising agent before employing his own, and even resorted to hiring a spy to observe their meetings. Disgruntled but undeterred, the Ladies sidestepped Early's efforts at domination and would continue to affect the progress of the Richmond Lee monument until its manifestation nearly two decades later.[14]

The Lexington-based Lee Memorial Association also thwarted Early's power grab in 1870, underscoring the difficulty of reducing Lee symbolism to one particular slant. Early insisted to Lexington members, in private, that Lee's statue should be a "Confederate" rather than a "state monument" at Richmond. Hypocrisy aside, given that Early's version of Confederate history likewise elevated Virginia, the comment again revealed that Early sought to use the former Confederate capital to centralize his myopic historical narrative. While the Lexington contingent accepted the Richmond statue, they also refused to yield on their own. After months of acrimonious back-and-forth with former Confederate officers at Washington College, including William Preston Johnston, William Allan, and William Nelson Pendleton, it was Early who compromised. He accepted Mary Anna Custis Lee's decision to retain Lee's remains on the college campus, offered the Lexington fund the sum of ten dollars (admittedly paltry since he would later give well over a thousand to the Richmond monument), and allowed the Lexington Lee Memorial Association to publish his contribution as a show of solidarity. He also agreed to provide speeches, an important element of commemoration, to raise additional funds for the Washington College monument. Several years later, in April 1875, he even chose to accompany sculptor Edward Valentine's Recumbent Lee sarcophagus on the final leg of its journey from Richmond to Lexington. The question is: Why did Early yield?[15]

From 1870 through 1875, Early learned that dominating the democratic sphere of commemoration was untenable. To begin with, he received a torrent of letters complaining that the various Lee memorialization schemes unnecessarily divided the Confederate ranks when they ought to be united in historical purpose. A particular missive from his most detested Confederate rival, John B. Gordon, capitalized on the unseemly infighting with a promise to send out his own agents to diminish and appropriate Early's power. Early attempted to unify former Confederate soldiers by deeming loyalty a basic litmus test for postwar commemoration, claiming "all who have *deserted since the close of the war*—however high their former position may have been," should be rooted out to assure "a bond of union not only among the survivors, but among their descendants for many generations." But he found that however viciously he attacked those who did not meet his requirements in public articles or private correspondence, he could not prevent competitors from interfering in Lee memorialization.[16]

In another lesson learned about the difficulties of controlling commemoration, particularly given its relationship to partisan politics, Early's attempt to use political authority to legitimize his Lee Monument Association failed to pack a punch. Following up on Early's November 1870 promise to involve the Virginia state government in the incorporation of his association, Bradley Johnson helped to charter it on January 25, 1871—using connections to Virginia senator and Early's former staff officer John W. Daniel—but to no discernible cowing effect on Early's rivals. Six years later, when Early made an even bolder attempt to exclude the Ladies' Lee Monument Committee by turning over his memorial association to the state of Virginia under the male leadership of the governor, treasurer, and state auditor, the Ladies continued to successfully fundraise and investigate potential city locations and sculptors without any regard for the man who sought to silence them.[17]

A final incident concerning the participation of Black Southerners in Confederate memorialization reveals Early's failure to control public commemorations. While in Lexington in April 1875 celebrating the placement of the Recumbent Lee sarcophagus, Early received word that he would become president of the Jackson Memorial Association, providing him an opportunity to shape memorialization of the second most-important figurehead in Lee's army. Because of Early's position, Confederate major general turned governor James L. Kemper invited Early to join a state commission, which was to receive a bronze statue of Jackson sculpted by recently deceased Irish sculptor and Confederate sympathizer John Henry Foley. From the outset, Early quibbled with Kemper by overemphasizing Virginia in the inscription and refusing to acknowledge Kemper's former rank in the Confederate army, perhaps because Early judged Kemper a powerful competitor. After much debate over text, location, and timing of the unveiling ceremony, the commission determined to place the statue in Richmond's Capitol Square on October 26, 1875. Even then, Early hoped to manipulate planned orator Moses D. Hoge's address, insisting that Jackson be lauded second-best beneath Lee and that references to Jackson's religiosity not overshadow his militarism.[18]

When Early learned that Kemper planned to allow Black militia units to march in the ceremonial parade—which Early declared an "indignity to the memory of Jackson, an insult to all Confederates who have any respect for themselves left"—he ignited an ugly row with the governor. Via frantic telegram, Early alleged that Kemper would promote the mixing of races, the flaunting of Lincoln's image, and the flying of Fifteenth Amendment banners, all overtly political concerns. Kemper fumed in private to mutual friend Fitzhugh Lee, "My indignation and wrath have known no bounds . . . my blood boils." To Early the governor curtly replied, "The programme is fixed. All Hell can't change it." Kemper went on to explain his reasons for including Black militiamen. He sought to assuage Northerners, who were suspicious of the memorialization of rebel generals, with a peaceful, segregated celebration that included freedpeople—not to mention he also hoped to avoid handing to the Radicals another "bloody shirt." Kemper also informed Early that he had "fully" considered the "propriety" of the "very humble request" of the militia units "to be allowed to honor Jackson's memory," arguing that because Jackson "for many years taught negro Sunday schools," Black Southerners had "turned out in great numbers" at his funeral and burial and should be allowed to celebrate his statue. Determined to allow Black participation in commemoration but to prevent racial mixing, Kemper exhaustively detailed a "procession of whites several miles long," and "then in the rear of all this . . . come the negroes." Moreover, he had even excluded the legislature, because it was integrated. Despite Kemper holding his ground, Early won his object when the Black units refused to march because of their place in line, while Early attended to much fanfare.[19]

Vexed by wearying competition in the memorial sphere, Early found more success when he intermingled commemorative oration with the dependable tools of scientific history. Importantly, it was his Lexington opponents who gave him a tremendous opportunity to fuse memory and history around the symbol of Lee, providing the most compelling explanation for Early's concessions to them. When Preston Johnston first invited Early to speak at Washington College on Lee's birthday, January 19, 1872, Early demurred; the Lexington group, after all, seemed determined to co-opt Lee symbolism away from Early's control. He warned that his address would spurn reconciliation, but Johnston proved surprisingly soothing, assuring Early that "you are not the man nor this the occasion for pretty talk. The world is full of people able to make that, and Purgatory is too: but there are not many who by nature, education, sympathy and knowledge of the facts can do what we wanted done." Not only was the Lexington group apparently open to Early's historical message and methods, but they also confirmed "a general expression of satisfaction that you are to speak." Apparently, they, too, saw the benefit in restoring harmony among former Confederate officers who sought to memorialize Lee.[20]

Early's 1872 Lee birthday speech, which elided evidence-based history with memory, proved to be among the most important he ever made. In the oration Early reinforced the odds thesis, presented to unify Confederate veterans, and employed seemingly indisputable science to elevate Lee. He declared that his US numbers were based on Federal primary sources—"taken from their own reports and statements"—while conferring upon his Confederate figures incontestable authority from the "last interview I had with General Lee." Though at first Early appeared to exonerate Virginia alone by blaming military loss on events in the West and Southwest, he mitigated even this censure by stressing "the [overall] disadvantage of overwhelming numbers" for all Confederate armies. The odds thesis thus became a blanket pardon for failure. Moreover, confirmed by science and reason, Lee emerged the blameless victor: "General Lee had not been conquered in battle, but surrendered because he had no longer an army with which to give battle. What he surrendered was the . . . mere ghost of the Army of Northern Virginia, which had been gradually worn down by the combined agencies of numbers, steam-power, railroads, mechanism, and all the resources of physical science." The clever use of scientific method and logic proved rhetorically forceful, but Early, ever the lawyer, recognized the simple counterargument to be made: Lee *had* been defeated in battle. And nowhere was this more apparent than at the battle of Gettysburg.[21]

Thus, continuing in the birthday oration, in an even more alarming example of obscuring memory with scientific history, Early combined verifiable fact with utter fabrication to put to bed Lee's most egregious battlefield error—failing to defeat the Army of the Potomac at Gettysburg after a stunningly successful first day. This speech generated the influential First Corps sunrise attack thesis, which blamed Lee's subordinate James Longstreet for defeat because he failed to assault at first light on the second day, thereby allowing Union troops time to get into position. As Early explained, this time based on no documented evidence that could confirm the scheduled hour of the assault, Lee ordered "Longstreet's corps . . . to begin the attack at dawn." But Longstreet failed to take his position until 4 p.m., by which point "Meade's whole army had arrived on the field. . . . Had the attack been made at daylight, as contemplated, it must have resulted in a brilliant and decisive victory." Implicit, as well, was the idea that if Longstreet had followed orders on the second day, then Lee would not have had to launch the disastrous assault—known to posterity as Pickett's Charge—on the third day.[22]

Early had, in fact, tried to source the sunrise thesis by corresponding with Lee's staff officers, but none of them could confirm a specifically timed order. They could agree only on the fact that Longstreet, who had defected to the Republican Party postwar, was an abominable turncoat. At best a vague and loosely recorded postwar conversation between Lee and Preston Johnston suggested that Longstreet was "often slow," in Lee's opinion. But when in the birthday speech Early nestled in this canard alongside so many properly sourced statements, it resolutely lodged in the historical record.[23]

Another reason for the sunrise thesis's longevity was the birthday oration's successive incarnations. It lived on as a published pamphlet and was reprinted nearly intact, save the intro and conclusion, in John William Jones's influential *Personal Reminiscences of Robert E. Lee* (1874). Perhaps even more important, William Pendleton, Early's former Washington College rival and Lee's former chief of artillery, began to parrot the ill-founded interpretation in his own lecture circuit on Lee—never mind that it contradicted Pendleton's contemporary 1863 report. In this way, the sunrise thesis allowed Early to resolve bitterness with the Washington College contingent, bonding over their shared historical exploits, while revealing to Early the power his historical approach afforded. Longstreet suffered so gravely over the next few years, as Early wrote and encouraged defamatory article after article, that Early became increasingly feared as a historian not to cross, wielding power equal to a politician but longer lasting.[24]

Early could not have been more affirmed by the paeans he received in response to the Lee birthday speech, reinforcing his historical leadership after an arduous slog through the commemorative field. His longtime friend Fitzhugh Lee admired Early's scientific methods and was "pleased to see the stress put upon figures—They never lie and are uncontestable when correctly set down." But even soldiers whom Early had never met praised him for remaining "firm and unyielding in defense of the 'Lost Cause,' Constitutional liberty, and the Supremacy of the Anglo Saxon over the gizzard footed Africans," contrasting Early to the "truckling drones, who . . . abandon principle." Confirming the underlying politics of Early's historical work, such sentiments taught Early that he could most successfully memorialize Lee from the obscuring platform of scientific history.[25]

As Early continued to discredit competing historical narratives in the 1870s, his growing fame gained him increasing access to primary documents, a foundational element of scientific history. He began to develop ideas about the preservation and dissemination of sources to shape the historical record over the long term. To William H. Payne, a former brigadier general in Early's Army of the Valley, Early explained, "I think our people ought to be very particular as to whom they furnish material for writing anything about the war"—in other words, he advocated withholding sources to bolster only favored accounts. Yet when Early believed a document supported his desired narrative, he felt no hesitation in copying it out for publication, regardless of ownership, as revealed by a dispute with the editor of New York's *Historical Magazine*, Henry B. Dawson.[26]

Early and Dawson had miraculously maintained cordial relations during the famous debacle when Dawson published William Mahone's authorized autobiography in June 1870. The piece had manifestly insulted Early's generalship, nearly sparking a Mahone-Early duel. But now Early and Dawson fell out when Early copied Lee's report on Gettysburg from the *Historical Magazine*'s spring 1872 issue for republication in the Baltimore-based *Southern Magazine*. Dawson argued that the document, long presumed lost until found in the papers of war correspondent William Swinton, could not be copied without his consent because he had published it first. Early, however, was busy establishing himself as the preeminent expert on Gettysburg and, therefore, felt ownership of Lee's report.[27]

Early's interest in primary documents soon burgeoned into a career in archives construction thanks to his association with the Southern Historical Society. This was the missing piece in his methodology that solidified the reach and longevity of his historical legacy. The Southern Historical Society, founded May 1, 1869, in New Orleans, Louisiana, and with auxiliaries across the South and mid-Atlantic, initially enjoyed only modest success securing subscriptions, collecting primary accounts, and publishing documents and articles with the goal of preserving Confederate history. After multiple failed attempts to entice Early to speak in New Orleans, the society finally secured Early's oratory skills for its 1873 reorganizational meeting in White Sulphur Springs, West Virginia. This would mark the start of Early's archivist activities. At the August 14 convention, Early angled to move the parent society to Richmond, the symbolic center of his own historical exploits, while retaining the state branches. During his address he praised the society's "efforts to preserve and place before the public the materials for an authentic history of our cause" and was rewarded with yet another presidency.[28]

At the first meeting of the reorganized society in Richmond in 1873, Early openly relished presiding over what would soon become a flourishing repository for Confederate documents and a central producer of Confederate history. In his speech he insisted that Confederate devotees remained firmly at war with the United States, only their weapons were now "the pen and the tongue of truth." This rallying cry moralized the production of "objective" history. As the *Richmond Daily Dispatch* reported on the event, Early assumed the role of commanding general in this war of words. He "'went for' the so-called historians of the war in his characteristic style" and "exhorted all to rally who were not willing to have their sons and brothers branded for all time as 'rebels and traitors.'" Moreover, the *Dispatch* noted, Early cleverly positioned himself as the highest historian in the land, for "it was not proposed to *appoint* a historian—historians are not *appointed*—but to collect material for the grand work," work in which Early had surpassingly excelled. By a number of reasonable markers, Early had become the chief historian of the Confederacy.[29]

As president of the Southern Historical Society until his death in 1894, Early would exert considerable influence over its publications of primary documents, historical interpretations, and book reviews in the *Southern Historical Society Papers*. At fifty-two volumes and continuing in some form from 1876 to 1959, these volumes featured primary accounts from common soldiers to generals and politicians and reached an international audience; still used today, they must rank as a profoundly important Confederate archive. Though Early and society secretary John William Jones, who served from 1875 to 1887, often clashed over how to present documentary evidence in the *Papers*—Jones favored publishing all firsthand accounts to serve future historians, while Early endorsed curating sources to present only "correct" facts, according to his interpretation—Early's influence thrived most behind the scenes. In correspondence he wooed would-be authors over to his facts, figures, and arguments before publication, even correcting or omitting portions of primary documents. The most glaring example to appear in the *Papers* featured Early's pet subject of Longstreet's tardiness at Gettysburg. In a series of articles, which appeared in issues from 1877 to 1878, Early labored tirelessly to recruit authors and evidence, much of which was questionable or even hearsay, to condemn Longstreet archivally. In short, the *Papers* were rife with invisible Early fingerprints, which edged the primary evidence toward his preferred interpretation.[30]

As Early's fame as historian continued to swell in the late 1870s and 1880s, he occasionally reentered the commemorative sphere to confront the continuing saga of the Richmond Lee equestrian statue, a nagging, unfinished business that might crown his achievements. The Ladies remained an unwelcome reminder that historical production could not be neatly confined to Early's chosen disciples. Early's brainchild, the all-male Lee Monument Association, which had been run by a state commission since 1877, had raised only $31,000 and produced two failed contests to solicit a sculptor in 1877 and 1878. Meanwhile, the all-female Lee Monument Committee continued to thrive, raising $21,000 and investigating promising European sculptors. When Robert E. Lee's nephew Fitzhugh Lee became Virginia's governor in

November 1885, he vigorously resurrected the monument effort, attracting Early's renewed involvement. Because Early considered Fitz Lee a steadfast confidant—and indeed, Lee had always tolerated Early's acidity with remarkable good humor—Early set out to vanquish the committee once and for all by taking his case to his friend. After the newspapers (correctly) portrayed the Ladies' efforts as preceding Early's, Early wrote to Fitz Lee in March 1886, "I saw the action of some ladies, who claim to represent the Lee Monument Association," seeking to instigate a new contest for the statue design. "There is but one Lee Monument Association in Virginia, and that was incorporated by an act of the Assembly." He allowed that "there was a Lee Memorial Association" at Lexington, "but its work has been accomplished." Fitz Lee, who was used to cheerfully stepping around Early's more malodorous schemes, instead unified the two remaining Lee monument associations, even inviting three women to serve on the state board. At last, the Ladies helped stage a sculptor competition with a sizable prize that resulted in the selection of Ohioan Charles H. Niehaus, but Early chided Fitz Lee that if the Northerner's design was built, he would "get together all the surviving members of the Second Corps and blow it up with dynamite." Ultimately the project of sculpting Lee fell to a runner-up, whom the Ladies but not Early endorsed, French artist Jean Antonin Mercié.[31]

Despite these continuing constraints on Early's vision for Lee memorialization, his considerable success at weaving together diverse elements of Confederate historical production was evident at the two commemorative dedications of the Mercié Lee statue on Monument Avenue in Richmond. First, at the cornerstone ceremony on October 27, 1887, Fitz Lee introduced Early as "the officer who first organized the move to form within the ranks of the Confederate soldier an association to perpetuate the memory of the army commander, who was the first president of the Lee Monument Association, and whose heart to-day beats as steady and strong for the living as it throbs tender and true for the dead." The sentiment captured Early's reputation as the most stalwart living Confederate and dedicated historian, and the "applause with which General Early was greeted showed the warm place he has in the hearts of old Confederates." Next, at the unveiling of the statue on May 29, 1890, amid a crowd of 100,000 onlookers and a military parade that powerfully overshadowed the civilian theme of Lee's funeral, Early was in evident ecstasy. He received a standing ovation wherever he moved, and when he entered the circle surrounding the monument the soldiers let loose a great rebel yell and escorted him to the stand. The newspapers reveled in recounting that when "General Fitz Lee saw that General Early was standing up and all the seats around him were occupied ... [Early] took the old cavalry commander on his lap, and the two joked with each other in a pleasant manner for some time." The masculine bonds of military service to the Confederacy, and the public's enthusiasm to consume such spectacle, lived on, despite the Ladies' manifold contributions to the day.[32]

The Richmond Lee monument thus embodied Early's struggles but also his profound success at consolidating Confederate history and commemoration. Though Early had come a long way from his original historical partnership with Lee, his work had done more to vindicate his chieftain and enshrine the Army of Northern Virginia at the center of Confederate history than Lee could have ever hoped. As Early explained in 1872, near the beginning of his crusade to construct Lee's image, "Fidelity to the cause in adversity as well as in prosperity, is the motto which will govern my life to the close." He held true to this promise as historian and maintained partisan advocacy for the Confederate cause in his writing. Moreover, he profoundly influenced how Americans, scholars and the public alike, view Confederate history to this day, by cloaking this advocacy in the apparently disinterested and factual garb of objective history.[33]

NOTES

1. I would like to thank Caroline E. Janney, Peter S. Carmichael, and Aaron Sheehan-Dean for inviting this essay, and Janney and Peter C. Luebke for editing numerous drafts. Keith S. Bohannon provided helpful comments on a conference paper version of this essay. Gary W. Gallagher sparked this project by passing along his personal Jubal A. Early archives, and I am extremely grateful for his incomparable mentorship sixteen years and counting.

2. Cadet William Nalle to Mother (Mrs. Thomas Botts Nalle [Lexington]), October 16, 1870, William Nalle Letter, MS-0042, Virginia Military Institute Archives, Lexington, http://digitalcollections.vmi.edu/digital/collection/p15821coll11/id/1559 (accessed March 9, 2020); John E. Cooke, *A Life of Gen. Robert E. Lee* (New York: D. Appleton, 1871), 498. In this chapter, references to Lexington are to Lexington, Virginia, unless otherwise noted.

3. Robert E. Lee to David McConaughy (Lexington), August 5, 1869, David McConaughy Papers, Gettysburg College, Musselman Library Special Collections and Archives, digital copy in Lee Family Digital Archive, Stratford Hall, Stratford, VA, https://leefamilyarchive.org/9-family-papers/861-robert-e-lee-to-david-mcconaughy-1869-august-5 (accessed March 10, 2020); Nalle to Mother, October 16, 1870, Virginia Military Institute Archives; Douglas S. Freeman, *R. E. Lee: A Biography*, 4 vols. (New York: Scribner and Sons, 1934), 4:526.

4. The famed White Sulphur Spring Manifesto (1868), for example, featured Lee's signature on a document that expressed that "the people of the South entertain no unfriendly feeling towards the government of the United States" and "the idea that the Southern people are hostile to the negroes, and would oppress them if it were in their power to do so, is entirely

unfounded"; *Staunton Spectator*, September 8, 1866; Lee, Farewell Address, April 10, 1865, Library of Congress, www.loc.gov/item/2003677965/ (accessed March 10, 2020). William Preston Johnston alleged that Lee abandoned writing a history of the Army of Northern Virginia because "of the difficulty of getting the documents to verify his statements, and his wish to be able to prove all he said." Johnston, "Memoranda of Conversations with General R. E. Lee," May 7, 1868, in *Lee, the Soldier*, ed. Gary W. Gallagher (Lincoln: University of Nebraska Press, 1996), 30. Lee corroborated this fact to Early in a letter (Lee to Early, November 22, 1865, Mss1L51c737, Lee Family Papers, Virginia Museum of History and Culture, Richmond [hereafter VMHC]). See also Keith Bohannon, "Many Valuable Records and Documents Were Lost to History: The Destruction of Confederate Military Records during the Appomattox Campaign," in *Petersburg to Appomattox: The End of the War in Virginia*, ed. Caroline E. Janney (Chapel Hill: University of North Carolina Press, 2018), 170–91. Several historians have pointed out the disjuncture between Lee's public and private legacies to the South; see Gaines M. Foster, *Ghosts of the Confederacy: Defeat, the Lost Cause, and the Emergence of the New South, 1865–1913* (New York: Oxford University Press, 1987), 51; Gary W. Gallagher, "Shaping Public Memory of the Civil War: Robert E. Lee, Jubal A. Early, and Douglas Southall Freeman," in *The Memory of the Civil War in American Culture*, ed. Alice Fahs and Joan Waugh (Chapel Hill: University of North Carolina Press, 2004), 40–41; and Elizabeth Brown Pryor, *Reading the Man: A Portrait of Robert E. Lee through His Private Letters* (New York: Penguin, 2007), 449–50. To understand the national prominence of Lee and his army during the Civil War, see Gallagher, *The Confederate War: How Popular Will, Nationalism, and Military Strategy Could Not Stave Off Defeat* (Cambridge, MA: Harvard University Press, 1997), 63.

 5. Lee to Early (Lexington), March 15 and October 15, 1866, George H. and Katherine M. Davis Collection, Howard-Tilton Memorial Library, Tulane University, New Orleans; Lee to Early (Lexington), March 15, 1866, Mss1Ea765b59, Early Family Papers, VMHC; Jubal A. Early, *A Memoir of the Last Year of the War for Independence in the Confederate States of America*, ed. Gary W. Gallagher (1866; repr., Columbia: University of South Carolina Press, 2001); Jubal A. Early, *Narrative of the War between the States*, ed. Gary W. Gallagher (1912; repr., New York: Da Capo Press with Broadfoot Publishing, 1989). For the famous newspaper duel with Sheridan, see Philip H. Sheridan, "To the Editors of the New Orleans Daily Crescent," *New Orleans Daily Crescent*, January 8, 1866; and Early, "To the Editor of the New York News," *New York News*, February 5, 1866, in "Clippings Concerning Controversy between Sheridan and Early," January–February 1866, Scrapbook, Early Papers, Library of Congress, Washington, DC (hereafter LC); and Gallagher, "Jubal A. Early, the Lost Cause, and Civil War History," in *The Myth of the Lost Cause and Civil War History*, ed. Gary W. Gallagher and Alan T. Nolan (Bloomington: Indiana University Press, 2000), 37, 40–41. This essay helps to bridge scholarship on the importance of impartiality to historical credibility in the nineteenth century by addressing the Civil War era. For the construction of scientific history as truth before the Civil War, see Eileen Ka-May Cheng, *The Plain and Noble Garb of Truth: Nationalism and Impartiality in American Historical Writing, 1784–1860* (Athens: University of Georgia Press, 2008). For after, see Peter Novick, *That Noble Dream: The "Objectivity Question" and the American Historical Profession* (Cambridge: Cambridge University Press, 1988); and Bonnie G. Smith, *The Gender of History: Men, Women, and Historical Practice* (Cambridge, MA: Harvard University Press, 1998). For Early's developing use of scientific history in the 1860s, see

Kathryn J. Shively, "Duty to My Country and Myself: The Jubal A. Early Memoirs," in *Civil War Writing: New Perspectives on Iconic Texts*, ed. Stephen Cushman and Gary W. Gallagher (Baton Rouge: Louisiana State University Press, 2019), 139–70. Finally, it is important to note that Early's scientific historical work existed within a much larger, international context of historians who used the sheen of objectivity to obscure political objectives; see Monika Baár, *Historians and Nationalism: East-Central Europe in the Nineteenth Century* (Oxford: Oxford University Press, 2010); Umet Uzer, *An Intellectual History of Turkish Nationalism: Between Turkish Ethnicity and Islamic Identity* (Salt Lake City: University of Utah Press, 2016); Lisa Yoshikawa, *Making History Matter: Kuroita Katsumi and the Construction of Imperial Japan* (Cambridge, MA: Harvard University Press, 2017); and Priya Satia, *Time's Monster: How History Makes History* (Cambridge, MA: Harvard University Press, 2020).

6. Lee to Early, November 22, 1865, Mss1L51c737, Robert E. Lee Papers, VMHC; William Garrett Piston, *Lee's Tarnished Lieutenant: James Longstreet and His Place in Southern History* (Athens: University of Georgia Press, 1988), 108. After Lee's death, former Lee staff officer Charles Venable confirmed to Early that since Lee had not produced a history of the Army of Northern Virginia, the task devolved onto Early; Venable to Jubal A. Early (Charlottesville), February 16, 1871, box 5, Chronological File (hereafter CF), Early Papers, LC.

7. For more on the political workings of commemoration, see William A. Blair, *Cities of the Dead: Contesting the Memory of the Civil War in the South, 1865–1914* (Chapel Hill: University of North Carolina Press, 2004), 1–3. For a sample of white women's and Black people's involvement in commemoration, see Caroline E. Janney, *Remembering the Civil War: Reunion and the Limits of Reconciliation* (Chapel Hill: University of North Carolina Press, 2013) and *Burying the Dead but Not the Past: Ladies' Memorial Associations and the Lost Cause* (Chapel Hill: University of North Caroline Press, 2008); Paul A. Shackel, *Memory in Black and White: Race, Commemoration, and the Post-bellum Landscape* (Lanham, MD: Altamira Press, 2003); and David W. Blight, *Race and Reunion: The Civil War in American Memory* (Cambridge, MA: Harvard University Press, 2001).

8. To understand Confederate emotionalism at monument dedications, see Foster, *Ghosts of the Confederacy*; and Charles Reagan Wilson, *Baptized in Blood: The Religion of the Lost Cause, 1865–1920* (Athens: University of Georgia Press, 1980). For the masculinization of scientific history, see Smith, *Gender of History*, 9–11. Though the literature on Early has well established his importance to the construction of the predominant Confederate memory, termed the Lost Cause, this essay takes a different approach to understanding how and why Early's historical legacies were so dominant and enduring by focusing on his blending of commemoration with scientific history and archives building. For the best work on Early and the Lost Cause, see Gary W. Gallagher's "Jubal A. Early, the Lost Cause, and Civil War History: A Persistent Legacy," in *Lee and His Generals in War and Memory* (Baton Rouge: Louisiana State University Press, 1998), 199–226; *Jubal A. Early, the Lost Cause, and Civil War History: A Persistent Legacy* (Milwaukee: Marquette University Press, 1995); and "Jubal A. Early, the Lost Cause, and Civil War History," in *Myth of the Lost Cause and Civil War History*, 35–59.

9. Early to William N. Pendleton (Big Lick), October 13, 1870, William Nelson Pendleton Papers, Southern Historical Collection, University of North Carolina Library, Chapel Hill (hereafter SHCUNC).

10. *Official Souvenir of the Dedication of the Monument to General Robert E. Lee* (Richmond: R. Newton Moon and Co., 1890), 1–3, Library of Virginia, Richmond.

11. "To the Surviving Officers and Soldiers of the Army of Northern Virginia," *Lynchburg Daily Virginian*, October 25, 1870. See also J. William Jones and R. A. Brock, eds., *Southern Historical Society Papers*, 52 vols. (1876–1959; repr., with 3-vol. index, Wilmington, NC: Broadfoot, 1990–92), 17:188–89 (hereafter *SHSP*); "To the Survivors of the Army and Navy of the Confederate States and to All the Admirers of the Character of the Late General Robert E. Lee, Wherever They May Reside," November 1870, Robert F. Hoke Papers, North Carolina State Archives, Raleigh. To understand Early's relegation of women to an inferior sphere, see Janney, *Burying the Dead*, chapter 4; and for broader context on the gendering of history, see Smith, *Gender of History*, 103, 113, 128.

12. Bradley T. Johnson to Early (Richmond), December 20, 1870, box 5, CF, Early Papers, LC. In desiring a national rather than a regional veterans' organization, Early and Johnson were not alone; see Charles Marshall to Early (Baltimore), October 31, 1870, box 5, CF, Early Papers, LC. At the meetings, Early would be confirmed as president of both, though the Lee Monument Association also featured an honorary leadership committee with Jefferson Davis as president; see *Organization of the Lee Monument Association and the Association of the Army of Northern Virginia, Richmond, Va.*, November 3 and 4, 1870 (Richmond: J. W. Randolph and English, 1871), 4, 10–12, Library of Virginia.

13. Lee to Early, November 22, 1865, Lee Family Papers, VMHC, msslL51c737, p. 48–50; Lee to Early (Lexington), March 15, 1866, George H. and Katherine M. Davis Collection, Howard-Tilton Memorial Library, Tulane University, New Orleans. The fact that Early and his defenders, such as Bradley Johnson and Dabney Maury, staked a public claim to Lee's bones was not outlandish for the nineteenth century. As historian Michael Kammen explains, famous Americans of the period were often interred or disinterred in order to achieve political or nationalistic goals; Dabney H. Maury to Early (Charlottesville), October 26, 1870, and Bradley T. Johnson to Early (Richmond), October 30, 1870, box 5, CF, Early Papers, LC; Michael Kammen, *Digging up the Dead: A History of Notable American Reburials* (Chicago: University of Chicago Press, 2010), 8, 85–86.

14. Janney, *Burying the Dead*, 108, 113, 116, 111; *Sheperdstown (WV) Register*, October 20, 1866; Early to the Editor of the *Galveston News*, March 17, 1871, Lee Monument Association Records, Library of Virginia; Sarah N. Randolph to Fitzhugh Lee (Richmond), April 15, 1873, box 6, CF, Early Papers, LC.

15. Early to Pendleton (Big Lick), October 13, 1870, (Lynchburg) October 24 and December 8, 1870, and Pendleton to Early (Lexington), March 10, 1871, William Nelson Pendleton Papers, SHCUNC; William Preston Johnston to Early (Lexington), December 16, 1870, William Allan to Early (Lexington), October 25 and December 16, 1870, and March 15, 1871, box 5, CF, Early Papers, LC. Though Valentine's sarcophagus arrived in 1875, in 1877 Washington College accepted a design for an addition to the chapel, which would contain the Lee family crypt. In 1878 the cornerstone was laid, and by 1883, the Recumbent Lee sarcophagus was unveiled with Lee's reinterred bones in the mausoleum; "Washington and Lee University, Lee Chapel," Historical American Buildings Survey No. VA 568-c, National Park Service, Department of the Interior, Washington, DC, 2, http://lcweb2.loc.gov/master/pnp/habshaer/va/va0900/va0910/data/va0910data.pdf (accessed May 4, 2020).

16. Emphasis Early's. Early to Edward McCrady (Lynchburg), December 1, 1870, Survivors Association Papers, Correspondence 1870, South Carolina Historical Society; Early to Dabney Maury (Lynchburg), December 14, 1870, with broadside "Association to Erect a Monument of Robert E. Lee," box 5, CF, Early Papers, LC; John B. Gordon to Early (Atlanta), November 24 and December 26, 1870, box 5, CF, Early Papers, LC. For additional letters discussing division over Lee memorialization, see Joseph E. Johnston to Early (Savannah), October 29, 1870, Mss1Ea765/6/54, Early Family Papers, VHMC; John C. Breckinridge to Early (Lexington, KY), December 20, 1870, box 5, CF, Early Papers, LC; and Early to Pendleton (Lynchburg), February 20, 1871, William Nelson Pendleton Papers, SHCUNC.

17. *Official Souvenir of the Dedication*, 3–4; *Journal of the Senate of the Commonwealth of Virginia* (Richmond: C. A. Schaffter, Superintendent Public Printing, 1870), 104–5, 113; *Journal of the House of Delegates of the State of Virginia for the Session of 1870–71* (Richmond: C. A. Schaffter, Superintendent Public Printing, 1871), 138; Janney, *Burying the Dead*, 108, 116, 111.

18. Kemper to Early (Richmond), July 8 and October 11, 1875, box 5, Early Papers, LC. One debate was over whether to place the statue at Virginia Military Institute or Winchester's Stonewall Cemetery; see "Local Matters," *Baltimore Sun*, September 10, 1875; and William Allan to Early (Baltimore), January 16, 1873, box 5, CF, Early Papers, LC. Another debate featured a conflict with the Ladies' planned Richmond parade for George Pickett's funeral; Kemper to Early (Richmond), September 30 and October 6, 1875, boxes 7 and 8, CF, Early Papers, LC. Hoge agreed not to "exalt the former [Jackson] over the latter [Lee]" nor to attribute Jackson's military abilities solely to his religiosity; Hoge to Early (Richmond), October 14, 1875, box 8, CF, Early Papers, LC.

19. Kemper to Lee (Richmond), November 4, 1875, Fitzhugh Lee Papers, Swem Library, William and Mary University, Williamsburg, VA; Virginius Dabney, *The Last Review: The Confederate Reunion* (1932; repr., Chapel Hill, NC: Algonquin Books, 1984), 5, 7; Kemper to Early, July 8, September 30, and October 6, 11, 23, 26, 1875, boxes 7 and 8, CF, Early Papers, LC; *Daily Virginian* (Lynchburg), April 29, 1875; *Lynchburg Daily News*, June 1, 1883; Roger D. Cunningham, "'They Are as Proud of Their Uniform as Any Who Serve Virginia': African American Participation in the Virginia Volunteers," *Virginia Magazine of History and Biography* 110, no. 3 (2002): 321n56. While Kemper and Early never resumed cordial relations, Fitz Lee coped with Early's embarrassing behavior with humor, as usual, playfully jabbing at Early for his "colored troops fit"; Fitz Lee to Early (Richland), December 24, 1875, box 8, CF, Early Papers, LC. It is important to recognize that not all Lost Cause purveyors were so viciously opposed to Black participation in politics and the public square during this period; see, for instance, Edward Pollard, "Romance of the Negro," *Galaxy Magazine* 12 (1871): 470.

20. Johnston to Early (Richmond), December 20, 1870, box 5, CF, Early Papers, LC; *Official Souvenir of the Dedication*, 3; Johnston to Early (Lexington), March 14, 1871, box 6, CF, Early Papers, LC; Early to Johnston (Lynchburg), March 10, 1871, William Nelson Pendleton Papers, SHCUNC. For another example of a speech, see Early to William H. Payne (Lynchburg), January 8, 1873, Jubal A. Early Collection, 1816–94, Jones Memorial Library, Lynchburg, VA. See also Christopher R. Lawton, "Constructing the Cause, Bridging the Divide: Lee's Tomb at Washington's College," *Southern Cultures* 15, no. 2 (Summer 2009): 8–12.

21. J. William Jones, *Personal Reminiscences of General Robert E. Lee* (New York: D. Appleton, 1874), 43–44.

22. Jones, *Personal Reminiscences*, 32; Carol Reardon, *Pickett's Charge in History and Memory* (Chapel Hill: University of North Carolina Press, 1997), 63, 85. Importantly, the sunrise thesis had not appeared in Early's previously penned memoirs.

23. Johnston, "Memoranda of Conversations with General R. E. Lee," 29. For examples of Early's correspondence with Lee's staff officers, see Charles Marshall to Early (Baltimore), March 15, 1870, Early Family Papers, VMHC; Charles Venable to Early (Charlottesville), April 5, 1872, box 6, CF, Early Papers, LC; Early to A. L. Long (Lynchburg), April 3, 1874, Armistead L. Long Papers, SHCUNC. Notably, this was not Early's first historical attack on Longstreet, though it ranks as one of his most influential; see correspondence between Early and Francis Lawley regarding Lawley's article, "General Lee," *Blackwood's Edinburgh Magazine* 111 (March 1872): 348–63; William Allan, Charles Venable, and Early discussed Lawley's article in Allan to J. A. E. (Lexington), March 26, 1872, and Venable to J. A. E. (Charlottesville), April 5, 1872; Francis C. Lawley to J. A. E. (Kent, Eng.), May 14 and August 16, 1872, box 6, CF, Early Papers, LC.

24. Jones, *Personal Reminiscences*, 1–51; Susan P. Lee, "Personal Recollections of General Robert E. Lee," in *Memoirs of William Nelson Pendleton* (Philadelphia: J. B. Lippincott Company, 1893), 522–23; US War Department, *The War of the Rebellion: A Compilation of the Official Records of the Union and Confederate Armies*, 127 vols., index, and atlas (Washington, DC: Government Printing Office, 1880–1901), ser. 1, 27(2):346–54; Jeffrey D. Wert, "James Longstreet and the Lost Cause," in *Myth of the Lost Cause and Civil War History*, ed. Gallagher and Nolan, 127–46; Piston, *Lee's Tarnished Lieutenant*, 119, 121–22. Lee's staff officers wrote directly to Longstreet to refute the sunrise thesis, though they refused to defend Longstreet in public; their letters are compiled in Helen D. Longstreet, *Lee and Longstreet at High Tide: Gettysburg in Light of the Official Records* (1904; Gainesville, GA: published by the author, 1905), 58–60.

25. Fitzhugh Lee to Early (Stafford County), March 15, 1872, and E. Milligan Dennison to Early (St. Louis Crossing, IN), January 27, 1872, box 6, Early Papers, LC. See also W. T. Walthall to Early (Mobile), August 26, 1872, box 6, Early Papers, LC.

26. Early to William H. Payne (Lynchburg), June 28, 1872, box 6, CF, Early Papers, LC.

27. Early to Dawson (Lynchburg), March 22, August 6, and December 16, 1872, Miscellaneous Mss., E, "Early, Jubal A.," New-York Historical Society, New York, NY; Kevin M. Levin, "William Mahone, the Lost Cause, and Civil War History," *Virginia Magazine of History and Biography* 113, no. 4 (2005): 384–86. Examples of Early denouncing rival historians in the 1870s are replete and involve authors from the North, the South, and abroad, such as William Mahone, Joseph E. Johnston, John Imboden, John S. Mosby, Adam Badeau, George Frederick Holmes, the comte de Paris, and Francis Lawley. Early's insistence on publishing Lee's 1863 Gettysburg report was bold, as it made no mention of a sunrise order since there had not been one; Piston, *Lee's Tarnished Lieutenant*, 130.

28. *Transactions of the Southern Historical Society* (Baltimore: Turnbull Brothers, 1874), 1; John W. Caldwell to Early (New Orleans), May 27, June 6, and June 10, 1873, box 7, CF, Early Papers, LC.

29. *Richmond Daily Dispatch*, October 30, 1873, p. 1, col. 1; "The South in the War: Annual Meeting of the Southern Historical Society," *New York Times*, October 28, 1874.

30. Early to Dawson (Lynchburg), December 29, 1874, New-York Historical Society; Early to Jones, March 20, 1876, and W. H. and Browne to Early (Baltimore), July 29, 1873,

Southern Historical Society Correspondence, formerly housed in the Eleanor S. Brockenbrough Library, Museum of the Confederacy, Richmond, VA, and now at the VMHC. For examples of Early's behind-the-scenes corrections, see Dabney Maury, Walter H. Taylor, and the comte de Paris in Early to Jones, March 20, 1876, and March 8, 28, 1878, Southern Historical Society Correspondence, VMHC. For an example of Early editing primary documents that would then appear in the *SHSP*, see Early to Armistead L. Long (Lynchburg) April 3, 1874, Armistead L. Long Papers, SHCUNC; and *SHSP*, July 1877, 4:66–68. For an excellent summation of the Gettysburg series in the *SHSP*, see Piston, *Lee's Tarnished Lieutenant*, 133–35. For the importance of the *SHSP*, see Richard D. Starnes, "Forever Faithful: The Southern Historical Society and Confederate Historical Memory," *Southern Cultures* 2, no. 2 (Winter 1996): 179.

31. Dabney, *Last Review*, 7; Early to Fitz Lee (Lynchburg), March 27, 1886, and "Monument to General Lee," news clipping in Correspondence of the Lee Monument Association as Maintained by the Virginia Treasurer's Office, 1871–1893, Library of Virginia; Ann Hunter McLean, "Unveiling the Lost Cause: A Study of Monuments to the Civil War Memory in Richmond, Virginia, and Vicinity" (PhD diss., University of Virginia, 1998); *SHSP*, 17:206–7. Early continued to prefer Edward Valentine as sculptor; Valentine declined to even participate in this latest contest after so much acrimony had stalled the monument for nearly two decades.

32. *SHSP*, 17:237, 18:294; *Fort Worth Daily Gazette*, May 30, 1890.

33. Early to Henry B. Richardson (Lynchburg), September 7, 1872, Richardson-Farrar Papers, SHCUNC.

From the Field of Battle to the Field of History

*White Northern Veteran-Writers and
Their Narratives of the Civil War*

PETER C. LUEBKE

In 1884 the American Historical Association met for the first time. To many academics, this date marks the start of the American historical profession. But a focus on the professional origins and consolidation of academic history overlooks how hundreds of white Northern Union soldiers helped inaugurate the modern field. Historians Gary W. Gallagher and Kathryn Shively have pointed out that the military history of the Civil War "began with works written by the wartime generation." Indeed, the wartime generation wrote copiously. One estimate places the number of regimental histories written by white Union authors at more than 800. The hundreds of histories that these veterans authored laid the groundwork for the academic discipline. In this case, the popular practice of history helped create the scholarly.[1] In the process of writing their regimental histories, veterans engaged in many of the methods that the American Historical Association would later adopt as the hallmarks of professionalism: reliance on primary documents, the creation of archives, and peer review. Thus, the amateurs behaved as professionals and helped construct the profession. These Civil War veterans embedded their own conceptions of history in their works, shaping the field for later generations of historians who would use these eyewitness histories as important primary sources. And so, the field of Civil War history began as military history written by amateurs armed with modern methods.

Scholars have long looked at academic historians to chart the burgeoning "professional" consensus about the field of history. While Peter Novick addressed the late-nineteenth-century crystallization of the field, Eileen Ka-May Cheng identified origins in the antebellum period, in which historical writers embraced "impartiality and originality" while also grappling with the subjectivity inherent in historical narrative. According to Cheng, historians employed empirical evidence to establish historical fact, which in turn demonstrated truths about the world; antebellum historians understood this as a scientific approach to history. Lindsay DiCuirci and David D. Van Tassel have also explained how antebellum historians concentrated on the identification and preservation of source documents. Aware that an impartial and scientific approach to history required a wide array of primary documents, antebellum historians devoted much of their energy to the creation of an archive. Thus, the transformation of the information in the archive into "knowledge" remained largely incipient before the Civil War. Tools had been developed—such as impartiality, archives, reflections on subjectivity—but not yet employed by many people.[2]

The Civil War transformed the practice of history in America. White Northern veterans stepped into a field of knowledge production that had undergone shifts immediately before the war and would later find consolidation in the halls of academia with the emergence of history departments. Before the war, Americans had concentrated on collecting primary source materials, publishing moralizing histories, or writing impressionistic accounts; a handful of writers crafted narratives based on close readings of primary sources. The Civil War changed that state of affairs: suddenly millions of Americans witnessed events of self-evident historic importance and had access to primary sources.

The Civil War provided both a subject for histories and ample documentation on which writers could draw. During the conflict, soldiers not only witnessed events but also had in hand an emerging historical method. Soldiers knew how to use sources to derive facts and compare sources in a search to find a truth. White Northern Union veteran-writers therefore simultaneously had a precedent for practice and an unprecedented archive at their fingertips. Their position in the mainstream of antebellum society and their ability to access resources for both research and publications gave white veteran writers advantages not available to others who sought to capture the historical importance of the Civil War—namely African American historians and writers. Narratives by African American veterans, such as those of Joseph T. Wilson and George Washington Williams stood as important works, but overall, the number of works written by white veterans dwarfed those by African American writers. While a full consideration of African American contributions to the formation of the historical profession in the nineteenth century lies outside the scope of the present essay, the importance of their narratives must be acknowledged.[3] Just as much as academic historians who would become the doyens of the field of history beginning in the 1880s, these veteran-writers demonstrated a sophisticated understanding of the use of primary sources and problems of interpretation. The birth of the field of history owes as much to these veteran-writers as it does to academic professionals.[4]

Critically, white Northern veterans could combine documents and practice with dissemination. In the mid-nineteenth century, America enjoyed a remarkable expansion of the publishing trade. Printers, binders, and booksellers proliferated and became increasingly linked into a nationwide trade. The middle decades of the nineteenth century saw a steady increase in printing-related firms. The trajectory of printing and publishing firms—one central sector of the overall printing industry, which included bookbinding, print engraving, ink production, papermaking, tool production, and type foundries, among other areas—shows the vast expansion of the industry. The 1850 census enumerated 673 printing and publishing firms (value of products roughly $11.6 million); in 1860 there were 1,666 (value of products roughly $31 million); in 1870 there were 1,550 (value of products $66.5 million); and in 1880 the number had climbed to 3,467 (value of products $90.8 million). Print, like most American industry, expanded dramatically.[5]

Although national networks of distribution evolved, Northern firms and markets dominated the trade. New York City became the center of the trade, followed by Philadelphia, Boston, and Chicago. The scale of print production and distribution in the North outdid that of the South. In 1870, for instance, a standard trade publication sent to every bookseller, newsdealer, music dealer, and stationer went to 797 firms in the former Confederate states as compared with 807 copies to Illinois alone. More than 1,000 copies of the same publication went to firms in Pennsylvania, while nearly 1,900 went to companies in

New York. Likewise, in 1870 there were 835 periodicals or newspapers printed in New York State, versus 917 total across all the former Confederate states. In 1878, only one of twenty-seven type foundries was in the ex-Confederate South (with two located in Baltimore and two in Missouri). Out of 329 bookbinders (identified by their affixed binders' tickets) before 1876, only 13 came from Confederate states. Apart from whatever these numbers may demonstrate about the demand for books and bookmaking appurtenances, these figures demonstrate that those people in Northern states not only had easy access to print but also had easy access to the means of production.[6]

Combined with the means of production, the men who went to war could read and write at an unprecedented rate. After the war, when Northern Union veterans wanted to record their deeds and write histories, they had ready access to print their books. In addition, they had access to an archive of unprecedented scale and scope. The accumulation of documents over the course of the war—through methods both public and private—gave veteran-historians access to an archive. The Civil War archive encompassed both informal and formal collections of war-related documents. Thus, after the Civil War, white Union veterans could draw upon varieties of archives, interpret them with a critical and sophisticated historical method, and then arrange for them to appear in narrative books.

Widespread literacy and education combined with a burgeoning postal system, which meant that soldiers kept up a steady flow of correspondence during the Civil War, leading to ample material for future archives. The flow of this correspondence led to several proto-histories—essentially scrapbooks composed of soldier letters—as well as regimental histories written during the war years. One study of letter-writing during the war puts the number of such letters around 500 million, with about 300 million of those coming from Northern soldiers' pens. The number of personal letters sent throughout the war created an immense archive, which vastly outstripped any antebellum archive. In addition, the letters added new voices to the archive; as scholar Christopher Hager has noted, "The war pushed ordinary Americans to stretch themselves as writers, to expand what their letters could do." The distance the war created between soldiers in the field and loved ones at home, as well as the novel experiences of life as a soldier, gave increased reason to pen missives. Most often, letters went to friends and family; though some of these letters remained private, oftentimes the letters would be shared within families or neighborhoods.[7]

Beyond the letters sent home for private and semiprivate audiences, correspondence also went to local newspapers, which relied upon soldiers' mail to inform the reading public of events at the seat of the war. Letters from regiments and units raised in the area also provided news directly pertinent to the home community. While a comprehensive tabulation of soldier letters remains impossible, some facts and figures have been collated. Together, the *Wabash Intelligencer* and *Wabash Plain Dealer* in Indiana printed more than several hundred letters during the war years. A New York weekly, the *Sunday Mercury*, printed several thousand soldier letters.[8]

While most readers treated newspapers as disposable and ephemeral publications, others clipped articles and compiled them into scrapbooks. Wisconsin bureaucrat Edwin B. Quiner, a former clerk to the Wisconsin assembly and secretary to the governor during the Civil War, made it his mission to document the war. In his effort to preserve the record, he subscribed to every newspaper in the state. With the aid of his daughters, he assiduously clipped out letters from the front lines, primarily those written by soldiers. His collection grew, so that by the end of the war, his scrapbooks bulged with nearly 10,000 letters that filled about 4,000 pages. The number of letters Quiner collected, along with the suggestive figures from the Wabash and New York papers, gives some indication of the paper trail the war left in local newspapers, which became archives in and of themselves.[9]

Families and interested people preserved newspaper correspondence, but so did the newspapers themselves. Letters and printed sheets went into newspaper files for future use. When soldiers returned home from the war, they could secure copies of wartime writing from the local newspaper. Few made as extensive a use of newspaper files as George G. Benedict, a Vermont reporter who enlisted and went to war. During the conflict, he sent letters about once every two weeks to the *Burlington Free Press*. Much later, when he wrote his history of the Twelfth Vermont Infantry Regiment, he turned to this previous material. He assembled his wartime letters and published them in a volume printed because "a number of my army comrades . . . have expressed a desire to preserve in permanent form what happened to be almost the only record published at the time." Benedict reproduced his letters as a book, but the thousands of letters in newspaper files would likewise serve veteran-historians.[10]

Individuals wrote the letters that preceded them home and kept diaries that often traveled home with them or made it back instead of them. But Northern writers enjoyed a special benefit: state adjutants general and administrations both North and South, by virtue of the way that armies had been raised through state enlistments, maintained bodies of official papers. Tasked with raising regiments and contributing men to the various drafts, states kept detailed track of their contributions. State files encompassed a variety of information, from basic demographic data of soldiers who enlisted to more descriptive narrative reports. In the North these state archives survived the war intact, while in the South they did not. State officials understood that value of these records; a former governor of Vermont explained that "it is our duty to furnish the Historian with everything of interest that came under our cognizance during the war."[11]

Veterans grasped the importance of the state archives. Early after the war ended, Lt. Col. P. T. Washburn, Vermont's former state adjutant general, explained the significance of these state records to a gathering of veterans: "The history of Vermont in the war for the preservation of the Union remains to be written. Its minutest details, yet fresh in your memories, are preserved of record in the official archives of the State, their most sacred deposit, for the use of the future historian." Washburn also predicted that "the future historian ... shall require their reproduction in the enduring form which literature gives to facts, and time shall furnish a standpoint, free from partisan prejudice and personal partiality, from which the past may be viewed in connected panorama." This prediction made evident that Washburn recognized that personal testimony could contribute to a history but on its own provided insufficient information for a complete narrative. He also saw that using the primary documents in the archive would enable authors to write from a stance of impartiality, as the documents would establish the facts. Conversely, Washburn also demonstrated that he understood personal experience would be a necessary complement to the masses of unprocessed data within the state files. Veteran-historians could take the atomistic facts of the state adjutant general records, arrange those facts, and interpret them to write a history: an "enduring form" of historical knowledge via "literature" (narrative).[12]

To the resources of the respective state archives, Northern writers could add those of the national archive. Veteran-writers could enrich their narratives with official documents. Soldiers understood that their diaries and correspondence gave only pieces of the puzzle; the reports and other official documents that the army bureaucracy generated provided important information. In a sense, the military hierarchy itself composed a limited form of history: company officers prepared narratives of what they had done for their regimental officers; regimental officers in turn used these reports to compose their narratives, which they then passed on to the brigade commander; the brigade commander used these reports as the basis for his account, which then got sent to the division general; the division reports informed the corps commanders of what their units had done; the corps commanders' summary reports informed the general commanding the army; and then the general commanding the army based his report to the secretary of war and the president on what he received from the corps commanders. At every one of these stages, the officers functioned as historians. They collected information, assembled archives of documents, weighed the evidence, and wrote a narrative statement of what they believed had happened. At each of these levels, printed versions of the reports found their way beyond army ranks, either serialized in newspapers or, in the case of final reports, printed by the Government Printing Office. To this mass of narrative paperwork could be added the official documentation that governed army life, such as general orders, special orders, messages, and dispatches. Many of these functional official documents appeared in mass printings; the Army of the Potomac, for instance, had a printing department from 1862 until the end of the war that had been equipped with several portable printing presses and sets of type.[13]

Thus, any white Northern veteran who wished to write a history could draw upon a number of sources. A look at one writer reveals the depth and scope of the research process that many of these veterans used. Chaplain Louis Napoleon Beaudry of the Fifth New York Cavalry Regiment provided a detailed account in his journal. Beaudry began writing his book while the regiment still remained in Virginia; he commemorated the start of the endeavor in March 1865, when he noted in his diary, "This evening I commenced writing." He reflected that "it is a work which will require some time and considerable, careful labor." Beaudry revealed the scientific thinking that went into his work. Not content to rely on memory alone, he realized that he would "have to base my calculations on diaries in the Regiment." Beyond depending on individual memories and diaries, he consulted personal letters, inspected the official documentation of the regiment (copies of which would later be accessioned into the files of the New York state adjutant general), employed primary sources found in newspapers, and otherwise behaved as a professional historian. A typical diary entry noted that he had been "busy with historic records, all day." As his work progressed, Beaudry cast his net wider for reliable information. He recorded writing "to Cols. Hammond and Johnstone for documents and information." He collected additional material from headquarters staff, getting "statistics from the Regiment and its records," and also copied "rosters of Companies from the Adjutant's Descriptive Book." In an entry that would not be out of place for any historian today, Beaudry confided in his journal, "I have more work to do than I ought to." Beaudry took advantage of his placement within the regimental hierarchy to gain access to people and records on which to base his history.[14]

Veterans also started collecting and using published materials on the Civil War. The proliferation of books about the Civil War began almost with the war itself. Like most other people in America, soldier writers consumed them for accounts of events. Moreover, the general accounts that appeared during the war created a larger historical context for the war itself. These books provided a framework for engagement: veteran-writers could begin to orient their work to the emergent historiography, either to support extant accounts or to refute what they saw as mistakes.[15]

Joshua Lawrence Chamberlain, later to become recognized as the hero of Little Round Top at Gettysburg, provides one example of a veteran author attuned to general works appearing in print. Always jealous of his reputation, Chamberlain erupted upon reading an account of the Battle of Gettysburg in J. R. Sypher's 1865 *History of the Pennsylvania Reserve Corps*. Sypher—a lawyer and sometime newspaper correspondent and all-around Pennsylvania chauvinist—attributed victory at Gettysburg to home-state heroes. Sypher wrote about Little Round Top that "fortunately, General Meade was present, and promptly ordered his old command, the Pennsylvania Reserves to charge upon the enemy, and retrieve the day, by turning defeat into victory." In a letter to the self-appointed battlefield historian of Gettysburg John B. Bachelder, Chamberlain accurately remarked that both of Sypher's claims "are without warrant." Chamberlain asserted that he knew better and could "give . . . the *real* truth & very nearly the whole truth" because he had been "an eye & ear witness to the whole operation." Chamberlain's correspondence hints that even as early as 1866, veteran-writers sought out published sources to inform their claims. Though Chamberlain did not say so himself, he had likely encountered Sypher's work when collecting sources for a history on which he had been working.[16]

Others besides Chamberlain realized that they wrote within a larger context of historical knowledge and weighed differences in methodological approaches. Veteran-writers consciously situated their work within a growing body of knowledge and responded to other writers. James H. McKee, formerly of the 144th New York Infantry Regiment, framed the necessity for his history in reference to the works of Benson Lossing, who had published "pictorial field books" of the American Revolution, the War of 1812, and the American Civil War. McKee recounted how Lossing had set about writing his books: "[He] went up and down through the country visiting old battlefields, deciphering moss-covered inscriptions in the old graveyards, interviewing men and women especially those who had participated in or who knew about those who had participated." Lossing's works preserved American history that would otherwise have been lost; on site Lossing would sketch "an old fort ... an old weather beaten building, a room with a history or some pieces of furniture." Although those at the time had failed to document the historical moment, Lossing could still find the vanishing traces of the recent past. Lossing, writing decades after the fact, had to rely upon whatever people he came across and the traces on the landscape. As McKee stated, Lossing's vignettes "were only mosaics which inlaid a story of wondrous interest."[17]

McKee introduced Lossing to tie his book into the larger field but also to tell readers how he would surpass Lossing. McKee's readers would have been well aware of Lossing's works, which had appeared first as cheap installments in pamphlet form before reissuance in book format. McKee, writing of Lossing, remarked that "we feel with the author constant regret that so much was lost, so little known of individual history and of the several organizations in which these heroes served." Lossing, writing at such a remove from the events, had "lost" much "individual history" and the broader context to which those individual histories related and the "several organizations" referred to, such as the Continental army. McKee, concerned that the same would happen to the history of the Civil War, wrote the history of his regiment to ensure that individual stories would be preserved. He remarked that "it is in the interest of history ... that this effort is made to gather up the scattered records of the 144th N.Y. Vol. in the war of 1861 and put them in permanent form." A book—a "permanent form" based on "scattered records"—presented a coherent history. Moreover, a book exhibited a sustained synthetic narrative of events, all based upon carefully collected and evaluated primary sources. McKee thought his history would stand the test of time, while Lossing's travelogues gave interesting fragments of a much larger story. Through the process of research and writing, McKee found that "scenes enacted so long ago have not all held their rightful sequence in memory." Through the course of writing, he opined how "elusive the evidence of facts" were "that seemed so easy to secure at the first outlook."[18] McKee found that only through a thorough consideration of the past could "elusive" facts be pinned down, which in turn demonstrated the superiority of his method as opposed to that of Lossing.

Many white Northern writers saw regimental histories as a way to create building blocks for future historians. They understood that their narratives would present an accurate description of their units' participation, which in turn would serve as the basis for further historical narratives. Col. William Holbrook, late of the Seventh Vermont Infantry Regiment, told fellow veterans that "the general historian cannot enter so much into the particulars, give the part taken, in large actions, by each regiment and detached company without making a story so voluminous as to be unreadable." Therefore, Holbrook declared that "it is the province of the regimental histories to treat of individual achievements, and to deal with the interesting and important details incident to the movements of the battalion and the company." Such works served a vital purpose, because only through them could "the personal services rendered by these officers and soldiers . . . be fully and perfectly understood by the present and future generations." Though he neglected to point it out to his audience, a regimental history also provided space for historians to discuss the activities of the common men. Their services took place not only on the battlefield but in the camps and the "movements" that took place in between battles. While the "general historian" could focus on a single battle, narrating the grand action in broad sweeps, the regimental historian would provide more of the personal account, which was important in telling the story of the veterans and what they had experienced.[19]

Holbrook knew of which he spoke because he had written the history for his regiment. Frustrated by a lack of good information, he wrote because "the history of the Seventh Vermont Regiment during the late war has never been written, and to this day the services which that gallant regiment rendered, and the severe experiences which it passed, are not, I am persuaded, fully understood or appreciated by those not connected with it." With some misgivings as to his own capabilities, Holbrook embarked on producing the narrative. As was typical with veteran writers, he sought to compile as much information as possible so that he could produce a factual account. He received "material and data" from several former officers, as well as "letters written from the regiment contemporaneously with the events which they chronicle" that had appeared in the *Rutland Herald* newspaper during the war. Holbrook, as did most others, knew that accounts written in proximity to the events that they described could prove more reliable than what someone remembered years later. He employed other contemporaneous documents, such as official reports, records of courts of inquiry, and reports of the state adjutant general. When necessary to fill in gaps or provide context, he drew upon previously published histories.[20]

Both McKee and Holbrook put their projects in discussion with other historical texts. They understood their individual works to be part of a larger field. Other white veteran-historians gave more reflective comments on the practice of history. George G. Benedict, the historian for the state of Vermont, offered his thoughts on history at a reunion of Vermont officers. Even in 1882, Benedict could tell a knowing audience that the Civil War was "a war about which more was written and printed in the time of it than any other way,—the very abundance of materials for the historian adds immensely to the labor and duration of his task." Benedict noted the publication of the *Official Records*, as well as histories of campaigns and battles. The mass of information required historians who would "sift fact from fancy, in all this mass of statement; to clear away the rubbish and let the solid truth appear; to decide the disputed claims; to determine the event of absolute importance." This task would also require "time, and of not a little time." Benedict thought that "the fermentation of the seventeen years since the close of the war has been a process of unsettling." By this, Benedict meant that early narratives of the war had been revised. Generals who had once been lauded for wartime success suffered a deflation of their reputation as more material came to public light, especially Confederate records. The opening of the Confederate archives captured during the war gave both sides of the story, "enabl[ing] us to see many events from two sides which before were only visible from one; and as the years go on and facts develop and theories disappear many things take on a different aspect."[21]

Benedict, as perhaps the most important white veteran-historian in the state of Vermont, had ample opportunity to make his views known. He delivered a paper to the Military Order of the Loyal Legion in which he gave a lengthy oration on his ideas about history and historical writing. Benedict began his talk with a definition of history, that is, "a narrative of actual events—a true story in distinction to a romance." History, for Benedict and his listeners, depended upon relating the facts of the past rather than on simply a good story.[22]

In order to narrate facts, Benedict explained that writers needed to search far and wide for them. Using himself as an example, he told his audience of the lengths to which he had gone both to secure facts and to corroborate them, including traveling to Washington, DC, to collect material. Benedict also understood that sources differed in accuracy. Speaking of the *Official Records*, Benedict pointed out that even "official reports vary in reliability... and it is a melancholy fact that many official reports contain as much fact as fiction." Accuracy depended upon comparison and impartial consideration. Benedict recommended that "the careful historian must sit constantly, like a judge in court, weighing opposing evidence, examining and cross examining the official and other witnesses, and sifting from the bushel of statements the kernel of exact fact." Over the course of his research, Benedict detected variations in the documentary evidence he used, including gaps, and had to marshal his resources to work through those problems.[23]

To drive his point home, Benedict described an instance where romance had triumphed over history. He mused that "at best all men do not see alike; not every man knows how to tell what he has seen; and truthful persons will give very different descriptions of incidents witnessed plainly by all and which they have no interest in misrepresenting." Benedict explained further, using an example from his own work. In preparing his history of the Vermont troops, Benedict had discovered an oft-repeated account of a private named William Scott who fell asleep while on sentinel duty in 1861. Court-martialed for his dereliction of duty, Scott received a sentence of death. But, at the last moment before his execution, a pardon arrived from President Abraham Lincoln. Seven months later that same soldier led a Vermont regiment during a charge on a Confederate earthwork outside of Yorktown, Virginia. "Mortally wounded in the affair," Scott, before expiring, prayed for Lincoln and expressed his gratitude for the president's mercy, or so the story went.[24]

Benedict dug deeper into the story. He found that contemporary newspaper articles had mentioned the affair, but it had grown in retelling. Eventually, Private Scott's redemption became the subject of a popular poem. Politicians then began to make much of the anecdote for their own purposes. But, as Benedict found, the soldier in question had been "shot in the abdomen" and "sank into a state of collapse, and died about a day later." Benedict assessed, unsurprisingly, that "being in a semi-conscious state he would not have been very likely to make any speeches or offer any prayers." In other words, few writers had let the truth stand in the way of a good story.[25]

The story of Private Scott served as an extended illustration for Benedict, but he offered other examples to his audience. He noted several occasions where incorrect information had found its way into the record, in some cases apparently in all innocence. Benedict concluded that "these instances of the truth of the adage 'to err is human' as well as that 'a lie will travel a mile when truth is putting on his boots' may teach us a lesson of charity for uninspired historians, whose works, resting on imperfect human testimony, are necessarily and easily liable to unintentional error."[26] Benedict's experience in unraveling the event with Private Scott led him to a deeper understanding of historical practice and how historians needed sagacity when approaching sources. He understood that part of the role of the historian would be to evaluate sources and account for the role of imperfect testimony.

While Benedict may have reflected more on the obstacles of writing history than most, other white veteran-authors realized the inherent difficulties in crafting a faithful narrative representation of the past. Capt. Lucien B. Crooker, Capt. Henry S. Nourse, and Sgt. Maj. John G. Brown of the

Fifty-Fifth Illinois Infantry wrote the history of their regiment. Selected by the Fifty-Fifth Illinois veterans' committee in 1884, they set about a "careful collation of numerous army letters and diaries of soldiers." To this they added research at the office of the state adjutant general, "a complete file of the Chicago *Tribune*," and other sources. The authors noted that they consulted the "earliest dispatches and latest official reports." They studied them "diligently" but remarked that they had not been "blindly followed, for those who have helped make the history of which they write, rarely acknowledge newspaper correspondents, or even generals, to be infallible." In addition to this judicious approach to their sources, they also noted that they would cover the entirety of the history of the Fifty-Fifth, even the times when "antagonisms rankled and human passions raged, even when not aroused by the frantic charge or in the fume of desperate strife." As the trio wrote, "It seems axiomatic to the writers of this volume that the revealing of truth and not its suppression is the proper purpose of history." Though not as lengthy in their discussion of the matters as Benedict, Brown, Crooker, and Nourse all acknowledged that primary sources had to be reconciled with each other and that "truth" served as the end goal.[27]

S. Millett Thompson of the Thirteenth New Hampshire Infantry laid out the broader importance of his regimental history and how he wanted to tell the story of everyone in the unit and what the war had meant for them. He stated that "it is desired that the reader of this book shall gain some idea of what it cost, in labor, fighting and suffering, to re-unite the dissevered States of the American Union; for every regiment in the Northern army had experiences similar to those of the Thirteenth." Thompson explained that he drew only from authoritative sources. He eschewed "cheap newspaper accounts, popular yarns or realms dimesque." As with many others, Thompson began his account as a personal memoir for his family. When he discussed the idea with former members of the regiment, they encouraged him to pen a history. Once resolved to write the book, Thompson embarked on his work. He examined "the many letters, diaries and papers required in the work, after reading every reliable publication I could obtain bearing upon the particular service in which the Thirteenth took part." Thompson consulted statements, letters, and diaries of more than thirty members of the Thirteenth, ranging from those of the former colonel of the regiment on down to those of privates, showing that he wanted to cover not only the sweeping movements of campaigns or the tactical clashes of battle but also the granular level of soldier experience. He also examined manuscript histories of other regiments. Published authorities consulted included adjutants general reports from

Connecticut, Maine, Massachusetts, New Jersey, New York, Rhode Island, Vermont, and New Hampshire. Visits to battlefields and camps in Virginia also aided in writing an accurate account.[28]

Thompson announced the impending publication of his regimental history at the 1887 reunion to raise money to finance the volume. He told his listeners that "nearly a quarter of a century ago you were engaged in making American history—volumes of it—far more volumes of it than can ever be written by the pen of a mortal man." A distributed circular gave the model of the book, and Thompson requested that a subscription be taken. Thompson and others remained conscious of a difference between the personal memoirs and their regimental histories. Doubtless, memoirs contained more of private stories, whereas histories gave a public facing account. The distinction that veterans drew between the privately circulated memoirs and the histories they wrote also hinged on the types and number of sources used. For memoirs, personal memory sufficed, while for a history, the facts needed to be confirmed and accurate information presented.[29]

The accounts of Benedict and Thompson also highlight how historical writing helped knit white veterans together. Northern veterans remained in conversation with one another, circulating sources and texts. They delved into archives, public and private, and sought out primary source materials. When dealing with sources, veterans employed similar methods or "rules" of interpretation and modified those methods as challenges became apparent. In other words, veterans who wrote histories constituted a professional group in and of themselves, with methods and narratives similar to those produced by the emerging academic field of history. Because Novick looked almost exclusively at professional historians and Cheng ended her narrative in 1860, the important role these veteran-historians played in American historical practice.[30]

The white Northern veteran aimed to craft an impartial and scientific narrative about his own experience; this in turn limited the Northern veteran to a panoply of primary sources written by similar people for similar ends. The standpoint that veteran-authors adopted—telling the stories of their regiments—placed their own stories at the center of the book. The sources that they drew upon to write their narratives had been created by men such as themselves. Letters to family, letters to the hometown newspaper, diaries scribbled in the field, official reports lodged after battles, records maintained by an army of clerks within the army proper, muster rolls maintained in the state repositories—all placed the white Northern soldier at the center of the story. The similarity of perspectives and methods—the veterans aimed to write an impartial narrative but one rooted in eyewitness status—led to the creation of a consensus that became a basis for the field of Civil War history. Thus, by the time professional historians began producing scholarly accounts in the late nineteenth century, the ground had already been prepared for a narrative rooted primarily in the commonalities of wartime experiences of white soldiers. Unsettling for historians today, the popular convention in the nineteenth century that informed the foundation of the field was white men writing about white male military service. The white veterans' "truth," rooted in the use of professional methods, served as the foundation for the modern field of Civil War history.

NOTES

I presented versions of this chapter at both the Society of Civil War Historians Conference in 2018 and at a John L. Nau III Civil War Center event at the University of Virginia. I gratefully acknowledge the comments I received on both of those occasions, especially the suggestions of Keith Bohannon, John Coski, Caroline E. Janney, Kathryn Shively, and Yael Sternhell. Both Caroline Janney and Kathryn Shively closely read this manuscript, and their careful attention improved it.

1. Gary W. Gallagher and Kathryn Shively Meier, "Coming to Terms with Civil War Military History," *Journal of the Civil War Era* 4, no. 4 (December 2014): 491, 498; Stephen Z. Starr, "The Grand Old Regiment," *Wisconsin Magazine of History* 48, no. 1 (Autumn 1964): 22. As Gallagher has also noted, the academic and popular sides of history overlapped, starting with the wartime generation. Former Confederate general Edward Porter Alexander, when penning his memoirs, sought guidance from some of the most prominent historians of his day, including Columbia professor William Dunning. *Fighting for the Confederacy: The Personal Recollections of General Edward Porter Alexander*, ed. Gary W. Gallagher (Chapel Hill: University of North Carolina Press, 1989), xx.

2. Peter Novick, *That Noble Dream: The "Objectivity Question" and the American Historical Profession* (Cambridge: Cambridge University Press, 1988); Eileen Ka-May Cheng, *The Plain and Noble Garb of Truth: Nationalism and Impartiality in American Historical Writing, 1784–1860* (Athens: University of Georgia Press, 2008), 58–61, 79–83, 132–38, 254–55; Lindsay DiCuirci, *Colonial Revivals: The Nineteenth-Century Lives of Early American Books* (Philadelphia: University of Pennsylvania Press, 2019), 1–13; David D. Van Tassel, *Recording America's Past: An Interpretation of the Development of Historical Studies in America, 1607–1884* (Chicago: University of Chicago Press, 1960), 95–110. For more on the effort to preserve manuscripts and primary sources, see Sean R. Busick, *A Sober Desire for History: William Gilmore Simms as Historian* (Columbia: University of South Carolina Press, 2005), 29–35.

3. Historian John Hope Franklin discussed the significance and importance of the work of George Washington Williams; historian Elizabeth R. Varon has written on the importance of Joseph T. Wilson. See John Hope Franklin, "George Washington Williams and Beginnings of Afro-American Historiography," *Critical Inquiry* 4 no. 4 (Summer 1978): 657–72; John Hope Franklin, *George Washington Williams: A Biography* (Chicago: University of Chicago Press,

1985); and Elizabeth R. Varon, "Joseph T. Wilson's *The Black Phalanx*: African American Patriotism and the Won Cause," in *Civil War Writing: New Perspectives on Iconic Texts*, ed. Gary W. Gallagher and Stephen Cushman (Baton Rouge: Louisiana State University Press, 2010), 13–41. For discussions of African American historians and history in the nineteenth century, see John Ernest, *Liberation Historiography: African American Writers and the Challenge of History, 1794–1861* (Chapel Hill: University of North Carolina Press, 2004); Stephen G. Hall, *A Faithful Account of the Race: African American Historical Writing in Nineteenth-Century America* (Chapel Hill: University of North Carolina Press, 2009); and Benjamin Quarles, "Black History's Antebellum Origins," pt. 1, *Proceedings of the American Antiquarian Society* 89 (April 1979): 89–122. Chad L. Williams has written eloquently about the challenges that W. E. B. Du Bois and African American historians faced after World War I, when, much like the period after Civil War, access to source materials and monetary resources hampered writing. Chad L Williams, *The Wounded World: W. E. B. Du Bois and the First World War* (New York: Farrar, Straus and Giroux, 2023).

For the remainder of this chapter, the veteran-authors discussed fit the following demographic described: they were white and Northern and supported the Union. In the interests of readability, shorter versions of the description will be used, but every instance should be understood to refer only to the described demographic.

4. Charles Camic, writing about the genesis of the academic study of economics, also underway in the same time frame as the academic study of history, has pointed out that the creation of a knowledge field relies upon participants seeking truth through correct theories and a unified method of scientific research. Camic noted that "people who make up a field are cognizant of other group members and relate to one another around the issues that define the field." He also remarked that common practices and resources help define the creation of a "field." Veteran-writers exhibited those characteristics, shared practices, and used resources in similar ways. Charles Camic, *Veblen: The Making of an Economist Who Unmade Economics* (Cambridge, MA: Harvard University Press, 2020), 26–29. Camic also pointed out that studies of a field or discipline typically "have tracked the story of knowledge specialists forward in time by examining their role in the struggles underway in their discipline over opposing truth claims." Put differently, stories of "fields" have looked at arguments within the field after it has been constituted rather than at the dynamics of what went into the creation of the field itself. Camic's observation well describes Novick's *That Noble Dream*. Camic, *Veblen*, 32.

5. The 1850, 1860, and 1880 censuses provide figures for "printing and publishing." The four categories used in the 1870 census—"printing and publishing, not specified"; "printing and publishing, book"; "printing and publishing, newspaper"; and "printing and publishing, job"—have been combined in order to compare like with like. Scott E. Casper, "Introduction," *The Industrial Book, 1840–1880*, vol. 3 of *A History of the Book in America*, ed. Scott E. Casper, Jeffrey D. Groves, Stephen W. Nissenbaum, and Michael Winship (Chapel Hill: University of North Carolina Press, 2007), 10–11, 12–13, 14–15, 16–17.

6. Michael Winship, "The National Book Trade System," in *Industrial Book*, ed. Casper et al., 124; Jeffrey D. Groves, "Periodicals and Serial Publication," in *Industrial Book*, ed. Casper et al., 226–27; Michael Winship, "Manufacturing and Book Production," in *Industrial Book*, ed. Casper et al., 44; Willman Spawn and Thomas E. Kinsella, *American Signed Bindings through 1876* (New Castle, DE: Oak Knoll Press and Bryn Mawr College Library, 2007).

7. Christopher Hager, *I Remain Yours: Common Lives in Civil War Letters* (Cambridge, MA: Harvard University Press, 2018), 4–6, 13; Karen Lystra, *Searching the Heart: Women, Men, and Romantic Love in Nineteenth-Century America* (Oxford: Oxford University Press, 1992).

8. *A Leaf of Voices: Stories of the American Civil War in the Words of Those Who Lived and Died, 1861–1865*, ed. Jennifer McSpadden (Indianapolis: Indiana Historical Society, 2014), xv–xvi; *Writing and Fighting the Civil War: Soldier Correspondence to the New York "Sunday Mercury,"* rev. ed., ed. William B. Styple (Kearny, NJ: Belle Grove, 2004), 8.

9. *This Wicked Rebellion: Wisconsin Civil War Soldiers Write Home*, ed. John Zimm (Madison: Wisconsin Historical Society Press, 2012), ix. Quiner used his scrapbooks as a basis for his *Military History of Wisconsin: A Record of the Civil and Military Patriotism of the State in the War for the Union* (Chicago: Clarke and Co., 1866).

10. George Grenville Benedict, *Army Life in Virginia: Letters from the Twelfth Vermont Regiment: Personal Experiences of Volunteer Service in the War for the Union, 1862–63* (Burlington, VT: Free Press Association, 1895), preface. For the text of the wartime letters themselves, see *Army Life in Virginia: The Civil War Letters of George G. Benedict*, ed. Eric Ward (Mechanicsburg, PA: Stackpole Books, 2002).

11. Redfield Proctor at the 1880 meeting of the Reunion Society of Vermont Officers, in W. G. Veazy et al., *Proceedings of the Reunion Society of Vermont Officers, 1864–1884, with Addresses Delivered at Its Meetings* (Burlington, VT: Free Press Association, 1885), 357.

12. Lt. Col. P. T. Washburn's oration at the 1869 meeting of the Reunion Society of Vermont Officers, in Veazy et al., *Proceedings of the Reunion Society of Vermont Officers*, 83.

13. Joan Boudrea, "The Portable Press and Field Printing during the American Civil War," *Printing History*, n.s., 12 (July 2012): 3–26. For a discussion of the process behind the mammoth compilation of primary sources, *The War of the Rebellion: A Compilation of the Official Records of the Union and Confederate Armies*, see Harold E. Mahan, "The Arsenal of History: The *Official Records of the War of the Rebellion*," *Civil War History* 29, no. 1 (March 1983): 5–27; and Yael A. Sternhell, "The Afterlives of the Confederate Archive: Civil War Documents and the Making of Sectional Reconciliation," *Journal of American History* 102, no. 4 (March 2016): 1025–50. For an account of the destruction that befell many Confederate sources, see Keith Bohannon, "Many Valuable Records and Documents Were Lost to History: The Destruction of Confederate Military Records during the Appomattox Campaign," in *Petersburg to Appomattox: The End of the War in Virginia*, ed. Caroline E. Janney (Chapel Hill: University of North Carolina Press, 2018), 170–91.

14. Journal entries, March 13; May 13, 24, 31; and June 11, 1865, in Louis N. Beaudry, *War Journal of Louis N. Beaudry, Fifth New York Cavalry: The Diary of a Union Chaplain, Commencing February 16, 1863*, ed. Richard E. Beaudry (Jefferson, NC: McFarland, 1996), 208–9, 223, 225, 227, and 231. Beaudry began his work on March 13 and recorded working on his regimental history constantly through June. Journal entries, April 8, 18, 22; May 3, 10, 18, 22; and June 3, 5, 8, 9, 10, 12, 1865, in Beaudry, *War Journal*, 214, 217, 218, 220, 222, 224, 225, 228, 231.

15. The best study of the popular press during the Civil War, from newspaper accounts to lengthy tomes, remains Alice Fahs, *The Imagined Civil War: Popular Literature of the North and South, 1861–1865* (Chapel Hill: University of North Carolina Press, 2001). That veterans created networks of knowledge rooted in both experience and primary sources suggests

that the now-dominant paradigm of Civil War "memory" might need adjustment, as the concept of "memory" seems insufficient to encompass the ways in which veterans wrote about their experiences. For recent summaries of Civil War memory, see David W. Blight, *Race and Reunion: The Civil War in American Memory* (Cambridge, MA: Harvard University Press, 2001); and Caroline E. Janney, *Remembering the Civil War: Reunion and the Limits of Reconciliation* (Chapel Hill: University of North Carolina Press, 2013).

16. J. R. Sypher, *History of the Pennsylvania Reserve Corps: A Complete Record of the Organization...* (Lancaster, PA: Elias Barr, 1865), 460; Joshua L. Chamberlain to John B. Bachelder, November 10, 1865, in *The Grand Old Man of Maine: Selected Letters of Joshua Lawrence Chamberlain, 1865–1914*, ed. Jeremiah E. Goulka (Chapel Hill: University of North Carolina Press, 2008), 8. Chamberlain never completed his planned official history of the Fifth Army Corps of the Army of the Potomac. Eventually, the Fifth Army Corps Association selected Lt. Col. William H. Powell to finish a manuscript partially completed by Col. Carswell McClellan. Chamberlain himself spoke and wrote much about the war, apparently completing his manuscript of the Fifth Army Corps's role in the last days of the war sometime in 1899. Despite its completion in 1899, this manuscript appeared in print only after Chamberlain's death. William H. Powell, *The Fifth Army Corps (Army of the Potomac): A Record of Operations during the Civil War in the United States of America, 1861–1865* (New York: G. P. Putnam's Sons, 1896); Joshua L. Chamberlain, *"Bayonet! Forward": My Civil War Reminiscences* (Gettysburg, PA: Stan Clark Military Books, 1994); Joshua L. Chamberlain to Sarah (Sae) Farrington, April 4, 1899, in Goulka, *Grand Old Man of Maine*, 169; Joshua L. Chamberlain, *The Passing of the Armies: An Account of the Final Campaign of the Army of the Potomac, Based upon Personal Reminiscences of the Fifth Army Corps* (New York: G. P. Putnam's Sons, 1915).

17. Fahs, *Imagined Civil War*, 304–7; James Harvey McKee, *Back "in War Times": History of the 144th Regiment, New York Volunteer Infantry, with Itinerary, Showing Contemporaneous Date of the Important Battles of the Civil War* (New York: Times Office, 1903), 21. As Fahs points out, though Lossing's publishers had intended for the Civil War volumes to appear during the war, Lossing missed deadlines and the first volume appeared in 1866.

18. McKee, *Back "in War Times,"* 21, 7.

19. Col. William Holbrook at the 1883 meeting of the Reunion Society of Vermont Officers, in Veazy et al., *Proceedings of the Reunion Society of Vermont Officers*, 413.

20. W[illia]m C. Holbrook, *A Narrative of the Services of the Officers and Enlisted Men of the 7th Regiment of Vermont Volunteers (Veterans), from 1862 to 1866* (New York: American Bank Note Company Commercial Department, 1882), iii, iv.

21. George G. Benedict at the 1882 meeting of the Reunion Society of Vermont Officers, in Veazy et al., *Proceedings of the Reunion Society of Vermont Officers*, 385, 386.

22. George G. Benedict, "The Element of Romance in Military History," War Paper No. 4, Vermont Commandery of the Loyal Legion, read March 13, 1893, in *Vermont War Papers and Miscellaneous State Papers and Addresses for the Military Order of the Loyal Legion of the United States* (Wilmington, NC: Broadfoot, 1994), 59.

23. Benedict, "Element of Romance in Military History," 66, 67.

24. Benedict, "Element of Romance in Military History," 62, 68.

25. Benedict, "Element of Romance in Military History," 71. The story of the sleeping sentinel proved controversial far beyond Benedict; in the 1930s, the Vermont Historical Society published a booklet intended to "examine everything and suppress nothing." Waldo

F. Glover, *Abraham Lincoln and the Sleeping Sentinel of Vermont* (Montpelier: Vermont Historical Society, 1936), 12.

26. Benedict, "Element of Romance in Military History," 77.

27. [John G. Brown, Lucien B. Crooker, and Henry S. Nourse], *The Story of the Fifty-Fifth Regiment Illinois Volunteer Infantry in the Civil War 1861–1865* (Clinton, MA: W. J. Coulter, 1887), 5–6.

28. S. Millett Thompson, *Thirteenth Regiment of New Hampshire Volunteer Infantry in the War of the Rebellion, 1861–1865: A Diary Covering Three Years and a Day* (Boston: Houghton, Mifflin, 1888), v, vii–viii

29. Thompson, *Thirteenth Regiment of New Hampshire Volunteer Infantry*, 689. Others followed the reverse course; Abner R. Small wrote his personal memoirs drawing upon the material collected for his history of the Sixteenth Maine Infantry Regiment. *The Road to Richmond: The Civil War Memoirs of Major Abner R. Small of the Sixteenth Maine Volunteers*, ed. Harold Adams Small (Berkeley: University of California Press, 1939), viii.

30. Novick, *That Noble Dream*; Cheng, *Plain and Noble Garb of Truth*. Historians who have written about Civil War memory have confined their analysis to examining the written works of Civil War leaders that appeared in commercial magazines, such as the famous "Battles and Leaders" series that appeared in *Century Magazine* or the memoirs of general officers. While providing valuable analysis of those genres, this approach overlooks the grassroots historical effort among white Northern veterans. For instance, see Paul H. Buck, *The Road to Reunion, 1865–1900* (Boston: Little Brown, 1937), 220–61; and Blight, *Race and Reunion*, 140–254.

Epilogue

Taking the Shape of the Civil War

AARON SHEEHAN-DEAN
CAROLINE E. JANNEY
PETER S. CARMICHAEL

The scale of the US Civil War and the variety of ways it changed America and the world make it resistant to a single holistic interpretive scheme. The historiography is massive and detailed, but in nearly every instance, these are branches rather than the trunk.[1] Why did the North endorse emancipation? How did class conflict shape the Confederate experience? What was the war's impact on American economic growth and state development? Why did the Union win? Why did the Confederacy lose? What role did gender play in the conflict? These questions, and many more like them, have generated rich topical historiographies, but the frameworks that govern each subfield remain separate.

The first question posed above—about the Union's decision to adopt emancipation—has generated decades of fruitful scholarship. It has attracted scholars of slavery and race who uncovered the persistence of enslaved people to seek freedom, scholars of the army interested in strategic and manpower policies, and scholars of the state tracking the nature of federal authority in the nineteenth century. The most fully developed topical historiography is the one surrounding the war's origins. The traditional and still dominant framing tracks debates among traditionalists and revisionists.[2] What unifies these studies is a focus on explaining secession and the rush to war, but the causation school labels offer little analytical value for the nature of the conflict as it evolved over the next four years.

For instance, knowing whether authors regard the war as irrepressible cannot predict their opinions about the war's effect on racial ideologies. To be fair, the question of whether the Civil War was avoidable leads to the one meta-framing that gives shape to assessments of the war itself. Reductively, this can be phrased as "Was the war worth the cost?" The critical posture of World War I era historians toward the political system of the 1850s led them to interpret the war as fundamentally unnecessary, a perspective rekindled in the 1970s and early years of the twenty-first century. Despite their callous misreading of the actual experience of slavery, Yael Sternhell identifies a set of Revisionist concerns that resonate with many contemporary historians: "a commitment to nonviolence, disgust with war, and frustration with the shortcomings of democracy."[3] She juxtaposes this perspective with the dominant neo-abolitionist reading of the conflict as "a just war, for a just cause, that gave the United States, as Lincoln had said, a new birth of freedom."[4] The tension between these positions emerges from disagreements about both the process and the consequences of the Civil War. On the former, historians argue about whether the war was fought according to prevailing ethical norms and over the scale of bloodshed, which is sometimes interpreted as prima facie evidence of the war's immorality. On the topic of outcomes, first-generation Revisionists doubted that slavery was bad enough to justify a war, while modern Revisionists argue that given postwar failures to establish equality and protect true freedom, the war's net effect was to increase rather than relieve suffering. Moral judgment forms the backbone of this approach and a peculiarly ex post facto moralizing of the kind not usually sanctioned by historians. The classic binary, as Sternhell shows us, consists of explanatory frameworks structured by teleological value judgments.

Civil War historians have never constructed an overarching historiographical framework for the war itself, rather than moral frameworks, and we do not propose one here. Indeed, a holistic interpretive structure would flatten out the very richness that makes the Civil War such a productive venue for scholarship. The Lost Cause is, in a way, such a holistic interpretive scheme, and its gross misrepresentations, to say nothing of its moral odium, suggest the serious drawbacks that come from reading the whole conflict through a single lens. Still, the lack of a central question that organizes scholarship on the US Civil War has inhibited efforts to make sense of changes over time in the literature.[5] The important changes in the field have not occurred along the traditionalist-revisionist axis but along the branching lines of the web that connect our scholarship to fields adjacent or distant to the US Civil War in space and time. Attending to the ebb and flow of various subfields reveals a broader pattern.

Between the mid-1980s and 2010, the breadth and sophistication of these fields expanded significantly. Several influences converged in these decades to generate a much more diverse and intellectually rewarding area of study. The social history revolution of the 1960s reached Civil War scholars two decades later.[6] Maris Vinovskis's famous 1989 article, "Have Social Historians Lost the Civil War?," encouraged historians who might not have been drawn to military conflict to study the war in order to better understand behaviors in American life.[7] The new military history of the 1970s, which sought to integrate military and civilian experiences by positioning war within its broader social context, spurred historians to think more capaciously.[8] The civil rights movement and the accompanying scholarly attention to race likewise generated a new focus on slavery and emancipation. New histories of women and gender inspired Civil War scholars to think seriously about the implications of the war for conceptions and practices of gender in the United States. Historians of class drew attention to nonslaveholders in the Confederacy and workers in the North, both communities that sometimes challenged the reigning dogmas of their sections. These complementary forces intersected in fruitful and novel ways, generating a wave of scholarship that centered previously marginalized historical actors—ordinary civilians, African Americans (both enslaved and free), poor people, women, and children—in the historical process. Because this scholarship enabled deeper and more precise explanations of the war, we call members of this generation the Internalists.

All of these analytical perspectives—social history, military history, and the critical study of race and gender—continue to attract attention, but since 2010, Civil War historians have tended to work horizontally rather than vertically, seeking breadth rather than depth. They have focused on different topics or reconceptualized older ones—memory studies, laws of war debates, global and transnational histories of the conflict, economics, civil-military relations, environmental history, western and Native American history—to connect the war to the nineteenth century and to the world. These methods have compelled Civil War historians to use tools from other fields. For instance, Stephanie McCurry has creatively applied theories of subjecthood and political action from subaltern studies, and many scholars have used James Scott's ideas about "infrapolitics" and the "weapons of the weak" in studies of slavery and supposedly powerless people.[9] Where the Internalists addressed questions about who won the war and why, the current generation is generally inclined to explore processes that span the century and the globe—abolition, capitalism, scientific racism, empire, and violence. For this reason, we term members of the succeeding generation the Externalists. Like all summary judgments, the distinction we are drawing between these schools is a fluid one. The presence of wide-angle studies in the 1990s and the persistence of traditional social history in the 2010s challenge our chronology, but the basic difference between these scholarly approaches seems borne out by a reading of the literature.

From the 1980s through the first decade of the twenty-first century, the leading publisher of academic Civil War history was the University of North Carolina Press, in particular the Civil War America series established and edited by Gary W. Gallagher. This series played a key role in fostering new work in the field. Its output, 115 titles during his tenure as series editor from 1987 to 2012, far surpasses that of other leading presses in the field.[10] The books published in the Civil War America series and through other outlets during this period can be roughly grouped into the following categories: biographies (mostly military and political leaders), social histories, campaign studies, soldier studies, political histories, cultural histories, and memory studies. A hallmark of many of these books is that they combined elements from these different categories, especially the integration of social and cultural questions, into more traditional military and political narratives.[11]

Biographies, especially of generals and leading politicians, have long been a staple of Civil War studies. This subfield shows the most continuity between post–World War II scholarship and what emerged in the 1980s. Historically, these studies emphasized personality and individual ability, sometimes at the expense of the broader context. Internalist approaches adopted more diverse analytical approaches and sought especially to elaborate the relationship between individuals and their social context.[12] Chester Hearn's biography of Ben Butler is representative of the era. It focuses on the Union general's wartime career, engaging with the contested memories of his occupation of New Orleans. It integrates military, political, and social history to assess both Butler and the US practice of occupation.[13] T. Michael Parrish's biography of Confederate general Richard Taylor, like Butler another combatant famous for his service in the trans-Mississippi theater, was grounded in the social context of antebellum plantation life in Louisiana.[14] Parrish's designation of "soldier prince" is not laudatory. To the contrary, Parrish shows how Taylor's cultivated image and battlefield success established a romantic, cavalier memory that played an important role in postwar reconciliation. Still, the focus remained on figures regarded as traditionally important—political and military leaders.

Social historians, whether motivated by Vinovskis's clever challenge or not, created a sharper break with past practice. Their influence could be seen in the many ways that Civil War scholars attended to issues of class, race, and gender that had remained hidden in the post–World War II literature. Iver Bernstein's study of the New York City draft riots, for instance, combined all these features to reveal one of the era's most horrible moments in all its complexity, while in other cases, such as labor studies, scholars focused on one particular angle.[15] "Battlefront," a word that only came into use during World War I, was joined by "home front," a concept popularized during World War II. Whether interested in logistics, workers, government contracts, wealth, or women, historians turned their analytical focus on households. As a part of this attention to the war's lived experience, a new subfield in gender history sprang up where previous historians had paid little attention to issues of femininity and masculinity per se. Historians plumbed wartime sources to answer questions about the experience of women, men, and gender that had taken center stage in American history more generally but had not yet been incorporated into the Civil War. George Rable, Catherine Clinton, Nina Silber, LeeAnn Whites, and Drew Gilpin Faust published influential books in the late-1980s and mid-1990s, helping establish frameworks around women's experiences that connected them to politics, military affairs, and the economy.[16] Subsequent studies by Stephen Berry, Peter Carmichael, Aaron Sheehan-Dean, and Lorien Foote built on this foundation to ask similar questions about men and manhood.[17] In all of these cases, historians both explained new elements of the Civil War and contributed to the histories of gender more broadly.

Campaign studies, typically pitched at the operational level, had long been a mainstay of Civil War history. The original Battles and Leaders series, when published in *Century Magazine* and as a four-volume book series, was organized around major military campaigns and battles.[18] Historians of the 1980s and 1990s pioneered much more comprehensive treatments of campaigns, incorporating local and regional history, social and cultural experiences, and civilians and soldiers and often extending the story well beyond the actual campaign itself. Joseph Glatthaar's analysis of Sherman's Carolinas Campaign, Kenneth Noe's study of the Battle of Perryville, and Michael Ballard's study of Grant's Vicksburg Campaign stand out as models of this new approach.[19] George Rable's *Fredericksburg! Fredericksburg!*, published in 2002, remains the gold standard, elegantly combining a detailed narrative of the pivotal clashes between the Union and Confederate armies along the Rappahannock River in late 1862 with a clear-eyed analysis of the experience of all the civilians exposed to the terrible violence of this campaign.[20] Some studies, like Jacqueline Campbell's and Lisa Frank's analyses of Sherman's marches in the Carolinas and Georgia, respectively, used the framework of a campaign to examine the war's impact on civilians, especially women.[21] A related approach could be found in the rise of place-based histories, some covering whole regions, others several counties or cities and their hinterlands. Robert Tracy McKenzie's study of Knoxville is a model in this respect, combining a close reading of the political and social dynamics in a contested city within a contested region, a perfect metonym for the larger civil conflict.[22]

The new military history, a movement that garnered the attention of historians of various places and times, spurred Civil War historians to rethink an exclusive focus on the battlefield. In addition to the new approaches to traditional military history topics like battles and campaigns, this involved pioneering studies of occupation, guerrillas, soldiers, and the relationship between the war and civilian morale.[23] The latter topic generated a robust and productive debate between historians who reckoned with the range of social and political discontent on the Confederate home front and a series of critics who interrogated Confederate nationalism with new attention.[24] The framework for both sides in this debate presumed a close connection between military and civilian affairs. It generated new insights into the nature of nationalism and civil-military relations. These arguments were framed across a narrow span of time (typically the four years of war), and the result was, in some respects, a missed opportunity, though one that scholars of a new generation are taking on as they connect the wartime and postwar era more tightly. The voluminous literature on soldiers and sailors, in contrast, enabled historians to tackle discrete changes experienced by men at war. Joseph Glatthaar's study of the racial attitudes of Sherman's men, Lorien Foote's analysis of class conflict and discipline within the Union army, and Susannah Ural's history of Irish Americans and ethnicity all produced new insights that spanned the broader era, even as the books primarily focused on the war itself.[25]

Just as military historians concerned themselves with politics, so political historians integrated military events into their accounts. George Rable's explanation of Confederate politics offered a framework to accommodate both the committed ideologues (such as Alexander Stephens) and those politicians (like Jefferson Davis and his cabinet officers) who responded to the pressures of war to devise new policies.[26] Mark Neely showed how the demands of war compelled both Union and Confederate leaders to abridge civil liberties.[27] Richard Bensel's comprehensive political economic analysis of the Union and the Confederacy generated few imitators at the time, though a more recent cohort of historians of American political development have returned to his arguments.[28] One of the virtues of political history as it came to be practiced in the 1990s was its engagement with histories of slavery and emancipation. This was a salutary and long-overdue change. A good example of this perspective appears in William Link's *Roots of Secession*.[29] Because of its centrality to the broader process of Confederate secession, scholars have investigated Virginia's ambivalent exit from the Union at repeated intervals over the twentieth century. Most of those studies centered on the decision-making by white elites in Richmond or in regional power centers around the state.[30] Link's book, in contrast, paid careful attention to the role played by enslaved people, especially those who fled to freedom over the Ohio River or via the land route along the Great Valley into Pennsylvania. Over the 1850s, slaveholders' very public efforts to reclaim escaped slaves generated legal battles between Virginia and Pennsylvania that stimulated the defensive political posture that defined the late antebellum South.

A wave of new work on antebellum abolitionists and studies of wartime emancipation reveals the deep connections between politics and slavery. Despite abolitionists' aversion to electoral politics, Stanley Harrold's work (among that of many others) shows their deep engagement with the broader process of policy and law.[31] This relationship gained even more importance during the war, as emancipation became a manpower policy, a partisan dispute, a foreign policy, and an exercise of central state authority. Initially, the debate shaped itself around a single question—"Who freed the slaves?"— though the limits of this framing were already showing in the 1990s.[32] Two important venues that have facilitated much of the new work in this subfield are the journal *Slavery and Abolition* and the documentary project organized by the University of Maryland's *Freedmen and Southern Society Project*, which began publication in 1980 and 1982 respectively. New primary sources, creative analytical approaches, and heightened public demand for these stories have energized a community of scholars who have conducted some of the most creative scholarship in any field since midcentury.

Although cultural histories emerged more fully in the period after 2010, a number of pathbreaking studies were published in the earlier period. Alice Fahs's study of popular literature during the war is one of these.[33] Responding to a still earlier generation of scholars who denigrated nineteenth-century popular literature, Fahs attended carefully to the ways in which that work "democratized" the war by dramatizing it in ways that reached ordinary readers. Fahs showed how novelists, poets, and playwrights, rather than retreating behind a one-dimensional patriotism, all confronted their audiences with the changes, particularly with regard to race and gender, that the war was producing. Like many cultural historians, Fahs investigated the act of depiction as a way of understanding cultural boundaries of race, gender, and class. Analysis of literature also played a key role in most of the studies of memory that emerged in this period, including the work of Nina Silber, David Blight, Sarah Gardner, and others.[34] In these works, as well as in studies of religion, authors identified new ways of understanding how the war's participants experienced and processed the war. Their process of deriving meaning gave us a much fuller view of the era. Thanks to this work, we can now see the extent to which the war challenged old ways of knowing and how people assimilated its violence and destruction into preexisting value systems.

The field of Civil War memory was effectively created in the 1980s and 1990s. Charles Reagan Wilson's and Gaines Foster's pioneering books opened the gates to a number of rich studies.[35] Some, like the work of Alan Nolan, Caroline Janney, and William Blair, focused on contextualizing the creation of the Lost Cause.[36] Other scholars attended to Northern memories, revealing a richer and more diverse memory landscape than today's popular culture reflects.[37] Nearly all agreed that memories of the war were constructed to meet the political needs of the present. David Blight's *Race and Reunion* established a framework—centered on Northern complicity in white Southern interpretations of the war at the expense of Black interpretations—that has generated productive debate and an increasingly nuanced portrait of American attitudes toward the past.[38] Part of what distinguished memory studies was the willingness of historians to venture beyond the normal boundaries of the era. Instead of 1844–77, the traditional framing of the "Civil War era," most historians of memory carried the story into the early twentieth century. For these scholars, the war was effectively the background, the thing about which later generations fought, and if anything united memory scholars it was an agreement that the context within which memory or history took root was as important, if not more so, than the past era being discussed. The more capacious chronology of memory studies anticipated and encouraged one of the key shifts in the decade that followed.

If there was an overarching issue driving much of the writing in the late twentieth and early twenty-first centuries, it was explaining *why* the war ended the way that it did. Historians of military strategy, class conflict, politics, and slavery all offered answers to this question, and each of these approaches has generated its own internal debates. What marks the question as representative of the Internalist generation is its close attention to cause and effect. Historians argued about a discrete moment—the cessation of major military hostilities in April 1865. In their books, they articulated arguments that offered precise, often singular, explanations. For instance, Herman Hattaway and Archer Jones argued that the North won the Civil War by waging a logistical campaign that weakened Confederate armies over time and by exploiting tactical defensive positions, while Brian Holden Reid credits the moments when the Union army pursued offensive operations, as at New Orleans, Vicksburg, and Atlanta.[39] David Williams, in a series of books, claimed that class dissension on the Confederate home front fatally weakened the South's war effort, while Gary Gallagher responded by showing the resiliency of Confederate nationalism and attributed Confederate defeat to Union military power.[40] Eric McKitrick argued that the Union's two-party system gave it flexibility and responsiveness, while the Confederacy's prohibition on political parties channeled opposition into a personal and counterproductive confrontation with Jefferson Davis. Mark Neely responded by showing how much the political opposition mobilized by Democrats weakened Lincoln in the North.[41] The overarching research question in this instance was predicated on a fixed chronology and tolerated little ambiguity.

Since 2010, Civil War historians have shifted their topical focus—with much recent writing on veterans, the environment, laws of war debates, emancipation, global and transnational histories of the conflict, economics, civil-military relations, and western and Native American history. But the more compelling innovation is the way this history is being written. Contemporary scholars have taken issue with their predecessors' approach to timing and consequently enabled an expansion of the narratives that describe change during the era. They also reject the Internalists' posture of certainty, instead chronicling half-steps, inconsistencies, ironies, and incomplete transformations. For instance, while previous historians of slavery showed that the Union's mobilization of African American manpower enabled Union victory, today's scholars focus more on the Black experience of war and how attitudes about race changed as a result.[42] Similarly, historians of politics have adopted equally broad framings, aiming to track the effect of the conflict on the rise of the Republican Party, the dimming fortunes of Democrats, and the ideological frameworks that underlay both parties, rather than just on whether Northern and Southern political systems enabled victory or defeat.[43] These perspectives reflect a shift away from the cause-and-effect model of the previous generation and toward an emphasis on longer time frames and more gradual change. In comparison to the earlier generation of intellectual histories, consider how a work such as Louis Menand's *Metaphysical Club* is concerned primarily with the long history of American philosophy. In contrast to histories that explained how Americans managed during the war, Menand emphasized the ways that it upset existing epistemologies, yielding a new pragmatism that extended across most spheres of life.[44] This change in chronological and causal framing owes a great deal to the influence of cultural history, which has itself become a major tool for historians of the Civil War era.

Veterans might not appear like a new topic. One of the first forms of Civil War history, after all, were unit studies written by veterans that explained their military service to their communities. Scholars writing between the 1980s and 2010 continued this approach, writing community studies that explored the social and political position of veterans.[45] More recent work focuses on veterans as individuals to assess the impact of the war.[46] In particular, a growing community of scholars use modern psychoanalytic and trauma theory to interrogate the interior dimensions of the veterans' experience.[47] These are social histories of a sort, though most of these scholars are as connected to histories of medicine as they are to traditional social history. Of equal importance, they speak much more directly to our current environment, in which newspapers regularly report on the challenges faced by veterans of the Iraq and Afghanistan wars. Recent histories show that Civil War military service, like that experienced in the twenty-first century, could generate profound psychological damage, leading to drug addiction, despair, and suicide.

The previously hidden personal costs of war have drawn scholars into still more intimate histories. Despite their seeming remove from the electoral politics and battlefield operations that interested post–World War II historians, new histories of emotions and senses connect the personal and the political, the individual and the macro. Michael Woods's pioneering study, *Emotional and Sectional Conflict in the Antebellum United States*, shows how the emotional regimes and expressions of antebellum men facilitated regional antagonisms and eventually war.[48] Recent work in this vein has excavated the impact of imprisonment on soldiers' attitudes toward themselves and their comrades and the bifurcated emotional inheritance of defeat and suffering for white Southern men who displayed new levels of vulnerability within their families even as they adopted an increasingly violent posture toward freedpeople.[49] Allied to these cultural approaches has been new academic interest in material culture, long the purview of museum and National Park Service personnel. Civil War historians have started drawing connections between the physical elements of the Civil War era—weapons, clothing, relics, and the landscape itself—and the ways that people experienced and understood the conflict.[50] These studies perform the useful service of both decentering people as autonomous agents of their lives and showing how people used objects to manage their worlds.

Environmental history likewise complicates older notions of rational actors by demanding that historians incorporate the natural world as a determinative force. And just as medical and psychological histories of veterans have drawn scholars primarily rooted in other fields to Civil War sources, environmental historians have investigated the 1860s as a moment of transition in attitudes and behaviors toward the natural world.[51] Historians have long been aware that armies consume and refashion resources and sometimes even the land itself. The US Army's campaign of logistical devastation across the South amplified this trend.[52] At the same time, Civil War environmental historians often adopt the longer time frames typical of the field. Erin Mauldin's *Unredeemed Land: An Environmental History of Civil War and Emancipation in the Cotton South*, for instance, focuses on land use and labor practices, especially in the wake of emancipation, in a story that extends well into the postwar period and connects, historiographically, to histories of agriculture and capitalism in the New South.[53] Other histories have combined environmental, medical, and military history, as in Kathryn Shively's innovative study of self-care practices among soldiers exposed to the hazards of Virginia's swamps.[54] New and forthcoming work on human-animal relations, weather, and the protection and exploitation of federal lands will continue all these salutary trends.

Recent investigations into the scale and extent of resource destruction during the war connect with an older tradition of analyzing the Union's "hard war." Recent writing has modified this framework to reveal a picture both of unnecessary killing, often directed against Black soldiers and civilians, and of cautious restraint. Where the debate of the 1990s assumed a binary shape characterized at its poles by Michael Fellman and Mark Neely's argument about whether the war was violent or restrained, more recent work exposes the roots of both violence and restraint and their long legacies.[55] The most celebrated book on this topic in recent years has been John Witt's *Lincoln's Code*, an investigation of the origins and legacy of the Lieber Code.[56] Witt's study, like others in the field, ranges beyond a simplistic assessment of whether the Civil War was "just" or not.[57] Instead, it shows how regular people, politicians, and military commanders applied and reinterpreted religious and philosophical traditions to shape their behavior toward guerrillas, prisoners, enemy soldiers, civilians, and slavery. Guerrillas, in particular, have become an important part of this new portrait of the war's nature. A host of scholars have crafted much more careful investigations of irregular warfare than prevailed in the first flush of guerrilla literature in the 1950s and 1960s. This work adds a degree of intentionality, even strategy, to understanding the decision-making of Civil War irregulars that was missing from previous generations of scholars who characterized guerrilla behavior as chaotic.[58]

Another binary framing that current scholars have abandoned is the preceding generation's debate about which historical actors led emancipation. The most influential recent histories presume a reciprocal relationship, initiated by enslaved people who exploited and accelerated the US Army's labor needs and sustained by the Lincoln administration's willingness to change its war strategy.[59] The question of responsibility for the policy change serves only as the beginning of investigations that center on how the process of emancipation affected the experience of being Black in America. Even as champions like Frederick Douglass tried to leverage African American soldiering into full citizenship and supporters like Abraham Lincoln publicly acknowledged the importance of that military service to Union victory, conservatives in the North and white Southerners undermined wartime gains.[60] The result is that the subfield of emancipation studies embodies most fully the Externalists' embrace of contingency and ambiguity. The title of Joseph Reidy's Bancroft-prize-winning history *Illusions of Emancipation* aptly summarizes the current perspective on the ambivalence and half-measures that defined the process.[61] Current histories of emancipation do much more than convey a sense of incompleteness. They reveal that the historical process of ending slavery was inseparable from every sphere of life—these histories incorporate politics, economics, social relationships, culture, and religion. In this sense, they represent the broader and more capacious analytical framings common to the Externalist generation.

Historians deploying a global or transnational approach to the Civil War are following the lead of scholars in other fields who have spent the past two decades "internationalizing" the US history curriculum more broadly. Some of these treatments are hemispheric, others trans-Atlantic, and still others global.[62] Regardless of the geographical scope, what unites these studies is a recognition of both real-time connections and structural similarities. US participants in the conflict monitored and actively shaped foreign impressions of the Civil War, hoping to generate support or at least forestall alliances with their enemies. The long tradition of diplomatic history focused on American relations with Britain and France; the newer scholarship shifts our gaze to other countries and beyond the ambassadors negotiating official relations.[63] Some of these scholars are also attentive to the insights that comparative history can generate, even if the historical subjects occupied separate spaces during the war years.[64] European histories of abolition, nationalism, war, and empire building have long recognized that these processes spanned geographic boundaries; American histories are discovering that the same changes in North America did so as well.

Over the last two decades, historians of capitalism have found the early American republic a particularly fertile ground for research, and Civil War scholars have expanded on that work.[65] Harking back to some of the questions raised by Richard Bensel in *Yankee Leviathan*, some scholars have addressed the state's role, from fiscal policy to development to banking and currency.[66] These studies provide additional windows onto the nature of the war but are more focused on the transition to an industrial capital economy in the United States. Where an earlier generation regarded postwar economic growth as the inevitable result of a fully free-labor United States, we can now see how intimately involved both federal and state governments were in structuring the patterns of growth that followed the conflict. We can also now see that free labor did not mean an equal and fair labor market. At the level of everyday individuals, the cultural history of capitalism reveals all the ironies and tensions produced by Northern victory, as Brian Luskey's recent history of employment contracts during the war shows.[67]

Civil-military relations have been an interest of scholars for some time, but more recent analyses center not on officers and their political counterparts but on the role of war in American life. As befits a generation of scholars whose professional lives encompassed America's "endless" wars, many of these accounts have been skeptical. In particular, they challenge the clear separation of wartime and peace (itself a hallmark of the preceding generation) as a way to test a key tenet of American exceptionalism—that our political and social development happened according to rules and reason rather than to violence and change. The refusal of Thomas Pressly and other historiographers to address the war's broader meaning in American life perhaps reflects the shock of the obvious. From their often-teleological position, the Union's persistence and the end of slavery were too self-evident to demand attention. That posture has collapsed in the past decade, most visibly in the reassessments of how to date the end of the war.[68] Even when they do not agree, scholars arguing over the appropriate chronology for the Civil War jointly investigate the relationship between war and peace in American life and the actual mechanisms that enable political and social change. The ends of war debate raises the deeper issue of how democracies fight and, distinguishing this field as contemporary, recover from civil conflicts.

Like other topics that illuminate the changing nature of Civil War history, the West as a field of study is not new. But where the literature of the 1980s and 1990s offered more traditional military histories of campaigns and politics, often in ways that distinguished the West from the rest of Civil War America, today's scholars integrate the region into broader narratives.[69] Stacy Smith's and Kevin Waite's recent books reveal the long reach of slavery and the unrelenting commitment by white Southern migrants to remake the West in the image of the South.[70] By exposing the overlap and continuities between Southern slavery and various forms of bondage and peonage in the West, these authors force readers to see slavery as truly national and to understand it as one part of a long history of coerced labor in North America. Ari Kelman, Megan Kate Nelson, and others have likewise integrated the experience of western Indigenous people into the Civil War narrative.[71] Rather than being solely subject to the US Army, Native Americans emerge in their work as actors in their own right, navigating the dangerous uncertainty of the middle decades. The trauma of state-sponsored violence and the vagaries of postwar memory, long preeminent themes in the larger Civil War literature, connect the western and eastern experiences in these accounts.

The distinction we have drawn between the literature of the 1980s through the first decade of the twenty-first century and that of the 2010s, is, like all historiographical divisions, somewhat arbitrary. Some of the changes we identify as typical of current scholarship emerged during the aughts (a few even earlier), and many historians continue to produce valuable research within the parameters established in the 1980s. Our description of the pattern of historical research over the last several decades does not presume an inevitable trajectory. We have deliberately avoided the word "progress." The Externalists, in most cases, do not come to bury Internalists but to build upon their work. Civil War history has changed, as does every field, in response to pressures both internal to academia and connected to broader social and cultural changes. Some of these changes are cumulative, such the shift from social histories of groups—workers, enslaved people, women—to cultural histories of how people within those communities thought and acted. Other changes reflect the resolution of questions, such as the movement away from investigations of why the war ended as it did and toward explanations of what that end meant for participants and the country more generally. Still other changes introduce new actors into the Civil War—from Apaches in the Southwest to Cubans in the Caribbean. In all these cases, the underlying structure of the field reveals not a binary or polar alignment—traditionalists versus revisionists—but a host of different ways of conceptualizing and explaining the historical changes of the Civil War era.

NOTES

1. Thomas J. Pressly's *Americans Interpret Their Civil War*, rev. ed. (1954; New York: Free Press, 1964), remains the only single-author book-length historiographical treatment of the conflict. First published in 1954, it set out to explain the "causes and character" of the conflict. Despite that claim, Pressly's narrative devotes nearly all its time to unpacking competing explanations of the war's origins. Pressly's last chapter is tellingly titled "The Confusion of Voices," because he saw nothing unifying midcentury historians—"the one common element in the rival interpretations was their disagreement with that tradition" (337). The modern echo of Pressly's literary shoulder shrug can be heard whenever a writer falls back on the virtues of "problematizing the past" or revealing its "complexity." Charles Beard and Mary Beard stand alone among the historians chronicled by Pressly as ones who focused on the war's broader significance. Their interpretation of the war as "'a social cataclysm in which the capitalists, laborers, and farmers of the North and West drove from power in the national government the planting aristocracy of the South'" speaks more to the postwar order than to its causes (238).

2. Pressly, *Americans Interpret Their Civil War*; Kenneth M. Stampp, "The Irrepressible Conflict," in *The Imperiled Union: Essays on the Background of the Civil War* (New York: Oxford University Press, 1980), 191–245; Frank Towers, "Partisans, New History, and Modernization: The Historiography of the Civil War's Causes, 1861–2011," *Journal of the Civil War Era* 1 (June 2011): 237–64; Michael E. Woods, "What Twenty-First-Century Historians Have Said about the Causes of Disunion: A Civil War Sesquicentennial Review of the Recent Literature," *Journal of American History* 99 (September 2012): 415–39.

3. Yael A. Sternhell, "Revisionism Reinvented? The Antiwar Turn in Civil War Scholarship," *Journal of the Civil War Era* 3 (June 2013): 241.

4. Sternhell, "Revisionism Reinvented?," 242.

5. The most recent historiography of the war did not advance a general framework but instead reflected the decentralized nature of the field by organizing its chapters around already discrete topical fields. Aaron Sheehan-Dean, ed., *A Companion to the U.S. Civil War*, 2 vols. (Malden, MA: Wiley and Sons, 2014). For similar treatment, see James M. McPherson and William J. Cooper Jr.'s introduction to *Writing the Civil War: The Quest to Understand* (Columbia: University of South Carolina Press, 1998), 1–7, and the chapter structure of that volume, which is organized topically. Two article-length historiographies likewise attend to new works without advancing an overall thesis: Joseph Glatthaar, "The 'New' Civil War History: An Overview," *Pennsylvania Magazine of History and Biography* 115 (July 1991): 339–69; and Aaron Sheehan-Dean, "The Long Civil War: Recent Writing on the Outcomes of the U.S. Civil War," *Virginia Magazine of History and Biography* 119 (June 2011): 107–53. The *Journal of the Civil War Era* has published an outstanding series of historiographical essays, though these too adopt a format organized around subfields. See, for instance, the forum "The Future of Civil War Era Studies," *Journal of the Civil War Era* 2 (March 2012): 3–10, www.journalofthecivilwarera.org/forum-the-future-of-civil-war-era-studies. Michael Woods's recent historiographical assessment lauded the ways that "efforts to capture the 'real war' have brought historians into fruitful conversation with scholars in other fields and disciplines," including the histories of emotions, medicine, and the environment. Michael E. Woods, "Interdisciplinary Studies of the Civil War Era: Recent Trends and Future Prospects," *Journal of American Studies* 51 (May 2017): 350.

6. This observation is not mean to slight the pioneering earlier social histories of the war, including Ella Lonn, *Desertion during the Civil War* (1928; Lincoln: University of Nebraska Press, 1998); Bell Irvin Wiley, *Southern Negroes, 1861–1865* (New Haven, CT: Yale University Press, 1938); Ella Lonn, *Foreigners in the Confederacy* (Chapel Hill: University of North Carolina Press, 1940); Bell Irvin Wiley, *The Life of Johnny Reb: The Common Soldier of the Confederacy* (Baton Rouge: Louisiana State University Press, 1943); Frank L. Owsley, *Plain Folk of the Old South* (Baton Rouge: Louisiana State University Press, 1949); Ella Lonn, *Foreigners in the Union Army and Navy* (Baton Rouge: Louisiana State University Press, 1951); Mary Elizabeth Massey, *Ersatz in the Confederacy: Shortages and Substitutions on the Southern Home Front* (Columbia: University of South Carolina Press, 1952); Bell Irvin Wiley, *The Life of Billy Yank: The Common Soldier of the Union* (Baton Rouge: Louisiana State University Press, 1952); Mary Elizabeth Massey, *Refugee Life in the Confederacy* (Baton Rouge: Louisiana State University Press, 1964); and Mary Elizabeth Massey, *Bonnet Brigades* (New York: Knopf, 1966).

7. Maris Vinovskis, "Have Social Historians Lost the Civil War? Some Preliminary Demographic Speculations," *Journal of American History* 76 (1989): 34–58.

8. Robert M. Citino, "Military Histories Old and New: A Reintroduction," *American Historical Review* 112, no. 4 (October 2007): 1070–90.

9. Stephanie McCurry, *Confederate Reckoning: Power and Politics in the Civil War South* (Cambridge, MA: Harvard University Press, 2010); James C. Scott, *Domination and the Arts of Resistance: Hidden Transcripts* (New Haven, CT: Yale University Press, 1990); James C. Scott, *Weapons of the Weak: Everyday Forms of Peasant Resistance* (New Haven, CT: Yale University Press, 1985).

10. The Louisiana State University Press series Conflicting Worlds, edited by T. Michael Parrish, which has published sixty-four titles, many of them signal contributions

to the field, began in 2002. Other key publishing venues—the UnCivil Wars series at the University of Georgia Press (2011), Civil War in the North at Kent State University Press (2015), and The North's Civil War at Fordham University Press (2002)—are likewise twenty-first-century creations. Many leading publishers—including Harvard and Oxford University Presses and the University Presses of Virginia, Kentucky, and Tennessee—have established records of publishing Civil War history. This essay considers relevant titles regardless of publisher.

11. In some respects, this approach was anticipated by James McPherson in his *Battle Cry of Freedom* and Philip Paludan in his *"A People's Contest,"* both published in 1988, which combined political, social, and military history in a synthetic treatment that spanned the period. James M. McPherson, *Battle Cry of Freedom: The Civil War Era* (New York: Oxford University Press, 1988); Philip S. Paludan, *"A People's Contest": The Union and the Civil War, 1861–1865* (New York: Harper and Row, 1988).

12. Lesley J. Gordon, *General George E. Pickett in Life and Legend* (Chapel Hill: University of North Carolina Press, 1998); Elizabeth D. Leonard, *Lincoln's Forgotten Ally: Judge Advocate General Joseph Holt of Kentucky* (Chapel Hill: University of North Carolina Press, 2011).

13. Chester G. Hearn, *When the Devil Came Down to Dixie: Ben Butler in New Orleans* (Baton Rouge: Louisiana State University Press, 1997).

14. T. Michael Parrish, *Richard Taylor: Soldier Prince of Dixie* (Chapel Hill: University of North Carolina Press, 1992).

15. Iver Bernstein, *The New York City Draft Riots: Their Significance for American Society and Politics in the Age of the Civil War* (New York: Oxford University Press, 1990); Grace Palladino, *Another Civil War: Labor, Capital, and the State in the Anthracite Regions of Pennsylvania, 1840–68* (Urbana: University of Illinois Press, 1990).

16. George C. Rable, *Civil Wars: Women and the Crisis of Southern Nationalism* (Urbana: University of Illinois Press, 1989); Catherine Clinton and Nina Silber, eds., *Divided Houses: Gender and the Civil War* (New York: Oxford University Press, 1992); LeeAnn Whites, *The Civil War as a Crisis in Gender: Augusta, Georgia, 1860–1890* (Athens: University of Georgia Press, 1995); Drew Gilpin Faust, *Mothers of Invention: Women of the Slaveholding South in the American Civil War* (Chapel Hill: University of North Carolina Press, 1996).

17. Stephen W. Berry, *All That Makes a Man: Love and Ambition in the Civil War South* (New York: Oxford University Press, 2003); Peter S. Carmichael, *The Last Generation: Young Virginians in Peace, War, and Reunion* (Chapel Hill: University of North Carolina Press, 2005); Aaron Sheehan-Dean, *Why Confederates Fought: Family and Nation in Civil War Virginia* (Chapel Hill: University of North Carolina Press, 2007); Lorien Foote, *The Gentlemen and the Roughs: Violence, Honor, and Manhood in the Union Army* (New York: New York University Press, 2010).

18. Robert Underwood Johnson and Clarence Clough Buel, eds., *Battles and Leaders of the Civil War: Being for the Most Part Contributions by Union and Confederate Officers: Based upon 'The Century War Series'* (New York: Century, 1887–88).

19. Joseph T. Glatthaar, *The March to the Sea and Beyond: Sherman's Troops in the Savannah and Carolinas Campaign* (New York: New York University Press, 1985); Kenneth Noe, *Perryville: This Grand Havoc of Battle* (Lexington: University Press of Kentucky, 2001); Michael B. Ballard, *Vicksburg: The Campaign That Opened the Mississippi* (Chapel Hill: University of North Carolina Press, 2004).

20. George C. Rable, *Fredericksburg! Fredericksburg!* (Chapel Hill: University of North Carolina Press, 2002).

21. Jacqueline Glass Campbell, *When Sherman Marched North from the Sea: Resistance on the Confederate Home Front* (Chapel Hill: University of North Carolina Press, 2003); Lisa Tendrich Frank, *The Civilian War: Confederate Women and Union Soldiers during Sherman's March* (Baton Rouge: Louisiana University Press, 2015).

22. Robert Tracy McKenzie, *Lincolnites and Rebels: A Divided Town in the American Civil War* (New York: Oxford University Press, 2006). Appalachia, both north and south, received extensive treatment in this era. See, for instance Kenneth W. Noe and Shannon Wilson, eds., *Civil War in Appalachia: Collected Essays* (Knoxville: University of Tennessee Press, 1997); John C. Inscoe, *The Heart of Confederate Appalachia: Western North Carolina in the Civil War* (Chapel Hill: University of North Carolina Press, 2000); Martin Crawford, *Ashe County's Civil War: Community and Society in the Appalachian South* (Charlottesville: University Press of Virginia, 2001); Brian McKnight, *Contested Borderland: The Civil War in Appalachian Kentucky and Virginia* (Lexington: University Press of Kentucky, 2006); and Robert M. Sandow, *Deserter Country: Civil War Opposition in the Pennsylvania Appalachians* (New York: Fordham University Press, 2009).

23. Stephen V. Ash, *When the Yankees Came: Conflict and Chaos in the Occupied South, 1861–1865* (Chapel Hill: University of North Carolina Press, 1995); Michael Fellman, *Inside War: The Guerrilla Conflict in Missouri during the American Civil War* (New York: Oxford University Press, 1989); Mark Grimsley, *The Hard Hand of War: Union Military Policy toward Southern Civilians, 1861–1865* (Cambridge: Cambridge University Press, 1995); William A. Blair, *Virginia's Private War: Feeding Body and Soul in the Confederacy, 1861–1865* (New York: Oxford University Press, 1998).

24. On the former, see Richard E. Beringer, Herman Hattaway, Archer Jones, and William N. Still Jr., *Why the South Lost the Civil War* (Athens: University of Georgia Press, 1986); and Drew Gilpin Faust, *The Creation of Confederate Nationalism: Ideology and Identity in the Civil War South* (Baton Rouge: Louisiana State University Press, 1988). On the latter, see Gary W. Gallagher, *The Confederate War: How Popular Will, Nationalism, and Military Strategy Could Not Stave Off Defeat* (Cambridge, MA: Harvard University Press, 1997); Anne Sarah Rubin, *A Shattered Nation: The Rise and Fall of the Confederacy, 1861–1868* (Chapel Hill: University of North Carolina Press, 2005); and Sheehan-Dean, *Why Confederates Fought*.

25. Glatthaar, *March to the Sea and Beyond*; Foote, *Gentlemen and the Roughs*; Susannah Ural Bruce, *The Harp and the Eagle: Irish-American Volunteers and the Union Army, 1861–1865* (New York: New York University Press, 2006).

26. George C. Rable, *The Confederate Republic: A Revolution against Politics* (Chapel Hill: University of North Carolina Press, 1994).

27. Mark E. Neely Jr., *The Fate of Liberty: Abraham Lincoln and Civil Liberties* (New York: Oxford University Press, 1991) and *Southern Rights: Political Prisoners and the Myth of Confederate Constitutionalism* (Charlottesville: University Press of Virginia, 1999).

28. Richard Franklin Bensel, *Yankee Leviathan: The Origins of Central State Authority in America, 1859–1877* (Cambridge: Cambridge University Press, 1990).

29. William A. Link, *Roots of Secession: Slavery and Politics in Antebellum Virginia* (Chapel Hill: University of North Carolina Press, 2003).

30. Charles Ambler, *Sectionalism in Virginia, 1776–1861* (Chicago: University of Chicago Press, 1910); Henry Shanks, *The Secession Movement in Virginia, 1847–1861* (Richmond: Garnett and Massie, 1934); Richard Orr Curry, *A House Divided: A Study of Statehood Politics and the Copperhead Movement in West Virginia* (Pittsburgh: University of Pittsburgh Press, 1964); William G. Shade, *Democratizing the Old Dominion: Virginia and the Second Party System, 1824–1861* (Charlottesville: University Press of Virginia, 1996).

31. Stanley Harrold, *Subversives: Antislavery Community in Washington, D.C., 1828–1865* (Baton Rouge: Louisiana State University Press, 2003) and *Border War: Fighting over Slavery before the Civil War* (Chapel Hill: University of North Carolina Press, 2010).

32. Barbara J. Fields, "Who Freed the Slaves?," in *The Civil War: An Illustrated History*, ed. Goeffrey C. Ward (New York: Knopf, 1990), 178–81; James M. McPherson, "Who Freed the Slaves?," *Proceedings of the American Philosophical Society* 139 (1995): 1–10.

33. Alice Fahs, *The Imagined Civil War: Popular Literature of the North and South, 1861–1865* (Chapel Hill: University of North Carolina Press, 2001); Jonathan H. Earle, *Jacksonian Antislavery and the Politics of Free Soil* (Chapel Hill: University of North Carolina Press, 2004).

34. Nina Silber, *The Romance of Reunion: Northerners and the South, 1865–1900* (Chapel Hill: University of North Carolina Press, 1993); David W. Blight, *Race and Reunion: The Civil War in American Memory* (Cambridge, MA: Harvard University Press, 2001); Sarah E. Gardner, *Blood and Irony: Southern White Women's Narratives of the Civil War, 1861–1937* (Chapel Hill: University of North Carolina Press, 2004).

35. Charles Reagan Wilson, *Baptized in Blood: The Religion of the Lost Cause, 1865–1920* (Athens: University of Georgia Press, 1980); Gaines M. Foster, *Ghosts of the Confederacy: Defeat, the Lost Cause, and the Emergence of the New South, 1865–1913* (New York: Oxford University of Press, 1987).

36. Alan T. Nolan, *Lee Considered: General Robert E. Lee and Civil War History* (Chapel Hill: University of North Carolina Press, 1991); William A. Blair, *Cities of the Dead: Contesting the Memory of the Civil War in the South, 1865–1914* (Chapel Hill: University of North Carolina Press, 2004); Caroline E. Janney, *Burying the Dead but Not the Past: Ladies' Memorial Associations and the Lost Cause* (Chapel Hill: University of North Carolina Press, 2008).

37. John R. Neff, *Honoring the Civil War Dead: Commemoration and the Problem of Reconciliation* (Lawrence: University Press of Kansas, 2005); Barbara A. Gannon, *The Cause Won: Black and White Comradeship in the Grand Army of the Republic* (Chapel Hill: University of North Carolina Press, 2011).

38. Blight, *Race and Reunion*; Caroline E. Janney, *Remembering the Civil War: Reunion and the Limits of Reconciliation* (Chapel Hill: University of North Carolina Press, 2013); Nina Silber, *This War Ain't Over: Fighting the Civil War in New Deal America* (Chapel Hill: University of North Carolina Press, 2018).

39. Herman Hattaway and Archer Jones, *How the North Won: A Military History of the Civil War* (Urbana: University of Illinois Press, 1983); Brian Holden Reid, *America's Civil War: The Operational Battlefield, 1861–1863* (Amherst, NY: Prometheus Books, 2008).

40. David Williams, *Rich Man's War: Class, Caste, and Confederate Defeat in the Lower Chattahoochee Valley* (Athens: University of Georgia Press, 1998); David Williams, *A People's History of the Civil War: Struggles for the Meaning of Freedom* (New York: New Press, 2005); David Williams, *Bitterly Divided: The South's Inner Civil War* (New York: New Press, 2008);

David Williams, Teresa Crisp Williams, and David Carlson, *Plain Folk in a Rich Man's War: Class and Dissent in Confederate Georgia* (Gainesville: University Press of Florida, 2002); Gallagher, *Confederate War*.

41. Eric McKitrick, "Party Politics and the Union and Confederate War Efforts," in *The American Party Systems: Stages of Political Development*, ed. William Nisbet Chambers and Walter Dean Burnham (New York: Oxford University Press, 1967), 117–51; Mark E. Neely Jr., *The Union Divided: Party Conflict in the Civil War North* (Cambridge, MA: Harvard University Press, 2002).

42. Compare, for instance, Armstead L. Robinson, *Bitter Fruits of Bondage: The Demise of Slavery and the Collapse of the Confederacy, 1861–1865* (Charlottesville: University of Virginia Press, 2005), with Kate Masur, *An Example for All the Land: Emancipation and the Struggle over Equality in Washington, D.C.* (Chapel Hill: University of North Carolina Press, 2010).

43. Mark Lause, *Race and Radicalism in the Union Army* (Urbana: University of Illinois Press, 2009); John H. Matsui, *The First Republican Army: The Army of Virginia and the Radicalization of the Civil War* (Charlottesville: University Press of Virginia, 2016); Matthew E. Stanley, *The Loyal West: Civil War and Reunion in Middle America* (Urbana: University of Illinois Press, 2017).

44. Louis Menand, *The Metaphysical Club: The Story of Ideas in America* (New York: Farrar, Straus and Giroux, 2001); Peter S. Carmichael, *The War for the Common Soldier: How Men Thought, Fought, and Survived in Civil War Armies* (Chapel Hill: University of North Carolina Press, 2018).

45. Donald R. Shaffer, *After the Glory: The Struggles of Black Civil War Veterans* (Lawrence: University Press of Kansas, 2004); Rusty Williams, *My Old Confederate Home: A Respectable Place for Civil War Veterans* (Lexington: University Press of Kentucky, 2010); Robert Hunt, *The Good Men Who Won the War: Army of the Cumberland Veterans and Emancipation* (Tuscaloosa: University of Alabama Press, 2010).

46. James Marten, *Sing Not War: The Lives of Union and Confederate Veterans in Gilded Age America* (Chapel Hill: University of North Carolina Press, 2011).

47. Kathleen Logothetis Thompson, "War on the Mind: Trauma and Coping among Union Soldiers and Veterans" (PhD diss., West Virginia University, 2017); Diane Somerville, *Aberration of Mind: Suicide and Suffering in the Civil War–Era South* (Chapel Hill: University of North Carolina Press, 2018); James Broomall, *Private Confederacies: The Emotional Worlds of Southern Men as Citizens and Soldiers* (Chapel Hill: University of North Carolina Press, 2019); Dillon Carroll, *Invisible Wounds: Mental Illness and Civil War Soldiers* (Baton Rouge: Louisiana State University Press, 2021); Jonathan S. Jones, "Opium Slavery: Veterans and Addiction in Civil War America" (PhD diss., Binghamton University, 2020).

48. Michael E. Woods, *Emotional and Sectional Conflict in the Antebellum United States* (Cambridge: Cambridge University Press, 2014).

49. Evan Kutzler, *Living by Inches: The Smells, Sounds, Tastes, and Feeling of Captivity in Civil War Prisons* (Chapel Hill: University of North Carolina Press, 2019); Mark M. Smith, *The Smell of Battle, the Taste of Siege: A Sensory History of the Civil War* (New York: Oxford University Press, 2014); Broomall, *Private Confederacies*.

50. Megan Kate Nelson, *RuinNation: Destruction and the American Civil War* (Athens: University of Georgia Press, 2012); Brian Luskey and Jason Phillips, eds., "Material Culture," special issue, *Civil War History* 63 (June 2017); Joan Cashin, *War Stuff: The Struggle*

for Human and Environmental Resources in the American Civil War (Cambridge: Cambridge University Press, 2018); Joan Cashin, ed., War Matters: Material Culture in the Civil War Era (Chapel Hill: University of North Carolina Press, 2018).

51. Jack Temple Kirby, "The American Civil War: An Environmental View," National Humanities Center, 2001, http://nationalhumanitiescenter.org/tserve/nattrans/ntuseland/essays/amcwar.htm; Brian Drake, The Blue, the Gray, and the Green: Toward an Environmental History of the Civil War (Athens: University of Georgia Press, 2015); Adam Dean, An Agrarian Republic: Farming, Antislavery Politics, and Nature Parks in the Civil War Era (Chapel Hill: University of North Carolina Press, 2015); Judkin Browning and Timothy Silver, An Environmental History of the Civil War (Chapel Hill: University of North Carolina Press, 2020).

52. Lisa M. Brady, War upon the Land: Military Strategy and the Transformation of Southern Landscapes during the American Civil War (Athens: University of Georgia Press, 2012).

53. Erin Mauldin, Unredeemed Land: An Environmental History of Civil War and Emancipation in the Cotton South (New York: Oxford University Press, 2018).

54. Kathryn Shively Meier, Nature's Civil War: Common Soldiers and the Environment in 1862 Virginia (Chapel Hill: University of North Carolina Press, 2014); Andrew McIlwaine Bell, Mosquito Soldiers: Malaria, Yellow Fever, and the Course of the American Civil War (Baton Rouge: Louisiana State University Press, 2010); Jim Downs, Sick from Freedom: African-American Illness and Suffering during the Civil War and Reconstruction (New York: Oxford University Press, 2012).

55. Fellman's Inside War was one of the chief targets in Mark E. Neely Jr., The Civil War and the Limits of Destruction (Cambridge, MA: Harvard University Press, 2010).

56. John Fabian Witt, Lincoln's Code: The Laws of War in American History (New York: Free Press, 2012).

57. Stephen C. Neff, Justice in Blue and Gray: A Legal History of the Civil War (Cambridge, MA: Harvard University Press, 2010); D. H. Dilbeck, A More Civil War: How the Union Waged a Just War (Chapel Hill: University of North Carolina Press, 2016); Aaron Sheehan-Dean, The Calculus of Violence: How Americans Fought the Civil War (Cambridge, MA: Harvard University Press, 2018).

58. Daniel E. Sutherland, A Savage Conflict: The Decisive Role of Guerrillas in the American Civil War (Chapel Hill: University of North Carolina Press, 2009); Barton A. Myers, Executing Daniel Bright: Race, Loyalty, and Guerrilla Violence in a Coastal Carolina Community, 1861–1865 (Baton Rouge: Louisiana State University Press, 2009); Brian McKnight, Confederate Outlaw: Champ Ferguson and the Civil War in Appalachia (Baton Rouge: Louisiana State University Press, 2011); Joseph M. Beilein Jr. and Matthew C. Hulbert, eds., The Civil War Guerrilla: Unfolding the Black Flag in History, Memory, and Myth (Lexington: University Press of Kentucky, 2015); Barton A. Myers and Brian D. McKnight, eds., The Guerrilla Hunters: Irregular Conflicts during the civil war (Baton Rouge: Louisiana State University Press, 2017); Joseph Beilein, Bushwhackers: Guerrilla Warfare, Manhood, and the Household in Civil War Missouri (Kent, OH: Kent State University Press, 2019); Andrew Fialka, "Controlled Chaos: Spatiotemporal Patterns within Missouri's Irregular Civil War," in Myers and McKnight, Guerrilla Hunters.

59. Chandra Manning, Troubled Refuge: Struggling for Freedom in the Civil War (New York: Knopf, 2016); Amy Taylor, Embattled Freedom: Journeys through the Civil War's Slave Refugee Camps (Chapel Hill: University of North Carolina Press, 2018); Brian Taylor, Fighting for

Citizenship: Black Northerners and the Debate over Military Service in the Civil War (Chapel Hill: University of North Carolina Press, 2020).

60. J. Downs, *Sick from Freedom*; Carole Emberton, *Beyond Redemption: Race, Violence, and the American South after the Civil War* (Chicago: University of Chicago Press, 2013); Kristopher A. Teters, *Practical Liberators: Union Officers in the Western Theater during the Civil War* (Chapel Hill: University of North Carolina Press, 2018).

61. Joseph P. Reidy, *Illusions of Emancipation: The Pursuit of Freedom and Equality in the Twilight of Slavery* (Chapel Hill: University of North Carolina Press, 2019).

62. Edward Bartlett Rugemer, *The Problem of Emancipation: The Caribbean Roots of the American Civil War* (Baton Rouge: Louisiana State University Press, 2009); Timothy M. Roberts, *Distant Revolutions: 1848 and the Challenge to American Exceptionalism* (Charlottesville: University of Virginia Press, 2009); Matthew Clavin, *Toussaint Louverture and the American Civil War: The Promise and Peril of a Second Haitian Revolution* (Philadelphia: University of Pennsylvania Press, 2011); Patrick J. Kelly, "The North American Crisis of the 1860s," *Journal of the Civil War Era* 2 (September 2012): 337–68; Andre M. Fleche, *The Revolution of 1861: The American Civil War in the Age of Nationalist Conflict* (Chapel Hill: University of North Carolina Press, 2012); Don H. Doyle, ed., *American Civil Wars: The United States, Latin America, Europe, and the Crisis of the 1860s* (Chapel Hill: University of North Carolina Press, 2017); Gregory P. Downs, *The Second American Revolution: The Civil War–Era Struggle over Cuba and the Rebirth of the American Republic* (Chapel Hill: University of North Carolina Press, 2019); Ann L. Tucker, *Newest Born of Nations: European Nationalist Movements and the Making of the Confederacy* (Charlottesville: University of Virginia Press, 2020).

63. Howard Jones, *Union in Peril: The Crisis over British Intervention and the Civil War* (Chapel Hill: University of North Carolina Press, 1992); Howard Jones, *Abraham Lincoln and a New Birth of Freedom: The Union and Slavery in the Diplomacy of the Civil War* (Lincoln: University of Nebraska Press, 1999); R. J. M. Blackett, *Divided Hearts: Britain and the American Civil War* (Baton Rouge: Louisiana State University Press, 2001); Howard Jones, *Blue and Gray Diplomacy: A History of Union and Confederate Foreign Relations* (Chapel Hill: University of North Carolina Press, 2010).

64. Enrico Dal Lago, *Civil War and Agrarian Unrest: The Confederate South and Southern Italy* (Cambridge: Cambridge University Press, 2018); Aaron Sheehan-Dean, *Reckoning with Rebellion: War and Sovereignty in the Nineteenth Century* (Gainesville: University Press of Florida, 2020); Amanda B. Bellows, *American Slavery and Russian Serfdom in the Post-Emancipation Imagination* (Chapel Hill: University of North Carolina Press, 2020).

65. Rosanne Currarino, "Toward a History of Cultural Economy," *Journal of the Civil War Era* 2 (December 2012): 564–85.

66. Mark K. Wilson, *The Business of War: Military Mobilization and the State, 1861–1865* (Baltimore: Johns Hopkins University Press 2006); Chad Morgan, *Planters' Progress: Modernizing Confederate Georgia* (Gainesville: University Press of Florida, 2005); John Majewski, *Modernizing a Slave Economy: Economic Vision of the Confederate Nation* (Chapel Hill: University of North Carolina Press, 2009); Nicholas Barreyre, *Gold and Freedom: The Political Economy of Reconstruction* (Charlottesville: University of Virginia Press, 2015); David K. Thomson, *Bonds of War: How Civil War Financial Agents Sold the World on the Union* (Chapel Hill: University of North Carolina Press, 2022).

67. Brian Luskey, *Men Is Cheap: Exposing the Frauds of Free Labor in Civil War America* (Chapel Hill: University of North Carolina Press, 2020).

68. William A. Blair, *With Malice toward Some: Treason and Loyalty in the Civil War Era* (Chapel Hill: University of North Carolina Press, 2014); Gregory P. Downs, *After Appomattox: Military Occupation and the Ends of War* (Cambridge, MA: Harvard University Press, 2015); Andrew Lang, *In the Wake of War: Occupation, Emancipation, and Civil War America* (Baton Rouge: Louisiana State University Press, 2017); Caroline E. Janney, *Ends of War: The Unfinished Fight of Lee's Army after Appomattox* (Chapel Hill: University of North Carolina Press, 2021).

69. Alvin Josephy, *The Civil War in the American West* (New York: Knopf, 1991); Donald Frazier, *Blood and Treasure: Confederate Empire in the Southwest* (College Station: Texas A&M University Press, 1995).

70. Stacy Smith, *Freedom's Frontier: California and the Struggle over Unfree Labor, Emancipation, and Reconstruction* (Chapel Hill: University of North Carolina Press, 2013); Kevin Waite, *West of Slavery: The Southern Dream of a Transcontinental Empire* (Chapel Hill: University of North Carolina Press, 2021).

71. Ari Kelman, *A Misplaced Massacre: Struggling over the Memory of Sand Creek* (Cambridge, MA: Harvard University Press, 2015); Megan Kate Nelson, *The Three-Cornered War: The Union, the Confederacy, and Native Peoples in the Fight for the West* (New York: Scribner, 2020).

CONTRIBUTORS

William A. Blair is Ferree Emeritus Professor of History at The Pennsylvania State University. He was the founding editor of the *Journal of the Civil War Era*. Author and editor of seven books, his most recent publication dealt with racial violence in early Reconstruction. He is currently working on a Black history of what became Arlington National Cemetery.

Peter S. Carmichael is Fluhrer Professor of Civil War Studies and the director of the Civil War Institute at Gettysburg College. He is the author of *The War for the Common Soldier: How Men Thought, Fought, and Survived in Civil War Armies*.

Andre M. Fleche is a professor of history at Castleton University. He is the author of *The Revolution of 1861: The American Civil War in the Age of Nationalist Conflict*.

Wayne Wei-siang Hsieh has authored *West Pointers and the Civil War: The Old Army in War and Peace* and various essays and articles on military history and military affairs and coauthored with Williamson Murray *A Savage War: A Military History of the Civil War*. He currently serves on the civilian faculty at the US Naval Academy as an associate professor of history.

Caroline E. Janney is John L. Nau III Professor of the American Civil War and the director of the John L. Nau Center for Civil War History at the University of Virginia. She has published seven books, including *Remembering the Civil*

War: Reunion and the Limits of Reconciliation and *Ends of War: The Unfinished Fight of Lee's Army after Appomattox*, winner of the 2022 Lincoln Prize.

Peter C. Luebke received his PhD from the University of Virginia in 2014. He has written and presented widely on American military history. He is the editor of a scholarly edition of Albion Tourgee's *Story of a Thousand* as well as *The Autobiography of John A. Dahlgren*.

Cynthia Nicoletti is a professor of law and history at the University of Virginia. She is the author of *Secession on Trial: The Treason Prosecution of Jefferson Davis* and is currently at work on a legal history of land redistribution during and after the Civil War.

Aaron Sheehan-Dean is Fred C. Frey Professor of Southern Studies and the chair of the history department at Louisiana State University. He teaches courses on nineteenth-century US history, the Civil War and Reconstruction, and Southern history. He is the author of *The Calculus of Violence: How Americans Fought the Civil War*, *Why Confederates Fought: Family and Nation in Civil War Virginia*, and most recently *Reckoning with Rebellion: War and Sovereignty in the Nineteenth Century*.

Kathryn J. Shively in an associate professor of history at Virginia Commonwealth University and the author of *Nature's Civil War: Common Soldiers and the Environment in 1862 Virginia*, winner of the Wiley-Silver Prize for best first book on the Civil War.

INDEX

abolition: in antebellum era, 233; and British Empire, 74, 77, 80; and comparative history, 51–52; and Confederate treaties with Native Americans, 19; in Indian Territory, 33; in Kansas, 22; post-emancipation experiences in West Indies, 49
Afghanistan war, 55–56, 236
Allan, William, 192
American empire, 96, 100
American Historical Association, 207–8
American republicanism, 6, 51, 69, 71
American Revolution, 2, 50, 70, 72, 116n76, 214
antebellum era: and abolition, 233; and archives, 208, 209, 210; Civil War era compared to, 46–47; and Lee's modernization of US Army, 94, 96, 101, 108; and primary sources, 208; slaveholders' political power during, 70
Apaches, 241
archives: in antebellum era, 208, 209, 210; building of, 12, 209, 210; correspondence in, 210–11; and Early, 189–91, 196–98, 202n8; and national archive, 212, 213; scrapbooks in, 210, 211, 223n9; and state records, 211–12, 213, 217; of Union army, 212–13; white Northern veteran-writers' access to, 209–13, 220
Argentina, 80
Arkansas, 19, 20, 25, 34n4
Arlington National Cemetery, 146
Armitage, David, 53–54
Army of Northern Virginia: Alexander on, 5;. Early on, 187, 188, 190, 191, 200, 202n6; and Lee, 3, 94, 107–10, 120, 125, 129, 131, 187, 195, 201n4, 202n6; parole of, 125; printing department of, 213; slave raiding in Pennsylvania, 111
Army of Tennessee, 78
Army of the Potomac, 180, 195, 224n16
Army of the Shenandoah, 123
Association for the Preservation of Civil War Sites (American Battlefield Trust), 4
Association of the Army of Northern Virginia (AANVA), 190–91, 203n12
Ayers, Edward L., 43, 55–56, 96, 106
Ayutla Revolution of 1854–55, 77

Bachelder, John B., 214
Baldwin, John B., 133

253

Ballard, Michael, 232
Barbour, B. Johnson, 133
Batson, Felix I., 27
Battle of Gettysburg, 195–96, 197, 205n22, 205n24, 205n27
Battle of Pea Ridge, 25
Bayly, C. A., 94–96, 111
Beaudry, Louis Napoleon, 213, 223n14
Bedenbaugh, Thomas, 13
Belize, 74
Bender, Thomas, 56
Benedict, George G., 211, 216–19, 220
Bennett v. Hunter (1869), 148, 149, 155
Bensel, Richard Franklin, 96, 233, 239
Beringer, Richard E., 42–43, 71
Bernstein, Iver, 231
Berry, Stephen, 231
Binns, Charles, 122, 124
Bishop, John, 130
Black, Jeremiah, 148
Black Codes, 135
Black landownership: and land redistribution, 143–44, 147, 154; and tax titles, 11, 142–44, 150–51, 158
Black people: Black women compared to white women, 46, 173; and comparative history, 47–48, 229; effect of emancipation on, 238; experience of war, 236; and historical memory in public sphere, 188, 193–94; interpretations of Civil War, 234; US government's recruitment as soldiers, 72; and voter suppression, 145
Black troops: Confederate refusal to acknowledge, 105; Confederate slaughter of, 109, 130; hanging of, 181; and historical memory in public sphere, 193–94, 204n19; importance of, 238; refusal of recruitment into Confederate army, 110–11; role in Civil War, 7; unnecessary killing of, 237; veterans' historical narratives, 209, 221–22n3
Blackwell, Robert, 155
Blazer, Richard, 123
Blight, David, 234

Bloch, Marc, 40, 43–44, 60n1
Booth, John Wilkes, 127
Botts, John Minor, 133, 135
Boudinot, Elias Cornelius: as Cherokee delegate to Confederate Congress, 25, 33; on Cherokee Nation Convention, 26; and Committee on Indian Affairs, 32; legislation introduced by, 17–18, 27–30, 31, 33; as secretary of Arkansas Secession Convention, 25; on white colonization in Indian Territory, 30–31
Boudinot, William, 32
Bowman, Shearer Davis, 48–49, 60n1
Bowman, S. M., 126, 133–34, 140n55, 140n58
Brazil, 48, 49–50, 53
British Empire, 56, 74
Brown, John, 104
Brown, John G., 218–19
Brown, Joseph, 44
Brown, Walter Lee, 23–24
Bryan, George S., 153
Buchanan, James, 75, 79
Bureau of Military Justice, 122
Burns, Ken, 7
Butler, Ben, 230

Calhoun, John C., 50
California, 19, 74, 77
Callahan, Samuel B., 18, 32, 33
Campbell, Jacqueline, 232
capitalism, 41, 97, 100, 113n18, 183, 239
Captured and Abandoned Property Act, 142
Caputo, Philip, 42
Caribbean, 49–50
Cass, Lewis, 75–76, 78–79
Catholicism, 48, 57
Catton, Bruce, 108
Central America, 74–77, 85
Century Magazine, 225n30, 231
Chaffin, Tom, 71
Chamberlain, Joshua Lawrence, 173, 180, 214, 224n16
Chapman, William H., 119, 127–29, 130, 135
Chappel, Cyrus, 130

Cheng, Eileen Ka-May, 208, 220
Cherokee Nation: government of Confederate Cherokees, 25–32, 33; National Committee and Council of, 26–27, 30; neutrality maintained by, 24; on protectorate status with Confederacy, 20, 21, 23, 25, 33, 35n11; on protectorate status with US government, 23; and representation in Confederate Congress, 17–18, 19, 21, 22; and representation in US Congress, 21, 36n13; rival governments of, 26–27, 30, 33; and Treaty of New Echota, 21, 36n13
Cherokee Nation v. Georgia (1831), 21
Chickasaw Nation, 18, 21–23, 28–29
Choctaw Nation, 18, 21–23, 24, 26, 28–29
Churchwell, William M., 79–80
civil-military relations, 46, 229, 232, 235, 239–40
civil rights movement, 229
Civil War art, 6–7
Civil War era: ambiguities of, 96, 234–35, 240; antebellum era compared to, 46–47; in Civil War history, 2, 9, 232, 235–36; as clash of state institutions, 95; and comparative history, 40, 46–48, 50–51, 59, 60, 108; and modernity, 12, 43, 59, 94, 96, 108, 117n85; physical elements of, 237; public memorial culture of, 58; and Society of Civil War Historians, 8
Civil War history: academic and popular sides of, 207, 221n1, 234; biographies in, 230–31; and causation studies, 228; and cessation of hostilities, 235; class relations in, 229, 231, 232, 235; and comparative history, 10, 39–40, 50–51, 52, 53–55, 56, 57; cultural representations in, 4, 6, 230, 234, 236; diplomacy in, 9, 10, 18, 239; emancipation in, 2, 7, 9, 227–28, 229, 233–34, 235, 238, 239; ethno-cultural conflict in, 1, 70, 79, 232; and Externalists, 230, 238, 241; gender history in, 2, 9, 227, 229, 231; and Internalists, 229, 230, 235, 241; interpretation of, 227, 241n1; lessons of, 111; memory studies in, 2, 9, 10, 11–12, 58, 225n30, 229, 230, 234–35; military histories in, 1, 2, 10, 207–8, 229, 230, 231–32, 236; Native Americans in, 229, 235, 240, 241; patterns of, 240–41; political history in, 1, 2, 9, 230, 233, 236; slavery in, 1, 2, 113n17, 228, 229, 230, 235–36, 240; social history in, 1, 4, 8–9, 229, 230, 231, 236, 241; subfields of, 227, 229, 230–31, 233, 238, 242n5; and traditionalist-revisionist axis, 228–29, 241; and transnational history, 12, 51–54, 113n17, 229, 235; veterans in, 235, 236–37; violence in, 182, 183, 237–38; as war between nations, 81–82; wartime generation's writings on, 207, 221n1; women in, 229, 231, 232, 241
Clarke, Beverly L., 75
class relations: in Civil War history, 229, 231, 232, 235; Civil War's effect on, 46, 227; and Confederate nationalism, 71; and cultural history, 234; Gallagher on, 5
Clinton, Catherine, 231
Coffron, Jeremiah, 118, 125–26
Coffron, John W., 119, 125–27
Comanches, 103
Comonfort, Ignacio, 77
comparative history: Marc Bloch on, 40, 43–44, 60n1; Shearer David Bowman on, 60n1; and change over time, 45–47, 53, 56, 58, 59; and Civil War era, 40, 46–48, 50–51, 59, 60, 108; and Civil War history, 10, 39–40, 50–51, 52, 53–55, 56, 57; and Confederate nationalism, 52, 232; differences exposed by, 40, 45, 51, 59, 60n1; and economics of war, 56, 229, 235; and emancipation, 47, 48, 49–50, 51, 52, 53, 56, 57, 58, 59; and exceptionalism, 41, 50, 51, 54, 239–40; explicit comparative framings, 40, 43, 51; and gender history, 46, 63–64n30; and guerrilla warfare, 42, 56; implicit comparative analyses, 40, 43, 51; and latent comparative thinking, 41–42, 43;

comparative history (*continued*)
likeness identified by, 40, 59; and Lost Cause, 57, 58–59; models of, 40–41, 60–61n1; and North, 43, 44, 45, 62n17; and race theory, 49, 57, 59; and Reconstruction, 47, 48, 55–56, 57, 67n85; and secession crisis, 51, 53, 56, 72; and South, 43, 44, 45, 58, 59, 62n17; and transnational history, 41, 50–51, 59, 229, 239; and women, 46, 63–64n30

Compromise of 1850, 77

Conant, John, 150–51, 161n36

Confederacy: and annuity payments of US government for Five Nations, 18, 20, 21, 29, 32, 34–35n4; and citizenship for Native Americans, 22, 31; and comparative history, 52, 58; consolidation of centralized power, 96; Early's narratives on, 12; and elections in Indian Territory, 17; expansion of, 19, 34; Federal authority in, 102; federal property tax in, 146; Gallagher on, 3–5, 45; and Indian Affairs, 20, 27, 28, 32; international recognition of, 81–82, 85; Lee's defense of, 187; military history of, 186–87; Monroe Doctrine renounced by, 75; morale of, 42–43; on Mosby's battalion, 123; as nation-state, 10, 69–70, 71, 72, 73, 74, 76–79, 81–85, 94, 96–97, 105, 107, 110; nonslaveholders in, 229; and reconciliation, 231; and self-government, 83; and slave uprising fears, 181–82; and states' rights, 79, 80

Confederate army: conscription in, 120; Early on, 195; fractiousness of generals in, 110, 117n79; and Hicksford Raid, 168–71, 172, 179, 181; and localized methods of military recruitment, 96; Native American units in, 26, 30–31, 32; partisans of, 121

Confederate Congress: Elias Cornelius Boudinot's legislation proposed to, 17–18, 27–30; Native Americans as nonvoting delegates of, 17, 18, 19–20, 22, 24, 33, 35n5; and racial bias in treaties with Native Americans, 23–24; US Congress compared to, 44

Confederate defeat: cause of, 227; and Confederacy as nation-state, 10; and Confederate nationalism, 72, 85, 107; and defeat empathy, 58–59; and dueling, 106; Early on, 195; and emotional studies, 237; Gallagher on, 3–4, 235; Lee on, 187–88, 195; and legitimate belligerents, 109; South's interpretation of, 55, 119

Confederate diplomacy: and Confederate nationalism, 72, 73, 78, 81, 83, 84; and Mexico, 84–85; and Southern envoys to Europe, 33–34, 72; and treaty relations with Native American communities, 10, 18–25, 34, 34n4, 35n5

Confederate history: Alexander on, 5, 221n1; Early's leadership on, 189–92, 196, 197–98, 199, 200; preservation of, 197; records of, 217

Confederate memory, 191, 202n8

Confederate nationalism: and comparative history, 52, 232; divisions within national identity, 71–72, 73; and John Forsyth Jr., 79; Gallagher on, 10, 45, 72, 235; and interests of slaveholders, 10, 71, 76, 85; and political power, 69–70, 73, 85; as response to Lincoln's election, 71, 73, 81, 84; and transnational framework, 10, 72–73

Confederates: and comparative history, 58–59; discharge of rebel prisoners of war, 130, 132, 139n43; Grant's order on former Confederates, 127; Andrew Johnson's pardoning of, 131, 132, 135, 142; military personnel as lawful belligerents, 105, 132; paroled, 127; and property seizures on nonpayment of taxes, 147, 148, 160n23; Radical Republicans on, 131; reactionary politics after Appomattox, 5; Union army's attitude toward, 125, 136; US citizenship reclaimed by, 135

Confederate veterans, 190, 195, 203n12

Confiscation Act of 1862, 159n6
consensus school, 41, 51
Cooke, John Esten, 186
Cooley v. O'Connor (1870), 148, 149, 155
Cooper, Douglas H., 28
Corbin, David T., 152–53, 154
Costa Rica, 74–76
Crawford, Martin J., 83
Crawford, Samuel, 177
Creek Nation, 18, 19, 24, 32
Crooker, Lucien B., 218–19
CSS *Planter*, 145
Cuba, 49, 53, 241
cultural representations: in Civil War history, 4, 6, 230, 234, 236; Gallagher on, 8
Curry, George H., 118–19, 127, 129
Cushing, Caleb, 148
Custer, George A., 124

Dal Lago, Enrico, 51–52
Daniel, John W., 193
Davis, Jefferson: and Elias Cornelius Boudinot's plan for Indian territory, 31; on Confederacy as nation-state, 69, 73; and Democratic Party, 45; and Early, 203n12; escape of, 131; inaugural address of, 73, 76; Lincoln compared to, 44, 62n19; and Lincoln conspirators' trial, 130; murder of William Nelson, 106; on Native Americans as nonvoting delegates, 22; on partisan warfare, 126; personal confrontation with, 235; and Albert Pike appointed as commissioner of Indian Affairs, 20; as politician, 233; on slave uprisings, 182; as US secretary of war, 73–74; and Stand Watie as brigadier general, 32
Dawson, Henry B., 197
Dean, Eric, 55
Declaration of Independence, 73
defeat empathy, 55–56, 58–59
Degler, Carl, 48–49
Deleuze, Gilles, 100
democracy, 45, 57

democratic capitalism, 41
Democratic Party, 45, 57, 235, 236
DeTreville, Richard, 149–56, 160n34, 161n37
DeTreville, William, 145, 149–50, 152
DeTreville v. Smalls (1879), 141–45, 151, 153–56, 158
DiCuirci, Lindsay, 208
Dimitry, Alexander, 75–77
diplomacy: in Civil War history, 9, 10, 18, 239. *See also* Confederate diplomacy; US diplomacy and Monroe Doctrine
Direct Tax Act of 1862, 11, 142–43, 145–50, 155, 158
Direct Tax Commission, 147, 156, 161n36, 162n61
Dodge, Grenville, 106
Dominican Republic, 83
Donald, David, 1
Donoghue, Denis, 40
Douglas, Stephen, 45
Douglass, Frederick, 238
Downing, Lewis, 26
Downs, Gregory P., 48, 53
Doyle, Don H., 52–53, 56, 72, 113n17
Du Bois, W. E. B., 52, 222n3
dueling, 106, 116n76, 197

Early, Jubal Anderson: and archives, 189–91, 196–98, 202n8; on Army of Northern Virginia history, 187, 188, 190, 191, 200, 202n6; birthday speech on Lee, 194–96; and commemoration of Lee, 188–94, 196, 198, 200, 202n8; on Gettysburg, 195–96, 197, 205n22, 205n24; historical leadership of, 189–92, 196, 197–98, 199, 200; on interment of. Lee in Richmond, 191, 192, 203n13; and Bradley T. Johnson, 190; and James L. Kemper, 193–94, 204n19; as lawyer, 187, 189, 195; on Longstreet, 195–96, 198, 205n23; on Lost Cause, 196, 202n8; and odds thesis, 187–88, 195; political objectives of, 5, 187, 188, 189, 191, 193, 196, 200, 202n5; postwar memoir of, 187, 191; and primary documents, 187,

Early, Jubal Anderson (*continued*) 190, 195, 196, 197, 198, 205n27; on racial mixing, 193–94, 204n19; and Richmond Lee equestrian statue, 191–92, 198–200; and rival historians, 189, 191, 192, 197, 205n27; and scientific historical writing, 12, 187–88, 189, 190–92, 194–97, 202n5, 202n8, 205n22; on sunrise attack thesis, 195–96, 205n22, 205n24, 205n27; and veterans, 190, 195, 203n12; on white supremacy, 196

economics of war: and comparative history, 56, 229, 235

Edling, Max, 56

Elliott, William, 157

Ellis v. Barnet, 150, 151, 152

El Salvador, 74

emancipation: in Civil War history, 2, 7, 9, 227–28, 229, 233–34, 235, 238, 239; and comparative history, 47, 48, 49–50, 51, 52, 53, 56, 57, 58, 59; and environmental history, 237; as epochal transformation, 60n1; and political history, 233, 238; and Union Cause, 45, 63n25, 227; white Northerners on, 6, 58

English Civil War, 50

enslaved people: in Civil War America series, 9; in Civil War history, 229, 241; and comparative studies of runaways, 47; and emancipation, 238; freedom sought by, 227, 233; hardships of Civil War experienced by, 46; and Hicksford Raid, 167, 168, 169, 171–72, 174, 175, 180; military affairs shaping quest for freedom, 10; state's power of renaming of, 100; transforming uncertainties of war into opportunities, 47, 238; uprisings of, 169, 182. *See also* formerly enslaved people; freedpeople

environmental history, in Civil War history, 2, 229, 235, 237

Escott, Paul, 57

ethnicity, 1, 70, 79, 232

ethno-cultural conflict, in Civil War history, 1, 70, 79, 232

European empires, 74, 77–78, 83–84

European nationalist movements, 72

European revolutions of 1848, 70, 72

Ex parte Milligan, 148

Fahs, Alice, 223–24n15, 224n17, 234

Faust, Drew Gilpin, 72, 231

Fellman, Michael, 42, 238, 247n55

Ferguson, Champ, 130, 133

Field, Stephen, 155

Fifteenth Amendment, 194

Fitzhugh, George, 84

Five Nations: Confederate alliances with, 18, 23, 24, 27, 33, 34n4; Confederate obligations for US annuity payments to, 18, 20, 21, 29, 32, 34–35n4; cultural affinities with South, 34n4; dispossession of lands in 1830s, 18

Foley, John Henry, 193

Foner, Eric, 143

Foote, Henry S., 27

Foote, Lorien, 231, 232

formerly enslaved people, 142, 144, 147, 158

Forsyth, John, Jr., 78–79, 83

Fort Harmar agreement (1789), 21

Foster, Gaines, 55, 234

Foucault, Michel, 95, 99, 100, 109, 110, 117n95

France, 58, 59, 77–78, 83, 84, 85, 239

Frank, Lisa, 232

Franklin, John Hope, 221n3

Frederickson, George, 49

Frederick II (king of Prussia), 95

Freedmen and Southern Society Project, University of Maryland, 233

Freedmen's Bureau, 142, 143, 144

freedpeople: as Cherokee Nation citizens, 33; "contraband" camps of, 100; forty-acre plots for, 142; and land redistribution, 142–47, 158; white Southern men's violent posture toward, 237

Freehling, William, 71

Free-Soilers, 73–74

French, W. M., 151
French Commune, 51, 54
French Empire, 53
French Revolution, 70, 110

Gadsden, James, 77–78
Gallagher, Gary W.: on academic and popular sides of history, 221n1; *Causes Won, Lost, and Forgotten*, 6; and changes in field of Civil War history, 2–4; and Civil War America series, 4, 8–9, 230; and comparative history, 45; on Confederate nationalism, 10, 45, 72, 235; *The Confederate War*, 4–5; essays of, 8; on guerrilla warfare, 136n2; on Lee, 9, 109; as mentor to graduate students, 7, 12, 13; on military histories, 3, 4, 7, 8, 9, 10–11, 207; and popular audience, 6, 7, 9; and primary source material, 5, 7, 10, 13; and Society of Civil War Historians, 7–8; *Stephen Dodson Ramseur*, 3, 4; *The Union War*, 6
Gardner, Sarah, 234
Garfield, James, 148
Garrison, William Lloyd, 51–52
gender history: in Civil War history, 2, 9, 227, 229, 231; Civil War's effect on, 46; and comparative history, 46, 63–64n30; and Confederate nationalism, 71; and cultural history, 234; Gallagher on, 5
German states, 70
Germany, 58, 59, 105
Gerrish, Luther, 174–75
Glatthaar, Joseph, 232
Glymph, Thavolia, 9, 46
Gordon, John B., 192
Grant, Ulysses S.: Alexander on, 5; on Army of Northern Virginia's parole, 125; destructive war strategy of, 43; on discharge of rebel prisoners of war, 130; and Fort Donelson, 100; Gallagher on, 5; and guerrillas, 123–24, 125, 126; and Hicksford Raid, 170, 172, 176, 178; and Lee, 99, 103, 108, 125; C. E. Willis McCue's correspondence with, 132, 134, 135; and John Willis McCue's release, 119, 134, 135–36, 140n58; on Mosby, 123–24, 125; name and initials of, 99–100; order on former Confederates, 127; progress associated with, 108; Vicksburg Campaign, 232; and West Point, 99
Great Britain, 71, 74–78, 80, 81, 82–83, 239
Greece, 54, 56, 82, 94, 98
Gregg, David, 170–71
Grimsley, Mark, 50
Guatemala, 74, 75
guerrilla warfare: in Civil War history, 232, 238; and comparative history, 42, 56; of Confederate Indian troops, 19, 33; defining of, 11, 119, 120–21, 122, 123, 136n2; Grant's efforts against, 123–24, 125, 126; and Hicksford Raid, 168, 169, 172, 173, 174–75, 176, 177, 178, 179, 180, 181, 182; and E. Lee, 94, 103, 104, 109; and Mexican-American War, 103; military commissions of Union army prosecuting, 122–24, 126, 127–31, 133–34, 136, 139n46, 140n48; and Mosby, 120, 121–24, 126, 134, 137n15, 138n17; Philip Sheridan's efforts against, 123–24, 138n17

Hager, Christopher, 210
Hahn, Steven, 71–72
Haiti, 70, 84
Haley, John, 173
Halleck, Henry, 120–21
Hampton, Wade, 170
Hancock, Winfield Scott, 128–29
Harrison, Benjamin, 157
Harrold, Stanley, 233
Harrover, Robert M., 123–24, 137n15, 138n16
Hattaway, Herman, 42–43, 71, 235
Haupt, Herman, 102
Hayes, Rutherford, 156
Hearn, Chester, 230
Hechter, Michael, 52
Herr, Michael, 42

Hicksford Raid (1864): accounts of, 167, 169, 173–75; and acts of reprisal, 12, 167, 169, 172, 178, 179, 181, 183; and breakdown in discipline, 169, 170–71, 172, 175, 176, 177, 178, 180, 182, 183; correspondence on, 168–69, 173, 174, 177, 178–81; and guerrilla warfare, 168, 169, 172, 173, 174–75, 176, 177, 178, 179, 180, 181, 182; historical narrative of, 170–72, 176, 177, 178–79, 180, 182–83; historical silences of, 168, 170, 175, 177, 178, 180, 181, 182, 183; homes destroyed by, 165, 166, 168, 172, 173–75, 178, 180; and mutilation of Union stragglers, 167, 169, 172–73, 174, 177, 179; Northern journalists on, 179–81, 182; official reports of, 168, 170, 172–73, 175–79, 182; sexual violence during, 12, 169, 173–74, 181; Southern journalists on, 181, 182; Sussex plantation owner killed in, 167–68, 174–75; as Union victory, 169, 176, 182; white Southern women's role in, 180–81

Hill, Ambrose Powell (A. P.), 116n79, 170–71

historical memory: and. Early, 195; and historical silences, 12, 168; and political history, 12, 234; postwar memory, 240; in public sphere, 188, 189–90, 191, 193–94, 204n19; and white Northern Union veteran-writers, 220, 224n15, 225n30

historical narrative: of Black veterans, 209, 221–22n3; creation of, 168; and Early's political objectives, 5, 187, 188, 189, 191, 193, 196, 200, 202n5; and Early's scientific historical work, 12, 187–88, 189, 190–92, 194–97, 196, 202n5, 202n8, 205n22; of Hicksford Raid, 170–72, 176, 177, 178–79, 180, 182–83; impartiality of, 201n5, 208, 212, 217–19, 220, 221; subjectivity inherent in, 208, 217–18; of Union army documents, 212–13, 216, 217, 220; of white Northern Union veteran-writers, 207, 210, 212, 213, 215–19, 220, 236

historical profession: hallmarks of professionalism, 208; and historical method, 12, 208–9, 210, 214–18; and primary sources, 208, 212, 219; and scientific thinking, 12, 187–88, 189, 190–92, 194–97, 202n5, 202n8, 205n22, 213, 220; and state archives, 211–12; white Northern Union veteran-writers laying groundwork for, 12, 207–8, 209, 213, 221, 222n4, 225n30. *See also* archives

Hodgson, Matthew, 8
Hoge, Moses D., 193, 204n18
Holbrook, William, 215–16, 224n19
Hollywood Memorial Association, 189
Holt, Joseph, 119, 121–23, 131, 134–35
Holt, Michael, 2
Honduras, 74, 75
Hotchkiss, Jedediah, 102
Hotze, Henry, 81
Hundred Years' War, 50
Hungary, 70

Imboden, John, 120, 133, 134, 140n58, 205n27
Indian Territory: abolition of slavery in, 33; Elias Cornelius Boudinot's proposal for white colonization of, 30–31; Confederacy's legislation regulating elections in, 17, 25, 28; and Confederate treaties with Native Americans, 19, 20, 24, 29, 32, 33, 35n5; and election of 1863, 17, 34n1; Federal army's withdrawal from, 23
Internal Revenue Commission, 152, 153, 156, 157
Iraq war, 55–56, 236
Ireland, 70
irregulars: and comparative history, 42, 56; definitions of, 11, 119, 121–22, 123, 129; and Mexican-American War, 103; strategy of, 238; as threat to Union war effort, 119, 120
Italy, 51–53, 56, 82, 105

Jackson, Thomas J. "Stonewall," 7, 102, 106, 108, 116n79, 190, 193–94, 204n18

Jackson Memorial Association, 193
Janney, Caroline E., 109, 191
Jefferson, Thomas, 50, 73
Jenkins, Bill, 166–68, 183
Johnson, Andrew, 119, 130–35, 139n47, 140n55, 142, 144
Johnson, Bradley T., 190, 191, 193, 203n12, 203n13
Johnson, Reverdy, 148
Johnson, Richard Mentor, 25
Johnson, Robert Ward, 25, 32
Johnson, William, 181–82
Johnston, William Preston, 192, 194, 196, 201n4
Jones, Archer, 42–43, 71, 235
Jones, John William, 196, 198
Jones, Richard M., 18
Jones, Robert M., 23, 28–29
Juárez, Benito, 77

Kalyvas, Stathis, 54
Kansas, 19, 22, 36n19
Kantrowitz, Stephen, 47
Keegan, John, 108
Kelly, Patrick, 75
Kelman, Ari, 240
Kemper, James L., 193–94
Kentucky, 122
Kerr-Ritchie, Jeffrey, 50
Kolchin, Peter, 46, 48–49, 51
Koselleck, Reinhart, 58

Ladies' Lee Monument Committee, 189, 190, 191–92, 193, 198–200, 204n18
Ladies' Memorial Associations, 191
Lamar, Mirabeau B., 75–77
land forfeiture, in Confederacy, 146
land redistribution: controversies of, 154, 158–59n6; failure of, 143–44; and freedpeople, 142–47, 158; and land confiscation schemes, 147; legal mechanisms of, 144; planters' lawyers working to roll back, 142, 143, 144, 148, 149, 153–54, 156; and Reconstruction, 11, 142; and tax sales, 11, 144, 147, 154; and tax titles, 142–43, 144
Lathrop, Barnes, 3
Latin America: nations of, 82, 83, 84; white Southerners on racial diversity of, 70, 79, 84–85; white Southerners serving in US embassies in, 70, 74, 75–81, 82, 85
laws of war, 109, 121, 147, 160n23, 229, 235
Lee, Custis, 146
Lee, Fitzhugh, 194, 196, 198–200, 204n19
Lee, Mary Anna Custis, 146, 191, 192
Lee, Robert E.: as advocate of state support for manufacturing, 112n14; as agent of state authority on frontier, 96, 98, 103; Alexander on, 5; and Army of Northern Virginia, 3, 94, 107–10, 120, 125, 129, 131, 187, 195, 201n4, 202n6; in Civil War art, 7; on Confederacy as nation-state, 94, 105; and Corps of Engineers, 100, 108; death of, 187, 188, 189, 190; Early's commemoration of, 188–94, 196, 198, 200, 202n8; and Early's historical writings, 187–88, 189, 191, 200; engineering background of, 93, 94, 98–103, 108; John Henry Foley's statue of, 193; funeral of, 187, 189, 199; Gallagher on, 9, 109; Gettysburg report of, 197, 205n27; and Grant, 99, 103, 108, 125; and honor, 97, 98, 106–7; and Jackson, 106, 116n79; lineage of, 98; and Longstreet, 195–96; Lost Cause on, 93, 107–8, 111; John Howard McCue's correspondence with, 131–32, 135; memorialization of, 188–93, 194; Jean Antonin Mercié's statue of, 199; and Mexican-American War, 93, 99, 101–4, 108; military career of, 94, 187; and military history of Confederacy, 186–87; Mississippi River improvements of, 93, 101–2; and modernity, 93, 94, 97, 104, 108, 109, 110, 111; odds thesis of, 187–88, 195; and Overland Campaign, 98; on partisan warfare, 126; and Ramseur, 3–4; on reconciliation, 187, 189, 190, 194; on Reconstruction, 188; Recumbent

Lee, Robert E. (*continued*)
   Lee sarcophagus in Lexington, 192, 193, 203n15; reputation of, 188; in retirement, 94; and Richmond Lee equestrian statue, 191–92, 198–200; and secession, 96, 105; slaves of, 107, 110; as soldier, 97; stroke of, 186; surrender at Appomattox, 32, 104, 109–11, 125–27, 130, 131, 195; as symbol of Confederacy, 4; and tax sales, 148; treason indictment of, 131; universal appeal of, 190; and US Army modernization, 94, 96, 101, 108; US Army resignation, 105, 116n67; and Washington College, 110, 111, 186–87, 189, 192, 194, 203n15; and Weldon Railroad, 167, 177; White Sulphur Spring Manifesto of, 200–201n4
Lee Memorial Association, 189–90, 191, 192, 194, 199
Lee Monument Association, 189–92, 193, 198, 199, 203n12
Lexington, VA: flood of 1870, 186, 189; and Lee Memorial Association, 189–90, 191, 192, 194, 199; Recumbent Lee sarcophagus in, 192, 193, 203n15
Lieber, Francis, 54, 120–21
Lieber Code, 104, 121–22, 137n8, 238
Lincoln, Abraham: assassination of, 119, 127, 131, 133, 134; and Black people's participation in public sphere, 193–94; on Civil War as new birth of freedom, 228; on Civil War as "People's contest," 94–95; Confederate nationalism as response to election of, 71, 73, 81, 84; conspirators' trial, 128, 129, 130; Davis compared to, 44, 62n19; guerrilla cases commuted by, 123, 137n14; political opposition to, 235; and John Ross on protectorate status of Cherokee Nation, 23, 25; William Scott pardoned by, 218; war strategy of, 238
Link, William, 233
Longstreet, James, 5, 195–96, 198, 205n23, 205n24
Lossing, Benson, 214–15, 224n17

Lost Cause: and Black participation in politics and public square, 204n19; and comparative history, 57, 58–59; context of, 234; and defeat empathy, 55–56; Early on, 196, 202n8; Gallagher on, 5, 6–7; interpretive scheme of, 228–29; on Lee, 93, 107–8, 111; on Union army, 108; on Union matériel predominance, 62n17, 108
Louisiana, 49
Loyola, Ignatius, 98
Luskey, Brian, 239

Mahone, William, 197, 205n27
Manuel de Rosas, Juan, 80
Marcy, William, 78
Marshall, Charles, 107
Marshall, John, 21
Maryland, 122
Mason, James, 83
Masur, Kate, 48
Mauldin, Erin, 237
Maximilian (emperor of Mexico), 83
Mazzini, Giuseppe, 51–52
McAllister, Robert, 173, 177, 179
McConaughy, David, 187
McCue, C. E. Willis, 119–20, 132, 135, 140n49
McCue, John Howard, 119–20, 128–30, 131, 132–35, 139n40, 140n49
McCue, John Willis: conscription in Confederate army, 120; cross-examination of witnesses, 128, 139n35; guerrilla charges against, 119, 125, 126, 130, 134–35; as member of Mosby's battalion, 11, 118–19, 120, 124–25, 128, 129–35, 140n61; military commission for case of, 119, 126, 127–31, 133–34, 135; motivations of, 120; murder of Richard N. Ryan, 119, 125–28, 129, 130–33, 135, 138n31; pardon requests for, 132; as prisoner, 118–19, 124, 125, 126, 130, 135, 138n23; raid on post office at Coffron's store, 119, 125, 126; release of, 135–36; scouting mission of, 124–25; sentence

of, 130, 131, 132–35; verdict of, 130, 131; and Nathaniel J. Watkins's trial, 129–30; witnesses of, 128–29
McCurry, Stephanie, 46, 71, 113n17, 229–30
McGregor, S. W. D., 179
McKee, Henry, 145
McKee, James H., 214–16
McKenzie, Robert Tracy, 232
McKitrick, Eric, 235
McPherson, James, 43, 96, 243n11
Meade, George Gordon, 170, 172, 175–76, 178, 195, 214
Meherrin River, 171
Meigs, Montgomery C., 101
Meiji Japan, 56
memory studies: in Civil War history, 2, 9, 10, 11–12, 58, 225n30, 229, 230, 234–35; and comparative history, 56–60; Gallagher on, 5, 6, 11, 12; and historical silences, 168. *See also* historical memory
Menand, Louis, 236
Mercié, Jean Antonin, 199
Mexican-American War, 74, 77, 93, 99, 101–4, 108
Mexico, 32, 53, 77–80, 83, 84–85
Military Campaigns of the Civil War series, 8
military histories: in Civil War history, 1, 2, 10, 207–8, 229, 230, 231–32, 236; and comparative history, 50–51; of Confederacy, 186–87; Gallagher on, 3, 4, 7, 8, 9, 10–11, 207; and nation-states, 70
Military Order of the Loyal Legion, 217
Mississippi River, Lee's navigation improvements to, 93, 101–2
Missouri, 19, 20, 42, 122
Mitchel, Charles Burton, 25, 32
modernity: and armies, 93, 94, 95, 96, 97–98, 103, 104, 105, 106, 110; and bureaucratization, 93, 94, 97, 98, 99, 106; and Civil War era, 12, 43, 59, 94, 96, 108, 117n85; defining of, 94; and discipline, 93, 94, 95, 97, 98, 100, 109, 110; and industrialization, 93; internal contradictions and limits of, 93–94; and Lee, 93, 94, 97, 104, 108, 109, 110, 111; and nationalism, 69; and nation-states, 93, 94, 96, 97, 103–5; and warfare, 11, 93, 94, 96, 109
Monroe Doctrine, 74, 75–76, 78, 84
Moore, Barrington, Jr., 60n1
Moore, Dominique, 13
Moore, J. Quitman, 81
Mora, Juan Rafael, 76
Mormons, 72
Morris, William W., 126
Mosby, John Singleton: and ambiguity of defining irregulars, 119, 121–22, 123, 129; as commander of Forty-Third Battalion of Virginia Cavalry, 120, 121–24, 128, 130, 131–32, 133, 134, 139n47; disbanding of battalion, 126–27, 128; as Early's rival, 205n27; as fugitive, 129; Grant's efforts against, 123–24, 125; and guerrilla warfare, 120, 121–24, 126, 134, 137n15, 138n17; John W. McCue as member of battalion, 11, 118–19, 120, 124–25, 128, 129–35, 140n61; men's treatment as prisoners of war, 124, 138n22; military commissions trying men of, 119, 122–23, 124, 126, 127–30, 134; and retaliation cycles, 124, 126; Sheridan's efforts against, 123–24, 138n17; surrender and parole terms for, 125, 126, 131, 132; Union army's efforts against, 136
Mosquito Coast, 74–75
Mott, Gershom, 170
Munford, Thomas, 126
Murphy, Joseph, 165

Napoleon, 95, 109
nationalism: and comparative history, 52–53, 59; and family of nations, 71; Gallagher on, 3, 10, 12; and modernity, 69; and self-government, 6, 70, 74, 76, 77, 79; and slavery, 97; of white Southerners, 4, 10, 70, 73, 74, 76–77, 83, 85. *See also* Confederate nationalism; Union nationalism

nation-states: in Central America, 74; and comparative history, 56; Confederacy as nation-state, 10, 69–74, 76–79, 81–85, 94, 96–97, 105, 107, 110; as dominant political organization, 69–70, 73, 74, 80; and interests as slaveholders, 10, 71, 76, 85; military institutions of, 95–97, 104, 105, 109, 113n18; and modernity, 93, 94, 96, 97, 103–5; and sovereignty, 73, 74, 76, 80, 82, 85

Native Americans: changes in governance, 35n5; citizenship of, 22, 23–24, 31; in Civil War history, 229, 235, 240, 241; Confederate respect for home rule of, 18, 21; Lee's army service subduing, 93; as nonvoting delegates of Confederate Congress, 17, 18, 19–20, 22, 24, 33, 35n5; protection against land grabs of Unionist whites, 22; protection of sovereignty, 22, 24, 25, 34–35n4; on protectorate status, 22–23, 25, 33; resistance strategies of, 10, 72; slaveholding practices of, 19, 20, 24, 28; state's renaming for land title registration, 100; and treaty relations with Confederates, 10, 18–25, 32, 33, 34, 34n4, 35n5; and treaty relations with US government, 22–23, 36n19; as troops in South's western flank, 19; violence used by white settlers in wars against, 109

Neely, Mark, 140n48, 233, 235, 238, 247n55

Neiman, Susan, 58

Nelson, William, 106

New Mexico Territory, 19

New South, 59, 237

newspapers: correspondence published in, 210–11, 216, 219, 220; primary sources in, 213

Nicaragua, 74–75

Niehaus, Charles H., 199

Noe, Kenneth, 232

Nolan, Alan, 234

North: antislavery beliefs in, 6; and comparative history, 43, 44, 45, 62n17; comparison of state-level politics, 44, 62n20; and memory studies, 234; as nation-state, 96; publishing trade in, 209–10; state archives in, 211–12; workers in, 229. *See also* Union

Nottoway River, and Hicksford Raid, 167–68, 170, 172, 175, 176

Nourse, Henry S., 218–19

Novick, Peter, 208, 220, 222n4

Oakes, James, 45, 63n25

O'Brien, Tim, 42

occupation, in Civil War history, 19, 56, 230, 232

Official Records (War Department), 177, 217

Opothleyahola (Creek chief), 24

Orr, James, 148

Osterhammel, Jürgen, 95–96

Ottoman Empire, 56

Ould, Robert, 124, 138n22

Owsley, Frank, 33

Parker, Geoffrey, 95

Parrish, T. Michael, 9, 230–31, 242–43n10

Partisan Rangers Act, 121

partisan warfare: in Civil War history, 1; Davis on, 126; defining of, 11, 121, 122; Grant's efforts against, 123–26; and military justice, 136

Payne, William H., 196

Peace Democrats, 72

Pendleton, William Nelson, 192, 196

Pennsylvania State University, 6, 7

Petersburg, VA, 165–67, 169–72, 175–76, 178

Phillips, Wendell, 52

Pickett's Charge, 107, 195

Pierce, Franklin, 77

Pike, Albert, 20–24

Poland, 54, 70, 82

political history: in Civil War history, 1, 2, 9, 230, 233, 236; and comparison of state-level politics, 44, 62n20; Gallagher's approach to, 4, 7, 8; and historical memory, 12, 234; and military histories, 11

Port Royal, SC: land redistribution in, 145–46; land tenure in, 154; tax titles in, 141–42, 143, 145–46, 147, 148–49, 153, 157
post-traumatic stress disorder, 55
Potter, David M., 1, 51, 69, 71
Powell, William H., 124, 224n16
Pressly, Thomas J., 240, 241n1
primary sources: and comparative history, 39, 40; and Gallagher, 5, 7, 10, 13; and historical profession, 208, 212, 219; and white Northern Union veteran-writers, 209, 213, 219, 220, 223–24n15
prisoner-of-war camps, 100

Quapaw, 23–24
Quarles, Benjamin, 1
Quigley, Paul, 72
Quiner, Edwin B., 211, 223n9

Rable, George, 231, 232, 233
race relations: Civil War's effect on, 46, 58, 228, 229, 231, 236; and Confederate nationalism, 71, 72; and cultural history, 234; and emancipation, 227; and imperialism, 10
race theory, 2, 5, 6–7, 49, 57, 59, 229
racial bias, 22, 23–24, 29–30
racial injustice, 7
Radical Republicans, 131
railroads: and Corps of Engineers, 100–101; and Herman Haupt, 102; Weldon Railroad, 167, 170–71, 176–78, 182; and westward expansion along thirty-second parallel, 19, 77
Ramage, James A., 122, 138n22
Ramseur, Stephen Dodson, 3–4
Randall, J. G., 147–48
Raum, Green B., 157
Reconciliationist Cause, 6, 58, 187, 189, 190, 194
Reconstruction: and comparative history, 47, 48, 55–56, 57, 67n85; and Early's voluntary exile, 188, 191; and land redistribution, 11, 142; Lee on, 188
redemption, 58

Reid, Brian Holden, 235
Reidy, Joseph, 9, 238
religion, 9, 48, 57, 59, 234
Republican Party, 22, 36n19, 51, 57, 70, 79, 236
Republic of Texas, 82
Revenue Act of 1861, 146
Richmond, VA, 189, 190, 191–92, 193, 198–200, 203n13
Rives, Alexander, 133
Rives, William C., 133
Roman, A. B., 83
Rome, 48, 53–54
Ross, John, 23–27, 30, 33
Rosser, Thomas, 126
Rubin, Anne Sarah, 72
Russell, John, 128–29
Russia, 48–49, 56
Rwanda, 57
Ryan, Richard N., 118, 125–28, 129, 130–33, 135, 138n31

Saint-Domingue, 169
Santa Anna, Antonio López de, 77
Schivelbusch, Wolfgang, 58–59
Scott, James, 99, 230
Scott, Rebecca, 49
Scott, Walter, 93
Scott, William, 218, 224n25
Scott, Winfield, 102–3, 105
Sea Island Lands (pamphlet), 149–50, 161n37
secession crisis: and comparative history, 51, 53, 56, 72; and Compromise of 1850, 77; and formation of nation-state, 69, 70, 71, 73, 74, 76, 79, 81, 85; and protectorate status of Native Americans, 22–23; separatist movements compared to, 72; slavery as uniform interest of, 80–81; Southern secession conventions, 26; studies of, 228, 233; and US Army officers, 96
sectionalism, 44, 57
Seminole Nation, 18, 32
Seneca, 23–24

Seward, William Henry, 22, 36n19, 83
Sewell, William H., Jr., 40, 61n1
Sexton, Jay, 74
Shawnee, 23–24
Sheehan-Dean, Aaron, 105, 121, 139n46
Sheridan, Philip, 108, 123–25, 138n17, 139n40, 187
Sherman, John, 153
Sherman, William T., 98–99, 102, 106, 142, 232
Shively, Kathryn J., 207
Silber, Nina, 46, 231, 234
Silbey, Joel, 2
Simpson-Vos, Mark, 13
Skelton, William, 96
Skowronek, Stephen, 95
slaveholders: in Kansas, 36n19; Native Americans as, 19, 20, 24, 28; political power during antebellum era, 70; and power of nation-states, 10, 71, 76, 85; rebellion of, 72
slavery: antislavery beliefs in North, 6, 34n4; British Empire's abolition of, 74, 77, 80; capitalist production linked to, 100; in Civil War history, 1, 2, 113n17, 228, 229, 230, 235–36, 240; and comparative history, 47, 48–49, 53; Davis on expansion of, 73; and formation of Confederacy as nation-state, 69, 71, 74, 76–79, 81, 83–84, 97, 107, 110; Gallagher on, 4–5, 45; land redistribution as partial compensation for, 144; and nationalism, 97; and political history, 233; regional divide imposed by, 46; Roman legacy of, 48; white Southerners' commitment to, 70, 72, 74, 75, 76–81, 83–84, 240. *See also* abolition; emancipation; enslaved people
Smalls, Robert: compensation legislation introduced by, 156–58; and *DeTreville v. Smalls*, 143, 145, 153–54, 155; and land purchased at tax sale, 11, 145, 149, 151, 158; wartime heroism of, 145
Smith, Boyd, 128–29

Smith, Daniel Huger, 154
Smith, Edmund Kirby, 32
Smith, Stacy, 240
social history: in Civil War history, 1, 4, 8–9, 229, 230, 231, 236, 241; and comparative history, 52; Gallagher on, 4, 5, 7, 8; granularity of, 41; and military histories, 11
Society of Civil War Historians, 7–8
South: and comparative history, 43, 44, 45, 58, 59, 62n17; comparison of state-level politics, 44, 62n20; home front of, 4, 5, 47, 232, 235; and interpretation of Confederate defeat, 55, 119; publishing trade in, 209–10; social order of, 46; state archives in, 211–12, 217. *See also* Confederacy
South America, 48, 74, 85
South Carolina Sea Islands, and tax sales, 11, 145–46, 148–51, 153–54, 158
Southern Historical Association, 7
Southern Historical Society, 197–98
Southwest, Confederate expansion into, 19, 34
Spain, 53, 57, 76, 83
Spanish Empire, 53
Stampp, Kenneth, 1
Stanton, Edwin, 119, 121–22, 125
state power, 48, 49, 72, 94, 96
Stephens, Alexander, 233
Sternhell, Yael, 228
Stewart, Frank, 106
Still, William N., Jr., 42–43, 71
Strong, William, 155
Stuart, Alexander H. H., 133
Surry County, VA, 167
Sussex County, VA: Civil War era structures surviving in, 166–67; destruction of homes in, 165–69, 172, 173–75, 176; destruction of records during Hicksford Raid, 165, 166, 174, 178, 179; historical silences in, 168, 183
Sweeny, Thomas, 106
Swinton, William, 197
Sypher, J. R., 214

Tacey v. Irwin (1873), 148, 149, 155
Taiping Rebellion, 51, 54, 105, 109
Tannenbaum, Frank, 48
tax sales: former landowners' challenges to, 141, 143, 144, 153–57, 159n20; irregular nature of, 141, 143, 147; and land redistribution, 11, 144, 147, 154; land transfers grounded in, 144, 146; legal challenges to, 148–53, 161n41, 161n42, 161n51, 162n61; and national cemeteries, 146, 159n20; and price of land, 155; and South Carolina Sea Islands, 11, 145–46, 148–51, 153–54, 158; and trespass suits, 150–51, 152, 156
tax titles: and attacks by planters' lawyers on, 143, 153, 157, 158; and Black landownership, 11, 142–44, 150–51, 158; durability of, 141–42, 151, 153–55, 157, 158; and land redistribution, 142–43, 144; in Port Royal, SC, 141–42, 143, 145–46, 147, 148–49, 153, 157
Taylor, Richard, 230–31
Temple, Henry John, 83
Texas, 19, 34n4
Thirty Years' War, 50
Thomas, Emory M., 70, 110
Thompson, S. Millett, 219–20
Thomson, Janice E., 95
Thornton, T. E., country store of, 166, 168
Tillman, George, 145
Tilly, Charles, 95
Towne, Laura, 150–51, 154
Trammell, Philip, 122–23, 137n14
trans-Mississippi frontier, 29, 32, 33, 231
transnational history: and Civil War history, 12, 51–54, 113n17, 229, 235; and comparative history, 41, 50–51, 59, 229, 239; and Confederate nationalism, 10, 72–73
Treaties of Friendship and Alliance, 23
Treaty of Guadalupe Hidalgo, 103
Treaty of Hopewell (1785), 21
Treaty of New Echota (1835), 21, 36n13
Trescot, William Henry, 142–43, 148, 156–57
Trouillot, Michel-Rolph, 168, 182

Tucker, Ann, 72
Turner, Henry, 130
Twigg, David, 103

Union: Cherokee Nation's relations with, 24, 26; and committees of vigilance and safety, 127; and Federal authority in Confederacy, 102; as inspiration for white Northerners, 6; and localized methods of military recruitment, 96; and modernity, 94, 110; Native Americans' relations with, 23; preservation of republican government, 51, 69
Union army: attitude toward Confederates in name of ending the war, 125, 136; and Confederate slavery, 47; discipline in, 232; and enslaved people, 238; and environmental history, 237–38; fractiousness of generals in, 110, 117n79; insubordination within, 106; and Lieber Code, 104, 121–22, 137n8, 238; Lost Cause on, 108; military commissions of, 119, 122–24, 126, 127–31, 133–34, 136, 139n46, 140n48; official documents of, 212–13, 216, 219–20; public perception of, 180; and tax sales, 146–47. See also Hicksford Raid (1864)
Union Cause, 6, 7, 45, 58, 63n25, 227
Union Indian brigade, 26
Union nationalism, 10, 52
University of North Carolina, Southern Historical Collection, 3, 5
University of North Carolina Press, 4, 8–9, 230
University of Texas, 2, 9
University of Virginia, 7
Ural, Susannah, 232
US Army: in antebellum era, 96; bureaucratic organizations of, 100; and dueling, 106; and industrialization, 101; Robert E. Lee's modernization of, 94, 96, 101, 108; and Mexican-American War, 103–4; and right of officers to resignation, 105, 116n67, 116n71; and

US Army (*continued*)
    taxation of insurrectionary states, 11; Union Indian ranks of, 26–27
US Congress: Confederate Congress compared to, 44; and tax sales, 141, 152, 153, 155, 156; treaties with Indigenous nations, 21, 22, 36n19
US diplomacy and Monroe Doctrine, 74, 75–76, 78
US government: and annuity payments for Five Nations, 18, 20, 21, 29, 32, 34–35n4; and Confederate diplomacy, 83; and Fort Harmar agreement, 21; racial and ideological differences in, 85; and treaty relations with Native Americans, 22–23, 36n19
US Justice Department, 152
US Supreme Court: and Direct Tax Act, 148–49, 162n56; on Native tribes as dependent nations, 18, 20–21; on Seventh Amendment, 161n41; and sovereign immunity doctrine, 161n51; on titles to land sold in insurrectionary districts, 141, 143, 148, 151, 153, 154–56, 157, 158, 161n51
US territorial expansion, and Monroe Doctrine, 74, 75–76, 78
US Treasury Department, 152, 157, 162n61
US War Department, 177

Valentine, Edward, 192, 203n15, 206n31
Van Buren, Martin, 25
Vance, Zebulon, 44
Van Tassel, David D., 208
Vattel, Emmerich de, 104
Vaughn, John C., 120
veterans: Black, 209, 221–22n3; in Civil War history, 235, 236–37; and comparative history, 55, 57; Confederate, 190, 195, 203n12. *See also* white Northern Union veteran-writers
Vietnam War, legacy of, 41–43, 55
Vinovskis, Maris, 1, 229, 231
Virginia Military Institute, 110, 120, 204n18

Waite, Kevin, 240
Wallace, Lew, 127, 129–31
Wardell, Morris L., 33
warfare: and civil conflicts, 240; and legitimate belligerents, 104, 105, 109, 121, 131, 132, 134; and modernity, 11, 93, 94, 96, 109; role in American life, 239–40. *See also* guerrilla warfare; partisan warfare
War of 1812, 214
Warren, Gouverneur K., 167–72, 174, 175–83
wars of German unification, 50
Washburn, P. T., 212, 223n12
Washington, George, 50, 187
Washington College, 110, 111, 186–87, 189, 192, 194, 196, 203n15
Watie, Stand, 25–27, 29–33
Watkins, Nicholas J., 128–30, 139n37, 139n41
Watson, Samuel, 96, 106
Weber, Max, 60n1, 95–96, 98, 105, 111
Weldon Railroad, 167, 170–71, 176–78, 182
western history, 229, 235, 240
West Indies, 49–50
West Point: and discipline, 98–100; educational system at, 114n33; and Lee, 94, 98, 99, 101, 107, 110; and Ramseur, 3; and Cadmus Wilcox, 97
Whig Party, 2
Whipper, William, 151
White, Hayden, 41
white Northerners, on emancipation, 6, 58
white Northern Union veteran-writers: access to archives, 209–13, 220; correspondence during Civil War, 210–11, 212, 213, 216, 219, 220; diaries of, 211, 212, 213, 219, 220; and historical method, 12, 208–9, 210, 214–17; historical narratives of, 207, 210, 212, 213, 215–19, 220, 236; and historical profession, 12, 207–8, 209, 213, 221, 222n4, 225n30; and larger context of historical knowledge, 214–15; personal memoirs of, 220, 225n29, 225n30; and primary sources, 209, 213, 219, 220,

223–24n15; and published materials on Civil War, 214, 216; and publishing trade, 210; regimental histories written by, 207–8, 210, 211, 215–16, 218–20

Whites, LeeAnn, 231

white Southerners: and Black Codes, 135; commitment to slavery, 70, 72, 74, 75, 76–81, 83–84, 240; and comparative history, 57, 59; on Confederacy as nation-state, 82; Confederate nationalism created by, 72, 73, 81; ethos of white supremacy, 59, 79; Gallagher on, 3, 4–5, 72; on Monroe Doctrine, 74, 75–76, 78; sense of nationalism among, 4, 10, 70, 73, 74, 76–77, 83, 85; in US embassies in Latin America, 70, 74, 75–81, 82, 84–85

white supremacy, 59, 72, 79, 196

Whitney, Milton, 139n37

Wilcox, Cadmus, 97

Williams, David, 235

Williams, George, 152

Williams, George Washington, 209, 221n3

Williams, G. F., 180

Willis, A. C., 124

Wilson, Abraham, 128–29

Wilson, Charles Reagan, 234

Witt, John, 238

women: Black women compared to white women, 46, 173; in Civil War American series, 9; in Civil War history, 229, 231, 232, 241; Civil War's effect on, 46, 63n28; and comparative history, 46, 63–64n30; white Southern women as political adversaries, 180–81; white women and historical memory, 188–91, 193

Woods, Michael, 45, 236–37, 242n5

Wool, John E., 101–2

Wooster, Robert, 96

World War I, 55, 117n85, 222n3, 228, 231

World War II, 56, 57, 231

Yancey, Benjamin, 80

Yancey, William Lowndes, 80

Yankee carpetbaggers, 188

Zeledón, Pedro, 75, 76

www.ingramcontent.com/pod-product-compliance
Lightning Source LLC
Chambersburg PA
CBHW031949230426
43672CB00010B/2101